The Politics of Ontario

The Politics of Ontario

EDITED BY
Cheryl N. Collier and Jonathan Malloy

UNIVERSITY OF TORONTO PRESS

LIBRARY AND ARCHIVES CANADA CATALOGUING IN PUBLICATION

The politics of Ontario / edited by Cheryl N. Collier and Jonathan Malloy.

Includes bibliographical references.

Issued in print and electronic formats.

ISBN 978-1-4426-0912-9 (paperback).—ISBN 978-1-4426-0913-6 (hardback).—
ISBN 978-1-4426-0914-3 (pdf).—ISBN 978-1-4426-0915-0 (html).

1. Ontario—Politics and government—1995–2003. 2. Ontario—Politics and
government—2003–. 3. Ontario—Social conditions—1991–. I. Malloy, Jonathan, 1970–, editor
II. Collier, Cheryl N., 1967–, editor

JL270.P65 2017   320.9713   C2016-903377-5
                                          C2016-903378-3

We welcome comments and suggestions regarding any aspect of our publications—please feel free to
contact us at news@utphighereducation.com or visit our Internet site at www.utppublishing.com.

North America   *UK, Ireland, and continental Europe*
5201 Dufferin Street   NBN International
North York, Ontario, Canada, M3H 5T8   Estover Road, Plymouth, PL6 7PY, UK
                                         ORDERS PHONE: 44 (0) 1752 202301
2250 Military Road   ORDERS FAX: 44 (0) 1752 202333
Tonawanda, New York, USA, 14150   ORDERS E-MAIL: enquiries@nbninternational.com

ORDERS PHONE: 1–800–565–9523
ORDERS FAX: 1–800–221–9985
ORDERS E-MAIL: utpbooks@utpress.utoronto.ca

Every effort has been made to contact copyright holders; in the event of an error or omission,
please notify the publisher.

This book is printed on paper containing 100% post-consumer fibre.

The University of Toronto Press acknowledges the financial support for its publishing activities of
the Government of Canada through the Canada Book Fund.

Printed in the United States of America

Dedicated to Graham White,
scholar of Ontario politics

Contents

Part 1: The Setting

Part 2: Institutions

Part 3: Politics

Part 4: Policy

Tables and Figures

Tables

Figures

Preface

CHERYL N. COLLIER AND JONATHAN MALLOY

IT HAS BEEN 20 YEARS since an edited volume on the government and politics of Ontario was published. Yet the province continues to have an important impact on the rest of the country and remains a frequent topic of research and teaching in universities and colleges, which offer well-attended courses on the subject. Ontario continues to set the pace for political, economic, and social change across the board in Canada, while still retaining, for better or for worse, many traditional links to the past. In many ways, the study of Ontario has never been more vibrant.

It is in the spirit of this continued interest in Canada's most populous province that we present this new edited volume, *The Politics of Ontario*. While we owe a huge debt of gratitude to *The Government and Politics of Ontario*, initiated by Donald C. MacDonald in 1975 and continued under the steady hand of Graham White up to its fifth edition in 1997, this book both continues with and differs substantially from its predecessors.

This book examines the major changes as well as the enduring continuities of Ontario politics from the 1990s on into the new millennium. Our volume includes authors from the last edition of *The Government and Politics of Ontario* to help reflect on these core continuities and to help us analyze the present landscape. We also include some of the leading current provincial experts in fields including fiscal and economic policy, the environment, labour, multiculturalism, and the complexities of the Greater Toronto Area (GTA)—issues that have risen to the top of the province's policy agenda.

The underlying theme of *The Politics of Ontario* is that Canada's most populous province is in a new era. It is no longer the economic engine indisputably driving the national economy, but remains the most populous province in Canada, home of Canada's largest urban agglomeration, and the centre of Canadian finance and media. It is a society that has undergone considerable change and disruption, but is also Canada's most multicultural and diverse province with the country's first openly gay premier. The chapters that follow chronicle these exciting changes in the province and weigh their related consequences for the future and their impact on the country overall.

The Politics of Ontario is organized into four sections: an introductory overview of the economic and political context, an examination of key governing institutions, a section on political actors and activity, and a final section on policy areas and challenges. Authors carefully weigh the changes and continuities from the late 1990s to the present day and ask what they all mean for the future. Each chapter includes a list of timely discussion questions that instructors of provincial politics courses will find useful to structure class debates and/or to establish term paper topics.

We are indebted to the hard work of the authors who not only wrote and provided timely edits to their chapters, but also demonstrated admirable patience with an edited volume that took much longer to produce than was first promised. They were also forced to contend with a somewhat surprising 2014 provincial election and other disruptions along the way. We thank them all for their professionalism and tenacity. We also thank Michael Harrison at the University of Toronto Press, Higher Education division, for his support of this book and gentle nudging to help it to completion.

Finally, both Jon and Cheryl thank their families for their enduring patience as we dealt with all of the bumps and roadblocks typical of edited volumes.

Contributors

Editors

Cheryl N. Collier is Associate Professor of Political Science at the University of Windsor and Co-Director of the university's interdisciplinary Health Research Centre for the Study of Violence Against Women. She teaches and researches in the fields of Canadian and provincial politics focusing on gender, federalism, social movements, and comparative social policy. She has published on these topics in the *Canadian Journal of Political Science*, *Politics and Gender*, and the *Canadian Political Science Review*.

Jonathan Malloy is Associate Professor and Chair of the Department of Political Science at Carleton University. His teaching and research focus on Canadian political institutions. Recent publications include the co-authored book *Fighting for Votes: Parties, the Media, and Voters in an Ontario Election*. He is a former president of the Canadian Study of Parliament Group and a former Ontario Legislative Intern.

Contributors

Gina Comeau is Assistant Professor in the Department of Political Science at Laurentian University. Her research interests centre on the role of civil society organizations in public policy formulation and on popular culture. She has published on these topics in the *International Journal of Sport Policy & Politics* and the *Journal of Sport and Social Issues*, as well as in the books *Gouvernance communautaire* and *The Politics of Popular Culture*.

Rand Dyck is Adjunct Professor of Political Science at Carleton University following a long career at Laurentian University. He wrote three editions of *Provincial Politics in Canada*; edited four editions of *Studying Politics: An Introduction to Political Science*; wrote six editions of *Canadian Politics: Critical Approaches* and co-authored two more; and wrote five editions of *Canadian Politics: Concise*. He was the recipient of teaching awards at both Laurentian and Carleton, and also teaches at Nunavut Sivuniksavut in Ottawa.

Anna Esselment is Assistant Professor in the Department of Political Science at the University of Waterloo. She has published on issues of federalism and intergovernmental relations, campaigns and elections, and political marketing. Recent works include "The Governing Party and the Permanent Campaign" in *Political Communication in Canada*, and "Designing Campaign Platforms" in the Special Issue, *Journal of Parliamentary and Political Law*.

Bryan Evans is Professor in the Department of Politics and Public Administration at Ryerson University. Recent publications include *Transforming Provincial Politics: The Political Economy of Canada's Provinces and Territories in the Neoliberal Era* (edited with Charles W. Smith); "Are Non-government Policy Actors Being Heard? Assessing New Public Governance" (with Halina Sapeha) in *Canadian Public Administration*; "Social Democracy in the New Age of Austerity" in *Orchestrating Austerity: Impacts and Resistance*, edited by Donna Baines and Stephen McBride; and "Tales of Policy Estrangement: Non-governmental Policy Work and Capacity in Three Canadian Provinces" (with Adam Wellstead) in the *Canadian Journal of Nonprofit and Social Economy Research*.

Daniel Henstra is Associate Professor of Political Science at the University of Waterloo and his research centres on public administration and public policy. His SSHRC-funded program of research investigates the multilevel governance of climate change adaptation, analyzing the ways in which policies and policymaking are affected by the relationships between levels of government and by the patterns of interaction between state and societal actors.

Martin Horak is Associate Professor of Political Science and Director of the Local Government Program at Western University. His research focuses on urban policy processes. He is particularly interested in the comparative dynamics of policy formation and implementation under conditions of multilevel governance. His books include *Governing the Post-Communist City: Institutions and Democratic Development in Prague*; *Sites of Governance: Multilevel Governance and Policy-Making in Canada's Cities* (co-edited with Robert Young); and *Urban Neighborhoods in a New Era: Revitalization Politics in the Post-Industrial City* (with multiple co-authors). He has published numerous journal articles on Canadian and comparative urban politics and governance.

Matthias Oschinski is a Senior Economist with the Office of Economic Policy at the Ontario Ministry of Finance. His research interests include income inequality, labour market policies, and the impact of technological change on the future of work. Among his recent publications is *Ontario Made: Rethinking Manufacturing in the 21st Century*.

Tracey Raney is Associate Professor in the Department of Politics and Public Administration at Ryerson University. Her research focuses on Ontario and Canadian politics, women and politics, and Canadian national identity. Her publications on Ontario include co-authorship of "Democratizing the Ontario Legislature: Change, but Change Enough?" (Canadian Study of Parliament Group), and "Breaking the Holding Pattern: Women in Ontario Politics" in *Stalled: The Representation of Women in Canadian Governments*. Her research has been published in *Nations and Nationalism*, *International Journal*, and the *Canadian Journal of Political Science*.

Larry Savage is Director of the Centre for Labour Studies at Brock University. His research interests revolve around the politics of organized labour. He is the author of *Socialist Cowboy: The Politics of Peter Kormos*; and co-editor of both *Rethinking the Politics of Labour in Canada* and *Public Sector Unions in the Age of Austerity*.

Myer Siemiatycki is Professor in the Department of Politics and Public Administration at Ryerson University, where he was founding director of the Graduate Program in Immigration and Settlement Studies. His research interests span identity politics, migration, and labour studies. He is co-editor of *Electing a Diverse Canada: The Representation of Immigrants, Minorities, and Women*; co-author of "Diverse Pathways to Immigrant Political Incorporation"; and author of *The Diversity Gap: The Electoral Under-Representation of Visible Minorities*.

Julie M. Simmons is Associate Professor in the Department of Political Science at the University of Guelph. She teaches and researches in the fields of Canadian politics, federalism, public policy, and administration. In particular, her research focuses on issues of democracy and accountability in federal-provincial relations. She is co-editor of both *Overpromising and Underperforming?* and *Understanding and Evaluating New Intergovernmental Accountability Regimes*. She has recently published in *Canadian Public Administration* and the *Canadian Political Science Review* and is co-editing (with James Farney) a book on regionalism in the Harper era.

Tamara A. Small is Associate Professor in the Department of Political Science at the University of Guelph. Her research focuses on digital politics, including the use and impact of the Internet by Canadian political actors. She is the co-author of *Fighting for Votes: Parties, the Media, and Voters in an*

Ontario Election, and the co-editor of both *Political Communication in Canada: Meet the Press, Tweet the Rest* and *Mind the Gaps: Canadian Perspectives on Gender and Politics*. Her work has been published in *Information, Communication and Society, Party Politics*, and the *Canadian Journal of Political Science*.

Graham White is Professor Emeritus at the University of Toronto Mississauga. His research and teaching focus on governmental institutions in the Canadian provinces and territories. Among his books are *The Ontario Legislature: A Political Analysis*, two editions of *The Government and Politics of Ontario*, and most recently *Made in Nunavut: An Experiment in Decentralized Government*. A former president of the Canadian Political Science Association, he is currently English co-editor of the *Canadian Journal of Political Science*.

Mark Winfield is Associate Professor of Environmental Studies at York University. He is also Co-Chair of the Faculty's Sustainable Energy Initiative and Coordinator of the Joint Master of Environmental Studies/Juris Doctor program offered in conjunction with Osgoode Hall Law School. Prior to joining York University, he was Program Director with the Pembina Institute, and prior to that Director of Research with the Canadian Institute for Environmental Law and Policy. His publications include the book *Blue-Green Province: The Environment and Political Economy of Ontario* as well as numerous articles, book chapters, and reports on a wide range of environmental and energy law and policy topics.

Peter Woolstencroft is Professor Emeritus in the Department of Political Science at the University of Waterloo. He has published essays on political geography, the politics of education, the federal and Ontario Progressive Conservative parties, Ontario politics, leadership conventions, international electoral co-operation, and (singly or jointly) election campaigns in Canada from 1993 to 2011.

PART I

The Setting

1

Ontario Then and Now

GRAHAM WHITE

O NE OF THE FEW THINGS THAT PRACTICALLY all political scientists agree
on is that social change leads to political change. Disagreement may be
rife as to why and how societal change produces political change, but in try-
ing to understand a political system such as Ontario's it is essential to know
about the society underpinning it as well as how that society has changed in
both the short and long term. This chapter thus offers an overview of major
social, economic, and political changes in Ontario since 1950.

Why 1950? Certainly there is nothing magical about starting an account
of the province's social and political changes in that year; indeed, to a significant extent, using 1950 as a baseline year is a function of available data (the
federal government conducts comprehensive censuses every 10 years and
thus we have extensive data for 1951). Though 1950 may seem like ancient
history to students born at the turn of the millennium, a substantial proportion of the Ontario population was alive then (including several contributors to this book). Choosing 1940 as a starting point would have been too
much of a stretch, not least because so much about the province that year
was determined by the exigencies of wartime. To have chosen 1960 would
have meant losing too many developments in the 1950s that remain relevant
to understanding present-day Ontario politics.

While the emphasis in this chapter is on the dramatic changes that have
transformed Ontario in the past six and a half decades, it is important to appre-
ciate the continuities evident in the province's society and politics over that
period. Indeed, it is worth asking whether the scale of social change evident
in Ontario since 1950 has been matched by a similar scale of political change.

Overview: A Province Transformed

Ontario in 1950 was a province in the midst of far-reaching changes. The
postwar baby boom was well underway and the province was experiencing
strong economic growth, in marked contrast to the all-too-recent unemployment and hardship of the Great Depression. Immigrants were flocking
to the province. Signs of growth, prosperity, and change were everywhere,
from the work progressing on Toronto's first subway to the homes for the
aged being built or planned in every county. The "Toronto Bypass" (later

christened Highway 401) was under construction and a pioneering if not especially effective Anti-Discrimination Act had been passed by the Legislature a few years earlier.

Six and a half decades on, the Ontario of 1950 seems almost unrecognizable. The very landscape—at least in the heavily populated southern reaches of the province—has changed. Open countryside, dotted with farms and woodlots connected by quiet rural roads, has been supplanted by endless sprawling suburbs linked by massive superhighways. The most profound changes, however, are those among the people of Ontario: the socio-demographic composition of the province's current population differs dramatically from that of 65 years earlier. So too the foundations of Ontario's economy have undergone extensive change in this period. Central elements of Ontarians' current lifestyles were scarcely imaginable in 1950. So too how Ontarians lived in 1950—no television (let alone computers or cell phones), but home delivery of bread and milk, often from horse-drawn wagons, and the Toronto Maple Leafs regularly winning the Stanley Cup— would astound their present-day counterparts.

Changes in Ontario's socio-demographic makeup, in its economy, and in other facets of the province have brought about far-reaching shifts in popular attitudes on all manner of social and political issues. No less far-reaching than socio-demographic, economic, and political changes characterizing Ontario over the past six decades—and of course closely linked in with them—have been changes in popular attitudes on social, moral, and political issues. Consider the biggest public events in Toronto. Sixty-five years ago the big crowds came out for the Santa Claus Parade and the Orange Parade on the "Glorious Twelfth" (a signal of the dominance in Ontario society of the Orange Lodge, a militantly Protestant organization). Santa Claus remains popular, but today the Pride Parade and the Caribbean Carnival (formerly Caribana), a celebration of black culture, draw crowds of equal or greater size. Consider also that in 1950 few Indigenous Ontarians even had the vote and were effectively prohibited, by the federal Indian Act, from launching legal actions against the government, whereas today Ontario has formally recognized Indigenous peoples' "inherent right to self-government" and a First Nations citizen has served as Lieutenant-Governor. In 1950, communities proudly featured smokestacks belching black smoke on their official documents as symbols of their progress; present-day governments stress their "green," "environmentally friendly" initiatives. Among other telling indicators of value change, few could be as noteworthy as the emergence of Kathleen Wynne, an openly gay woman, as Ontario's premier. In 1950, it would have been unthinkable that a woman could become premier and homosexuality was a criminal offence.

In the political-governmental realm, the state's regulatory reach and the range of its intervention into private spheres of activity have expanded greatly. In the postwar decades, it was "difficult to find any area of economic activity that was not subjected to some deliberate form of [state] intervention";[1] in social terms, behaviour such as racial and religious discrimination, family violence, and political donations, once deemed private in nature, are now vigorously regulated by the state. Both responding to and leading all these changes have been tectonic shifts in the province's governance: the size, shape, and operation of government; the jurisdictional and financial relations among federal, provincial, and municipal governments; and the citizenry's demands and expectations of their governments.

Social and Economic Change

Population Growth

Ontario's population has grown substantially, from 4.6 million people in 1951 to 13.8 million people in 2015; the population of the Greater Toronto Area now exceeds the entire province's 1950 population by more than a million people.[2] Although the postwar baby boom was hardly unique to Ontario, between 1945 and 1960 Ontario's population not only grew faster than did the population of any other province, but also of any industrialized country in the world.[3] Much of this and subsequent population growth reflects the province's continuing attractiveness to immigrants. During the 1950s and 1960s, migration was responsible for over 40 per cent of the province's population increase. In more recent decades, with significant decline in the rate of natural increase, international immigration and migration from elsewhere in Canada have become increasingly important sources of Ontario's population growth. Though it is no longer the case, as it was as recently as 2001–02, that Ontario has far more immigrants than births, international migration far outstrips natural increase (births minus deaths) in overall numbers. Whether it represents an enduring trend remains to be seen, but for the first time in decades, Ontario has in recent years lost more people to interprovincial migration than it has gained.

Most of the population increase has occurred in urban areas, most notably (but by no means exclusively) in what has come to be called the Greater Toronto Area (GTA). Whereas in 1950 just over half of Ontario's population lived in centres of more than 10,000 people,[4] this proportion had by 2011 surpassed 85 per cent with 66 per cent in the half dozen largest cities alone. In 1950 the municipalities that would shortly be melded into Metropolitan Toronto numbered slightly over a million souls. Extensive stretches of farmland were to be found within the future "Metro" boundaries, while getting to nearby towns such as Whitby, Brampton, and Richmond Hill—or even to the small airport at Malton—involved a journey into the country. Today the GTA's population has surpassed 6 million and urban sprawl has engulfed Brampton, Richmond Hill, and beyond. An unending conurbation runs from Oshawa to the south side of Lake Ontario east of Hamilton. Isolated pockets of open space can still be found between the northern reaches of Toronto and the south end of Barrie (which itself has grown exponentially, from a population of 12,514 in 1950 to over 200,000 in 2015), but they are contracting daily as development encroaches, constrained only by a provincially imposed Greenbelt. In 1950 Ontarians lived either in rural or in urban areas. Through the 1950s, 1960s, and 1970s, the larger centres developed extensive suburban fringes. While the suburbs continue to expand, Ontario has developed "edge cities," mixed-use urban communities contiguous with—indeed often with indistinguishable boundaries from—larger cities with extensive if diffuse employment in white-collar, often high-tech industries. Edge cities' spatial configurations—sprawling low-density housing tracts served by massive car-focused malls rather than identifiable central cores—little resemble traditional cities. So too their socio-economic profiles (neighbourhoods marked by striking homogeneity in their middle-class composition, and sometimes in the ethnic origins of their residents) and the political attitudes associated with them (e.g., opinions on funding and distributing public services) are often quite different from those found in long-established urban areas.

Changes in Ethnic and Religious Composition

Not only has the population grown and its spatial distribution evolved, its composition has also undergone substantial change. The age profile of Ontarians has changed continually, as the so-called boom, bust, and echo generations have moved onto the demographic stage, occasioning substantial variations in the proportions of the very young, the elderly, and those of working age. Changing immigration patterns have left an indelible impact on the province's social composition. The 1951 census revealed only minor departures from the long-standing Anglo-Celtic domination of Ontario: more than two-thirds of Ontarians were of British descent, with another sixth of French, German, or Dutch origin (many of whom had become all but entirely assimilated into the dominant Anglo-Celtic culture). For a few years after World War II, the traditional main sources of Ontario's immigrants, Britain and Northern Europe, continued to hold pride of place, but throughout the 1950s and 1960s, Southern and Eastern Europeans settled in Ontario in unprecedented numbers. Yet another sea change occurred in the 1970s, with most international immigrants to Ontario coming from Asia, the Caribbean, Africa, and Central America. During the period 1983–92 more people came to Ontario from both Poland and Jamaica than from Britain, while the United States (traditionally an important source of immigration) ranked after Vietnam, Portugal, and Guyana.[5] The countries sending the most immigrants to Ontario in the first years of the new millennium were India, China, Pakistan, the Philippines, and Sri Lanka. Not surprisingly, according to the 2011 National Household Survey, 26 per cent of Ontario residents are members of what have come to be termed "visible minorities."[6]

Immigration has not affected rural and small-town Ontario to nearly the same extent as it has the large urban areas, either in the sheer scale of population growth or in the shifting composition of the population brought about by the influx of visible minorities. Without overlooking important trends toward convergence—for example, in availability of communications media and access to top-quality primary and secondary education—the long-standing divide between urban and rural Ontario persists and has widened perceptibly in terms of the influence of immigration. Large-scale demographic shifts have had their effects on rural and small-town Ontario, and while changes are likely to continue in the coming years, the contrast currently is substantial and stark.

Urban myth holds that the United Nations has declared Toronto the world's most multicultural city. It hasn't, but the enormous numbers of visible minorities in Toronto—and the vast number of students entering the city's schools speaking languages other than English—explain why the claim rings true. The 2006 census revealed that over 40 per cent of immigrants to Canada in the period 2001–06 settled in the Greater Toronto Area and some 82 per cent of them were visible minorities. In two of Toronto's suburbs visible minorities in fact constituted the majority of the population: 57 per cent in Brampton (of whom 56 per cent were South Asian) and 65 per cent in Markham (of whom 52 per cent were Chinese). Nor is Toronto alone in experiencing dramatic shifts in the ethnic and cultural composition of its populace; all major cities give ample evidence of changing immigration patterns. A Statistics Canada report, released in early 2010, contained data and projections on visible minority populations that would have astounded Ontarians of all skin colours in 1950: by 2031 visible minorities will constitute over half the provincial population. More than 60 per cent of Toronto residents will be visible minorities and even in places like Kingston and Peterborough, "whites" will find themselves in the minority.[7]

The effects of immigration are also evident in the religious affiliations of Ontarians. In 1950 the province was overwhelmingly Protestant, with

Roman Catholics, at roughly 25 per cent of the population, accounting for most of the balance. By 2011 Catholics had become by far the largest religious denomination in Ontario, at 31 per cent of the population, compared to barely 21 per cent for all mainstream Protestant denominations combined. Nearly 3 million people (23 per cent) reported belonging to no organized religion and substantial numbers adhered to non-Christian faiths. Inconceivable to Ontarians of 1950, Statistics Canada's 2011 National Household Survey found that Ontario was home to nearly twice as many Muslims as Presbyterians.

Far more significant than shifts in the pattern of religious affiliation, however, has been the thoroughgoing secularization of Ontario. Simply put, religion is not the pervasive force in modern-day Ontario that it was 65 years ago. In 1950 Ontario provincial law forbade not only professional sports on Sunday, but also the serving of alcohol in restaurants or taverns on "the Lord's Day." To be sure, religion continues as a key element in many Ontarians' lives. Nor is controversy about religion in social and political realms unknown, but the nature of such controversy has shifted markedly. In 1950 religious issues in Ontario almost inevitably involved disputes between Protestants and Catholics; today religious disputes are far more likely to turn on accommodation of non-Christian practices—sharia law, the right of Sikh students to wear kirpans in school, and the like. Still, the influence of religion in the social and political realms is very much diminished; "who knew or cared in 1990," one analyst tellingly asked, "that [Premier] Bob Rae is part-Jewish?"[8]

Detailing the implications of these massive shifts in the province's ethnic composition and the influence of religious factors on the design and delivery of social services is far beyond the scope of this chapter (though see Chapter 15 in this collection.) The essential point, however, is clear: Ontarians' needs, values, and expectations on a host of issues of direct relevance to the social service community have changed massively in the six and a half decades this chapter covers.

A Changing Economy

In the economic realm, the transformation has been no less remarkable. Overall standards of living, whether measured in strictly monetary terms, in access to and availability of goods and services (luxuries as well as staples), or in life expectancies and levels of health, are dramatically higher than 65 years ago. Consider that in 1953 the percentage of Ontario households with TV sets (21.5) was only marginally higher than those without indoor toilets (18.3).[9]

The structure of the provincial economy has also evolved extensively. Resource sectors—agriculture, forestry and mining—which were central to Ontario's economy in 1950 have long since been eclipsed in total value (and even more so in the size of their workforces) by the service sector. So too manufacturing—the backbone of the provincial economy in 1950—must still be healthy for Ontario to prosper, but in both value and employment, services outpace manufacturing by an ever-widening margin. (As well, with precipitous declines in the manufacture of appliances, farm equipment, and similar products, autos and auto parts loom increasingly large within the manufacturing sector.) In 1955 primary industries (agriculture, forestry, fishing, and mining) were responsible for 14 per cent of provincial output and 13.7 per cent of provincial employment; these figures had declined to 6.1 and 4.7 per cent by 1975. By 2011 less than 2 per cent of the Ontario labour force worked in primary industries, and their contribution to provincial GDP was a like proportion. For secondary (i.e., manufacturing and processing) industries, the decline was less dramatic but substantial nonetheless, with their proportion of provincial GDP declining from 40.3 per cent in 1955 to 29.3 in 2008 as employment fell by half, from 38.3 per cent to 19.3 in 2010. Manufacturing, in decline for decades, has in recent years experienced particularly significant contraction: between 1997 and 2014, the contribution of manufacturing to provincial GDP fell from 22.3 to 13 per cent, and employment in manufacturing declined from 19.5 per cent of total provincial employment to 11.2 per cent. By contrast, the contribution of the tertiary sectors—retail, government, financial services, hospitality and tourism, health and education, and so on—to provincial GDP increased from 45.7 to 68.3 per cent while employment went from 48.0 to 78.6 per cent.[10] (See further discussion of economic trends in Chapter 2.)

A noteworthy consequence of these structural shifts has been a radical reorientation within organized labour. In 1950 the big, powerful unions in Ontario were such industrial stalwarts as the Steelworkers, Autoworkers, and Machinists. Today the largest and by times the most militant unions are found in the public sector; the Steelworkers organize university support staff; and Unifor (formerly the Canadian Auto Workers and the Communications, Energy and Paperworkers Union) attempts to organize employees in fast food outlets. These developments are partially tied in with substantial growth in the rate of women's participation in the workforce.

Change in the Public Sphere

Just as Ontario's socio-demographic composition and its economy are barely recognizable 65 years on, so too, in scope, structure, and operation, government looks very different now than it did in 1950. To be sure, the fundamental structural underpinnings are unchanged since 1950, though many aspects of on-the-ground operations have been radically trans- formed. Ontario remains a British-style "responsible government," with power concentrated in the premier and the cabinet; the elected Legislature has a modicum of influence in holding the government accountable and in framing public debate on the great issues of the day, but precious lit- tle policy clout. Governance in Ontario is still very much determined—at once constrained and empowered—by federalism, through a complex web of federal-provincial policy and financial arrangements. Municipalities and local governments continue to provide essential services to the public but remain politically and financially subservient to the province. One funda- mental structural change has wrought far-reaching change to governance throughout the province: the grafting of the Canadian Charter of Rights and Freedoms onto the constitution in 1982.

Politically, for more than half the period it seemed that Ontario was impervious to change. One wag dubbed the province "the longest-lasting one-party state this side of Albania" in reference to the Progressive Con- servative Party's unbroken hold on power from 1943 to 1985. This appar- ent continuity, however, masked far-reaching change, as the Conservatives adroitly and continuously recast themselves to match Ontario's changing needs, composition, and outlook; important continuities notwithstanding, programmatically and attitudinally, the government of Bill Davis (1971–85) differed a good deal from that of Leslie Frost (1949–61). That Ontario was not immune to more dramatic political change became evident when, in the decade after Davis retired, all three major political parties—Liberals, New Democrats, and Conservatives—won majority governments. Electorally, the province remains highly competitive.

The Ontario State in 1950

Though small by current standards in size, budget, and scope, the Ontario government was nonetheless a substantial operation in 1950. In March 1950 it numbered some 13,685 employees; this included staff of provincial mental hospitals, penal institutions, the Ontario Provincial Police, and the Liquor Control and Liquor Licence Boards.[11] Most departments had networks of regional offices but all "headquarters" functions were located in Toronto, with virtually all head office staff housed either in the Legislative Building or in the stolid, almost Stalinesque Whitney Block across the street.

According to the *Public Accounts*, in the fiscal year 1950–51, the Ontario government spent in "ordinary expenditures" (what we now term program spending plus interest on the public debt) $264 million and realized revenues of $265 million for a surplus of roughly a million dollars. However, accounting procedures of the day, with "sinking funds," curious treatment of capital spending, accounts payable and receivable, and the like, were apparently designed to maximize the likelihood of producing a budgetary surplus on paper if not necessarily in reality. If the figures are reorganized in accordance with the accounting methods employed from the late 1960s on—in other words, made comparable to figures in current budgets—then it becomes clear that Ontario was incurring deficits—substantial deficits—in the early 1950s.[12]

By far the largest spending department was the Department of Highways, which accounted for some 32 per cent of the province's program expenditures. The Departments of Education (22 per cent) and Health (13 per cent) were the other big spenders; the Department of Public Welfare consumed 9 per cent of the provincial budget.[13]

Ontario received virtually nothing in federal transfers (having just opted out of the dominion-provincial "tax rental agreement"). The province declined to levy personal income taxes, though it was entitled to do so, but did raise 28.5 per cent of its revenue from corporate tax. The next largest source of provincial income was the gas tax, which contributed 24.3 per cent of government revenue. The only other significant revenue sources were profits and fees from the liquor boards (15.3 per cent), transportation licences (7.8), and succession duties (6.6).

Women were a marginal force in the public service, numerically and substantively. Just 9 per cent of those employed by the Ontario government in 1950 were women—and almost all were single, since married women were only hired if no men or single women were available.[14] Women were paid substantially less than men for similar jobs. Women were plentiful among the ranks of secretaries and clerks, but few and far between in the higher echelons of the government in either the administrative or political realms, beyond a smattering of professional staff in social policy departments such as health and education. When a woman was appointed as a Civil Service Commissioner in 1957, it was sufficiently noteworthy to warrant special mention in the Throne Speech.[15] Only two women had ever served in the Ontario Legislature; one lost her seat in 1945, the other in 1951, and no more were elected until the 1960s. It was only in 1974 that the first female deputy minister was appointed, and it was only at the end of the 1960s that the annual reports of the Civil Service Commission ceased to present data on women employees according to their marital status. Numbers and positions of women in government may not have been a concern, but one group was singled out for special attention in hiring: veterans. The annual Civil

Service Commission reports of this era were careful to document how veterans fared in government hiring; in 1950–51, they comprised 56 per cent
of the men appointed to the service.

Government ran on a rigid command-and-control model, shot through
with paternalism; by way of illustration, for a provincial employee to leave
work early required written permission from the deputy minister.[16] The
principal employee organization, the Civil Service Association of Ontario
(CSAO) sometimes engaged in discussions with the government over pay
and conditions of work, but devoted much of its energy, especially at the
local level, to morale-building social events. Notions of transforming the
CSAO into a union were vehemently rejected by leaders and members alike;
loyalty to the service and camaraderie between bosses and workers within
work units trumped any stirrings of class solidarity.

Local government organization had not changed appreciably since the
Baldwin Act of 1849. Some 954 municipalities dotted the province—29 cities, 38 counties, 306 towns and villages, 572 townships, and 19 "improvement
districts" in Northern Ontario.[17] Plans were in train to erect a federal-style
metropolitan government out of 13 Toronto-area municipalities, with
"Metro" coming into existence in 1954. The province's stance toward
local governments was very much laissez-faire (even creating Metropolitan
Toronto was rather less intrusive than might appear since no local entity
disappeared—just some of their powers).[18] Municipalities received modest
financial support from the province in the form of rigidly controlled conditional grants but relied largely on property taxes for revenue—no small burden considering that municipalities raised and spent almost as much money
as the province (and were prohibited from running deficits lest the Ontario
Municipal Board take control of them).

Socially, the province provided limited services to those in the direst
need but little beyond. The federal government and charitable organizations
shouldered most of the load; in the 1950s the United Appeal movement
"was still consistently raising and spending on a per capita basis more money
for services (other than income maintenance) than was the Public Welfare
Department."[19] Means-tested welfare support was available to "the destitute"
and doctors were paid partial fees from the public purse for looking after
"old age pensioners and other indigents." In addition to a vigorous public
health system focused on disease prevention, Ontario operated mental hospitals and provided grants to community hospitals, tuberculosis sanatoria,
and "various institutions for deprived young and old." Child welfare policy was administered by local children's aid societies, private organizations
funded by the province. The workmen's compensation system was publicly
mandated but entirely financed by employers.

In both financial and policy terms, Ontario took a more activist role in education, though many aspects of the system were left in local hands. Primary and high school curricula were prescribed in authoritative detail by the Department of Education, which dispatched inspectors to ensure adherence to the required curriculum and conducted "provincial," province-wide examinations for Grade 13 that determined 100 per cent of students' final marks. At the same time, locally elected trustees were responsible for almost all operational aspects of the school system. Extensive consolidation of school boards had occurred in the 1940s and continued through the 1950s, mostly involving amalgamating tiny "school sections" (often responsible for a single school) into township boards. In 1950 there were still over 2,000 school boards in Ontario; 71 per cent of elementary schools—some 4,400—comprised one teacher in one room and 40 per cent of the one-room schools lacked indoor toilets.[20] Teachers were ill paid and often lacked formal training; they were required by law to belong to teachers' associations, but these evinced little involvement in labour relations issues or political activity.

Only a very small proportion of young Ontarians attended the province's five universities; nor did they have the option of enrolling in a college of applied arts and technology, for none existed in Ontario.

The Ontario State Today

Structure and Operations   A sketch of the Ontario state 65 years later offers myriad contrasts, although important continuities are also evident. The Ontario government is, in terms of size, budget, and scope, larger and more intrusive by several orders of magnitude than it was in 1950.

The Ontario Public Service (OPS) is an immense and organizationally complex institution, numbering over 60,000 people, though it is significant that fewer people are now employed in the OPS than was the case at the end of the Robarts era in 1971.[21] Its composition as well as its operating norms and procedures only vaguely resemble those of 1950. Structurally, it comprises 27 ministries and three secretariats dedicated to target groups such as seniors and women. The list of provincial agencies runs to many pages and includes hundreds of organizations engaged in all manner of commercial, regulatory, advisory, and adjudicative functions and employing tens of thousands of staff (who are not included in the OPS count).

The OPS and Ontario's agencies, boards, and commissions, along with most of the "broader public sector" (schools, universities, municipalities, and hospitals) are heavily unionized. Scarcely imaginable in 1950, Ontario's occasionally militant public sector unions have not hesitated to exercise their right to strike.

The Ontario government's budget for 2015–16 projected spending of $133 billion ($121 billion on programs and capital projects, the balance on debt interest) and revenue of $124 billion, for a deficit of $9 billion. The provincial debt by the end of fiscal 2016 was expected to stand at $311 billion. Consuming nearly 40 per cent of the provincial budget, the Ministry of Health and Long-Term Care dwarfed all other ministries in spending. The next largest were the Ministries of Education (19 per cent) and Community and Social Services (8 per cent), with another 3 per cent for the Ministry of Children and Youth Services; the Ministry of Transportation, the leading spender in 1952, was allocated a paltry 2.6 per cent. On the revenue side, federal transfer payments—including an embarrassing $2.4 billion in equalization payments—were to account for 18.3 per cent of provincial revenues and corporate tax another 9.1 per cent. Close to half the Ontario government's revenues for 2015–16 were to come from two taxes that did not exist in 1950, personal income tax (24.4 per cent) and retail sales tax (13 per cent). The gas tax, a key revenue source in 1950 was expected to contribute less than 2 per cent to provincial coffers. Such comparisons underplay the extent to which the revenue mix changed over the decades. Perhaps the most striking example lay in the shift toward reliance on personal over corporate income as a tax source. In the early 1960s, when (following the expiration of the federal-provincial tax-sharing agreements) Ontario first effectively set its own tax rates, the province raised substantially more from corporate than from personal income taxes ($187 million versus $114 million in 1961–62); by 2015, a dramatic reversal had taken place ($30.4 billion in personal income tax; $11.3 billion in corporate income tax).

Across all governments in Ontario, a third or more of senior officials, up to and including the deputy minister level provincially and the chief administrative officer level municipally, are women. In terms of ethnicity and culture, the composition of government bureaucracies is increasingly coming to reflect the province's highly diverse population. Political patronage in public service hiring and promotion may surface on rare occasions but is essentially extinct, save to some extent in the agency sector and in politicians' offices.

All governments in Ontario have taken huge steps—culturally as well as logistically—to treat the citizenry as "customers," who expect and deserve exemplary "service" from their public institutions. Access to government services has increased exponentially and routine citizen-government transactions have been greatly simplified. Many dealings—processing of permits and licences, registration of businesses or commercial transactions, and the like—which not so long ago required either a trip to an often distant government office (open only during the day) or a slow exchange of mailed correspondence can now be done instantaneously over the Internet from home or office at literally any time. "One-window" approaches to providing government services and extensive information about services and policies posted on government websites are only some of the means by which government fosters a "customer service" ethic. Technology has made many of these innovations possible, but they are also very much a function of shifting attitudes about the role and orientation of government.

Ontario has fewer than half the municipalities it had in 1950, 444 all told: 6 regions, 23 counties, 11 districts (all in Northern Ontario), 49 cities; most of the balance are towns and townships.[22] Dozens of small townships, villages, and towns have been absorbed into larger governmental units, virtually all against their will. Not all amalgamations and consolidations have involved small rural or semi-rural communities; most populous urban areas have also seen formerly independent municipalities or contiguous suburbs absorbed into large cities. Moreover, the jurisdictional scope of municipalities has widened as well, with municipal governments being assigned responsibilities well beyond the norm of 65 years ago. In return, the province provides substantial funding for municipalities in the form of unconditional block grants, though they still remain heavily dependent on property taxes.

Changes in educational governance have been even more dramatic. The number of local school boards has been repeatedly slashed, so that now they number only 79. Though much larger and with professional capacity undreamed of in 1950, school boards' powers have been in other ways severely circumscribed, on the one hand by powerful, militant teachers' unions and on the other by a centralizing provincial government that has removed their access to the local tax base and imposed standards on everything from literacy testing to allowable hallway dimensions.

An Activist Welfare State Over the past decades the minimalist state that Ontarians knew in 1950 has been transformed into an activist welfare state, though, to be sure, it has experienced periods of backtracking and retrenchment, such as the slashing of social assistance payments by the Harris government in 1995.

The Ontario government of the 1950s was activist but not interventionist, concentrating on providing the facilities necessary to encourage economic development, but not to direct or regulate it. Nor was social policy a prime concern during the premiership of Leslie Frost (1949–61). A crusading journalist commented, "Nothing symbolized the administration of Leslie Frost more than the fact that the disgraceful, crowded and smelly hospital for retarded children at Orillia, subject to pleas for help for years, could be reached by the most modern and expensive four-lane boulevard expressway."[23]

In the 1960s and 1970s, under Conservative premiers John Robarts and Bill Davis, Ontario developed into a full-fledged welfare state, marked by such measures as the adoption of medicare; extensive enhancements to services and benefits for the poor, disabled, and elderly; massive construction of public housing; and the establishment of legal aid and student loan programs. The same period saw a remarkable expansion of postsecondary education, through the creation not only of several universities but an entire system of community colleges. Accordingly, with over half a million full-time students enrolled in the province's 20 universities and 24 community colleges in 2013–14, postsecondary education in Ontario is no longer the elite preserve it was six and a half decades earlier. Roughly 42 per cent of Ontarians aged 18 to 24 attend postsecondary institutions[24]—one of the highest rates in the world.

If the Ontario welfare state has not changed fundamentally since the 1970s—some would argue that it has in fact contracted since then—the Ontario state has become highly activist and interventionist, involved in a far wider range of policy fields than in 1950. Beyond welfare state measures, most notably a panoply of remarkable health services delivered at no cost to patients, Ontario provides services far beyond those available 65 years ago—to name just a few, tough-minded enforcement of court-imposed family support orders, commuter trains in the GTA, a bilingual television network, and business advice and loans. Of at least equal significance, the Ontario state is also involved in a host of regulatory activities in fields thought well outside the ken of government in 1950, including pollution control, interpersonal relations (through human rights legislation, landlord and tenant legislation, and the like), gambling, and local zoning and development processes.

Conclusion

This chapter has highlighted the profound and multi-dimensional changes that have transformed Ontario in recent decades. Whether the focus is on the province's socio-demographic composition, its economy, the role of government and the citizenry's expectation of government, the size and scope of the provincial government, the number and nature of municipal governments, or the attitudinal make-up of the populace, change has been far-reaching, if not always consistent in direction or at a steady pace.

This is more than slightly ironic for a province whose official motto—*Ut Incepit Fedelis, Sic Permanet* (Loyal She Began, Loyal She Remains)—emphasizes stability and continuity. And indeed, important features of present-day Ontario would be familiar to the province's residents in 1950: the continuing dominance, notwithstanding some inroads by visible minorities, of

Anglo-Celtic elites in all aspects of Ontario society, economy, and politics; the self-confident belief (non-Ontarians would call it smugness) that the province is the centrepiece of Confederation; the preference for progressive, middle-of-the-road politics; the tension between Toronto and the province's several distinctive regions; the continuing subservience of local and municipal governments to Queen's Park, despite their greatly enhanced importance in people's everyday lives. Other continuities could be cited.

Overall, though, the contrast between the Ontario of today and the Ontario of 1950 is remarkable. The changes outlined in this chapter tell us a good deal about why present-day Ontario politics unfold as they do.

Discussion Questions

1. Does the Ontario of 1950 indeed seem almost unrecognizable today? Why or why not?
2. Has the scale of social change evident in Ontario since 1950 been matched by a similar scale of change politically? Explain.
3. Is the divide between urban and rural Ontario (or between the Greater Toronto Area and the rest of the province) significant politically? Why?
4. How has the provincial economy evolved since 1950?
5. What changes might you expect for Ontario in the future? Imagine you are writing in the year 2050 and discuss how Ontario may have changed between now and then.

Notes

1 K.J. Rea, *The Prosperous Years: The Economic History of Ontario 1939–1975* (Toronto: Ontario Historical Studies Series and the University of Toronto Press, 1985), 17.
2 Unless otherwise indicated, demographic and economic figures are taken from Statistics Canada data. To avoid cluttering the text, specific references are not included; these are available from the author on request.
3 D.R. Richmond, *The Economic Transformation of Ontario* (Toronto: Ontario Economic Council, 1974), 3.
4 Lionel D. Feldman, *Ontario 1945–1973: The Municipal Dynamic* (Toronto: Ontario Economic Council, 1974), 7.
5 Rand Dyck, "The Socio-Economic Setting of Ontario Politics," in *The Government and Politics of Ontario*, 5th ed., ed. Graham White (Toronto: University of Toronto Press, 1997), 44, Table 10.
6 It is worth noting that Indigenous people are excluded from the Statistics Canada definition of "visible minorities."
7 Statistics Canada, *Projections of the Diversity of the Canadian Population*, Catalogue no. 91–551-X (Ottawa: Statistics Canada, 2010).

8   Nelson Wiseman, "Change in Ontario Politics," in *The Government and Politics of Ontario*, 5th ed., ed. Graham White (Toronto: University of Toronto Press, 1997), 427.

9   Ontario Economic Council, *Ontario: A Society in Transition* (Toronto: Ontario Economic Council, 1972), 61.

10   Figures for 1955 and 1975 are from Rea, *The Prosperous Years*, 83, Table 15. Output data for 1999 based on author's calculations from Statistics Canada, *Provincial Gross Domestic Product by Industry 1984–1999*, Catalogue no. 15–203-XIB (Ottawa: Statistics Canada, 2000), Table 1, and *Provincial and Territorial Economic Accounts Review*, Catalogue no. 15–203-XIB (Ottawa: Statistics Canada, 2008). Employment data are calculated from the 1996 census, Statistics Canada, *Profile of Census Divisions and Subdivisions in Ontario*, Catalogue no. 15–203-XIB, vol. I, plus "Employment by Major Industry Groups, Seasonally Adjusted by Province." Data on manufacturing 1997–2014 from Chapter 2 of this book.

11   Ontario Civil Service Commission, *Report for the Year Ending March 31, 1951* (Toronto: Queen's Printer, 1952). All data in this chapter on civil service staff levels are taken from commission reports.

12   For example, in fiscal 1951–52, the province reported a surplus of just under a million dollars but by current standards, incurred a deficit of $34.3 million. My thanks to Ken Leishman, former assistant provincial auditor of Ontario, for this calculation. He is responsible for the figures, but not for my interpretation of them, or of then-current accounting procedures.

13   Data on revenue and expenditure have been taken or calculated from various Ontario budgets; the *Public Accounts*; Richmond, *The Economic Transformation of Ontario*; and D.K. Foot, *Provincial Public Finance in Ontario: An Empirical Analysis of the Last Twenty-five Years* (Toronto: Ontario Economic Council, 1977).

14   Wayne Roberts, *Don't Call Me Servant: Government Work and Unions in Ontario 1911–1984* (Toronto: Ontario Public Service Employees Union, 1994), 62.

15   J.H. Hodgetts, *From Arm's Length to Hands-On: The Formative Years of Ontario's Public Service, 1867–1940* (Toronto: Ontario Historical Studies Series and University of Toronto Press, 1995), 189.

16   Roberts, *Don't Call Me Servant*, 47.

17   Ontario Department of Municipal Affairs, *1951 Municipal Directory* (Toronto: Queen's Printer, 1951), xxii.

18   *1951 Municipal Directory*, 11.

19   The summary in this paragraph is based on Vernon Lang, *The Service State Emerges in Ontario 1945–1973* (Toronto: Ontario Economic Council, 1974), 4–5; the quotations are also taken from this source.

20   R.D. Gidney, *From Hope to Harris: The Reshaping of Ontario's Schools* (Toronto: University of Toronto Press, 1999), 13–14.

21   In the early 1990s, the Civil Service Commission (now the Public Service Commission) replaced reporting OPS complement size by head count with full-time equivalent (FTE) figures. The FTE complement as of March 31, 2014 was 62,960, which would translate into a somewhat higher number of actual people. This figure includes "regular" (i.e., permanent) and fixed-term employees but excludes students, seasonal staff, and employees of Crown corporations and independent agencies, boards, and commissions, such as the Liquor Control Board of Ontario, the Workplace Safety and Insurance Board, and Hydro.

Ontario Public Service Commission, *Annual Report 2013–14*, 4, https://www.
ontario.ca/document/public-service-commission-annual-report-2014

22 Association of Municipalities of Ontario, "Ontario Municipalities," http://
www.amo.on.ca/AMO-Content/Municipal-101/Ontario-Municipalities.
aspx. A small number of "cities" are such in name only, such as the City of
Kawartha Lakes and the City of Prince Edward, which are in reality coterminous
with the former counties of Victoria and Prince Edward.

23 Quoted in Joseph Schull, *Ontario Since 1867* (Toronto: McClelland and Stewart,
1978), 347.

24 Ontario Ministry of Training, Colleges and Universities, *Results-Based Plan
Briefing Book, 2013–14*, Part I, 20, http://www.mtc.gov.on.ca/en/about/
rbp_2013_14.shtml

2

The Political Economy of Ontario

MATTHIAS OSCHINSKI*

Introduction

Over the past 15 years, Ontario's economy experienced significant structural changes and business cycle effects that have contributed to a plethora of economic policy challenges, most markedly in the once-vibrant manufacturing sector, leading to the loss of well-paid jobs and international competitiveness. In fact, as this chapter will show, Ontario's tradable sectors contributed very little to recent job growth. Instead, employment grew rapidly in the nontradable sectors of the economy, in part due to a rapid increase in broader public sector jobs. As a consequence, Ontario is confronted with a widening trade deficit.

Moreover, the 2008 recession left the province with a hefty fiscal deficit, rendering it unlikely that job growth in the broader public sector can be sustained at past levels. In addition to public sector debt, private household debt has soared in recent years, threatening to dampen private consumption, which, in turn, might affect the nontradable sector negatively.

Overall, then, Ontario's current macroeconomic outlook appears to be rather bleak, creating a number of challenges for public policy—including high unemployment and underemployment, a rise in nonstandard employment, perceived skills shortages in emerging industries, and growing demand for public services in a context of high debt and deficit.

All of this suggests that Ontario confronts a critical juncture in its economic trajectory. Given the scope of the economic challenges it faces, Ontario needs to re-evaluate its value proposition in the global economy and ensure that its economic policies are aligned accordingly. The realignment of economic policies faces several barriers, however. The first is a highly charged partisan environment in the province and the absence of a coherent economic vision. The second is that changing many of the framework economic policies is subject to intergovernmental bargaining, which requires a more instrumental Ontario in the federation—a role that Ontario has been reluctant to play.

The State of Ontario's Economy

Industry and Employment Shares

In 2014 Ontario's economy contributed about 36.7 per cent to Canada's overall GDP (see Table 2.1 below). While this share has fallen slightly compared to 1997 and 2007, a disaggregated view shows that it has been declining more sharply for specific industries. In particular, in construction and manufacturing it appears to have diminished most steadily. Information and cultural industries, educational services, health care, and public administration, in contrast, have seen their respective shares increase or at least remain stable during this time period.

Within Ontario, the finance, insurance, and real estate sector has become the most vital contributor to the province's GDP, accounting for 23.2 per cent

Table 2.1 Ontario GDP as Share of Canadian GDP

	1997	2007	2014
All industries	39.9	40.3	36.7
Accommodation and food services	35.9	35.9	34.0
★AWMR	47.5	47.7	43.6
Agriculture, forestry, fishing, and hunting	18.7	19.0	18.9
Arts, entertainment, and recreation	41.9	42.3	38.4
Construction	36.5	34.9	27.8
Educational services	39.7	40.2	40.4
Finance, insurance, and real estate	44.8	45.6	51.9
Health care and social assistance	37.7	39.1	37.1
Information and cultural industries	41.7	44.5	43.4
Manufacturing	51.8	49.5	44.9
Mining and oil and gas extraction	5.5	4.3	6.3
Other services (except public administration)	38.4	38.4	36.3
Professional, scientific, and technical services	46.2	46.8	43.8
Public administration	38.0	37.8	39.4
Retail trade	38.7	37.9	37.1
Transportation and warehousing	34.7	33.5	33.5
Utilities	32.1	32.1	29.9
Wholesale trade	42.3	44.8	43.7

★AWMR = Administrative and support, waste management and remediation services.

Source: Statistics Canada, CANSIM Tables 379–0025 and 379–0030.

in 2014 (see Table 2.2). While manufacturing accounted for the largest share in 1997 at 22.3 per cent, the sector's contribution declined significantly to 18.3 per cent in 2007 and fell further to 13.0 per cent in 2014. Next to public administration, health care and wholesale trade have the highest GDP shares in the province, while the biggest gain appears to have occurred in professional, scientific, and technical services. In sum, a look at disaggregated GDP shares shows the decline in importance of the goods sector, that is, agriculture, construction, manufacturing, mining, and utilities. Of these sectors, only construction and mining had a higher GDP share in 2014 than in 1997.

As Table 2.3 below illustrates, this structural change is also reflected in employment figures. Between 1993 and 2014, the percentage share of total employment in goods-producing industries fell from 24 per cent to 17.7 per cent. As a closer look reveals, however, the decline actually started after 1997. In fact, between 1993 and 1997 employment in manufacturing and

Table 2.2 Ontario GDP by Industry

Industry	GDP Percentage Share		
	1997	2007	2014
Finance, insurance, and real estate	21.3	22.4	23.2
Manufacturing	22.3	18.3	13.0
Public administration	5.8	5.3	7.2
Health care and social assistance	6.5	6.1	6.8
Wholesale trade	5.1	6.4	6.6
Professional, scientific, and technical services	4.4	5.7	6.4
Educational services	5.5	4.8	5.7
Retail trade	4.8	5.6	5.5
Construction	4.6	5.2	5.4
Transportation and warehousing	4.2	3.9	3.8
Information and cultural industries	3.1	4.1	3.8
AWMR★	2.4	3.0	3.0
Other services (except public administration)	2.3	2.5	2.0
Utilities	2.6	2.1	2.0
Accommodation and food services	2.2	1.9	1.9
Mining and oil and gas extraction	0.8	0.5	1.4
Agriculture, forestry, fishing, and hunting	1.3	1.1	0.8
Arts, entertainment and recreation	1.0	1.0	0.7

★AWMR = Administrative and support, waste management and remediation services.

Source: Statistics Canada, CANSIM Tables 379–0025 and 379–0030.

Table 2.3 Employment by Industry in Ontario

Industry	Total Employment by Industry				Employment Share by Industry			
	1993	1997	2007	2014	1993	1997	2007	2014
Goods-producing industries	1,020,247	1,106,637	1,131,412	1,033,100	24.0	24.6	20.4	17.7
Manufacturing	792,347	876,650	797,057	653,215	18.6	19.5	14.4	11.2
Construction	146,596	157,113	258,014	305,486	3.5	3.5	4.7	5.2
Utilities	46,663	42,059	46,787	45,073	1.1	0.9	0.8	0.8
Mining, quarrying, and oil and gas extraction	23,767	22,690	23,222	24,620	0.6	0.5	0.4	0.4
Forestry, logging, and support	10,873	8,125	6,332	4,706	0.3	0.2	0.1	0.1
Service-producing industries	3,228,516	3,397,573	4,413,675	4,803,915	76.0	75.4	79.6	82.3
Trade	741,515	785,307	968,512	1,030,025	17.5	17.4	17.5	17.6
Health care and social assistance	413,382	431,105	531,731	644,373	9.7	9.6	9.6	11.0
Educational services	352,634	326,718	414,711	462,564	8.3	7.3	7.5	7.9
Accommodation and food services	293,569	306,245	366,718	428,440	6.9	6.8	6.6	7.3
Public administration	285,444	261,940	371,217	387,985	6.7	5.8	6.7	6.6
Professional, scientific, and technical services	162,228	202,357	312,949	350,071	3.8	4.5	5.6	6.0
AWMR*	135,432	186,613	357,859	341,950	3.2	4.1	6.5	5.9
Finance and insurance	x	x	282,147	317,108			5.1	5.4
Transportation and warehousing	186,925	202,473	246,089	259,552	4.4	4.5	4.4	4.4
Other services (except public administration)	160,114	169,005	183,739	202,455	3.8	3.8	3.3	3.5
Information and cultural industries	120,766	124,439	134,147	138,046	2.8	2.8	2.4	2.4
Real estate, rental, and leasing	x	x	103,651	109,272	x	x	1.9	1.9
Arts, entertainment, and recreation	63,983	72,488	93,434	94,026	1.5	1.6	1.7	1.6
Unclassified businesses**			78,312	84,022			1.4	1.4
Management of companies and enterprises	16,753	23,482	46,770	38,049	0.4	0.5	0.8	0.7

*AWMR = Administrative and support, waste management and remediation services.

**Unclassified businesses are businesses for which the industrial classification (NAICS) has yet to be determined.

Note: x = Suppressed to meet confidentiality requirements of the Statistics Act.

Source: Statistics Canada, CANSIM Table 281–0024 (SEPH).

construction increased quite significantly. As a consequence, the employment share of goods-producing industries rose from 24 per cent in 1993
to 24.6 per cent in 1997 before falling to 20.4 per cent in 2007. To a large
extent this decrease was driven by massive employment losses in the manufacturing sector, which saw its employment share decline from 19.5 per cent
in 1997 to 11.2 per cent in 2014.

In contrast, the employment share in service-producing industries
increased quite considerably, from 76 per cent in 1993 to more than 82 per
cent in 2014. A disaggregated look at the data reveals that total employment has increased in all service-producing industries since 1993. The largest
employers in the service sector are wholesale and retail trade followed by
health care and social assistance. Also noteworthy, between 1997 and 2014
public administration saw a steady increase in employment, from around
262,000 in 1997 to almost 388,000 in 2014, an increase in employment
share from 5.8 per cent to 6.6 per cent.

To a certain extent, the shift in employment from goods producing
industries to services producing industries in developed countries reflects
the new division of labour in a globalizing economy. With the creation of
the World Trade Organization (WTO) in 1995 and the subsequent inclusion of strong emerging markets, labour-intensive tasks of the production
chain were increasingly outsourced from economically advanced countries. Yet, as the next section reveals, Ontario also experienced a decline
of its overall tradable sector, which might be a more alarming trend in
the medium and long term.

In the context of shifts in employment it seems appropriate to address
the issue of nonstandard employment in Ontario. Following H. Krahn,
nonstandard employment can take a variety of dimensions.[1] More specifically, the term encompasses workers in part-time employment, those with
multiple jobs, employees on temporary contracts, and the self-employed
without additional employees. Studying these categories for the period of
the late 1970s up to 1994, Krahn finds that nonstandard employment in
Canada has indeed increased during that time, probably exacerbated by
the deep recession in the early 1990s. His results indicate that although
women are more likely to be involved in nonstandard employment, during the 1980s part-time jobs and temporary work arrangements became
increasingly common for male employees as well.

Following Krahn's methodology, Table 2.4 below shows the dimensions
of nonstandard employment for Ontario between 1997 and 2014. As the
figures indicate, nonstandard employment has remained fairly stable for
most categories with the marked exception of temporary work. Here, the
employment share rose from 7.8 per cent in 1997 to 10.7 per cent in 2014.

Table 2.4   Types of Nonstandard Work in Canada as Percentage of Total Employment, by Sex and Age Group

Sex	Age-Group	Part-Time		Multiple		Temporary		Own-Account	
		1997	2014	1997	2014	1997	2014	1997	2014
Male	15–24	43.4	43.6	5.1	5.3	22.3	30.9	4.9	3.1
	25–34	6.0	7.9	4.9	5.4	7.0	10.9	8.5	9.3
	35–44	3.4	4.9	4.3	4.7	4.3	5.6	11.6	11.8
	45–54	4.1	4.7	3.7	4.1	3.3	4.9	12.8	14.0
	55–64	10.3	10.4	3.8	3.5	4.1	6.2	18.1	17.8
	65–69	32.7	31.0	2.9	3.9	8.1	9.7	30.4	29.3
Female	15–24	58.4	60.5	8.0	8.8	20.7	31.8	6.4	2.0
	25–34	21.2	19.3	5.2	7.2	7.5	10.8	6.9	6.8
	35–44	22.5	18.0	5.9	5.7	5.8	7.8	9.8	8.5
	45–54	22.8	17.9	4.5	5.0	5.4	5.7	9.8	9.7
	55–64	30.0	24.3	3.5	4.6	4.7	6.6	12.8	13.0
	65–69	56.9	45.4	3.3	4.9	5.4	11.2	27.9	23.9
Total % of All Employment		**18.9**	**19.0**	**4.9**	**5.3**	**7.8**	**10.7**	**10.0**	**10.4**

Notes and Definitions:

- Methodology was reproduced from H. Krahn, "Non-standard Work on the Rise," *Statistics Canada, Perspectives,* Catalogue no. 75–001E (1995). Note that Krahn excludes the age category of workers 65–69, whereas they are included here.
- Part-time workers are defined as individuals who usually work less than 30 hours a week in all jobs; multiple workers are tabulated based on individuals who hold more than one job, whether full-time, part-time, or self-employed; temporary workers include persons working in seasonal, contract, or other casual employment; and own-account workers are defined as self-employed persons without paid employees.
- Totals for all nonstandard work will not sum to 100 per cent given that jobs are not necessarily mutually exclusive (e.g., an individual working part-time may also hold multiple jobs, etc.).

Source: Statistics Canada, Labour Force Survey.

Moreover, the increase in temporary work appears to be consistent in all age categories.

A.M. Noack and L. Vosko corroborate these findings.[2] However, they extend their analysis to include precarious employment, which takes into account the drop in unionized jobs in the private sector. According to the authors, a lower rate of unionization is commonly correlated with lower job security, fewer or no employment benefits for health and pension, and lower salaries. Workers affected by this are usually part-time employees. In fact, as Noack and Vosko report, in 2009, seven out of every 10 part-time private sector employees in Ontario were in precarious jobs. Industries most affected by this were "other services" (which includes companies in repair and maintenance services, personal care and laundry, and civic and professional organizations) and business, building, and other support services.

As the next section will show, in recent years Ontario has experienced large employment losses especially in the tradable sectors, such as manufacturing. This contributed to a loss of unionized positions in the private sector.

Tradable versus Nontradable Industries

In order to illustrate the fundamental changes in Ontario's economy since the late 1990s, it is helpful to distinguish its economic sectors into tradable and nontradable industries. Tradable industries produce commodities and services, which don't have to be consumed at or near the location where they are being produced. Hence, mining and financial services can be seen as tradable industries.

In the case of nontradable industries, in contrast, the location of production and consumption does not differ too much. Hence daycare centres and barbershops, for instance, are more widely dispersed in an economy. Measuring the locational concentration of businesses and employing input-output tables to establish trade shares allows us to categorize industries according to the tradability of the commodity or service they produce.

Table 2.5 below lists each industry according to its tradability. As can be seen, the vast majority of Ontario's employment in 2014 was in the nontradable sector, around 39.3 per cent in fully nontradable industries, and another 31.4 per cent in mainly nontradable industries. In other words, less than 30 per cent of Ontario's workforce is employed in tradable industries.

As Figure 2.1 below illustrates, Ontario has experienced a rapid increase in nontradable employment since 1997. In fact, of the total number of jobs created between 1997 and 2014, more than 90 per cent were in nontradable industries compared to a mere 9.2 per cent in tradable sectors. Moreover, around 40 per cent of all new jobs created in the nontradable sectors were broader public sector jobs, that is, health care, educational services, and public administration. Given Ontario's current fiscal situation, it is unlikely that job growth in the broader public sector can continue at this level.

As a consequence of Ontario's meagre performance with regard to its tradable industries, its shares in total imports and exports also dropped significantly between 1997 and 2014. As Figure 2.2 illustrates, Ontario's imports and exports as a total of Canadian imports and exports peaked at 66 per cent and 55 per cent, respectively, in 1999 before falling to 57.7 per cent and 39.4 per cent, respectively, by 2014.

Table 2.5   Tradable and Nontradable Industries in Ontario

Fully Tradable	Fully Nontradable
(Employment Share 2014: 18.6%)	*(Employment Share 2014: 39.3%)*
Agriculture, forestry, and fishing	Construction
Mining, oil, and gas	Wholesale trade
Food and beverages manufacturing	Transportation and warehousing
Textiles and leather	Real estate, rental, and leasing
Wood manufacturing	Legal services
Pulp and paper manufacturing	Management of companies and enterprises
Printing and related	Office administrative services
Petroleum and coal manufacturing	Facilities support services
Chemicals	Employment services
Plastics and rubber	Business support services
Computer and electronics	Investigation and security services
Electrical equipment	Waste management and remediation
Automobile manufacturing	Arts, entertainment, and recreation
Aerospace	Accommodation and food services
Accounting and tax preparation	Other services
Architectural, engineering, and related services	Public administration
Specialized design services	
Computer system design and services	
Management, scientific, and technical services	
Scientific research and development services	
Advertising and related services	
Other professional services	
Travel arrangement and reservation services	
Service to buildings and dwellings	
Other support services	
Mainly Tradable	**Mainly Nontradable**
(Employment Share 2014: 10.8%)	*(Employment Share 2014: 31.4%)*
Non-metallic mineral products	Utilities
Primary metal manufacturing	Retail trade
Fabricated metal manufacturing	Educational services
Machinery manufacturing	Health care and social assistance
Furniture manufacturing	
Information and cultural industries	
Finance and insurance	

Source: Author's calculations.

Figure 2.1 Employment Change in Tradable and Nontradable Industries

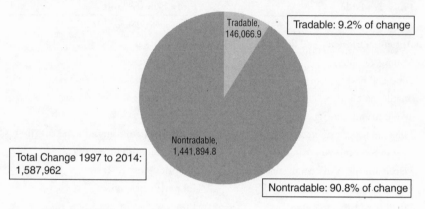

Tradable, 146,066.9

Tradable: 9.2% of change

Total Change 1997 to 2014: 1,587,962

Nontradable, 1,441,894.8

Nontradable: 90.8% of change

Source: Author's calculations.

Figure 2.2 Ontario's Share in Canada's Exports and Imports

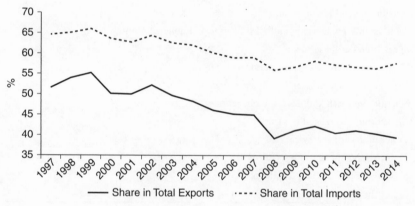

— Share in Total Exports   ····· Share in Total Imports

Source: Industry Canada.

Structural Changes and Business Cycle Effects

When analyzing Ontario's economic performance and the resulting political and socio-economic consequences, two main factors can be discerned. Structural changes affect the economy over the long term, transforming a country's employment pattern and industry composition. Business cycle effects, in contrast, impact the economy over the short and medium term, usually leaving the long-term economic structure largely untouched. This section discusses the reasons for, and effects of, structural changes and business cycles in Ontario in turn.

Structural Changes in Ontario's Economy

Similar to most other developed economies, Ontario has been experiencing a shift from goods-producing industries and occupations to service-producing industries and occupations. Figure 2.3 depicts the ratio of service-producing employment to goods-producing employment in Ontario from 1997 to 2014. As the graph illustrates, the ratio of service-producing jobs to goods-producing jobs increased slightly between 1997 and 2001. From 2001 to 2004 it remained somewhat stagnant before increasing rather strongly up until 2014.

Why did this change occur? R. Schettkat and L. Yocarini identify three major dimensions of structural change.[3] First, a shift in the inter-industry division of labour can lead to changes in the occupational employment structure. In other words, outsourcing of specific jobs from goods-producing to service-producing industries can increase the number of service-producing employees while decreasing the number of goods-producing employees. This can happen, for instance, when manufacturers outsource service-related tasks. Due to the nature of industry classifications, jobs in manufacturing industries are often classified as manufacturing employment (i.e., goods-producing) while jobs in specialized service firms are defined as service-producing occupations. Hence, changes in relative employment might simply be a matter of re-classification due to outsourcing.

Figure 2.3 Ratio of Service-Producing Employment to Goods-Producing Employment in Ontario, 1997–2014

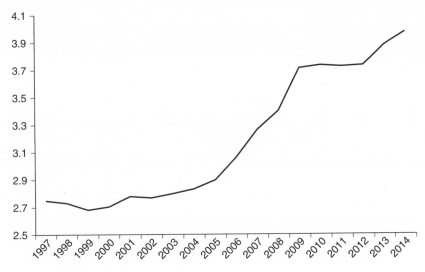

Source: Statistics Canada, Labour Force Survey.

A second reason why demand for labour might shift to service-producing occupations is due to productivity differentials between industries. As A. Woelfl points out, higher productivity growth in manufacturing relative to the services sector can lead to a reallocation of employment from the former to the latter.[4] The rationale behind this is that if productivity growth is consistently higher in manufacturing, as is the case for most OECD countries, companies are able to produce the same amount of output with fewer employees, which, in turn, can contribute to job losses in manufacturing industries.

Finally, shifts in final demand can result in occupational changes in the labour market. As R. Schettkat finds, there is evidence that, as countries grow richer, final demand for goods decreases relative to final demand for services.[5] In this context, D. Pilat and colleagues point to the importance of demographic changes in developed economies.[6] As with most developed countries, Canada is facing the challenges of an aging population. This demographic trend can give rise to different demand patterns, especially with regard to health care and social services and, in some cases, at the expense of manufacturing. As a consequence, employment would shift from the manufacturing sector toward the services sector.

Analyzing these three channels, Schettkat and Yocarini find that though outsourcing has been a common feature in a globalizing world economy, it cannot explain much of the rise in service-producing occupations.[7] Rather, their study points to the increasing importance of shifts in final demand as a major cause for structural changes in the labour market.

In recent years, increased automation and digitization have contributed to structural changes in the economy and will significantly transform occupations over the next decades. Advances in artificial intelligence, increased machine-to-machine communication and progress in robotics will affect almost all industries. In a recent book, E. Brynjolfsson and A. McAffee argue that these new developments are leading to an inflection point at which the rate of technological change is going to destroy more jobs than it creates.[8] Studying the effects of automation on US occupations, D. Autor and D. Dorn find that technological changes have contributed to a polarization of the labour market.[9] More specifically, they find that increased automation leads to job losses in routine middle-skilled occupations (e.g., most occupations in the manufacturing sector) as the tasks performed by those employees are easy to automate. In contrast, relatively higher paid occupations requiring creativity and abstract thinking are fairly protected from automation as are relatively lower-paid service jobs such as occupations in personal care or protective services. The result is an "hour glass" job market, with rising employment in high-skilled and low-skilled jobs and an eroding middle. This development, then, also contributes to the rise in income inequality witnessed over the past two decades. Faster technological change might exacerbate this situation.

Business Cycle Effects

In addition to the structural changes discussed above, business cycle effects affected Ontario's economy over the past decade. Two main events might be distinguished here: first, the commodities boom in the early 2000s; second, the bursting of the housing price bubble in the United States in 2008.

Between 2002 and 2008 global commodity prices experienced a steep increase mainly due to a rapid expansion of economic activity in emerging markets. This, in turn, led to an increase in primary products from Canada's mining sector. As a consequence, the Canadian dollar sharply appreciated vis-à-vis the US dollar in the following years. Since primary commodities are unevenly spread among Canadian provinces, the economic consequences of the commodity boom were rather unbalanced. While the mining sectors in Alberta and Saskatchewan profited greatly, Ontario's economy was largely negatively affected. This is illustrated in Figure 2.4 below, which depicts changes in Ontario's manufacturing employment vis-à-vis the changes in the exchange rate between the Canadian and US dollars.

With the Canadian dollar appreciating, Ontario's manufactured goods became more expensive in US dollar terms and hence less competitive in international trade. Manufacturing employment as a share of total employment in Ontario started to decline, from around 18 per cent in 2002 to 11.2 per cent in 2014.

The bursting of the US housing bubble in 2008 and the subsequent global financial crisis further aggravated this negative trend. As a consequence of this crisis, the United States, Ontario's most important export destination, had lost significant steam; consumer spending declined and negatively affected the demand for imports from Ontario.

Economic Policy Challenges

The early 2000s brought two challenges to Ontario's then rather vibrant industrial base. First, a resource boom contributed to a rise in the value of the Canadian dollar, lowering the competitiveness of Canadian exports. Then, appreciation of the Canadian exchange rate increased competitive pressure for domestic manufacturers.[10] In fact, the favourable exchange rate during the late 1990s gave manufacturers a price advantage over US products, making Canadian commodities more attractive abroad. Things changed, however, in the early 2000s. A resource boom, driving up prices of

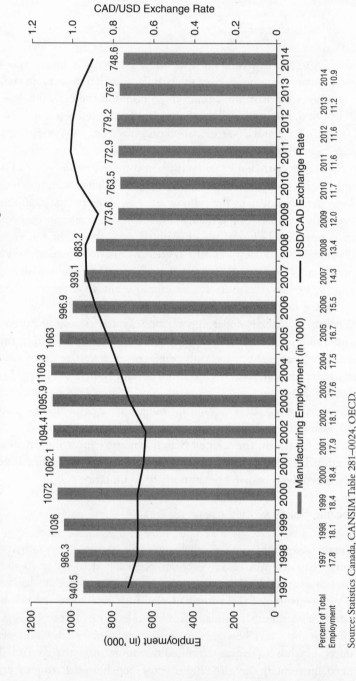

Figure 2.4 Employment in Ontario Manufacturing and CAD/USD Exchange Rate

Source: Statistics Canada, CANSIM Table 281–0024, OECD.

primary goods, started to affect the Canadian economy. Being rich in natural resources, Canada's mining sector profited from increased global demand for primary commodities, resulting in an appreciation of the Canadian exchange rate. The strength of the Canadian dollar, in turn, drove up prices of Canadian manufactures, thus decreasing the sector's international competitiveness.

The 2008 recession that first hit the US economy before turning into a global phenomenon exacerbated the woes of Ontario's manufacturing industry. As credits dried up, private consumption plummeted in the United States, leading to a decrease in demand in Ontario's largest export market. Additional problems in the Eurozone also lowered demand for Canadian products in EU member states and uncertainty about the future led to a drop in Canada itself. In this context, the so-called Detroit Three—GM, Chrysler, and Ford—came to the brink of bankruptcy. In Ontario, home to roughly one-fifth of North America's total auto production, this generated a fear of massive unemployment as the woes of the big carmakers also threatened the livelihood of a large number of suppliers. In light of this, the governments of the United States, Canada, and Ontario coordinated a bailout (through the purchases of equity stakes in GM and Chrysler) in an attempt to help the companies restructure and survive. The federal government and the provincial government contributed a total of $14.4 billion to this effort. It has been estimated that around 52,000 Canadian jobs were saved due to this measure.[11] The bailout was an easy sell for both the federal and provincial government since numerous well-paying jobs were at stake in municipalities already hit hard by job losses in manufacturing.

While the bailout was criticized by some as a waste of taxpayers' money and a blatant subsidy to two companies that were largely responsible for their own troubles, an empirical study by Shiell and Somerville comes to a somewhat different conclusion.[12] In their view, the total cost of the auto bailout was markedly less than the total economic losses of $20 billion Canada would have incurred, and two-thirds of which Ontario would have borne, without government action. Chrysler committed to maintain 20 per cent of its North American production in Canada until 2014, while GM vowed to keep 16 per cent of its operations until 2016. In addition, GM promised to invest a total of $2 billion in its Canadian operations and $1 billion into research and development.[13] Surprising many critics, by 2011 both Chrysler and GM had successfully restructured, turned fortunes around, and reported small profits. Both governments also stand to recoup much of their investments as a result.

More recently, the Canadian dollar dropped significantly in value vis-à-vis the US dollar. This is mainly the result of two developments. First, with the US economy recovering from the financial crisis, confidence in the US dollar is rising. In addition, reacting to the slowdown in the Canadian economy, the Bank of Canada started to lower interest rates to make the Canadian dollar a less attractive investment vehicle. This takes pressure off the exchange rate and thus supports international competitiveness of the nonresource tradable sectors. That said, Canada faces a second issue that would, in effect, require exactly the opposite reaction, that is, an increase in interest rates. Over the past decade, household debt in Canada has been rising steadily, from around 110 per cent of personal disposable income in 2002 to around 165 per cent of personal disposable income in 2015.[14] As a result, Canada's private household debt as a ratio of personal disposable income was higher in 2015 than that of the United States. Lower interest rates in this situation might further aggravate the problem with dire consequences for the economy in the medium and longer term.

An additional challenge for Ontario's economic policy is the province's public debt burden. As Figure 2.5 below illustrates, Ontario's net debt to GDP ratio has increased considerably from around 26.8 in 2007–08 to 39.4 in 2014–15. While Ontario had a surplus of $668 million in 2000, it reported a deficit of around $10.5 billion in 2013–14. In July 2015 the rating agency Standard & Poor's downgraded Ontario's credit rating from AA- to A+ due to a combination of a very high debt burden and a very weak budgetary performance.

The Political Economy of Economic Transformation

The ratings downgrade is symptomatic of a general souring of opinion on Ontario's economic future. Recent discourse on Ontario, in fact, has been dominated by a narrative of declinism. A decline in manufacturing

Figure 2.5 Ontario Net Debt to GDP Ratio, 1997–2014

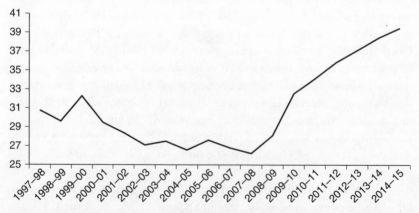

Source: Ontario Financing Authority, 2015.

employment, a ballooning public deficit and lagging labour productivity are symptomatic of diminished international competitiveness. Public commentators ponder whether or not the province will become an extension of the US Rust Belt.[15] Ontario's admission to the club of equalization recipients has further contributed to a souring of sentiment (see Chapter 8 in this volume).

Overall employment in the broader public sector, a driver in employment growth in the past 12 years, is likely to stagnate or turn negative given the size of the debt. At the same time, consumer spending might adjust to lower levels with negative effects on other nontradable sectors of the economy. Over the near and medium term, it is vital, then, for Ontario to revive its tradable sector to stimulate both economic and employment growth in the province. This contributes to two economic policy imperatives. The first is a reordering of key national economic policies. The second is the need for a coherent postindustrial economic vision for Ontario.

The first imperative is a rewiring of Ontario's economic relationship with the rest of Canada. Much of national economic policy is predicated on the old logic of a uniquely prosperous Ontario. For example, even though Ontario's unemployment rate has hovered above the national average in recent years, its workers and employers still make a large net contribution to the national Employment Insurance (EI) program—$1.2 billion in 2012.[16] The percentage of unemployed in Ontario covered by EI in 2012 was 38 per cent, far below the national average.[17] Furthermore, even though Ontario's fiscal capacity (the ability of the provincial government to raise revenues) has declined relative to that of the other provinces, Ontarians still make a substantial net payment into the equalization program—$4 billion in 2012. These are but two examples across a suite of federal public policies that serve the province poorly.

The result, however, is a net distribution of wealth from Ontario. According to the Mowat Centre, there is a $12-billion gap between what Ontarians pay into the federation versus the resources they receive.[18] This gap was (perhaps) justifiable during periods when Ontario's prosperity far outstripped other regions. But, in a context of slow growth and high unemployment, the net transfer remains a tremendous constraint on Ontario's economic transformation.

Ontario also needs a clear vision of its economic future. Digitization, artificial intelligence, and automation are going to be the drivers of a new industrial revolution. To prepare for this, Ontario needs to align public policies accordingly. A highly skilled, entrepreneurial, and adaptive labour force is a necessity to succeed in this new environment. Skills training should, however, not be restricted to younger-age cohorts. As technological developments will render skills redundant at a faster pace, life-long-learning is going to be a key issue in labour market politics.

Fostering a truly entrepreneurial labour force and creating an inviting environment for innovative ideas can help Ontario reap the benefits of the digital revolution.

Conclusion

This chapter presents a decidedly pessimistic view of the Ontario economy and the economic policy challenges confronting Ontarians, though that is not the primary intent. Ontarians should find some comfort in the fact the province has many of the framework conditions right. Ontario's population is among the most educated in the world. According to most measures, its cities are among the most livable in the world. And it still is a magnet for international talent. Combined, these factors should give pause to those betting against Canada's most populous province.

The primary argument, however, is that Ontario faces a critical juncture in its economic history. Given the scope of the economic challenges it faces, urgent and coordinated action is required across a range of public policies. Absent this, Ontario will be poorly positioned to compete in the global economy and the standard of living for Ontarians will fail to keep pace with the province's international peers.

Discussion Questions

1. What are Ontario's economic prospects? Will Ontario retain its status as a global player in manufacturing?
2. What public policy adjustments are required to help Ontario emerge stronger from the economic downturn that began in 2008?
3. The chapter contends that many federal public policies are hindering Ontario's economic transition. What explains the persistence of these policies? How can the federal government help Ontario?

Notes

*   The views expressed in this chapter are those of the author and do not necessarily reflect the views of the Ontario Ministry of Finance or the Government of Ontario. Any remaining errors are the author's responsibility.

1   H. Krahn, "Non-standard Work on the Rise," *Statistics Canada—Perspectives*, Catalogue no. 75–001-XPE (Ottawa: Statistics Canada, 1995).

2 A.M. Noack and L.F. Vosko, *Precarious Jobs in Ontario: Mapping Dimensions of Labour Market Insecurity by Workers' Social Location and Context* (Toronto: Law Commission of Ontario, 2011).

3 R. Schettkat and L. Yocarini, "The Shift to Services Employment: A Review of the Literature," *Structural Change and Economic Dynamics* 17 (2006): 127–47.

4 A. Woelfl, "The Service Economy in OECD Countries," Working Paper No. 3 (Paris: OECD Directorate for Science, Technology and Industry, 2005).

5 R. Schettkat, "Why Economies Slow: US Sclerosis?" *Challenge* 47, no. 2 (2004): 39–52.

6 D. Pilat, A. Cimper, K. Olsen, and C. Webb, "The Changing Nature of Manufacturing in OECD Countries," Working Paper No. 9 (Paris: OECD Directorate for Science, Technology and Industry, 2006).

7 Schettkat and Yocarini, "The Shift to Services Employment."

8 E. Brynjolfsson and A. McAfee, *The Second Machine Age* (New York: W.W. Norton, 2014).

9 D. Autor and D. Dorn, "The Growth of Low-Skill Service Jobs and the Polarization of the US Labor Market," *American Economic Review* 103, no. 5 (2013): 1553–97.

10 J.R. Baldwin and R. Macdonald, "The Canadian Manufacturing Sector: Adapting to Challenges," Statistics Canada, Economic Analysis Research Paper No. 57 (Ottawa: Statistics Canada, 2009). See also J.R. Baldwin and B. Yan, "Exchange Rate Cycles and Canada/US Manufacturing Prices," *Review of World Economics* 143, no. 3 (2007): 508–33.

11 M. McClearn, "Autopilot Bailout," *Canadian Business* 84, no. 11/12 (2011): 12–14.

12 L. Shiell and R. Somerville, "Bailouts and Subsidies: The Economics of Assisting the Automotive Sector in Canada," Institute for Research on Public Policy Study No. 28 (Montreal: IRPP, 2012).

13 McClearn, "Autopilot Bailout."

14 Statistics Canada, "National Balance Sheet and Financial Flow Accounts, Fourth Quarter 2015," *The Daily*, http://www.statcan.gc.ca/daily-quotidien/160311/dq160311b-eng.htm

15 Gordon, "Dutch Disease?"

16 Josh Hjartarson and Liam McGuinty, *A Federal Agenda for Ontario* (Toronto: Ontario Chamber of Commerce, 2012).

17 Ibid.

18 Noah Zon, *Filling the Gap: Measuring Ontario's Balance with the Federal Government* (Toronto: Mowat Centre, 2013).

3
The Social and Economic Context
of Ontario Politics

RAND DYCK

THIS CHAPTER SKETCHES THE BASIC SOCIAL AND ECONOMIC CONTEXT of the Ontario political system, including such characteristics as geography, economy, class structure, language and ethnicity, religion, gender, and age. In the process, it seeks to identify typical demands raised in the politics of the province and some of the responses made. Many of these subjects are examined in greater detail in chapters of their own.

Geography

Physiography

With an area of just over 1 million square kilometres, Ontario is the second-largest province in Canada, about one-third smaller than Quebec, and slightly bigger than British Columbia.[1] If Ontario were an American state, it would be second in size to Alaska, and if it were a separate country, it would rank close to South Africa or Egypt, being twice as large as Spain or France, and four times larger than Britain.

The Hudson Bay Lowlands immediately adjacent to that body of water are marked by muskeg, peat bogs, and conifer forest. Otherwise, the northern two-thirds of the province is part of the geological formation known as the Canadian or Precambrian Shield, characterized by rugged bare rock, rivers, lakes, trees, and a harsh winter climate. The Shield extends as far south as an imaginary line drawn roughly between the tip of Georgian Bay and Renfrew. Below this, the fertile Great Lakes and St. Lawrence Lowlands constitute a large amount of prime agricultural land, much of which is rapidly disappearing into urban development.

Regionalism

Given its large area, Ontario can be divided into regions. Except for the Precambrian Shield, however, physical geography does not dictate any natural regional boundaries. Instead, its other regions are based on the distances involved as well as certain distinctions in natural resources, demography, economic development, and psychological orientations. Although the regional designations and specific boundaries are rather arbitrary, it would seem best to employ five—North, East, Southwest, Central, and the Greater Toronto Area—or six if the North is considered as two regions rather than one.

The Northern region, essentially everything north of Muskoka, is the one most securely anchored in law as well as physiography, primarily so that it can benefit from special government programs designed for its distinctive needs. It is the only region to have a ministry (Northern Development and Mines) unto itself; the provincial government also operates the Northern Ontario Heritage Fund, which parallels FedNor, the federal economic development agency for the region. Individual residents of the North are eligible for such privileges as reduced vehicle licence fees and the Northern Ontario energy tax credit.

The Northern region contains about 775,000 residents, 6 per cent of the province's population, compared to 88 per cent of its area. Such a huge territory sometimes requires the recognition of a subdivision between the northwest, centred on Thunder Bay, and the northeast, containing the urban centres of Sault Ste. Marie, Sudbury, Timmins, and North Bay. But whether it is considered to be one region or two, the North can also be identified in terms of the peculiarities of its ethnic mix, its natural resources, its political culture, and its social and economic problems. The North's settlement pattern is characterized by isolated, resource-based, single-industry mining or forestry communities, which are subject to great fluctuations in economic prosperity. Chapter 10 of this book provides a more detailed discussion of the North.

Where to draw the lines between the various regions of Southern Ontario is a more difficult question. The Toronto region is primarily identifiable, of course, as heavily urbanized, but its actual boundaries vary. For some purposes, the region corresponds with the megacity of Toronto; for others, such as Statistics Canada's Census Metropolitan Areas, it is the labour market area stretching from Oakville to Ajax. Increasingly, however, the four surrounding regional municipalities of Peel, Halton, Durham, and York are lumped with Toronto under the designation "Greater Toronto Area" or GTA. This region ranks first in almost every aspect of economic life in Canada, such as size of labour force in, and value of, manufacturing, finance, retail sales, services, and real estate. It is therefore not surprising that "Toronto" dominates the economic and political life of the province and justifies having its own chapter in this book.

Eastern Ontario, centred on Ottawa, Kingston, and Pembroke, also has its own provincial economic development agency, the Eastern Ontario

Development Fund. Next to the North, the East is generally the least prosperous region, but the fact that it contains the national capital gives it a more
federal orientation than the rest of the province.

The Central region consists of the territory immediately north, east, and
west of the Greater Toronto Area, including Barrie, Muskoka, and Peterborough to the north and northeast; Kitchener-Waterloo and Guelph to the
northwest; and Hamilton and the Niagara peninsula to the southwest. This
area is probably the least well defined, and in a sense, consists of what is left
over after the other more distinct regional boundaries have been drawn.
Alternatively, the "Golden Horseshoe" is the label sometimes applied to the
GTA as well as the area around the western end of Lake Ontario including
the Niagara Peninsula, while the "Greater Golden Horseshoe" essentially
combines the central region and the GTA.

The last region is the Southwest, which contains such large urban centres as London, Sarnia, and Windsor, as well as a large stretch of first-class
agricultural land from the Bruce Peninsula to the southwestern tip of the
province. As in the case of Eastern Ontario, it sometimes suffers economically and its boundaries are recognized for purposes of the Southwestern
Ontario Development Fund.

Thus, although universal agreement on the actual regional divisions within
the province is regrettably absent, there is no doubt that Ontario is marked
by regional cleavages. Distinctive demands arise from different regions, varied
voting patterns are often apparent, and governments are acutely aware of the
necessity to distribute cabinet posts and other appointments, public works, and
public finances on a reasonably equitable regional basis.

Transportation and Communications Systems

Given that such a large proportion of the Ontario population lives along
the Windsor-to-Cornwall corridor, that part of the province is particularly
well served by transportation systems. The 401 or Macdonald-Cartier Free-
way provides a vital highway connection here, as do the Via Rail passenger
service and a variety of airlines. The rates charged by the privatized toll
highway 407 that runs parallel to the 401 throughout the GTA have often
generated political controversy.

Given the geographic and population size of Toronto, that city operates
an extensive network of public transit services under the Toronto Transit
Commission, while a provincial government agency, Metrolinx, provides an
integrated transit system for the entire GTA. Even so, traffic gridlock in the
region is usually identified as one of the most serious problems in the province and is explored further in Chapter 17 on Toronto and the GTA.

Besides its corridor run, Via Rail provides a passenger service from Toronto to the Manitoba border and beyond, while Canadian Pacific and Canadian National operate extensive freight train services throughout the province. A Crown corporation, Ontario Northland, used to connect Toronto by rail to North Bay and Cochrane, but was recently discontinued except for the Polar Bear Express, which travels from Cochrane to Moosonee on James Bay. Otherwise, however, it serves northern communities by bus.

In an experience somewhat similar to the closure of the Ontario Northland Railway, the Harris government closed the government-owned NorOntair airline in 1996. On the other hand, Toronto's Pearson International is by far the biggest airport in Canada, and the Toronto Island airport is frequently a controversial issue. The idea of a major airport east of Toronto has recently been resurrected, and Metrolinx began operating an express rail service between Pearson airport and Toronto Union Station in 2015.

Marine transportation in the province is centred on the St. Lawrence Seaway, the world's largest canal system, including the Welland Canal that bypasses Niagara Falls. The Seaway has converted Thunder Bay into an ocean-going port, and in transferring western grain from trains to ships, it is the world's largest grain-handling facility.

Distances and divisions within the province are also overcome by various forms of communications. These include radio, television (including the government's own TVOntario), telephones, and the Internet.

While many aspects of transportation and communication fall within federal jurisdiction, numerous demands on the provincial government arise from this field as well. As in other provinces, concerns about better highways have been a constant of Ontario political life, while demands for the expansion of public transit systems are also common.

Population Distribution

Statistics Canada's 2015 estimate of the Ontario population was 13,750,000, such that the province continues to constitute about 38.4 per cent of the Canadian population. The population increased by 5.7 per cent between 2006 and 2011, but the downturn in the Ontario economy in recent years has caused the rate of increase to decline: immigrants are often settling in other provinces; Alberta has topped Ontario in terms of internal migration; and laid-off Ontario workers are often moving westward. About 86 per cent of Ontario's residents are classified as urban and 14 per cent rural, making Ontario the second most urbanized province in the country (next to BC). Sixteen urban centres in Ontario have populations of over 100,000 residents,

Table 3.1   Metropolitan Areas in Ontario over 100,000—2006 and 2011 Censuses

	2006 Census	2011 Census
Toronto	5,113,149	5,583,064
Ottawa*	846,802	921,823
Hamilton	692,911	721,053
Kitchener-Cambridge-Waterloo	451,235	477,160
London	457,720	474,786
St. Catharines–Niagara	390,317	392,184
Oshawa	330,594	356,177
Windsor	323,342	319,246
Barrie	177,061	187,013
Greater Sudbury	158,258	160,770
Kingston	152,358	159,561
Guelph	127,009	141,097
Brantford	124,607	135,501
Thunder Bay	122,907	121,596
Peterborough	116,570	118,975
Chatham-Kent	108,589	104,075

*I.e., the part of Ottawa-Gatineau on the Ontario side of the border.

Source: Statistics Canada, 2006 and 2011 Census, adapted by author.

as seen in Table 3.1, while the province contains another 25 or so communities with a population of over 10,000.

Each of these urban communities and others naturally does its best to attract new industry to boost its tax base and employment. They also seek federal and provincial government favours such as special grants and the establishment of government offices, and put pressure on private firms to locate in their area. Municipal politicians spend a great deal of their time at Queen's Park and even in Ottawa, activity that is likely the most obvious evidence of regional demands being made on the higher levels of government.

Probably because the rural population is declining, nonurban Ontario has sent louder and more radical messages to Queen's Park in recent years. The Ontario Landowners Association has taken a strong stand in favour of various aspects of rural property rights and against environmental legislation and rural amalgamations. In an attempt to reverse the decline in support for the Liberal Party in rural Ontario, when Kathleen Wynne first became premier she assumed the agriculture portfolio herself.

Economy

Ontario's economy was originally based on the abundance of three primary resources—agriculture, mining, and forestry—along with hydroelectricity. It then became the manufacturing core of the country; but as that industry has seriously declined in recent years, the province's economy has come to be dominated by the services sector. Historically one of the richest provinces in the country, Ontario now has a fiscal capacity below the national average and qualifies for annual equalization payments from the federal government.[2]

Beginning with the primary sector, Ontario often leads the other provinces in the total value of farm cash receipts, but the number of census farms declined by 9.2 per cent between 2006 and 2011. Ontario farm cash receipts amounted to $11.1 billion in 2011, almost equally divided between livestock and crops, with the leading industries being dairy products, cattle, hogs, poultry and eggs, corn, and vegetables.

If petroleum is excluded, Ontario also ranks among the leading provinces in the value of mineral production, led by nickel, copper, and gold. The nickel and copper are primarily found in the Sudbury area, the largest mining centre in Canada, while the gold mines are concentrated in the Timmins, Kirkland Lake, Red Lake, and Hemlo areas. A diamond mine near Attawapiskat opened in 2008, and the "Ring of Fire" in the Hudson Bay Lowlands is a new mining exploration development promising chromite, nickel, copper, and other minerals.

About two-thirds of Ontario is covered by trees, largely deciduous in the south and conifers in the boreal forest in the Canadian Shield. Ontario ranks third among the provinces in forestry production, after BC and Quebec, and jumps to second place in terms of pulp and paper alone. About 90 per cent of the forested area is owned and controlled by the provincial government, so that logging is mostly done by private firms on Crown land under the authority of forest resource licences. As in other provinces, the forest industry has been in a state of decline in Ontario for nearly a decade and has lost thousands of jobs.

Turning to the secondary sector of the economy, Ontario has specialized in electricity as a form of energy, and was the first province to establish a Crown corporation to provide it. The province's electricity production is now based primarily on nuclear power (over 50 per cent) and hydroelectric installations (over 20 per cent), with natural gas coming third. The largest of the hydroelectric stations are located at Niagara Falls and on the St. Lawrence and Ottawa rivers, while the nuclear-powered generating stations are at Bruce, on Lake Huron, and Pickering and Darlington east of Toronto.

The last of the coal-fired plants have been closed or converted to other feedstocks.

The energy industry has been a source of great political controversy. The heavy reliance on nuclear power has raised issues of expensive construction and refurbishing costs and of the absence of a solution for disposing of nuclear waste. Subsidization of wind and solar power, opposition to nearby windmills, and the expensive and politically motivated relocation of gas-fired electricity plants were major issues in the 2011 provincial election campaign and contributed to the loss of the McGuinty government's majority.

Ontario annually produces about half of all the manufactured goods in Canada, and leads other provinces in almost every major manufacturing sector—transportation equipment; primary and fabricated metals; chemicals, petroleum, and chemical products; food; electronic products and appliances; and machinery. Ontario's historic advantages in this respect included raw materials, cheap and abundant electricity, a pool of skilled workers, good transportation facilities, close proximity to the US automobile production industry, and the national tariff, which protected Ontario manufacturing from cheaper imports, although the tariff and electricity are no longer positive factors.

The automobile industry has been the backbone of Ontario's manufacturing sector. In addition to the principal car assembly plants, hundreds of smaller firms spread throughout Southern Ontario manufacture auto parts. Under the 1965 Auto Pact signed between Canada and the United States, cars and car parts could flow freely across the border subject to meeting certain Canadian value-added requirements. The main plants are GM in Oshawa and Ingersoll, Ford in Oakville, and Chrysler in Windsor and Brampton, but they have been joined by Toyota in Cambridge and Woodstock, and Honda in Alliston. While the "Big Three" American producers all announced cutbacks between 2006 and 2008, Honda and Toyota boomed.

The whole of Ontario's manufacturing sector began to face serious problems around 2005, primarily caused by increased energy costs, the high value of the Canadian dollar (discouraging exports), and cheap foreign competition, especially from China. The industry took an additional hit with the worldwide economic meltdown starting in 2008, the auto sector most of all. Thousands more employees lost their jobs, hundreds of firms shut their doors, and the automobile industry desperately pleaded for cash, loans, loan guarantees, and lines of credit. Because of the Canada-US integration of the Big 3 in particular, rescue efforts were coordinated among the Ontario, Canadian, and American governments. The three companies eventually all survived in a different and much downsized state.

Among the prominent parts of the tertiary sector of the Ontario economy are banking, insurance, investment, trade, education, computer services, hospitals and health care, tourism and recreation, and government. Toronto in particular houses outstanding educational, health and shopping facilities; in addition, that city is home to the main production facilities of the national English-language radio and television networks, is a key wholesale and retail distribution centre for both domestic and imported goods, and its many cultural, athletic, and recreational activities attract millions of tourists annually. Toronto is also the financial capital of Canada: all five of the main chartered banks have their operational headquarters there; the largest Canadian investment dealers are gathered around the Toronto Stock Exchange, which in turn carries out the great majority of share trading activity in the country; and trust and insurance companies are located nearby.

The services sector also includes the government, without which no account of the Ontario economy would be complete. If all levels of government are combined, the total number of people employed by government in 2011 was over 1 million. In fact, in almost every community, public or semi-public bodies are among the largest employers—federal, provincial, and municipal governments; school boards; hospitals; and community colleges and universities.

Class

An analysis of social class in Ontario society is not as clear-cut and straight-forward as that of the other main characteristics examined in this chapter. One approach to this question would be to examine the distribution of income. Like other provinces, Ontario contains stark disparities in income among individuals, families, communities, and regions. In 2010, the top one-fifth of the population earned 52.6 per cent of market income, while the bottom fifth took in only 1.0 per cent. When government transfers and taxes were added to the picture, the top fifth still received 44.2 per cent of the total income, while the income of the bottom fifth rose to 4.7 per cent.[3]

Another approach would be to divide Ontario residents into the corporate elite or upper class, the middle class, the working class, and the poor. Other perspectives offer different combinations and permutations of these groupings, such as dividing the working class into public and private sector components, but individuals often behave according to the interests of the class they think they belong to—usually the middle class—rather than the one into which social scientists would place them.

The Corporate Elite

Ontario contains some of the richest entrepreneurs and families in the world. In November 2012, *Canadian Business* magazine found that Ontario-based families were well represented among the 69 billionaires in Canada, including the following with their national ranking in parentheses: Thomson family (1), $20 billion; Galen Weston (2), $8 billion; Rogers family (4), $6 billion; Carlo Fidani (9), $4 billion; and Barry Sherman (13), $3 billion. In total, Ontario contained 39 of the richest 100 Canadians. Among the largest annual compensation packages received by corporate chief executive officers in 2011 were those of Frank Stronach (Magna), $41 million; Gerald Schwartz (Onex), $14 million; and the five big bank presidents, all in the $11 million range.[4]

Toronto has already been identified as the financial capital of Canada, but the nonfinancial Canadian corporate sector is only slightly less concentrated in the province. Even though many energy companies have moved to Alberta, 25 out of the 50 largest private employers in Canada still have their head offices in Ontario. These include the major banks, along with Onex, Weston, Loblaws, Magna, Canadian Tire, Celestica, Extendicare, Maple Leaf Foods, Sun Life, Rogers Communications, Barrick Gold, Sears Canada, Brookfield Asset Management, and Manulife.[5]

Many of the large corporations with headquarters in the Toronto region are national and transnational in scope, but they also press the Ontario government to adopt policies at the provincial level that are most favourable to themselves. They, along with hundreds of other companies with their head offices close to Queen's Park, are well situated to do so. Generally speaking, the corporate elite argues for lower taxes and more tax breaks, reduced spending (on others), reduced regulation (including environmental controls), and more flexible labour laws. They sometimes threaten to pull out of the province if their demands are not satisfied.

The Middle Class

The middle class, in objective social science terms, includes affluent farmers, small business people, and self-employed professionals, all of whom could be called the "old middle class," and civil servants, teachers, and other salaried professionals, who are often termed the "new middle class." To some extent, these two factions of the middle class have different economic interests and therefore different identities and political demands. For example, the new middle class is largely composed of those working in the public sector, and actually makes up a substantial portion of the union membership in the province.

Although the middle class is therefore far from being a unified force, its members are typically well educated and have comfortable incomes, and although they may pay a disproportionate amount of taxes, they take advantage of public education and health care programs and have money left over for considerable consumption. Some parts of the middle class have even benefited in recent years from structural changes in the economy, such as in the sectors of management, administration, and health care. On the other hand, many members of the middle class have suffered from the effects of technological change, globalization, downsizing, recession, and concern with government debt, which have significantly reduced employment opportunities in many areas. Moreover, the deregulation of tuition fees in such professional schools as business, law, and medicine, has had a more serious impact on middle class students than on other groups. It is therefore common to speak of the shrinking or hollowing out of the middle class as it declines in numbers relative to those above and below it, and the fate of the middle class is now a priority in the rhetoric of many politicians, stretching from Barack Obama to Justin Trudeau.

The Working Class

The working class has always faced economic insecurity, and this insecurity has increased in the past two decades, meaning increasing numbers of working people can find only part-time, short-term, or contract jobs. Those conscious of their class position generally believe that, apart from voting appropriately, the best way to address working class employment concerns has been to form or join a union (although, as mentioned, unionization is also widespread among an increasing segment of the middle class).

In fact, as a result of the economic shift from primary and secondary to tertiary industry, the largest labour unions in the province are no longer industrial, but rather in the services sector. Overall in Canada in 2015, 75 per cent of the public sector is unionized but only 17 per cent of the private sector.[6] Unions representing both public and private employees have joined forces in the Ontario Federation of Labour, a branch of the Canadian Labour Congress, giving the OFL a membership of about 1 million.

As noted in Chapter 16 on labour relations, only 28.2 per cent of all employees in Ontario are unionized, the second lowest rate in the country. The OFL calculates that on average, union members in the province made $6 per hour more than nonunion members, were twice as likely to have a workplace pension plan, and also more often had nonwage benefits like drug, vision, and dental plans.[7]

The labour movement is never short of political issues in which it has an interest. Not surprisingly, though, the NDP government (1990–95) was receptive to labour's demands, such as with Bill 40, which made it easier to form a union and unlawful to hire replacement workers during a legal strike. On the other hand, the NDP's social contract legislation, which over-rode collective agreements to freeze public sector wages, alienated much of the labour movement. After 1995, the new Harris Conservative government repealed Bill 40, laid off public servants, diluted safety and compensation legislation, and required all workplaces to post notices of how unions could be decertified. The McGuinty Liberal government initially made minor amendments to many labour laws and, as discussed in other chapters, attracted the support of many public sector unions, while most private sector unions remained loyal to the NDP.

The Poor

Poverty is measured in different ways, but by most accounts at least 10 per cent of the Ontario population lives below the poverty line,[8] and in 2009, Toronto had the fourth highest poverty rate among larger Canadian cities, at 12.2 per cent. Otherwise, as in the rest of the country, among the leading at-risk groups are lone-parent families, women, seniors, Indigenous people, persons with disabilities, recent immigrants, the unemployed, and visible minorities. Restricting eligibility for federal Employment Insurance benefits has led to an increased dependence on provincial social assistance programs.

After the 1995 election campaign, the Harris government reduced social assistance rates, introduced work for welfare or "workfare" (Ontario Works), and trumpeted its reduction of the social assistance caseload by 500,000 people. It also made cuts to many other programs that previously benefited the poor in a disproportionate way, all of which precipitated one of the most violent of the many confrontations of the Harris era.

The McGuinty government softened some of the Harris legislation with respect to social assistance recipients, re-entered the social housing field, made improvements in child care, and brought in postsecondary grants for low-income students. In 2008–09, it adopted a poverty reduction strategy, hoping to reduce the number of children living in poverty by 25 per cent over 5 years, but the economic decline strained the government's resources. Kathleen Wynne reiterated poverty reduction as one of her priorities when she assumed office in 2013.

Language and Ethnicity

French and English

In 2011 English was the mother tongue of 8.7 million Ontarians (68.2 per cent); close to 500,000 (3.9 per cent) had French as their mother tongue;

and the other 3.3 million (25.7 per cent) first learned some other language. Although the percentage claiming French as a mother tongue dropped from 5 per cent in 1991, the absolute number of francophones remained fairly constant. In 2011, 11.3 per cent of Ontario residents claimed they could speak French, while 97.3 per cent reported themselves capable of speaking English.

The French were the first non-Indigenous group to settle in Ontario, and the French-English cleavage has been a prominent generator of political activity, especially since the Quiet Revolution in Quebec in the 1960s. After 1968, the Progressive Conservative government encouraged the development of publicly financed French-language high schools, and gradually expanded the range of other French-language provincial services, starting with the courts. In 1986, the Peterson Liberal government introduced Bill 8, the French Language Services Act, which guaranteed provincial government services in French on a regional basis, that is, in any community that had at least 5,000 francophones, or in which at least 10 per cent of the population was French-speaking.[9] In the same year, simultaneous interpretation was introduced into the provincial Legislature and francophones gained exclusive governance of French-language schools. A year later, TVOntario established a French channel, Télévision française de l'Ontario (TFO), and in 1988, the first French-language school boards were created, of which there are now 12. Three French-language community colleges were set up between 1990 and 1995, as were several French-language community health centres.

The strengthening of French-language services sparked heated disputes in many localities. Later, in its efforts to restructure hospitals in the province, the Harris government slated Ontario's only French-language teaching hospital—the Montfort Hospital in Ottawa—for severe shrinkage. But when the decision was subject to a legal challenge, the courts claimed that the province had a constitutional duty to preserve the Franco-Ontarian identity and protect it from assimilation, a pronouncement going well beyond the actual words of the constitution.

Other Linguistic and Ethnocultural Groups

At 3.9 per cent of the population, French continues to exceed every language other than English in Ontario, although taking all Chinese languages together, they rank a close third, at 3.1 per cent. Italian is the next most popular language, at over 2 per cent, while several languages are about equal in numbers: Spanish, Punjabi, Tagalog, Portuguese, Arabic, German, and Urdu, all over the 1 per cent mark.[10]

According to the 2006 census, about 62 per cent of Ontarians were born in the province, another 9 per cent were born elsewhere in Canada, and

28 per cent were born abroad. Ontario has absorbed about 2.5 million immigrants over the past 25 years. The Philippines, China, and India provided the bulk of new immigrants in recent years, but given the province's economic decline, the number of immigrants choosing Ontario and Toronto fell off after 2001.[11] In 2006, nonwhite "visible minorities" (not all of whom are recent arrivals) constituted 23 per cent of the Ontario population, and the National Household Survey of 2011 put this figure at 26 per cent. Most of the "visible" immigrants settled in the Toronto region, transforming the Greater Toronto Area into a highly diversified ethnocultural community. As discussed in Chapter 15, visible minorities make up nearly half of the Toronto population.

Such a development has obvious implications for public services, the educational system, and public finance, as well as for Ontario's political culture, political parties, and elections. All political parties now scramble to attract the support of various new ethnic groups in the province, and multiculturalism raises such questions as adequate representation of such groups in public employment (e.g., police forces) and discrimination in the private sector. Since many recent immigrants speak neither English nor French, Toronto in particular faces many linguistic issues. In this regard, starting in 1989, school boards in the province were required to provide Heritage Language classes when a request to teach a particular language was made by the parents of at least 25 students of that board.

The Rae government enacted the most comprehensive employment equity legislation in the country, providing preferential employment access for women, Indigenous people, visible minorities, and people with disabilities. When the law ignited a backlash in the 1995 election campaign, the new Harris government quickly repealed it.

Indigenous Ontarians

In the 2006 census, 242,495 Ontarians (2 per cent) declared themselves to have an Indigenous identity, broken down as follows: 158,395 North American Indians (First Nations); 73,605 Métis; and 2,035 Inuit. The 2011 National Household Survey placed the figure at 300,000 or 2.4 per cent. Alternatively, in 2006, some 410,000 or 3.4 per cent claim an Indigenous origin. As in Canada as a whole, a majority of Ontario's Indigenous people live in urban areas rather than on reserves.

The Indigenous population of the province is outnumbered by many other ethnic groups and is generally subject to federal rather than provincial jurisdiction. Nevertheless, Indigenous issues increasingly require the attention of provincial politicians, particularly with respect to Indigenous land claims. The NDP government and Indigenous leaders signed a statement of political relationship in 1991 that recognized the First Nations' inherent right to self-government within the Canadian constitutional framework. Even though the Harris government preferred to leave Indigenous issues to Ottawa, it was forced to get actively engaged in negotiating land claims, seeing them as incentives to the economic development and self-reliance of Indigenous communities, clarifying access to and use of Crown land, and removing barriers to the development of natural resources. Nevertheless, many Indigenous peoples of the province continue to suffer from dismal economic prospects, poor government services, and widespread discrimination. One of their number, Dudley George, was killed by an OPP officer in a legitimate but heated land claim demonstration at Ipperwash in 1995. The judicial inquiry into the tragedy later laid most of the blame on the federal and provincial governments as well as the OPP.

Small advances, including the teaching of Native languages in certain public schools and the establishment of a Native health centre, have been made. Another positive development was the new Native-owned Rama casino near Orillia, although there, too, First Nations had to fight to retain their promised share of the take, and the Supreme Court of Canada ruled that the provincial Métis did not have a right to a share of the proceeds. Other individual and collective Indigenous accomplishments in Ontario are exemplified by the former Lieutenant-Governor, James Bartleman, an Indigenous man who initiated a major program of raising literacy levels by providing books to native communities. The McGuinty government signed the largest land claim yet in Ontario with the Rainy River First Nation, while the provincial minister of Indigenous affairs succeeded in handing Ipperwash Provincial Park back to its original inhabitants and in negotiating a casino deal. But in 2005, a long, ugly dispute broke out at Caledonia (near Hamilton) over a subdivision being built on land claimed by the Six Nations Confederacy, and even the government's purchase of the land from the developer did not end the confrontation.

Meanwhile, several members of First Nations in northwestern Ontario were convicted of contempt of court for failing to obey injunctions that prohibited them from interfering with private companies holding mining claims on disputed land. About this time the virtual absence of Indigenous people on Ontario juries also became an issue. The government asked retired Supreme Court Justice Frank Iacobucci to investigate the situation, and in a scathing report in early 2013, he wrote that First Nations in Ontario face a justice and jury system in a state of crisis that required urgent action.[12] While slow progress was being made in land claims negotiations in many locations in the province, the chief of the Attawapiskat First Nation went on a hunger strike in Ottawa in 2012 to protest against federal inaction on a whole range of Indigenous issues, coinciding with the countrywide protest of the Idle No More movement. Indigenous issues are discussed further in Chapter 15 of this book.

Religion

The religious identity of Ontarians was not surveyed in either the 2006 or 2011 census, but the 2011 National Household Survey indicated that 65 per cent of Ontarians classify themselves as Christians, about half of whom are Roman Catholics; 23 per cent report having no religious affiliation; and most of the remainder fall into the following five groups: Muslim, Hindu, Jewish, Sikh, and Buddhist.

Schools

The main historical implication of this religious distribution relates to the educational system: the Constitution Act, 1867, guaranteed Roman Catholic separate schools. Catholic school funding was gradually extended to grade 10, after which, if Roman Catholics wanted to attend private denominational schools, they had to pay tuition fees as well as support the public system through their taxes. It was not until 1984 that Premier Bill Davis responded to Catholic demands to extend full public support to the separate system, a controversial move that had major electoral consequences for the Conservative Party. Later, when the law was challenged as being discriminatory against other religions, the Supreme Court of Canada cited the clause in the 1982 Charter of Rights and Freedoms that allowed a continuation of such pre-Charter constitutional protection. This issue took many years to settle at the local school board level in terms of teachers, students, school buildings, and school boards. Since then, the autonomy of the Roman Catholic school system has occasionally come into question, such as in its teachings on homosexuality.

While the Harris government ignored increasing pressure to provide public support to all denominational schools, the 2001 budget included a tax credit for parents who paid tuition at private schools, whether or not they were faith-based. Upon obtaining office, however, the McGuinty government repealed this measure before it was ever implemented. In the 2007 election, wanting to treat all religious minorities equally and make them all conform to the same curriculum and standards, the PCs promised public support for all denominational schools, but this proved to be highly unpopular and contributed to their loss of the election. Thus, in addition to private schools, Ontario is left with a maze of four publicly funded school systems: English public, French public, English Catholic, and French Catholic.

Repeatedly denied the right to mount their own publicly supported school systems, other religions at least wanted to ensure that the public system was genuinely nondiscriminatory. Through court action, for example, they forced changes in opening and closing exercises that formerly required the Christian Lord's Prayer, and a variety of religious expressions are now reflected in such exercises.

Other Religious Issues

Restriction of Sunday shopping was another controversial issue related to religion that has been laid to rest, although in 1986 the Supreme Court of Canada upheld a Davis-era law on this issue based on the desirability of having a common pause day, rather than treating Sunday as a Christian holy day. A new religious question, however, confronted the McGuinty government. The Jewish community had been allowed to settle family disputes according to religious principles outside the judicial system if all parties involved were in agreement. But when a Muslim organization asked for the same privilege, that is, to allow the use of Sharia law based on Islamic principles as a method of religious arbitration, much opposition surfaced, and McGuinty put an end to all such practices in the province.[13] In the Legislature itself, MPPs voted to retain the recitation of the Lord's Prayer, but supplemented it with a rotating series of seven prayers of other faiths, a nondenominational prayer, and a moment of silence.

Gender

According to the 2011 census, Ontario contained 6,588,680 females and 6,263,140 males, for a ratio of 95.1 men for every 100 women. Such "gender-related" issues as child care, abortion, pay equity, and employment equity programs have become of increasing political importance since the "second wave" of the women's movement started around 1970, as noted in Chapter 12.

While the rate of female participation in the labour force in Ontario is about 62 per cent,[14] the proportion of women in senior officer and top earning positions at the 500 largest companies in the province in 2012 was only 20.7 per cent.[15] The highest proportions of women in such positions were found in the public sector, including Crown corporations, health care, and social assistance, and in accommodation and food services. In an effort to reduce the residual wage gap between men and women, the Pay Equity Act was proclaimed in 1988 and is overseen by the Pay Equity Commission.

In 2010, the average earnings of Ontario women were 72 per cent of men's earnings, but among those in full-time employment, women made 76 per cent as much as men.[16]

Women in Ontario were historically subject to the same constraints as their counterparts elsewhere when it came to active political participation. The first woman (Agnes Macphail) was not elected to the Ontario Legislature until 1943, and the first female cabinet minister was not appointed until 1972. After 1970, however, the number and proportion of women in the political and bureaucratic elites gradually increased, with substantive policy gains. But with the election of the Harris government in 1995, women's representation declined, as did their influence on public policy. For example, as part of the government's program of hospital consolidation, Women's College Hospital was merged with Sunnybrook Hospital in Toronto. The McGuinty government restored the independence of the former as a "leading-edge" women's health institute, and also signed a temporary child care agreement with the federal Martin government.

Equal Voice, a group working toward electing more women, has been modestly successful in recent elections, and by 2015, the 38 women MPPs constituted 35 per cent of the Ontario Legislature (see further discussion of women's representation in Chapters 5 and 12.) Between 1992 and 1995, the Liberal Party had a female leader, Lyn McLeod; in 2009, Andrea Horwath was elected leader of the Ontario NDP; and in 2013, new Liberal leader Kathleen Wynne made history when she became the first female premier of the province.

Sexual orientation has become a political issue in recent years. A clause was added to the Ontario Human Rights Code in the 1985–87 minority government period to protect homosexuals from discrimination. The Rae government extended spousal employment benefits within the public service to same-sex partners, but failed to pass a general law on the issue in a free vote. With only limited success at the political level, LGBT activists took their cause to the courts, and in the 1998 Rosenberg and 1999 *M v. H* cases, the Supreme Court of Canada ordered the government to treat same-sex partners the same as any common-law couples with regard to benefits and financial support and to amend other discriminatory laws. As a result, in 1999, the Harris government amended 67 provincial statutes by adding "or same-sex partner" wherever they said "spouse." Ontario was then the location of the major Charter challenge regarding same-sex marriage. The Ontario Court of Appeal ruled in the 2003 Halpern decision that the federal act on marriage discriminated against same-sex couples and ordered that such marriages be performed without delay.[17] The Ontario Legislature passed a bill to provide for the solemnization of such marriages as soon as the Supreme Court of Canada upheld the federal law on the subject.

LGBT issues continue to arise on the political agenda. In recent years, for example, high school bullying has gained much public attention, often involving sexual orientation and occasionally leading to suicide. In November 2011, Premier McGuinty introduced an anti-bullying bill, including the promotion of student clubs called "Gay-Straight Alliances" in the province's high schools. When the Catholic separate system preferred to employ the term "diversity clubs" instead, the premier told Catholic authorities to use the "gay" label, even if their faith frowned on the practice.[18] In 2013, Kathleen Wynne became the first openly gay or lesbian provincial premier in Canadian history, and the transgender issue made its way onto the political agenda shortly afterward.

Age

The 2011 census revealed that 14.6 per cent of Ontario residents were under the age of 15, 68.3 per cent were between the ages of 15 and 64, and 17.0 per cent were aged 65 or older. The aging of the population was confirmed when the median age rose by 1.4 years between 2006 and 2011 to 40.4. This increasing number and proportion of seniors is particularly significant for the political system.

A large proportion of the senior population is not financially self-sufficient, leading in part to demands for better pension programs. Indeed, fewer than half of those aged 65 and over have registered pension or savings plans to supplement federal public pension plans. Ontario provides such income-support programs as the Guaranteed Annual Income System (GAINS), targeted at very low-income seniors, and small tax credits related to the sales and property taxes, home renovation, and energy costs.

The growing pool of retirees is also making additional demands for health care spending, exacerbating the budgetary woes of all provincial governments. The inadequate supply of nursing home facilities frequently leads seniors to occupy expensive acute-care hospital beds when they do not really need them. In response to past demands, the Ontario government subsidizes seniors' costs for drugs and assistive devices; it also regulates the operation of retirement homes and promotes home care as a less expensive alternative to institutional solutions.

Conclusion

For many years it was commonly said that Ontario was an easy province to govern. That was largely because it was a relatively homogeneous province, at least in terms of the demands that were articulated, and because its prosperity readily provided the means to satisfy those demands. Economic downturns in the first part of the 1990s and since 2008 have seriously diminished the province's prosperity. Meanwhile, the salient provincial political issues have only increased: persistent regional disparities, serious unemployment, and more visible and vehement expression of class, ethnic, religious, gender, and age-related concerns. Many of these demands overlap: region with economy, economy with class, class with ethnicity, ethnicity with religion, religion with gender, and so on. The government elected in 1995 and re-elected in 1999 chose to ignore many such demands in an effort to reduce the size and significance of government. No doubt it was partly because the Harris-Eves government was unresponsive to such concerns that it lost the 2003 election, and the successor McGuinty government tried to accommodate a much broader set of demands. On the other hand, the economic difficulties of the province were a factor that persuaded Dalton McGuinty to resign as premier in 2012. Governing the new Ontario remains a challenging task for leaders of any political stripe.

Discussion Questions

1. In regional terms, do you feel that "Toronto" gets too much attention in Ontario politics? Why or why not?
2. Do you feel that Ontario governments cater too much to business at the expense of labour and the poor? Explain your position.
3. Should the province give continuing preference to the Franco-Ontarian minority in the face of increasing ethnic diversity? Why or why not?
4. How much autonomy should be given to the Roman Catholic separate school system? Alternatively, should all faith-based schools be publicly financed or should none?
5. Contrasting gender and age, which interest is most in need of government support? Why?

Notes

1   Ontario is actually the third largest province in terms of land, but because it contains much water, it is slightly bigger than British Columbia in total area.
2   Matthew Mendelsohn, *Back to Basics: The Future of the Fiscal Arrangements* (Toronto: Mowat Centre for Policy Innovation, 2012), http://mowatcentre.ca/back-to-basics-future-fiscal-arrangements
3   Statistics Canada, CANSIM Table 202–0701, "Market, Total and After-tax Income, by Economic Family Type and Income Quintiles, 2010 Constant Dollars," http://www5.statcan.gc.ca/cansim/a26?lang=eng&retrLang=eng&id=2020701&&pattern=&stByVal=1&p1=1&p2=-1&tabMode=dataTable&csid=

4 "The Rich 100: The Richest Canadians in 2012," *Canadian Business Magazine* (December 2012), http://www.canadianbusiness.com/lists-and-rankings/rich-100-the-richest-canadians-in-2012; Canadian Centre for Policy Alternatives, *Overcompensation: Executive Pay in Canada* (January 2013), http://www.policyalternatives.ca/publications/commentary/overcompensating

5 "Top 1000 Canadian Companies," *Globe and Mail, Report on Business Magazine* (July/August 2012).

6 Statistics Canada, CANSIM Table 282-0220, "Labour Force Survey Estimates (LFS), Employees by Union Status, Sex and Age Group, Canada and Provinces Annual (persons)."

7 Ontario Federation of Labour, *President's Report* (Winter 2013), 5, http://ofl.ca/wp-content/uploads/2013.01.28-OFLPrezReport-Web1.pdf. This claim is substantiated by Sharanjit Uppal, *Unionization 2011* (Ottawa: Statistics Canada, 2011), http://www.statcan.gc.ca/pub/75-001-x/2011004/article/11579-eng.htm

8 Conference Board of Canada, *Canadian Income Inequality: Is Canada Becoming More Unequal?* (2013), http://www.conferenceboard.ca/hcp/hot-topics/caninequality.aspx?pf=true

9 See the Schedule to the French Languages Services Act, http://www.e-laws.gov.on.ca/html/statutes/english/elaws_statutes_90f32_e.htm. The original 22 areas involved have since been joined by the cities of London and Kingston and the town of Callander.

10 2011 Census.

11 See Mowat Centre for Policy Innovation, *Expanding Our Routes to Success: The Final Report by Ontario's Expert Roundtable on Immigration* (2012), http://mowatcentre.ca/expanding-our-routes-to-success; See also https://mowatcentre.ca/immigration-to-ontario-declined-due-to-federal-government-rule-changes

12 Frank Iacobucci, *First Nations Representation on Ontario Juries* (Toronto: Ministry of the Attorney General, 2013).

13 Marion Boyd, *Religion-based Alternative Dispute Resolution: A Challenge to Multiculturalism* (Montreal: Institute for Research on Public Policy, 2007), http://irpp.org/research-studies/boyd-2007-12/

14 Statistics Canada, Table 282-0087, "2016 Labour Force Survey Estimates, by Sex and Age Group, Seasonally Adjusted and Unadjusted," http://www5.statcan.gc.ca/cansim/a26?lang=eng&retrLang=eng&id=2820087&&pattern=&stByVal=1&p1=1&p2=-1&tabMode=dataTable&csid=

15 Catalyst, *2012 Catalyst Census: Financial Post 500 Women Senior Officers and Top Earners*, Appendix 4—Women's Representation by Province/Territory, http://www.catalyst.org/knowledge/2012-catalyst-census-financial-post-500-women-senior-officers-and-top-earners

16 Statistics Canada, CANSIM Table 202–0102, "Average Female and Male Earnings, and Female-to-Male Ratio, by Work Activity, 2010 Constant Dollars."

17 *Halpern v. Canada (Attorney General)*, (2003–06–10) ONCA C39174, http://www.canlii.org/en/on/onca/doc/2003/2003canlii26403/2003canlii26403.html

18 Accepting Schools Act, 2012.

4

Political Culture in Ontario: Old and New

PETER WOOLSTENCROFT

THE CONCEPT OF POLITICAL CULTURE asks us to think not about the here and now, the latest policy controversy, scandal, or event, but about how people interpret such things, what underlies the immediate and the surface. People will have opinions, but political culture analysis focuses on the standing assumptions and the attitudes that underlie opinions and behaviour. The former is akin to weather; the latter, climate. Another metaphor is snow on mountaintops: a person who lives in the vicinity won't see yearly changes, but one returning after 10 years away will easily see differences in the snow cover. Generally the significance of change will take a long time to be appreciated. What caused change will be arguable.

This chapter will discuss political culture; review the roots of Ontario's politics; examine two overarching interpretations of the province's political culture; and close with a discussion of the contemporary scene, with a focus on identifiable changes and emerging ones. The fundamental theme to follow is the leading role of an activist provincial government—the "state"—in Ontario politics, with a secular trend of centralization, and the emergence of attitudes of fairness, inclusiveness, and equal treatment, the essentially contested and changing dynamics of contemporary politics.

Political Culture

Studies of political culture cover an enormous range of materials; they also entail important analytical issues.[1] For researchers, one important question is what kind of materials will be the basis of analysis. The first political culture studies employed survey data to delineate the pattern of attitudes, which were deemed to be essential for understanding how mass publics perceived things and thought about their role in politics.[2] Formally, the analytic focus was on what people knew (cognition), felt (affection), and thought (evaluation). Questions were designed to ascertain how people think they connect or should connect to politics. Do citizens think that their opinions matter, that they can be effective in political action, and, indeed, that they are obliged to be informed and to participate? One fundamental criticism was that the micro-approach resting upon survey data (the proverbial "snapshot in time") could not speak to the issue of change.[3]

In the Ontario case, historical narratives have been developed to describe its political culture; the emphasis, almost inevitably, has been on elites and principal political actors, with the presumption that there is considerable congruence between elites and the mass public. It is also presumed that recent and contemporary politics are traceable to distant political events, which are taken to be formative in the province's political culture—that is, there has been a bias in favour of continuities rather than change. Political culture analysis will have at least an implicit comparative tone, looking for similarities and dissimilarities between jurisdictions and looking much less at changes. One important analytical issue confronting those following this line of political culture analysis is the weighing of the importance of issues and decisions: what is the pattern and what is the exception?

In the late 1960s, A.R.M. Lower, an eminent historian, asked in the title of an essay, both playfully and seriously, "Does Ontario Exist?"[4] Legally and physically, of course, it does, but as for identity, the answer is "no." Quebec's debates about its identity and its role in Canada provided a clear and dramatic contrast to Ontario, at once highly regionalized and seemingly undifferentiated from anywhere else because of urbanization and industrialization, suburbs of any Ontario city being indistinguishable from any other in the province or, indeed, the rest of Canada, except, perhaps, for Quebec.[5] However, looking at the beginnings of Ontario has led analysts to identify what is distinctive (indeed, what is unique). If there are identifiable hallmarks to Ontario's formative political culture, are they pertinent in the twenty-first century? Is there a new Ontario political culture?

Historical Roots of Ontario's Political Culture

One dominant theme in studies of Ontario's political culture focuses on the province's birth as Upper Canada in the pre-Confederation period. The roots of its institutions reach back to the Constitutional Act of 1791.[6] The movement of Loyalists to the northern British colonies after the American Revolution has been taken by many as being essential for defining political culture, especially in Upper Canada. S.M. Lipset famously argued that 1776 marked the birth of two nations—one built on revolution, the other on counter-revolution. One consequence was that the British north had institutions readily captured by elites and not easily accessed by ordinary people. Although there were conservative and reform forces, the former were ascendant.[7]

Another consequence of 1776 was that the two countries embodied different value orientations. The values of the United States were best expressed in the American Declaration of Independence's phrase "life, liberty, and the pursuit of happiness"; Canada's by the phrase in its Constitution, "peace, order, and good government." American political culture comprised individualism, anti-statism, populism, and egalitarianism; in contrast, the northern British colonies, especially the Maritimes and Upper Canada, were heavily influenced by the Loyalists and their devotion to the British model, the monarchy, the established church, the superiority of elite leadership, and social order and cohesion.[8]

The central role of the Family Compact—Upper Canada's ruling elite—in the colony's economic and political life was strongly reinforced by two contextual factors. Ontario's rulers—separated from the Atlantic colonies by French-speaking Lower Canada, and conscious of the proximity of the United States—were increasingly insecure. Further, immigration was changing Upper Canada's society so that by the War of 1812 it was populated by non-Loyalist Americans. The effect, as argued by Wise, was that the "War of 1812, which struck Upper Canada far more severely than any other colony, hardened the already powerful forces of conservatism into a fierce and aggressive Tory ideology that become the foundation block of the Ontario political culture."[9]

One important element in Tory ideology was antipathy to the United States and its vulgar democratic ethos and overarching materialism. W.T. Easterbrook, in his examination of North American economic development in the 1800s, produced differentiations in economic life for the northeastern United States (the heart of its extraordinary economic expansion) and Canada, as presented in Table 4.1.

While it is arguable that in the United States there was a separation between economy and the state, this certainly was not the case to the north. Before and after Confederation, "the state was a rule-maker and regulator of economic activities, a financier and a promoter, a participant in the processes of credit and exchange, and a guarantor of structures of order." Further,

Table 4.1 Differences between Northeastern United States and Canada

Northeastern United States	Canada
Competitive	Constricted
Innovative and Dynamic	Conservative and Protective
Open and Democratic	Highly Regulated, Centralized
Independent of Government	Government Directed
Secure and Confident	Insecure and Defensive

Source: Author's summation of argument presented in W. T. Easterbrook, *North American Patterns of Growth and Development* (Toronto: University of Toronto Press, 1990).

despite ostensible commitment to market ideals, "it is intriguing that state involvement in resource development should so often be required."[10] The fact that so much of Ontario's land was held in the name of the Crown meant that state and resource extraction businesses were closely linked.[11] The early bias in Ontario, then, was for state institutions; what was important required not just state intervention but state direction and control.

A specific manifestation of this cultural precept is found in the history of banking in the pre-Confederation period. Upper Canada's Legislative Assembly had approved the creation of a new and independent bank. However, the idea met with fierce opposition from the Tory establishment: "The directors of the Bank of Upper Canada and government officials opposed the Bank on the grounds that chartering of more banks would create the danger of filling the country with local banks in every district as in the United States. They all would be liable to failure owing to inadequate funds and inefficient and dishonest management."[12]

Education provides another dramatic instance of the leading role of the state. In 1816, reflecting the interests and concerns of the newly arrived Loyalists, "Upper Canada became one of the first jurisdictions in the modern world to pass a common school act with provisions for the publicly aided schooling of the entire population."[13] Over the following decades, subsequent education leaders, notably John Strachan and Egerton Ryerson, developed the system, culminating in the 1846 School Act, the cornerstone of the modern public system. A central institution of society—the school—became primarily a state institution manifested in four publicly funded school systems.[14] Private schools existed, but they were rare and were the preserve of the well-connected and wealthy. In the last part of the twentieth century, interest in various forms of nonpublic school education developed across Canada, following developments in the United States. Ontarians have not shown great interest in publicly funding independent schools, including religious ones, even though Roman Catholic schools are so funded.[15] In a ranking of "education freedom" (i.e., state support for nonpublic schooling), Ontario stands in the middle of Canadian provinces and has allowed a foothold for independent schools to receive public dollars.[16]

The origin of Ontario's education system was state-centred, with private providers squeezed out and with Queen's Park over time dominating education policies (with the concomitant formation of province-wide teacher unions); and, in 1977, following much agitation about escalating local property taxes owing in part to provincially mandated policies and programs, the provincial government began to control education finances.[17]

In the early 1900s, actions of the first Conservative administration after three decades of Liberal governments showed the elusive character of political culture analysis. "Progressive" conservatism was evidenced by the reform of financing and governance of the University of Toronto; reversal of the Workman's Compensation Act, so that the employer had to show it was not negligent in the event of a work injury; compulsory smallpox vaccination; and electoral reforms.[18] The state-centred ethos is evident in the Ontario government taking the lead in introducing tractors to the agricultural community.[19] Another indicator is the early passage, starting in 1849, of various public health acts, the effect of which was province-wide standards, and serving as a model for the rest of Canada.[20] However, the central issue that preoccupied the province in the period was whether electrical power should be publicly or privately owned. Against vociferous opposition from Ontario's establishment—private electric power operators and big business—Adam Beck, a Conservative MPP and the foremost advocate for public power, marshalled support across a wide range of Ontario society, including small manufacturers, trade unionists, and municipal leaders, especially in towns and cities which feared that privately owned companies would bypass them. He used populistic devices, such as demonstrations at Queen's Park, to buttress the case. By the adroit building of a political coalition, the supporters of public power overcame the charge of "state socialism" and established the Hydro-Electric Power Commission (the first instance of a state-owned electrical utility in North America) that became the centrepiece of the province's economic development.[21] Was this the mindset identified by Easterbrook at work—a state-centred institution and its promise of certainty and fair treatment—in a polity not prepared to allow private institutions to dominate economic activity? Nelles argues that the answer lies elsewhere, in the intimate relationship between material and political interests. Ontario's politics of development meant that the state received revenue while appearing to control what happened and "industrialists used the government—as had the nineteenth-century commercial classes before—to provide key expenses at public expense, promote and protect vested interests, and confer the status of law upon private decisions. If public institutions such as the distribution of hydroelectricity were to the advantage of industry, this expansion of political control was eagerly sanctioned; whereas, if businessmen resented interference (mineral royalties and forest protection regulations, for example), then the scope of government intervention narrowed."[22]

It cannot be said that Nelles's observations apply uniquely to Ontario. In fact social science research would suggest his observations are the rule without exception. But the history of Ontario, as far back as its early settlement and through the nineteenth century and into the twentieth, meant that the state generally was not an enemy, a problem that had to be pruned and constrained; to the contrary, sometimes it was the first option, other times a second, but never, perhaps until recently, a nonstarter.

Consider the matter of the distribution and selling of alcohol, contentious throughout Canada. Since 1896, following rulings by the Judicial Committee of the Privy Council, the provinces have had primary control over alcohol. Perhaps how a province handles the issue of whether the alcohol trade should be state- or market-centred speaks to its political culture. In recent decades, most provinces have liberalized alcohol policies, but with Alberta being alone in having only private vendors. Ontario, however, has maintained control of the alcohol trade through the Liquor Control Board of Ontario (LCBO). Furthermore, it has continued the policy, established in 1927, that a consortium of three breweries (all currently owned by multinational companies) controls the selling of beer.[23] The Liberals in the 1985 election and the Progressive Conservatives in 1995 both promised liberalization of alcohol retailing but backed off. Although the issue was invisible in the 2014 election, the re-elected Liberals somewhat liberalized alcohol retailing by allowing selected grocery stores to sell beer. The limited academic literature suggests that most Ontarians are happy with the status quo.[24]

The (understudied) Ontario Municipal Board (OMB) is a critical example of the centralization of decision making in Ontario. Established in 1906 as an administrative tribunal (its members appointed by the cabinet), it has jurisdiction over property disputes entailing appeals from municipalities, expropriation compensation disputes, and municipal financing proposals, among other things.[25] The OMB has done much to change the face of Ontario; indeed, it "has played a commanding role in the land use planning process in Ontario from the introduction of planning controls prior to World War I to the present day."[26] The OMB has been criticized for its reputed penchant to overturn decisions made by municipal and regional governments in favour of developers.[27]

In the late 1960s the Ontario government began consideration of the regionalization of a wide range of policy areas, including land use, education, health, policing, and water.[28] By the 1970s various towns and cities had lost much control of education, many municipal services, and policing on the grounds of improvement in efficiency and program effectiveness. Although proposals were controversial (and, in some cases, derailed), and the Conservative Party perhaps paid a price (forming minority governments after the 1975 and 1977 elections), no party has championed a return to the past; indeed, Ontarians have more or less accepted the regionalization that has occurred despite the absence of data pointing to better results in terms of efficiencies and delivery of services and an apparent decline in responsiveness to community members and needs.[29]

On the face of it, then, the interpretation of Ontario's political culture as being state-centred (with its intimations of Tory presuppositions) leading to centralized public policies has prima facie merit. Consider the Liberal government of Dalton McGuinty, which, in its second term introduced a policy for the establishment of wind turbines across the province regardless of the views of the people in the municipality affected by the siting decisions. (See also discussion of the wind turbine issue in Chapters 13 and 14 of this book.)

It must be stressed that Ontario has never been homogeneous. Even before Confederation, agricultural producers, especially in the southwest, called for various reforms. The United Farmers of Ontario (UFO) government from 1919 to 1923 represented both a populistic turn in the province's politics, albeit a brief one, and the perversities of the single-member plurality system, with the third party in terms of popular vote forming a coalition government.[30] The 1943 election almost produced a CCF government (with a manifesto that called for the abolition of capitalism); subsequently, social democracy and its party—first the CCF, then the NDP—became an established force in the province, forming the government in 1990.[31]

Did the Progressive Conservatives Define Ontario's Political Culture?

From 1905 to 1985 the Conservative Party dominated Ontario, forming government 19 times, only three times with a minority; the only breaks in the party's hold on the province came with the UFO government of 1919 to 1923 and two Liberal governments from 1934 to 1943. The Progressive Conservatives (PCs), under the leadership of George Drew, Leslie Frost, John Robarts, and William Davis won 12 consecutive elections from 1943 to 1981, one of the longest streaks in Canadian politics, both federal and provincial.[32] The ability of the PCs to win office and to manage successfully the transition in leaders raised the question of what underlay the party's success. John Wilson, following his examination of election results focusing on defeats, made two points: Ontarians wanted a party that would provide "adequate leadership" and maintain "an equitable balance between the principal interests of the province."[33] Leadership, Wilson argued, reflected the province's agricultural heritage, in which producers placed a premium on sound financial management; fiscal mismanagement would lead to defeat. The central issue that Wilson identified as requiring balancing was the clash between labour and capital, the inevitable heart of the politics of an industrialized society. The PCs had been willing to accommodate at least some of the demands of the widening and strengthening working class. Wilson cites such things as George Drew's determination to prepare the province for industrial development, Leslie Frost's introduction of public hospital insurance, and John Robarts' acceptance of bilingualism.[34] Wilson's summary characterization: Ontario was a "Red Tory" province, with a "progressive conservative" political culture, which made it unique, "because of the special circumstances in which the province began its life."[35]

Election results must be treated very carefully in deciphering a region's culture. The PCs controlled Ontario from 1943 to 1985 (with minorities in 1943, 1975, and 1977) but never received a majority of votes cast, despite sometimes holding an overwhelming legislative majority. The singular fact of the Ontario party system is that three parties are sufficiently competitive to be considered as potential governments.[36] Of course, there are fluctuations in party support levels—three parties have formed government since 1943 (all in the period from 1985 to 2015). What is also telling is that in seven of 20 elections no party has received more than 40 per cent of the vote, indicative of heterogeneity rather than homogeneity in political thinking; the competitive three party system has been steady for over 70 years.

From the end of World War II until the early 1970s, Ontario enjoyed sustained economic growth and prosperity, especially in southern Ontario where the Toronto area became Canada's centre for business, finance, manufacturing, and culture in all forms.[37] For Ontario politicians, this meant that the task of funding the ever-expanding public sector, broadly considered, did not raise significant concerns about taxation as a political issue.[38] However, all of that changed in the 1970s. Advanced industrial democracies around the world underwent a series of economic shocks, highlighted by high inflation and rising tax rates. Ontario was not exempted, and in particular felt the impact of rapidly rising energy costs. The imposition in 1980 of the National Energy Program (NEP) by the Liberal government of Pierre Trudeau—returned to office in Ottawa after a short-lived Progressive Conservative government—among other things, was intended to mitigate the effect of energy costs upon manufacturers and consumers in Ontario. The consequence was that budgets were under stress and the ability of the Ontario government to handle the many demands of its "stakeholders" was greatly limited: tough times, tight budgets.

Parliamentary systems since the end of World War II have been widely characterized as experiencing an increase in the power of the executive branch, culminating in the premier or prime minister holding extraordinary sway over the direction of government policies and programs, especially in majority governments.[39] Consider two of the major decisions of Premier William Davis: the cancellation of the Spadina Expressway in Toronto and the extension of funding to Roman Catholic secondary schools, which was a total reversal of the PC Party's long-standing policy.[40] Both were single decisions of the premier. The point is that Wilson's account assumes a close connection between society, party, and political leadership. While leaders do not have many degrees of freedom, there seems to be considerable latitude for leaders to make decisions, at least within the party, so long as political tides are favourable.

And if Wilson caught the essence of Ontario's political culture up to the 1970s, since then the province seems to be a very different place: the necessity for balancing capital and labour has eased, a function of the decline in the manufacturing sector and concomitant decline of union membership in the private sector. Labour Day parades used to be big events, but no more. Political discourse has changed: NDP rhetoric no longer references socialism or even social democracy; workers have been shunted aside in favour of "ordinary Canadians" and the "middle class." And the Conservatives project a chameleon-like image, from the rightist positioning and adversarial language of Mike Harris, Ernie Eves, and Tim Hudak to John Tory's centrist posture.

Ideational and Operative Norms in Ontario's Political Culture

Sid Noel provides a very useful distinction when he identifies political culture as comprising *ideational* and *operative norms*. The ideational component refers to political ideas and philosophy. Words like "conservative," "radical," "liberal," or "socialist" easily come to mind; "identity," "individualist," "collectivist," or "sovereignty" are more subtle instances of political discourse. Do people value freedom—action, association, speech—or place a premium on control and social order? Operative norms are more diffused, being part of "the generally unarticulated assumptions, expectations, and understandings of people—the norms they quietly hold—about the way that their politics ordinarily ought to be conducted, what they can reasonably expect of government, and their sense of their society's proper place in relation to other societies and the world at large."[41]

Noel identifies five operative norms in Ontario politics, as follows:

- The imperative pursuit of economic success
- The assumption of pre-eminence
- The requirement of managerial efficiency
- The expectation of reciprocity
- The balancing of interests[42]

Noel claims that these norms have deep historical roots but have not "congealed" (i.e., become bedrock features) and are evolving more or less in tandem with the province's economic development.[43] The following will discuss the norms in light of political events since Noel's important contribution appeared.

The Imperative Pursuit of Economic Success

Ontario is not alone in placing weight on economic success. Indeed, it is hard to imagine a liberal–democratic polity in which most politicians would not talk about and focus on economic development. From this perspective, the aim of public policy is twofold: improvement of individuals' economic wellbeing and overall increase in public prosperity.[44] Accordingly, it is not surprising that Ontario, in conjunction with the national government, provided massive loans to two automobile manufacturers—General Motors and Chrysler, large employers in the province, but on the verge of bankruptcy—in the wake of the financial collapse of 2008. Such interventions have continued through the years, including a large grant to Toyota, one of the world's most profitable companies, for expansion of its Cambridge plant. But more broadly, through the first decade of the 2000s Ontario suffered an enormous loss of manufacturing jobs. What is not evident is that Ontarians are prepared to punish the government party—the Liberals—for the dramatic reshaping of the province's economy.

The Assumption of Pre-Eminence

It is certainly the case that there has been an assumption that Ontario would necessarily have a pre-eminent role to play in national politics.[45] Christopher Armstrong observed in 1981 that Ontarians "have always considered themselves to be 'real' Canadians and assumed that their wishes are the wishes of the nation collectively. Any apparent conflict between national and provincial objectives may be dissolved by the conviction that the interests of Ontario are the interests of Canada."[46]

Ontario premiers have historically had a big role beyond the normative premise of importance because of the province's population size and economic weight. Premiers Davis, Peterson, and Rae were central figures in constitutional politics through the 1970s to the early 1990s. However, Premiers Harris and McGuinty were relatively quiet, perhaps because of the reduced emotional symbolism in federal-provincial issues after the defeat of the Charlottetown Accord in 1992. The economic and cultural upheavals of the last third of the twentieth century saw Quebec become more aggressive in federal-provincial relations, along with the rising prominence of energy-producing provinces, notably Alberta to the west and Newfoundland and

Labrador to the east. Ontario, then, had strong challengers to the presumption that it would define the national interest. Further, Ontario's presumption surely has been undercut by it becoming at times a "have-not" province and a recipient of equalization payments. (See also Chapter 8's discussion of Ontario's role in the Canadian federation.)

Perhaps there is something else at work that may be suggestive of a change in the province's culture (or its ability to be a major actor in Ottawa). From 1867 to 1948 (that is until the death of Ontario's Mackenzie King, who was prime minister for 22 years over three stints from 1921 to 1948), prime ministers in good measure (and their opponents in the other major party) came from Ontario.[47] From 1948 to the present day only one prime minister (Lester Pearson) could rightly be labelled an Ontarian.[48] Prime ministers from Quebec (St. Laurent, Pierre Trudeau, Mulroney, Chrétien, Martin, and Justin Trudeau) have held office for 46 years and counting. Leadership races for the Liberals and Conservatives have produced Ontario-based candidates, but with the exception of Liberal Michael Ignatieff in 2008, they have been unsuccessful. It is noteworthy that, since George Drew, no leader (including six premiers) of the Ontario Progressive Conservative Party, one of the most successful parties in the world, has entered federal politics; the same is true for the Liberals. Only of the NDP could it be said that Ontario has been important, with three prominent leaders (David Lewis, Ed Broadbent, and Jack Layton, who was born and raised in Montreal) being politically based in the province.[49]

The Requirement of Managerial Efficiency

The requirement of managerial efficiency (identified by both Wilson and Noel) seems to have been greatly tested in the 2000s. Ontario budgetary deficits soared, as did the province's accumulated public debt, with bond rating companies lowering their ratings of the province's credit worthiness.[50] The debt of Hydro One (part of the former Ontario Hydro) was so large that it necessitated a special imposition on consumers in order to retire the obligation. A series of scandals (eHealth, ORNGE, and gas plant cancellations) burdened the province's finances at a time when decades of inattention to the province's transportation infrastructure generated increasingly long travel times and on occasion gridlock, especially in the Greater Toronto and Hamilton Area.

The Expectation of Reciprocity

Sid Noel identified a central component of Ontario's political culture from its earliest days as being the development of patron-client relationships within the polity.[51] The pattern of land settlement and the nature of agriculture led to "complex reciprocal transactions of exchange" between "individuals of unequal status and resources but mutual interests."[52] Noel argued that this set the scene for lower-drawer patronage across the province, which had the effect of creating strong support from business and professional classes. However, this patronage system fell apart in 1985 with the election of Liberals long unaccustomed to the intricacies of patronage networks. The NDP for its part was mired in a sharp economic downtown and protracted internal battles about the direction of the province. Moreover, in a highly urbanized society, marked by high mobility and neighbourhood anonymity, the political value of having local notables speak on a party's behalf had diminished. Electronic politics and the concomitant focus on the personality and style of the party leaders undercut the need to develop networks of community leaders supporting the party because of benefits, often minor in the scheme of things.[53]

The Balancing of Interests

Both John Wilson and Sid Noel place a premium on the balancing of interests, with Wilson focusing on labour-capital interests and Noel taking a more expansive view, arguing that the norm means "that all legitimate interests were *entitled* to be included in the process of balancing."[54] One arena that Wilson does not address is language minorities and education, one of the most vexing areas of conflict in Ontario.

One important instance was Regulation 17, which limited the teaching of French to the early elementary grades, established by the Conservative government of James Whitney in 1913, an administration otherwise known for its "progressive" mindset. The successor Conservative administration, headed by William Hearst, rigidly resisted opposition to the regulation, expressed by heated rhetoric, strikes, and demonstrations (and great anger in Quebec, to the extent that it became an issue of national unity). However, the Conservative government of Howard Ferguson in 1927, after extensive negotiations with various stakeholders, produced a widely hailed agreement. Two kinds of politics are evident: one is the "old Ontario"—Orange Lodge, Protestant, anti-French, matched by voices decrying the anglicization of French Canada—and the other is the recognition that all sides had to "share the road"—that is, salient actors had to find a political solution to a political problem.[55] Similar attempts to find political solutions can be seen in Leslie Frost's rejection of the Hope Commission's recommendation to cut back the Catholic school system,[56] in John Roberts and the expansion of French immersion schools,[57] and in Bill Davis and the extended funding for Catholic secondary schools.

Bob Rae, in his account of his premiership, reports that many of his attempts to strike a balance between business and labour were character-ized by no gratitude when the latter got something it wanted and brutish hostility when it did not.[58] The Harris government had a very clear agenda and ideological commitment, and it was not at all interested in canvassing input from a wide range of Ontario society. It brought a strong business orientation to its decisions about public policy, though it backed off on the privatization of the LCBO.[59] The PCs, under Harris and his short-lived suc-cessor Ernie Eves, proudly went outside the world of group politics, except for business, railing against "special interests" and in favour of "taxpayers."

The McGuinty government in its first seven years or so established very congenial relations with the province's various teacher unions, but after McGuinty took a tough stance with the same unions they turned on the Liberals, which led to a poor showing in a critical by-election in Kitchener-Waterloo and the loss of three seats out of five by-elections in the summer of 2013, despite Premier Wynne's promise to work more cooperatively with the teachers in the future. Public sector unions rallied behind the Liberals in the 2014 provincial election against the threat of large job cuts promised by Tim Hudak's Progressive Conservatives, but the adversarial relationship soon returned at the negotiating table. At one time, business and labour had strong organizations to speak on their behalf; that does not describe mod-ern Ontario, where the broad public sector, including doctors, has strong union organizations but without comparable taxpayer organizations seeking to be recognized and heard as part of the balancing process. Outside of busi-ness, public sector unions, and the (diminished) private sector unions, most Ontarians are not organized. "Third-party advertising" is unregulated, even during elections, so that interest groups can fund advertising against a party. Labour groups have adroitly used their resources to attack the PCs, but there are no countervailing nonpartisan voices heard.

The New Ontario

Consider this question: What kinds of things are "private" and what is "pub-lic"? Is, say, racial discrimination or sexual orientation a matter of private interactions or a proper subject for state intervention? What about smoking? On these issues and others there has been an enormous shift in the thinking of Ontarians since the 1960s.

One aspect of life that was considered to be "personal" was one's views of different groups of people and their members. If one held racist views, so be it; and if one refused to hire a black person or allow a Jewish person to be in one's restaurant, so be it. Leslie Frost—an Orangeman, small-town lawyer, and "Old Man Ontario"—certainly thought that odious views were private matters. But after pressure from various groups (especially Jewish), his government passed the Fair Employment Practices Act in 1951 and the Fair Accommodations Act in 1954. Both anti-discrimination acts were revolutionary for Ontario, as they challenged the bedrock assumption that interpersonal relations were private, not public matters. And, as was to happen many more times, American examples and leaders were part of the pressure campaign. So another part of Ontario's political culture—the anti-Americanism of the Loyalists—was being eroded, though for desirable ends.[60]

The Frost government in 1961 established the Ontario Human Rights Commission, the first such institution in Canada. Since then, the OHRC has assumed a leading role in the province's politics in fulfilling its mandate to provide everybody equal rights and the freedom to move through life without discrimination. While there are instances of hostility from some elements of Ontario society, no party has made an election issue of the OHRC. It seems that Ontarians have accepted the logic of Leslie Frost's thinking that discrimination and harassment because of who you are have no place in Ontario society. In 2013 the OHRC published a new policy that would curtail use of the criterion of "Canadian experience" in hiring; that is, "employers and regulatory bodies need to ask about all of a job applicant's previous work—where they got their experience does not matter."[61] Globalization, in its many expressions, has led the province to consider deeply how it will operate.

To date, Ontarians seem to have welcomed the enormous number of immigrants to the province. And while there are undoubtedly issues of adaptation and integration, old Ontario and new Ontario seem to have produced policies and social arrangements that have accommodated differences between peoples more or less harmoniously. Ontario is by no means unusual in these matters. But an important component of a purportedly well-entrenched political culture—its exclusivist side—has long receded. The system of public education, extending to the postsecondary level with its many colleges and universities, has provided Ontarians with widening educational opportunities. The new Ontario is a province that responds to public policy claims through the lens of fairness, inclusiveness, and equal treatment.

Every year a number of festivals and community events are held across the province. One of the most notable is Toronto's Pride Week, held each June, and one of the world's largest celebrations of diverse sexual orientations. Born out of police raids on bathhouses, in itself it is remarkable if one thinks about the impossibility of such events before the 1980s. But what is telling is that, over time, leading actors in the LGBTQ community found ways to build community support and acceptance rather than rejection and hostility.[62] An element of Ontario's political culture previously identified—political actors working to find solutions to political problems, rather than falling back on hard positions—was manifested yet again. In the twenty-first century, the sexual orientation of politicians seemingly is a dead issue, of no public pertinence, even of comment. The complex and changing dynamics of police–society interactions were illustrated by two events in 2016. The first saw Chief of Police Mark Saunders apologize for police raids on bathhouses. The second was the critique offered by Black Lives Matter about the lethal use of force by the police and that the police should not be recognized participants in Toronto's Pride events.

The norms of equality and acceptance run deep within the new Ontario. A number of instances of bullying, especially in schools and social media, led the Ontario government to allow the formation of Gay-Straight Alliance (GSA) clubs in the province's high schools, even in the Roman Catholic system, which was in effect told that it was not separate from the public system of education, despite claims to the contrary from various Catholic educators and school trustees.

Ontario's political culture has an unsettling side. While voter turnout, compared to other provinces, has historically been in the middle of the range, it is now falling to the low end, along with Alberta and British Columbia. In the 2014 election, turnout was just over 52 per cent; and, as elsewhere, it is primarily younger citizens who are not voting (and, indeed, not participating in political parties). Visible minorities are beginning to appear on municipal councils and school boards, but in no way commensurate to their proportions in Ontario society. Toronto's much vaunted social heterogeneity has not manifested itself in those who hold the mayor's chair, which has yet to be held by a nonwhite person.

Ontario: A New State, a New Political Culture?

In 1998, Thomas Courchene and Colin Telmer published an interpretation of Ontario arising out of the increasing north-south trade between the province and the United States and the financial exigencies facing all governments. Ontario was seeking a new role, it was suggested, one that called for closer relations with the United States and a developing lack of interest in Canada. The political manifestation was the 1995 election of the Mike Harris government under the rubric of the "Common Sense Revolution" that promised tight financial controls, cutbacks to social welfare, and a focus on creating economic vibrancy.[63] Was there a concomitant shift in Ontarian political culture?[64] The four Liberal victories from 2003 to 2015 suggest that

Ontarians were not fixed on a new direction. Moreover, as Wiseman argues, there is no evidence that "Ontarians feel any closer to the US than in the past or that they are supportive of more economic or cultural integration with it. Indeed, Ontarians were more opposed to free trade with the US than were Canadians in any other province."[65]

Conclusion

Ontarians are conservative and politically indifferent people. Political interest is episodic and sporadic, and political conversations seem to be rare; federal politics are more important, but, even so, it is striking that most Ontarians seem to be unaware of the opposition leaders until the election is well underway.[66] The electoral reform referendum of 2007 (see Chapter 11) failed to generate much interest, with only 52 per cent of the electorate voting and many voters reporting they were uninformed about the referendum despite an abundance of materials publicly available.

The strong role of the state, a function of diverse motives, has been a constant throughout Ontario's history. When a party adopts a clear anti-state posture it runs a high risk of defeat. The Harris-Eves government of 1995 to 2003 did not recalibrate the political thinking of Ontarians, and, indeed, many of the things the Conservatives feared—high government spending, ballooning deficits, and escalating public indebtedness—came with the Liberals after 2003 to no great public discontent despite much discussion about Ontario's dire financial straits. There is no evidence that many Ontarians think that the state is a problem that requires a severe curtailment of its role. Privatization is not a preferred option for most Ontarians, even in the case of the liquor market, and certainly not in health care. On the other hand, to the dismay of the critics of advanced capitalism, there is no great call for another economic path or a serious restructuring of the economic system.

Donald MacDonald, a former leader of the Ontario NDP, found that the province's political culture had two strong components—one conservative and the other "progressive," understood as commitment to egalitarianism and spreading democracy.[67] Progressiveness in contemporary Ontario does not extend much to the economic system or the workings of political institutions, but more to interpersonal relations and the rights of individuals within society, a society that sees itself as valuing fairness, inclusiveness, and equal treatment. Religious prescriptions as ordinarily understood do not hold sway. The litmus test is same-sex marriage, which is still controversial in some quarters but has become common and accepted since the province recognized the institution in 2003 following various court judgments.

No party has sought reversal and no new party has risen around the issue, thus marking the end of another part of Ontario's political culture.

Discussion Questions

1. What does the concept of political culture mean? Do you feel Ontario has a clear and distinguishable political culture?
2. Review the five operative norms in Ontario politics discussed in the chapter. What is your own interpretation of each of them in today's Ontario?
3. Do you agree that Ontarians are essentially conservative and politically indifferent people? Why or why not?
4. To what extent can we identify distinct regional and/or local political cultures in modern day Ontario?
5. Has immigration and social change transformed Ontario political culture, or has the existing culture largely absorbed such changes to remain much the same?

Notes

1   For a very helpful discussion of political culture, see Nelson Wiseman, *In Search of Canadian Political Culture* (Vancouver: UBC Press, 2007), especially Chapters 1 and 2. Those who write about political culture often use language like Wiseman's ("search" or "elusive"). "Elliptical" is perhaps another appropriate term.

2   Gabriel Almond and Sidney Verba, *The Civic Culture: Political Attitudes and Democracy in Five Nations* (Princeton, NJ: Princeton University Press, 1963).

3   Wiseman, *In Search of Canadian Political Culture*, 39.

4   A.R.M. Lower, "Does Ontario Exist?" *Ontario History* 60, no. 2 (1968): 64–69.

5   Ontario would have no need to pass a bill such as Quebec's Bill 101 (The Charter of the French Language). In the twenty-first century, it seems inconceivable that Ontario would see a need to pass a law deeming illegal various forms of religious symbolization, as the Quebec government proposed to do in 2013.

6   Instructive discussions are found in S.F. Wise, "Upper Canada and the Conservative Tradition," in S.F. Wise, *God's Peculiar Peoples: Essays on Political Culture in Nineteenth-Century Canada*, ed. A.B. McKillop and Paul Romney (Ottawa: Carleton University Press, 1993), 169–84, and Donald C. MacDonald, "Ontario's Political Culture: Conservatism with a Progressive Component," *Ontario History* 36, no. 4 (1994): 297–317.

7   Wise describes the six northern colonies as having more or less identical political institutions "governed by imperial representatives in alliance with bureaucratic elites whose makeup varied marginally from colony to colony" and argues that "the official ideology of empire won support from the great majority of the politically articulate." S.F. Wise, "Conservatism and Political Development: The Canadian Case," in *God's Peculiar Peoples*, 186.

8   S.M. Lipset, *Continental Divide: The Values and Institutions of the United States and Canada.* (Toronto: C.D. Howe Institute, 1989), 1.

9   Wise, "Conservatism and Political Development," 214.

10 Douglas McCalla, "The Ontario Economy in the Long Run," *Ontario History* 90, no. 2 (1998): 109.

11 H.V. Nelles, *The Politics of Development: Forest, Mines, and Hydro-Electric Power in Ontario, 1849–1941* (Toronto: Macmillan, 1974). Nelles describes the Crown Timber Act of 1849 as having "exceptional authority" in that it was legislative entrenchment of the principle of state ownership that had been heretofore a matter of regulation (13).

12 Carol Lawrie Vaughan, "The Bank of Upper Canada in Politics, 1817–1840," *Ontario History* 60, no. 4 (1968): 193. There is a contemporary resonance to this issue. Since Confederation, Canadian banks have been the responsibility of the national government, unlike the United States where both levels charter and regulate banks. In the United States, from 2001 to 2012, almost 500 hundred banks collapsed. The last banks (two) to declare bankruptcy in Canada were in the 1980s; prior to that the last bank to collapse was in 1923. No Canadian bank went under during the Great Depression, whereas in the United States more than 9,000 did.

13 Anthony Di Mascio, *The Idea of Popular Schooling in Upper Canada* (Montreal: McGill-Queen's University Press, 2012), 3.

14 The four are the English-language public system, the English-language Catholic system, the French-language public system, and the French-language Catholic system.

15 The Progressive Conservative Party made public funding of independent schools its central promise in the 2007 election but lost despite its early lead in public opinion polls.

16 One study put Alberta, British Columbia, Quebec, and Manitoba at the high end of its "Canadian Education Freedom Index" and Ontario in the middle. In 2002 Ontario started to provide public funding to independent schools. See Claudia R. Hepburn and Robert Van Belle, "The Canadian Education Freedom Index," *Studies in Education Policy* (September 2003).

17 R.D. Gidney, *From Hope to Harris: The Reshaping of Ontario's Schools* (Toronto: University of Toronto Press, 1999), 198.

18 Charles W. Humphries, "The Sources of Ontario's 'Progressive' Conservatism, 1900–1914," *Annual Papers of the Canadian Historical Association* (1967): 118–29.

19 Margaret Evans and R.W. Irvin, "Government Tractors in Ontario: 1918 and 1919," *Ontario History* 59, no. 2 (1969): 99–109.

20 J.T. Phair, "Public Health in Ontario," in *The Development of Public Health in Canada* (Toronto: Canadian Public Health Association, 1940), 67–85.

21 The hydro commission became Ontario Hydro in 1973; for an excellent account, see Neil B. Freeman, *The Politics of Power: Ontario Hydro and Its Government, 1906–1995* (Toronto: University of Toronto Press, 1996).

22 Ibid., ix.

23 Beer can only be sold in LCBO outlets, brewers' own stores, and the consortium's stores, which are obligated to serve a wide range of beers. An academic study in 2013 argued that price differences between Quebec, which allows grocery stores to sell beer, and Ontario amounted to almost $700 million a year. Anindya

Sen, "An Empirical Analysis of Beer Price Differentials between Ontario and Quebec," Working Paper, Department of Economics, University of Waterloo, 2013. It is worth noting that, in 2016, some grocery stores in Ontario were granted permission to sell beer.

24   Norman Giesbrecht, Anca Ialomiteanu, Robin Room, and Lise Anglin, "Trends in Public Opinion on Alcohol Policy Measures: Ontario 1989–1998," *Journal of Studies on Alcohol and Drugs* 62, no. 2 (2001): 142–49.

25   Ontario, Municipal Board Act.

26   J.G. Chipman, *A Law Unto Itself: How the Ontario Municipal Board Has Developed and Applied Land Use Policy* (Toronto: University of Toronto Press, 2002), xi.

27   Martin Regg Cohn, "How the OMB Stifles Democracy in Ontario," *Toronto Star*, Tuesday, 27 August 2013. Chipman reports that developers in their appeals of councils' decision won between 50 and 60 per cent of appeals heard from the 1970s to 2000 (*A Law Unto Itself*, 53).

28   A.L. McDougall, *John P. Robarts: His Life and Government* (Toronto: University of Toronto Press, 1986), 213–16.

29   In the case of police in Canada, see Savvas Lithopoulos and George S. Rigakos, "Neo-Liberalism, Community, and Police Regionalization in Canada: A Critical Empirical Analysis," *Policing: An International Journal of Police Strategies & Management* 28, no. 2 (2005): 337–52.

30   A wave of farmer-centred movements appeared in a number of provinces after World War I and formed government in Alberta and Manitoba. In Ontario the great overrepresentation of rural areas resulted in a severe discrepancy between votes cast and seats won (Conservatives 34 per cent of the vote, 22.5 per cent of seats; Liberals, 29 and 26; UFO, 22 and 40.5); see Brian D. Tennyson, "The Ontario General Election of 1919: The Beginnings of Agrarian Revolt," *Journal of Canadian Studies* 4, no. 1 (1969): 34.

31   Communists were elected to the Ontario Legislature and to some Ontario city councils under the Labour-Progressive banner in the 1940s and 1951.

32   The provincial Conservative Party adopted the name "Progressive Conservative" following the lead of the national party in 1942.

33   John Wilson, "The Ontario Political Culture," in *Government and Politics of Ontario*, ed. Donald C. MacDonald (Toronto: Macmillan, 1975), 226. For a slightly altered version of the argument see his "The Red Tory Province: Reflections on the Character of the Ontario Political Culture," in *The Government and Politics in Ontario*, 2nd ed., ed. Donald C. MacDonald (Toronto: Van Nostrand, 1980), 208–26.

34   Wilson, "The Ontario Political Culture," 233. Two of Robarts's biographers do not explicitly discuss bilingualism but cover extensively his interest in national unity: McDougall, *John P. Robarts*, and Steve Paikin, *Public Triumph, Private Tragedy: The Double Life of John P. Robarts* (Toronto: Viking Canada, 2005). Wilson does not refer to Robarts's vehement opposition to the federal government's proposal in 1965 for national health insurance ("medicare"), to which Ontario eventually acquiesced because of Ottawa's imposition of taxes for the program, which Ontarians would pay even if the province was not participating (McDougall, *John P. Robarts*, 166–72).

35   Wilson, "The Ontario Political Culture," 233.

36 J. Wilson and D. Hoffman, "Ontario: A Three-Party System in Transition," in *Canadian Provincial Politics: The Party Systems of the Ten Provinces*, ed. M. Robin (Toronto: Prentice-Hall, 1972).

37 But, as Peter Oliver observes, Ontario "writers have failed to reproduce any comprehensive or distinctive sense of either the city or the countryside" and "have also failed to suggest the vigour and enthusiasm which have created a progressive civilization of great complexity in little more than a century." Peter Oliver, "Introduction: On Being an Ontarian," in Peter Oliver, *Public and Private Persons: The Ontario Political Culture, 1914–1934* (Toronto: Clarke, Irwin and Company, 1975), 3.

38 By "broadly considered" is meant municipalities, universities and colleges, schools, and hospitals as well as the Queen's Park bureaucracy. Overall, the public sector constitutes about 15 per cent of Ontario's workforce.

39 A study of parliamentary government in Ontario published in 1969 reported that cabinet proceedings "are entirely informal and completely under the control of the premier, who may choose which items on the agenda will be discussed and decided upon and which, if any, will be carried over." F.F. Schindeler, *Responsible Government in Ontario* (Toronto: University of Toronto Press, 1969), 50.

40 Gidney, *From Hope to Harris*.

41 Sid Noel, "The Ontario Political Culture: An Interpretation," in *The Government and Politics of Ontario*, 5th ed., ed. Graham White (Toronto: University of Toronto Press, 1997), 50.

42 Ibid.

43 Ibid., 65.

44 Ibid., 54. Noel argues that the Harris-Eves governments were found wanting on both counts, which led to the PCs losing office in 2003.

45 S.F. Wise, "The Ontario Political Culture," in *God's Peculiar People*. Wise writes that a peculiar feature of Ontarians is that they "have always regarded Confederation as chiefly their creation, and the province is pivotal to its maintenance." Further, they hold the "idea that the country as a whole is a field for the expression of Ontario's interests" (221). Another statement of the centrality of Ontario is Robert M. Krause, "Ontario: Canada Writ Small," in *Introductory Readings in Canadian Government and Politics*, 2nd ed., ed. Robert M. Krause and R.H. Wagenberg (Toronto: Copp Clark, 1995), 117–32.

46 Christopher Armstrong, *The Politics of Federalism: Ontario's Relationship with the Federal Government, 1867–1942* (Toronto: University of Toronto Press, 1981), 258.

47 John A. Macdonald and Mackenzie King, while clearly from and of Ontario, each for a period represented constituencies in western Canada, and, in fact, each represented Prince Alberta in Saskatchewan.

48 Paul Martin is an ambiguous case in that his family came from Windsor, Ontario, but most of his business life was in Montreal and he represented an electoral district in that city. John Diefenbaker and Stephen Harper were born in Ontario but their adult years were in Western Canada. John Turner had ties to Quebec, Ontario, and British Columbia and was elected at different times from all three provinces.

49   Bob Rae is anomalous; after serving as Ontario's NDP premier, he returned to Ottawa as a Liberal and twice sought leadership and then served as interim leader before Justin Trudeau became leader.

50   In July 2015 the credit rating agency Standard & Poor's downgraded Ontario to A+; in 1985 its rating for Ontario was AAA, the highest possible category.

51   S.J.R. Noel, *Patrons, Clients, Brokers: Ontario Society and Politics, 1791–1896* (Toronto: University of Toronto Press, 1990).

52   Noel, "The Ontario Political Culture," 61.

53   The author's wife, upon being nominated by the Progressive Conservatives for the 1985 election, was visited by many groups and individuals testing her interest and willingness to support their causes and interests.

54   Noel, "The Ontario Political Culture," 64, emphasis in original.

55   Peter Oliver, "Regulation 17: The Resolution of the Ontario Bilingual Schools Crisis, 1916–1929," in Oliver, *Public and Private Persons*, 92–124.

56   Roger Graham, *Old Man Ontario: Leslie M. Frost* (Toronto: University of Toronto Press), 182–84.

57   McDougall, *John P. Robarts*, 191–92.

58   Bob Rae, *From Protest to Power: Personal Reflections on a Life in Politics* (Toronto: Viking Canada, 1996).

59   One of the most egregious examples of the public interest being narrowly defined is found in the privatization of Highway 407, where the private operator was given a 99-year lease for a payment far less than the publicly funded highway cost; see Chandram Mylvaganam and Sandford Borins, *"If you build it …": Business, Government and Ontario's Electronic Toll Highway* (Toronto: University of Toronto Press, 2004).

60   James W. St. G. Walker, "The 'Jewish Phase' in the Movement for Racial Equality in Canada," *Canadian Ethnic Studies* 34, no. 1 (2002): 1.

61   Ontario Human Rights Commission, "Remove the 'Canadian Experience' Employment Barrier," 15 July 2013, http://www.ohrc.on.ca/en/removing-canadian-experience-barrier-brochure

62   Ontario is not alone in its acceptance of diverse sexual lifestyles. The national government, with the Conservatives in office, has been identified as having a "gay friendly" foreign policy. One explanation is that gay Tories, mostly Toronto-based, cast the issue of acceptance in terms of strong and loving families.

63   Thomas J. Courchene and C.R. Telmer, *From Heartland to North American Region-State: The Social, Fiscal and Federal Evolution of Ontario* (Toronto: University of Toronto Faculty of Management, 1998).

64   See Peter Woolstencroft, "Reclaiming the 'Pink Palace': The Progressive Conservative Party Comes in from the Cold," in *The Government and Politics of Ontario*, 5th ed., ed. Graham White (Toronto: University of Toronto Press, 1997), 365–401.

65   Wiseman, *In Search of Canadian Political Culture.*

66   Woolstencroft, "Reclaiming the 'Pink Palace,'" 365.

67   MacDonald, "Ontario's Political Culture," 298.

PART 2

Institutions

5

The Ontario Legislature: Living Up to Its Democratic Potential amidst Political Change?

TRACEY RANEY

PRESUMABLY A KEY REASON ONTARIO HIGH SCHOOL STUDENTS are required to take a mandatory civics education class would be to increase their understanding of the political process in Canada, which in turn might make them more engaged citizens. In 2013, however, an Ontario high school teacher drew attention to the fact that the province's civics education textbooks contained factual errors about Canada's parliamentary system.[1] It goes without saying that providing students with misinformation about how their government works is likely not helping the goal of improving the political knowledge and engagement of the next generation of young citizens in the province. The purpose of this chapter is to provide an overview of Ontario's Legislature, paying particular attention to how it has changed over the last few decades. The goal of the chapter is obvious: it aims to offer an account of the Legislature that Ontarians can use to critically assess whether various changes to it have enhanced or undermined democracy in the province.

The chapter is divided into three parts. The first part outlines the context in which Ontario's Legislature operates, and includes a discussion of party competition and minority government. The second part reviews the basic structure of the provincial Legislature and the actors who work within it. In the third part, three key functions of the Legislature are reviewed: representation, legislation, and scrutiny. The central argument of the chapter is that while some of the changes made to the Legislature have strengthened its democratic potential, others have left it a weaker institution with some of the core aspects of parliamentary democracy diminished.

Parliamentary Context: Party Competition and Governing with a Minority

A central feature of Westminster parliamentary systems is strong political parties, and Ontario is no exception. Since 1990, each of the three main political parties has formed government at least once (the New Democratic Party in 1990, the Progressive Conservatives in 1995 and 1999, and the Liberals in

2003, 2007, 2011, and 2014). A competitive three-party system is significant for the Legislature in a number of ways. First, it means that when a single-party majority government is in power the opposition is effectively divided between two political parties, each with a semi-reasonable chance at forming the next government.[2] The relative stability of Ontario's three-party system means that opposition parties are perpetually in "campaign" mode and are also in competition with one another as the "government-in-waiting" party. Even opposition parties that are ideologically opposed (the NDP on the left and the PCs on the right) are prone to attacking one another as they seek to form the next government. Second, three-way competitions increase the chances of electing a minority government, as votes are split three ways.[3] Indeed, four of the last 12 elections in the province (one-third) have produced minority governments: 1975, 1977, 1985, and 2011. Unlike majority governments where opposition votes are not required, minority governments need the opposition's support to pass their legislation. Compromise and consensus between the government and opposition are therefore necessary ingredients for minority governments to work. This was precisely the case in the 1985–87 minority government of Liberal premier David Peterson when he struck an accord with the NDP; in exchange for including some of the NDP's priorities in the government's agenda, the NDP agreed not to bring forward or support a vote of nonconfidence against the government for a period of two years.[4] This legislative alliance resulted in a rather stable and productive minority government, after which the Liberals were rewarded with a majority government in the 1987 election.

In 2011, the Liberals won 53 seats—one seat short of a majority in the 107 seat chamber. Although they lost 18 seats from the previous election and no longer controlled the House, the Liberals seemed either ill-prepared or unwilling to acknowledge the new realities of minority government. Indeed, after the election, Dalton McGuinty referred to the results as a "major minority" win for his party.[5] This statement obscures the reality that the Liberals no longer held a majority and would need to work with the opposition in order to pass their legislation. But this is not what happened. During the fall of 2012, the Legislature effectively ground to a halt and heated debates ensued across the floor over the government's decision to relocate two gas-fired power plants during the 2011 election. On 15 October 2012, McGuinty prorogued the Legislature and announced his resignation as premier.[6] His reasoning was that the Legislature had become far too rancorous to get anything accomplished; however, it did not help his case that the prorogation occurred at a time when his government faced two contempt motions in the House. Rather than try to work with the opposition parties in the Legislature, the government decided it would be best to shut it down completely.

In January 2013, the Liberals elected Kathleen Wynne as their new leader, and she was sworn in as Ontario's and Canada's first openly gay premier the following month. In the 2014 election she secured a Liberal majority government. Wynne appeared to approach politics differently than her predecessor. In February 2013, her government's Throne Speech stated that the government "intends to work with opposition parties, in a spirit of renewed cooperation, to get the people's business done."[7] In June 2013, Wynne made several concessions to the NDP in her budget in order to secure that party's support. Wynne's premiership highlights the importance of the parties and their leaders to the functioning of the Legislature: party leaders (and premiers) set the tone of debate, and they decide how much or how little they will work with the members of the other parties to ensure the smooth functioning of the Legislature. In addition to the premier, opposition leaders also bring their own approaches and styles to their positions. In the 2013 budget talks, the leader of the NDP, Andrea Horwath, was able to negotiate several issues (e.g., lower auto insurance rates) with Wynne in order to secure her party's support for the budget. This approach contrasted with that of Progressive Conservative leader Tim Hudak, who refused to negotiate with either party during the budget talks.

The Structure of the Legislature: Parliamentary Conventions and Actors

A central feature of Ontario's parliamentary system is responsible government, which means that the government (the cabinet) can only govern insofar as it maintains the confidence of the House (the Legislature). Within the Legislature, the chief presiding officer is the Speaker of the House. Since 1990, the Speaker has been elected by members of the House through a secret ballot held at the opening of the first session of a Parliament. The Speaker does not take part in the debate before the House and only votes in cases of a tie. He or she is responsible for preserving order and decorum in the House, and he or she decides on questions of privilege and points of order. Other presiding officers include the Deputy Speaker (appointed by the House), who performs the duties and exercises the authority of the Speaker when the Speaker is absent, and three deputy chairs of the Committee of the Whole House.

Similar to other Westminster-style parliamentary systems, party discipline, and indeed, political parties themselves, are dominant features of Ontario's Legislature. Practically all legislative business centres on the recognized political parties. In addition, the rights of independent members are more limited than those of members who belong to a recognized party. Independent members must request permission from the Speaker to ask a question during oral questions. Since 1999, the Standing Orders specify that in order for a party to be recognized in the Legislature, a party caucus must include at least eight or more members.[8] Within the Legislature, parties are hierarchically organized, and the leader allocates specific roles and duties for key legislative positions, such as the house leader and party whip (the exception is the NDP, which elects its whip). Political party caucuses and Members of the Provincial Parliament (MPPs) are provided support for office operations, travel, and research, though this has only increased modestly in recent years in inflation-adjusted terms and relative to the overall growth of government. Without sufficient resources, it becomes difficult for MPPs to fulfill the scrutiny function that is required of them in the Legislature.

Individual MPPs do the lion's share of the work in the Legislature. Both the Official Opposition and the third-place party form shadow cabinets, members of which act as critics of the various government departments to which they are assigned. MPPs also sit on legislative committees, which are discussed in more detail below. In addition, MPPs fulfill important duties outside Queen's Park in their own ridings. These include meeting with and responding to the concerns of their constituents, attending community events and functions, and performing public speaking engagements. When combined with their work in the Legislature, the demands on MPPs can be very taxing.

In 1996, the Harris government eliminated the MPP pension plan. Following a 25 per cent pay increase for MPPs in 2007, the McGuinty government imposed a two-year freeze on salaries in 2010, which was later extended. Base MPP salaries are $116,000 a year, while cabinet ministers and the premier earn $166,000 and $209,000, respectively.[9] Undoubtedly, these salaries are higher than the incomes of average Ontarians. However, when compared to the compensation of other Canadian legislators, they are average or low. The 2015 salary of federal MPs was $167,400, while federal cabinet ministers received $247,500 and the Canadian prime minister earned $334,800 (not including car allowances).[10] In recommending a pay hike for Ontario's MPPs in 2006, the provincial Integrity Commissioner noted that such a measure was necessary in order to ensure that the provincial Legislature did not become a "farm team" for Ottawa, where salaries are higher.[11]

Legislative Officers

Ontario currently has eight legislative officers that assist the Legislature in its oversight of government: the Auditor General of Ontario, the Ombudsman, the Chief Electoral Officer, the Integrity Commissioner, the Information and

Privacy Commissioner, the Environmental Commissioner, and the Provincial Advocate for Children and Youth. The eighth and most recent officer is the Financial Accountability Officer, a position filled in February 2015 and modelled on the federal Parliamentary Budget Officer's position. Importantly, legislative officers report directly to the Legislature and not to the government, which means that they cannot be removed from office by the government if it does not like something they have to say. Beginning with the McGuinty government, these positions were appointed by ad hoc, all-party legislative committees. The functions of legislative officers vary, but broadly they assist nongovernment members in their scrutiny of the government by providing valuable expertise and information on public policy issues or matters of government. In February 2015, the Liberal government announced that all legislative watchdogs must now reapply for their position in open competitions adjudicated by an all-party legislative committee when their contracts expire; prior to this rule change they could simply be reappointed.

As part of its democratic renewal agenda, in 2004 the McGuinty government expanded the mandate of the Auditor General to include a review of government spending on advertising prior to broadcast or publishing and extended its value-for-money audits into the broader public sector for organizations that receive government grants, including hospitals, universities, and thousands of other organizations. Combined, these constitute over 50 per cent of total government expenditures.[12] Comparatively, Ontario's Auditor General Office is now one of the most powerful among its provincial counterparts.

The Ombudsman of Ontario (created in 1975) acts on complaints received by the public or members of the Legislature and as such plays an important oversight role in the political process. He or she investigates matters that relate to "provincial government entities, including ministries, commissions, boards, and other 'administrative units'—actions that affect individuals or groups."[13] They may also investigate issues of their "own motion."[14] André Marin served as ombudsman from 2005 to 2015 and investigated a number of important issues, including the scope of police powers during the 2010 Toronto G20 Summit; the ORNGE scandal, in which millions of dollars in public funds were misspent by the province's air ambulance service; and the acceptable use of force in prisons. Given the high profile nature of these investigations, the ombudsman's recommendations are usually adopted by the government.

Previously, Ontario's ombudsman had no authority over the "MUSH" sector (municipalities, universities, school boards, and hospitals).[15] This changed in December 2014 when the Ontario government passed Bill 8 (the Public Sector and MPP Accountability and Transparency Act), which allows the ombudsman to oversee municipalities, universities, school boards, and police. Unlike in some other provinces, however, the bill does not provide the ombudsman oversight over the "H"—hospitals. (In contrast, the Auditor General has no audit powers over municipalities.) Instead, it created a "patient ombudsman" who will receive, respond to, and investigate complaints from patients and former patients of Ontario's health care sector, though this office will not be an independent legislative officer like the ombudsman.[16] While these changes go some distance toward building an "ethical infrastructure" in the province, Ontario remains the only province whose ombudsman specifically has no reach into hospitals, long-term care, or children's aid societies.

Generally, legislative officers play an increasingly important oversight role in government. The expansion of the scrutiny function of the Legislature to its officers is potentially good for democracy in several respects: through their reports and investigations, officers can assist MPPs in their scrutiny role—the more eyes and ears on government, the better. Yet the rise in the authority and stature of legislative officers may also signal the malaise of the Legislature itself, as it becomes less effectual in making government more transparent and accountable in its own right. One implication of an expanded and empowered suite of legislative officers and a weakened Legislature is that it may blur the lines of accountability essential to the functioning of responsible government. Ultimately, it is the democratically elected members of the Legislature who are responsible to the people, and not the unelected legislative officers.

Parliamentary Calendar and Timetable

In 2014, the Ontario Legislature sat for a total of 77 days—longer than any other provincial or territorial government in Canada, but 50 days less than the House of Commons.[17] Its estimated operating budget for 2013–14 was $158 million.[18] This is up from $118 million 10 years previously.[19] According to the Standing Orders, the Legislature sits from the third Tuesday in February to the first Thursday in June, and from the Monday following Labour Day to the second Thursday in December. Five "constituency weeks" per calendar year are provided, which allow members to return to their ridings to conduct local business and meet with their constituents.

Legislative proceedings are divided into two parts: routine proceedings and orders of the day. Routine proceedings include members' statements, reports by committees, the introduction of bills, motions, statements by the ministry and responses, and petitions. Members' statements allow up to nine members per day (other than a leader of a recognized party in the House or a minister of the Crown) to be recognized and make a statement not exceeding one and a half minutes. Reports by committees allow time for the chairs of standing or select committees to present their amendments to legislation on the floor of the assembly.

As the centrepiece of a typical parliamentary day, question period (or "oral questions") provides opposition and government private members (those not in the cabinet) the opportunity to pose questions to the ministers of the Crown. Ministers may take an oral question as notice to be answered more fully on a future day, they may refer a question to a colleague, or they may decline to answer any question put to them.[20] Ontario's question period is 60 minutes, more time than any other province.[21] As Chapter 9 in this volume on the media attests, question period tends to garner considerable media attention and, for that reason, sometimes draws out the more juvenile behaviour of some MPPs. In 2009, Conservative MPPs Bill Murdoch and Randy Hillier staged a "sit-in" over the government's refusal to hold province-wide consultations on harmonizing provincial and federal sales taxes. After they positioned themselves closer to the Speaker and refusing to take their own seats, the Speaker was forced to end question period.[22] This kind of unparliamentary behaviour, or "playing to the camera," was likely spurred on by the introduction of television in the House in 1986.

In 2008, question period was separated from the rest of the routine proceedings in the afternoon and moved to 10:30 in the morning. While this change was pitched as a "family-friendly" move that would shorten the legislative day, it also provided the government more time in the day to control any potential fallout that might arise from question period. Moreover, moving question period to the morning resulted in even less media coverage of the other, perhaps less entertaining, proceedings in the House. Even before these changes, most MPPs were absent from the floor of the House during debates. This can create embarrassing situations when, for instance, a member introduces a student group from their constituency and there are more visitors in the galleries than members in their seats. At the same time, MPP absences do not necessarily mean they are slacking off, but rather that they are at committee meetings or attending to constituency matters.

Routine proceedings are followed by orders of the day, which allow for government business. In addition, up to 10 "opposition days" are provided in each parliamentary session, which allows the opposition parties to choose subjects for debate. In addition, private members' business is allotted two and half hours on Thursdays.

Functions of the Legislature

Legislatures fulfill a number of important functions, but the three main ones include representation, legislation, and scrutiny.[23] Each of these is discussed below.

Representation

Representation is a crucial aspect of any Legislature in a democracy. Ensuring that citizens have a voice in important public policy issues (such as education and clean energy) is essential to a democracy, where decisions are made based on the will of the people. Today each MPP represents one of 107 constituencies that has roughly the same number of residents (representation by population) so that every citizen's vote counts equally (although there are some exceptions, including northern constituencies).

Compared to previous generations, the representational burdens placed on MPPs today are much heavier. This is due to the small size of the Legislature relative to the population of the province. As part of his "Common Sense Revolution," Premier Harris reduced the size of the Legislature by a third (from 130 to 103 seats) for the 1999 election in the Fewer Politicians Act. Prior to the act, the average constituency in Ontario had 77,576 people.[24] By the time of the 2014 provincial election, Ontario's average constituency size was approximately 127,838 people, the biggest of any province.[25] After the 2018 provincial election, the number of seats in Ontario's Legislature is expected to grow to 122 (in order to match the increased number of Ontario ridings in the federal House of Commons).[26] Based on population projections for Ontario in 2018, each MPP would then represent approximately 116,732 people.[27] Although an improvement from today, Ontario's most populous constituencies (in southern, urban areas where further population growth is anticipated) will continue to place considerable demands on MPPs to adequately reflect and respond to the needs of voters into the foreseeable future.

Relative to their share of the population, women and visible minorities are underrepresented at Queen's Park. Although women constitute 52 per cent of Ontario's population, they held only 35.5 per cent of the seats in Queen's Park (38 out of 107) after the 2014 election. This is a high-water mark for women in the province, yet it remains far below the percentage of women in the general population. Visible minorities are also underrepresented in Ontario's Legislature. As seen in Chapter 15, despite constituting 26 per cent of the population, visible minorities accounted for only 16 per cent of all MPPs (17 out of 107) after the 2014 election. Although it has improved over time, Ontario's Legislature continues to be dominated by older, mostly non-racialized male members. The underrepresentation of women and visible minority groups weakens the legitimacy of the Legislature to adequately represent Ontario's diverse population.

Passing Legislation

The Legislature also passes laws. Note that passing laws is not the same as making laws. As White notes, "The most important part of the lawmaking process is pre-parliamentary; meaning the development of policy in cabinet and the bureaucracy."[28] Potential legislation proposed by the cabinet (overseen by the Premier's Office) is vetted by a multistage cabinet committee process in the executive.[29] While these executive processes are explored further in Chapter 6, a significant alteration made in 2003 holds special significance for the Legislature: at that time, Premier McGuinty gave backbench MPPs a role in his cabinet committees. While this decision opened cabinet to a wider group of government members, it also potentially blurs the lines of accountability between the government and the backbenches by reducing the number of government private members who could hold the executive to account, a point we will return to below.

There are three types of public bills in Ontario: government bills, committee bills, and private members' bills. The most common of these are government bills, which are introduced by cabinet ministers. In 1999, a number of changes were made to the Standing Orders that allow committee chairs to introduce so-called committee bills on the floor of the House, as long as they receive the support of at least two-thirds of the committee (excluding the chair).[30] However, very few such bills have been introduced or passed.[31] Private members' bills are introduced by members who are not ministers.[32] A fourth type of bill is private bills (not to be confused with private members' bills). Unlike public bills, private bills provide for an individual or group of individuals to be exempt from the general law, and originate when an individual, company, church, charitable organization, or municipality is seeking an exemption from the law.[33]

In terms of moving bills through the Legislature, government and private members' bills are introduced on the House floor, in a first reading. The bill is then printed in English and French and made available on the parliamentary website (http://www.ontla.on.ca/). A second reading provides members with an opportunity to debate and vote on the bill in principle; the bill may not be amended at this stage. If a bill is referred to committee then this must occur before the third reading. While most bills are referred to a committee after second reading, changes to the Standing Orders in 1999 allow public bills to be referred before second reading. This change would increase the opportunity for private members to influence policymaking through the committee process. Out of hundreds of bills introduced on the floor since 1999, only 15 have been referred to committee after first reading.[34]

If a bill is amended by a committee, the chair of that committee reports the bill to the House, and if it is then adopted, it may be ordered for a third reading.[35] After receiving approval from the majority of MPPs in a third reading, the bill is presented to the Lieutenant-Governor for Royal Assent, whereupon it becomes an act. This stage is necessary as all acts of Parliament must be signed into law by the Lieutenant-Governor, who represents the sovereign. White observes that a final, critical step in the legislative process occurs when a bill comes into force, as almost all government bills contain a provision that authorizes the government to make regulations (administrative decisions) related to the implementation of the bill. Accordingly, this provision "gives the government enormous power to issue legally binding directives (also called delegated legislation) setting out details of the policy without requiring any approval from the legislature."[36] The powers of the cabinet to make administrative decisions about how the provisions of a bill will be regulated reduce the capacity of the Legislature to effectively scrutinize "vast areas of government policy."[37]

The government can push its agenda through the Legislature in a number of ways. Two of these measures include motions of closure (Standing Order 48), which end all debate and put the question to an immediate vote, and time allocation motions (Standing Order 47), which allow the government house leader to move "with notice the allocation of time to any proceeding on a government bill or substantive government motion." Time allocation motions were formally entrenched in the Standing Orders in 1992, and they may not be moved until second reading debate has been completed, or six and one-half hours of debate has taken place. Time allocation allows the government to timetable (or limit) debate on its proposed legislation, and for this reason it is sometimes referred to as a "guillotine" motion.

Table 5.1 shows that 36 per cent of government bills that received royal assent have been time allocated since 1992. The table also indicates that the Harris-Eves governments used time allocation more than any other government during its second mandate: over 60 per cent of government bills were time allocated between 1999 and 2003. By comparison, in his second mandate and in the first session of her majority government to date, Dalton McGuinty and Kathleen Wynne used time allocation on less than half (43.6 per cent) of their government's bills. Not surprisingly, during the McGuinty/Wynne minority government years, the use of time allocation dropped to 16 per cent of government bills being allocated. Since Wynne's majority government victory in 2014, however, its usage has returned to around the same level as that of McGuinty's second majority government.

Time allocation was introduced quite late in Ontario compared to the federal House of Commons, where it was first introduced in 1969.[38]

Table 5.1 Time Allocation Motions in the Ontario Legislature, 1992–2016*

Parliament (duration)	Premier– Party (government standing)	Government Bills Receiving Royal Assent	# of Time Allocation Motions	% Government Bills Time Allocated
35th (1990–95)	Rae–NDP (majority)	97	21	21.6
36th (1995–99)	Harris–PC (majority)	118	35	29.7
37th (1999–2003)	Harris/Eves–PC (majority)	111	67	60.4
38th (2003–07)	McGuinty–Lib (majority)	109	28	25.7
39th (2007–11)	McGuinty–Lib (majority)	94	41	43.6
40th (2011–14)	McGuinty/ Wynne–Lib (minority)	25	4	16.0
41st (2014-present)**	Wynne-Lib (majority)	48	21	43.8
Total		**602**	**217**	**36.0**

*These numbers include all bills introduced from the second session of the 35th Parliament onward, beginning with the introduction of time allocation in 1992;
**Up to and including 9 June 2016.

Its introduction by the Rae government also goes some way in explaining the rancour and polarization of Ontario's Legislature throughout the 1990s. For his part, Harris's use of time allocation is consistent with his government's "mandate" approach to governing, whereby it rationalized that its authority to govern derived from its electoral mandate to implement a neoliberal agenda to reduce the size and role of the Legislature.[39] Accordingly, it did not need the consent of the Legislature to govern because it had won the election, and therefore felt justified in using time allocation to fulfill its mandate.

At the same time, while Harris was more prone to use time allocation than McGuinty, his government was, somewhat ironically, less successful at getting its bills passed. While 79 per cent of Harris's bills received Royal Assent during his two majority governments, 96 per cent of Premier McGuinty's bills did the same, a difference of 17 percentage points. The success rate of the McGuinty minority government in 2011 is also noteworthy: in its first year it plummeted to 47 per cent. Undoubtedly, this must have been a great shock to a government accustomed to passing its bills through the Legislature with relative ease over the last decade. The overall difference between Harris and McGuinty may be attributed to a more ambitious legislative agenda on the part of the Harris government (it introduced 288 bills compared to McGuinty's 211). It might also be explained by a rise in opposition tactics to stall the government. Chris Charlton's research shows, for example, a significant increase in the amount of time required to pass a bill between 1975 and 1989 (1 hour and 57 minutes) and 1990 and 1995 (5 hours and 55 minutes).[40] Thus far, the introduction of time allocation into Ontario's legislative proceedings has not resulted in a more efficient Legislature; rather, it appears to have had the opposite effect by forcing the opposition to rely on other tactics (e.g., stalling and obstruction) to fulfill its legislative duties. At the same time, Kathleen Wynne's majority government has proven to be rather more efficient, passing around 83 per cent of its legislation in the first session of the 41st Parliament. It remains to be seen whether the current government's ability to pass its legislation will continue apace or whether the opposition parties will attempt to slow the legislative agenda down again as we near the next fixed election date in a few years' time.

Since the 1990s, a number of incidents have occurred where opposition members have attempted to delay or obstruct the government. As the opposition leader of the Progressive Conservatives in 1991, Mike Harris sought to derail the NDP government budget implementation bill by introducing a bill that included the name of every lake, river, and stream in the province. By the time the bill was introduced on the floor and read aloud by the clerk of the House, four hours had passed.[41] In response, the Rae government changed the Standing Orders to limit the introduction of bills to 30 minutes, and each individual bill to five minutes.

Just six years later, with the NDP now in opposition and the PC Party in government, the NDP sought to block the passage of Bill 103, which amalgamated Metropolitan Toronto into one large "megacity." For 10 days the Legislature sat around the clock as the NDP introduced thousands of amendments to the bill—each named after every street in Toronto—and proposed that residents of each street "be informed of the impact arising out of the bill affecting them."[42] None of the amendments succeeded. Afterward, the Harris government changed the Standing Orders to empower the Speaker to rule out of order any motion or precedent that he or she considers to be frivolous or vexatious for purposes of delay or contrary to the Standing Orders or precedents.[43]

These incidents raise the question of what counts as legitimate dissent versus blatant obstruction of the House. According to C.E.S. Franks, "legitimate dissent becomes obstruction when it has no other purpose than to delay, when it is not exposing weakness or moulding opinion, but simply preventing legislation from being passed."[44] Ultimately, while the opposition must be given the opportunity to have its say, the government also has the right to govern. At the same time, the increase in "bad" or unparliamentary behaviour is also likely a reflection of the frustration many MPPs feel about how poorly the Legislature is working in the first place.

These moments highlight the declining civility in the House over the last few decades. Political observers have noted that throughout the Progressive Conservative dynasty (1943–85), the Legislature operated in a club-like, male-dominated environment, where debate was relatively moderate and civil.[45] The election of the NDP majority government in 1990 changed the political dynamics in the Legislature, as all three political parties could feasibly form the government. In a competitive party system, each and every debate becomes an opportunity to embarrass the government. To be sure, bad behaviour is not uncommon in other Legislatures. However, the partisan antics that have come to characterize the Ontario Legislature mean that anybody born after 1990 would have no personal memory of a time when politicians conducted themselves in a more civil fashion.

Scrutiny and Accountability

In addition to passing legislation, the Legislature has another key function of scrutiny and holding government to account. In addition to question period, an important way in which it scrutinizes the government is through the committee system. Committees generally engage in three types of activity: they review and amend legislation, they consider government spending estimates, and they conduct special enquiries.[46] Generally, there are two types of committees, standing and select committees, both of which may be comprised of no more than nine members for each committee. A committee of the whole (when the House sits in the chamber as a committee) may also be used for less significant bills. Committee membership is proportionate to the representation of the recognized parties in the House. In 2015 there were nine standing committees: the Committees on Estimates, Finance and Economic Affairs, General Government, Government Agencies, Justice Policy, the Legislative Assembly, Public Accounts, Regulations and Private Bills, and Social Policy.

According to David Pond, between 1985 and 1995, Ontario's then-11 legislative committees were some of the most sophisticated in the country; most met regularly and they often launched their own inquiries into matters of public importance.[47] After the passage of the Fewer Politicians Act, this kind of committee activity became much more difficult in a smaller

Legislature. As a sign of the dysfunction in the 2011 minority government, legislative committees did not sit at all during the fall 2012 session before being suspended completely by the sudden prorogation of 15 October. This situation was unusual, but reflective of the heightened partisanship and animosity that characterized the House during this time. Once Wynne took office in the winter of 2013, the committees were struck again.

The power of legislative committees, vis-à-vis the executive, was the subject of some debate in the House in the fall of 2012. The source of controversy was the Liberal government's decision to relocate two gas-fired electricity plants originally slated for construction in Oakville and Mississauga (also the source of the contempt motions discussed above). The opposition parties argued that the Liberals made this decision in order to gain votes in key GTA ridings in the 2011 election, and they demanded a full accounting of government estimates for the relocations. While the government claimed the relocations would cost $230 million, an independent report estimated the costs could be as high as $1.3 billion.[48] After the minister of energy produced only some of the documents requested by the Standing Committee on Estimates, the committee recommended to the House that the minister should be compelled to provide the documents without delay. On 13 September 2012, Speaker Levac provided his decision, and found there was a "prima facie" (on the face of it) breach of parliamentary privilege when the minister refused to hand over all the requested documents to the committee.[49] Further, the Speaker stated that "the right to order production of documents is fundamental to and necessary for the proper functioning of the assembly. If the House and its committees do not enjoy this right, then the accountability, scrutiny and financial functions of Parliament—which go to the core of our system of responsible government—would be compromised."[50] Shortly thereafter, the premier prorogued the Legislature, effectively shutting down all business in the House.

A final consideration for the scrutiny function of the Legislature is its size. As previously mentioned, Ontario has the most people per constituency of any province in the country. Generally, a smaller Legislature with a large population places more time constraints on MPPs, thus impeding their ability to provide rigorous and detailed scrutiny of government activities. The size of the Legislature relative to the cabinet is also important to consider. Figure 5.1 shows the size of the Legislature relative to the cabinet since 1985.

Figure 5.1 shows three ratio lines: the size of all private members relative to cabinet, the size of the opposition relative to cabinet, and the size of the government backbench relative to cabinet. The higher the number, the greater the size of the Legislature relative to the cabinet. The highest ratio of private members to cabinet ministers was in 1995, Harris's first year in

Figure 5.1 Ratio of Legislature Size to Cabinet Size, 1985–2014

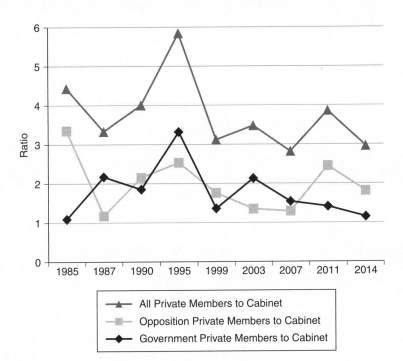

Source: Derived from the Ontario legislative website, http://www.ontla.on.ca

office. That year, there were 5.84 total private members, 2.53 opposition private members, and 3.32 government private members for every one cabinet minister. This makes sense, given that the 1995 Legislature predates the Progressive Conservative government's passage of the Fewer Politicians Act. Putting aside 1995, all three trend lines show that the ratio of private members to cabinet ministers has generally declined over time.

Looking at the Wynne majority government of 2014, we see fewer than three private members for every cabinet minister, and just slightly fewer government backbenchers than there are ministers (1.15:1). A small government backbench relative to the size of cabinet is significant for legislative democracy because it might curtail the willingness of government backbenchers to publicly vocalize their dissent of the government. If they behave according to the wishes of the government party and remain "whipped," then they have a good chance at securing a cabinet seat at some point in the future. Overall, the ratio of private members to cabinet ministers is at one of its lowest points today over the last 30 years in Ontario. It also constitutes the lowest ratio of private members to cabinet ministers in any of the provincial legislatures or the House of Commons. These trends are a function of an overall smaller Legislature, larger cabinets, and in the case of the 2011 and 2014 governments, smaller governing party sizes. These trends also limit the capacity of the Legislature to perform its scrutiny function effectively.

Conclusion

The Ontario Legislature has undergone a number of changes over the last few decades. While some of these changes have been positive, others underscore the reality that parliamentary democracy remains unfinished business in Ontario's Legislature. Many of these problems emerged with Ontario's competitive three-party system in the 1990s. The 2011 McGuinty minority government did little to resolve these issues, and, if anything, the shortcomings of the Legislature were amplified in a minority government that attempted to govern as though it had a majority. More positively, Premier Kathleen Wynne appeared to have taken a different tack in her minority by attempting to work with the other parties to pass the government's legislation, though this ended with her 2014 majority victory. The decline in decorum in the House also remains a problem. Given that Ontario high school students have been misinformed about how their government works, perhaps it is little wonder why they may be tuned out or turned off from provincial politics. The first step toward reaching the democratic potential of the Legislature begins with a properly informed and engaged citizenry.

Discussion Questions

1. Why do Ontarians have such low regard for politicians and the Legislature? What, if anything, can be done to improve their standing?
2. Should legislative officers like the ombudsman be given more power or less power to help make the government more accountable? Considering that these are unelected positions, do legislative officers weaken or strengthen democracy in the province?
3. Why are there so few women and visible minorities in the Legislature, and what are the best solutions to make the Legislature more representative of Ontario?
4. Is obstruction a necessary tactic for opposition parties today? What is the point at which legitimate dissent crosses into obstruction?
5. Should the size of the Legislature be increased to help it better perform its functions? Should Ontarians be supportive of such an option? Why or why not?

Notes

1   Caroline Alphonso, "Incorrect Textbooks Being Used to Teach Civics in Ontario," *Globe and Mail*, 14 April 2013, http://www.theglobeandmail.com/news/national/education/incorrect-textbooks-being-used-to-teach-civics-in-ontario/article11198218/

2   Graham White, "The Legislature: Central Symbol of Ontario Democracy," in *The Government and Politics of Ontario*, 5th ed., ed. Graham White (Toronto: University of Toronto Press, 1997), 83.

3   Ibid.

4   Peter Russell, *Two Cheers for Minority Government* (Toronto: Emond Montgomery, 2008), 153.

5   CBC News, "Ontario's Re-Elected Premier Touts 'Major Minority,'" 7 October 2011, http://www.cbc.ca/news/canada/ontariovotes2011/story/2011/10/07/ontario-premier-dalton-mcguinty.html

6   Prorogation means that all unfinished parliamentary business (including public and private bills, motions, and committee work) ceases unless a motion is passed to carry it over on the order paper to the next legislative session.

7   Robert Benzie, "Wynne's Hopes May Spring Eternal, But Spring Election Still Possible," *Toronto Star*, 15 March 2013, http://www.thestar.com/news/insight/2013/03/15/wynnes_hopes_may_spring_eternal_but_spring_election_still_possible.html

8   The minimum caucus size was adjusted from nine to eight in 1999 in order to accommodate the NDP and to reflect a smaller Legislature. In 2003 a similar concession was not granted to the NDP by the other parties when it won only seven seats and its official party status was revoked.

9   Ministry of Finance (Ontario), *Public Sector Salary Disclosure 2015 (Disclosure for 2014)*, http://www.fin.gov.on.ca/en/publications/salarydisclosure/2014/legassembly12.html

10 Parliament of Canada, "Indemnities, Salaries and Allowances," http://www.parl.gc.ca/ParlInfo/Lists/Salaries.aspx?Menu=HOC-Politic&Section=03d93c58-f843-49b3-9653-84275c23f3fb&Year=2015

11 Murray Campbell, "Ontario Urged to Give MPPs a Raise," *Globe and Mail*, 8 December 2006, http://www.theglobeandmail.com/news/national/ontario-urged-to-give-its-mpps-a-raise/article4092528/

12 Office of the Auditor General of Ontario, "Our History," http://www.auditor.on.ca/en/content/aboutus/historyofouroffice.html

13 Stewart Hyson and Gary Munro, "Ontario Ombudsman: A Game of Trust," in *Provincial and Territorial Ombudsman Offices in Canada*, ed. Stewart Hyson (Toronto: University of Toronto Press, and Institute of Public Administration of Canada, 2009), 191.

14 Ibid.

15 Ombudsman of Ontario, *2011–2012 Annual Report*, http://www.ombudsman.on.ca/Files/sitemedia/Documents/Resources/Reports/Annual/AR%202011-2012/Annual-Report-2011-2012-ENG.pdf, 14. Two exceptions are noted on page 17 of the report: closed-door municipal meetings and government supervisory appointments to replace a hospital board of directors (e.g., Niagara Health System).

16 Tara Deschamps, "Ontario Begins Search for New Health Care Watchdog," *Toronto Star*, 7 July 2015, http://www.thestar.com/news/gta/2015/07/07/new-ontario-health-care-watchdog-to-investigate-patient-complaints.html

17 Parliament of Canada, "Sitting Days of the Provincial and Territorial Legislatures by Calendar Year," http://www.parl.gc.ca/ParlInfo/compilations/ProvinceTerritory/SittingDays.aspx?Language=E

18 Ontario Ministry of Finance, *The Estimates—Office of the Assembly 2013–14*, http://www.fin.gov.on.ca/en/budget/estimates/2013-14/volume2/LEG.html

19 Ontario Ministry of Finance, *The Estimates—Office of the Assembly 2005–06*, http://www.fin.gov.on.ca/en/budget/estimates/2005-06/volume2/ola.html

20 Office of the Legislative Assembly of Ontario, *Standing Orders of the Legislative Assembly of Ontario, January 2009, Standing Order 37*, http://ontla.on.ca/web/go2.jsp?Page=/house-proceedings/supporting-content/files/standing_orders&menuitem=dandp_proceedings&locale=en

21 Michel Bédard, "Question Period in the Canadian Parliament and Other Legislatures" (Library of Parliament, 2011), http://www.parl.gc.ca/Content/LOP/ResearchPublications/2011-88-e.htm#a10

22 The Canadian Press, "Ont. Tories Stage Day 2 of Sit-In in Legislature in Protest of Harmonized Tax," 9 December 2009, http://www.cp24.com/ont-tories-stage-day-2-of-sit-in-in-legislature-in-protest-of-harmonized-tax-1.459912

23 C.E.S. Franks, *The Parliament of Canada* (Toronto: University of Toronto Press, 1987); David Docherty, *Legislatures* (Vancouver: UBC Press, 2005).

24 David Pond, "Imposing a Neo-Liberal Theory of Representation on the Westminster Model: A Canadian Case," *Journal of Legislative Studies* 11, no. 2 (2005): 171.

25 Statistics Canada, *Population Estimates by Year, by Province and Territory*, http://www.statcan.gc.ca/tables-tableaux/sum-som/l01/cst01/demo02a-eng.htm

26 While there are 121 Ontario seats in the House of Commons, the Ontario Legislature is likely to have 122 seats after the 2018 provincial election. The extra seat is allocated to the North to reflect the tradition of ensuring adequate representation in that region in the provincial Legislature. For more information, see Tracey Raney, Sasha Tregebov, and Gregory J. Inwood, "Democratizing the Ontario Legislature: Change, but Change Enough? A Paper Prepared for the Canadian Study of Parliament Group—Studies of Provincial and Territorial Legislatures" (Ottawa, 2013), http://cspg-gcep.ca/pdf/Ontario-e.pdf

27 Ontario Minister of Finance, "Ontario Population Projections. Fall 2014. Based on the 2011 Census," http://www.fin.gov.on.ca/en/economy/demographics/projections/projections2013-2041.pdf

28 White, "The Legislature," 84.

29 Raney, Tregebov, and Inwood, "Democratizing the Ontario Legislature."

30 Committee bills and private members' bills cannot impose taxes or directly allocate public funds.

31 Private email correspondence from the Office of the Deputy Clerk of the Ontario Legislative Assembly.

32 Legislative Assembly of Ontario (Legislative Research Service), "How an Ontario Bill Becomes Law" (August 2011), http://www.ontla.on.ca/lao/en/media/laointernet/pdf/bills-and-lawmaking-background-documents/how-bills-become-law-en.pdf

33 Legislative Assembly of Ontario, "How an Ontario Bill Becomes Law," 4.

34 Private email correspondence from the Office of the Deputy Clerk of the Ontario Legislative Assembly.

35 Unless the cabinet directs it to the Committee of the Whole. Legislative Assembly of Ontario, "How an Ontario Bill Becomes Law," 9.

36 White, "The Legislature," 86.

37 Ibid.

38 Robert Marleau and Camille Montpetit, "The Curtailment of Debate," in *House of Commons Procedure and Practice* (Ottawa: House of Commons, 2000), http://www.parl.gc.ca/marleaumontpetit/DocumentViewer.aspx?DocId=1001&Sec=Ch14&Seq=4&Language=E#fnB89

39 Pond, "Imposing a Neo-Liberal Theory of Representation," 172.

40 Chris Charlton, "Obstruction in Ontario and the House of Commons," *Canadian Parliamentary Review* 20, no. 3 (1997): 21–28.

41 Jacqueline Locke, "Obstruction in the Ontario Legislature: The Struggle for Power between the Government and the Opposition" (paper presented at the Canadian Political Science Association Annual Conference, London, ON, 2006), http://www.cpsa-acsp.ca/papers-2006/Locke.pdf

42 Ibid., 4.

43 Ibid., 5.

44 Franks, *The Parliament of Canada*, 131.

45 White, "The Legislature," 80.

46 Ibid., 88.

47 Pond, "Imposing a Neo-Liberal Theory of Representation," 185.

48 Canadian Press, "McGuinty Rejects Claim That Cancelled Gas Plants Cost $1.3 Billion," 1 November 2012, http://www.cbc.ca/news/canada/toronto/story/2012/11/01/ontario-mcguinty-gas-plants-cost.html

49 Legislative Assembly of Ontario, *Hansard Transcripts*, 13 September 2012, http://www.ontla.on.ca/web/house-proceedings/house_detail.do?Date=2012-09-13&Parl=40&Sess=1&locale=en

50 Ibid.

6
The Commanding Heights of Power and Politics in Ontario

BRYAN EVANS

THIS CHAPTER IS CONCERNED WITH THE PEOPLE who inhabit the upper reaches of the Ontario administrative state, and the structures through which their power is exercised. We term this region the "core executive" or "the centre." This refers to the "cabinet, the central agencies and related supporting institutions and personnel, such as ministerial political staff and deputy ministers of line departments."[1]

The beginnings of the modern Ontario core executive date to the 1969 Committee on Government Productivity (COGP), which launched a process leading to an enabled centre of government. The COGP's goal was to reassert the doctrine of the politics–administrative dichotomy through the establishment of a cabinet committee system designed to establish political control over the policy agenda. A clear separation between policy formulation and program implementation is at the heart of this concept. The role of the senior public service is to offer the best possible professional advice on policy matters, and it is the role of the political leadership, having been presented with the full spectrum of options, to decide. It is then the role of the public service to loyally implement the decision. This is the essence of the doctrine of the politics–administration dichotomy. The political leadership makes choices respecting policy, and the public service then determines the most efficacious means to implement that choice. What this perhaps blurred is the significant role senior public servants performed in framing policy problems and advocating for particular policy directions.

The result was Ontario's transition from "departmentalized" to "institutionalized" cabinet. Departmentalized cabinet refers to a structure composed of few cabinet committees with ministers enjoying significant decision-making autonomy. Collective cabinet deliberation was rare.[2] In contrast, the institutionalized cabinet is characterized by many standing committees and collective decision making, in which the premier shares power with cabinet committee chairs and the finance minister and is supported by robust central agencies such as the Cabinet Office and the finance ministry.[3] In the 1980s the Peterson Liberals initiated an expansion in staffing and functional sophistication at the centre that arguably constituted a paradigm shift toward a "new political governance." This paradigm is characterized by a concentration of power in the executive, an expanded role for political staff, and employing the public service to achieve partisan objectives.[4]

The history of Ontario's centre of government is one of oscillation between different points on a politics-administrative continuum. In the 1970s, a sharing of roles between the political leadership and the senior public service was clear. But as party competition and fiscal stress became more acute, efforts to assert a more traditional dichotomy were witnessed. And, in the twenty-first century, we observe a rebalancing of roles, allowing for significant public service roles in policy development, but without a return of the virtual fusion that evolved through four decades of one-party government. Since 1985, the political arm of government has become too significant an actor in the policy process for the roles to be completely delineated.

The Premier, the Premier's Office, and the Cabinet Office

Provincial premiers "dominate their respective governments."[5] Though constrained by various political and structural realities, "the raw power of the first minister is formidable."[6] Specifically, these powers include appointing and removing ministers, deputy ministers, the heads of arms-length agencies, boards, and commissions (though all require the formal approval of the Lieutenant-Governor); determining the structure of cabinet by establishing how many ministers will sit in cabinet, the number of cabinet committees, the formal procedures governing the cabinet decision-making process, which committees deal with which issues, and the role of the Cabinet Office in relation to the Premier's Office; and chairing the most important cabinet committee—policy and priorities—which determines what will go forward for cabinet decision. The premier also has, in practice, the sole authority to dissolve the Legislature. This power requires the approval of the Lieutenant-Governor and is particularly important during a minority government.[7] The premier can also establish or dissolve ministries, determine the content of legislation and regulations, as well as accord priority to each.[8] The degree to which a premier chooses to centralize power or to engage in power sharing depends on such variables as how he or she organizes the Premier's Office, personality, the political context (majority or minority government/distance from an election), and the degree of trust, reliability, and competence shared between the first minister and ministers.[9] The sources of the premier's power extend to his or her position as a party leader who cannot be removed by the caucus or ministers, as well as the availability of powerful central agencies and strategic ministries—notably the Cabinet Office and the finance ministry—to provide advice and support to his or her policy priorities.[10]

However, there are real constraints that mitigate against a "presidential" style of governing. For example, the premier cannot simply override ministers or interfere with their decisions in an ongoing way without alienating them. This is particularly the case where an authority is legally vested in an individual minister by a particular statute. In those cases, the power must be exercised by that minister with no interference from cabinet or the premier in order to avoid an allegation that the discretion of that minister has been improperly fettered. A premier needs ministerial energy and support, and maintaining this requires mutual respect and allowing space for ministers to exercise a real role in the decision-making process.[11]

The dominant position of the premier is buttressed by a key central agency, the Cabinet Office, whose capacity and power has grown significantly since the 1990s.[12] Together, the Premier's Office (PO) and the Cabinet Office (CO) constitute the very centre of government. These units provide policy and implementation support to the premier and cabinet. While it still holds true that "the two offices play distinct roles in the governing process, and are staffed by different types of people,"[13] they are required to work very closely with each other. The primary difference is that the PO is explicitly partisan and approaches policy decisions with a view to the political calculus of such. The CO is concerned with coordinating the decision-making process and ensuring that the best analysis is made available to the premier and ministers. That said, all aspects of policy are by definition political and, depending on the relationship between the premier and the cabinet secretary in particular, consultation between the two individuals can be highly political in nature. The Secretary of Cabinet is the chief public servant whose role is to serve as the interface between cabinet (the site of political decision making and leadership) and the administrative state. Since the 1970s, as the economic and political context shifted, different approaches to policy and administration emerged, and it has been the cabinet secretary's job to ensure the objectives of the political leadership are understood and implemented by the public service.[14] There is no set process for the selection of the cabinet secretary. Ultimately, who will be selected is the premier's choice since one of the primary roles is to serve as the deputy to the premier. The choice may be made in consultation with the current secretary, particularly if the selection is to come from the cadre of sitting deputies.[15]

As mentioned, what most clearly distinguishes the two offices is that the PO houses highly partisan staff whose loyalty is to the premier. In that role they provide the political/partisan analysis and strategy behind all policy initiatives. PO staffing has tended to increase during election years but most of this is not to expand policy advisory capacity. Instead, additional staff are hired to amplify communication of the government's accomplishments and to engage with key stakeholders to better assess their views of government initiatives.[16] As staff are identified with an individual premier, they will leave their positions when a new premier, even one from the same party, takes over. The PO is the central agency that provides the premier with the structural capacity to define and act on the policy agenda he or she wishes to pursue. In short, the PO "provides support to the Premier in achieving results on the government's priorities."[17] The key staff person in the PO is usually called the "chief of staff" or "principal secretary."[18]

In contrast, the CO is staffed by permanent, nonpartisan public servants who remain in place even when the premier is replaced. Most CO staff are seconded, or borrowed, from other ministries, and return to their home ministry after a year or two in the CO. The CO is "the Premier's Ministry" and is led by the Secretary of the Cabinet who is the chief public servant in a provincial government and serves as the deputy minister to the premier. As the premier's ministry, the CO will modify its structure and processes to conform to a premier's style of governing. Its main role is to enable the government and the premier specifically to implement his or her agenda. That agenda is set by the election platform of the winning party. The role of the CO in this respect is to work with the PO to map out a policy and legislative agenda and then to direct and facilitate the ministries responsible for writing the policy submissions that reflect the component parts of the agenda. CO staff support the cabinet decision-making structure, including cabinet committees. This entails agenda management, review and distribution of cabinet documents (especially cabinet submissions, which are policy decision documents) and related briefing documents, and recording decisions of cabinet. In addition, the CO acts as a liaison between the PO and line ministries as part of managing the government decision-making process. This entails ensuring items requiring cabinet approval are developed properly and delivered to the CO in a timely manner so that there is sufficient time for review and analysis by CO policy advisors prior to distribution to cabinet committees. In this capacity, the CO may arrange meetings between the PO and the political and public service staff in line ministries to discuss items going forward to cabinet or its committees. These are termed "four corners" meetings as they involve CO and PO staff as well as staff from the relevant minister's office and ministry staff. In addition, the CO works closely with the central agencies (Ministry of Finance, Management Board) to coordinate fiscal and policy decision-making. And finally, the CO works with ministries to implement decisions and develop communications.[19]

While the CO has tended to be larger than the PO, both have grown substantially since 1985. Staffing is indicative of a growing need for greater capacity at the "centre." Total PO staff in the 1970s was never more than 30 positions. CO staffing levels were similar. To a large degree this relatively modest staff complement reflected the height of Ontario's institutional-ized cabinet system, in which line ministries provided substantial input into policy formulation. Forty-two years of one-party government from 1943 to 1985 under the Progressive Conservatives had forged a close and trust-ing relationship between the premier, cabinet, and the senior public ser-vice.[20] The co-coordinative machinery established by the Committee on Government Productivity (COGP) was just that, coordinative rather than concerned with substantive policy issues.

The Liberals' 1985 Accord with the NDP allowed David Peterson to become premier and committed his government to a number of significant policy innovations. In functional terms, the CO and PO had been highly integrated during the Davis era, and Peterson's most significant change was to separate them. The PO and CO would each have its own executive lead rather than having the same person lead both.[21] CO staff levels increased to 80 positions. The PO grew slightly to 31 positions.

The trend accelerated with Bob Rae. The PO grew significantly to 85 staff members while the CO expanded to 126. Expansion of capacity enabled the centre of government to press forward with policy initiatives.[22] According to David Agnew, Rae's chief of staff, there was a need to build capacity to ensure execution of the government's agenda.[23]

The Progressive Conservatives returned to government in 1995 under Mike Harris and the "Common Sense Revolution" (CSR) manifesto, which, like the Accord, established the policy agenda. The sweeping program committed the government to rolling back taxes, regulations, and the role of the state in the province. The CSR thus reshaped the relationship between the political arm of government (specifically the premier) and the public service. This entailed a sharp reassertion of the politics-administrative dichotomy, under which the political executive would determine policy and the public service would ensure its faithful implementation. The Harris premiership acted quickly to gain con-trol over the public service by centralizing power in the hands of the elected executive and its advisors. Months before assuming power, Ontario's Conserva-tives began to determine which deputy ministers would stay and which would go, based on their "competence and comfort with the policy direction of the Common Sense Revolution."[24] The only question was whether the public ser-vice could be trusted to implement the platform. Two options were available: politicization of the public service or greater centralization to drive the agenda. Harris's inner circle chose the latter route.[25] Decisions over policy were absorbed into the "centre"—the Premier's Office and Cabinet Office. Perhaps counter-intuitively, for the first two years of Harris's premiership, the PO shrunk to 32 positions. In contrast, the CO continued its expansion, reaching 200 staff by the end of the Harris-Eves premierships in 2003. This expressed the revived politics–administration dichotomy, in which the challenge for the CO was to ensure policy implementation. However, between 1998 and 2003, the PO grew to more than 50 positions.

The CO began to take on a greater functional specialization to manage the CSR's large policy agenda. The number of senior executives rose from five to 10 persons with the rank of assistant deputy minister (ADM), deputy minister, or associate secretary. Three policy field units were established with six staff each. A new deputy minister responsible for public service restructuring was appointed and supported by two ADMs. In 1998–99, a new position of deputy minister of communications and associate secretary of the cabinet was established. Three ADMs responsible for "strategic communications" were also appointed. Policy was now joined by communications as a central and strategic function. And concern with revitalizing the policy capacity of the public service as a whole was reflected in the creation of a new unit, Policy Innovation and Leadership. And, further reflecting interest in greater control over policy, a deputy minister and associate secretary of the cabinet responsible for policy was appointed and supported by two new policy ADMs. Where the New Democrats had distrusted the public service, the Conservatives enlisted the centre as an instrument for implementing their agenda.

The McGuinty PO and its relationship to the CO expressed greater synergies. The relationship was shaped by the Third Way policy orientation of the McGuinty government, which saw the public service and the public sector as strategic instruments in delivering the Liberal agenda. This political orientation necessitated a robust centre with the coordinative and policy capacity to design and implement policy. But this is not to say that the centralization tendency abated or that politicization of the executive core was not part of the McGuinty style of governing.

Over McGuinty's premiership, his PO expanded substantially from 56 to 80 staff by the time of his resignation. The CO remained well staffed and fluctuated between 170 and 200 positions. The number of dedicated policy staff in McGuinty's PO was not unusual, numbering between 10 and 12 persons, largely consistent with the number of such functionaries since the Peterson government. What was different was the increasing functional specialization. Previous PO policy functions were rather generalized or did not exist, but in McGuinty's PO a sophisticated division of labour arose. This included appointing a policy and research director who directed policy advisors responsible for the full range of policy fields. In 2009 a deputy director of policy was added. The enhanced capacity of the PO to provide both political and strategic advice enabled the premier to extend his policy influence.

The CO would take on a greater role as a "system" coordinator responsible not only for policy design and implementation, but also for monitoring and measuring results achieved by public programs. Soon after the 2003 election, the new Liberal government announced a comprehensive plan for transforming government. The objective was to align and integrate services and program delivery. To monitor progress, a results-based planning process was introduced, with the objective to link politically determined priorities to policy and program achievements.[26] This process established the priorities and identified the measurable results, with related performance indicators to monitor progress. In most respects this was a continuation of the annual business planning process of the previous government.[27] The key difference was that the Liberal planning process "moved from ministry business planning to a government-wide results-based approach that aims to keep public services affordable, invest in the areas that matter most and live within our means."[28] The turn to a results focus necessitated some structural innovation. Results "tables" were created to monitor and report on progress. These structures brought together the appropriate ministers, political staff, deputy ministers, and Cabinet Office staff. Four were established to monitor outcomes in health, education, climate change, and poverty reduction. McGuinty, who had set clear objectives around health, sat at the health results table.

The roles and responsibilities of the Cabinet Office and Premier's Office demonstrate that both institutions are very much creatures of the premier. That is to say, his or her policy priorities and preferences will be reflected in how these institutions are structured and how they will work with one another and with the other structures and people inhabiting the executive core of the provincial government. Importantly, the expanding role of the centre enables the political arm of government to exercise significant control over the provincial state apparatus.

Cabinet, Ministers, and Cabinet Committees

A key debate concerns the centralization of power in the hands of the premier. One contention is that premier-centric government has replaced cabinet government. The key assumption is that power can only be located in one place and is finite. Ministers become nothing more than agents of the first minister and consequently the cabinet no longer serves as a forum for policy deliberation.[29] But this perspective is not without its critics, who counter that this confuses the premier's role as the "most important" actor with "dominance and dictatorship."[30] The emergence since the 1970s of an institutionalized cabinet has served to distribute power to other locations such as cabinet committees, central agencies, and indeed even individual ministers, whose stature and authority make the "dominant premier" model less likely.[31] A more nuanced view is that Ontario has "oscillated between institutionalized and premier-centred patterns."[32] Consequently, individual ministers make decisions within their respective ministries and within cabinet collectively. The premier certainly has strategic resources that are not available to ministers. That does not detract from cabinet as "the central locus of governmental power in our system."[33] For example, the work of Canadian cabinets and individual ministers is supported not only by key central agencies such as the Cabinet Office and the finance ministry, but also by the full spectrum of ministries composing the government. Deputy ministers, other ministry-based public servants, and ministers' political staff can all be mobilized to support cabinet decision-making processes.[34] In other words, ministers are not without their own power bases. Ministries are the "basic organizational unit of executive administration in the Westminster system"[35] and provide the minister with significant resources for policy development, stakeholder management, and communications.

Cabinets perform critical functions, including provision of advice and information to the first minister; achieving consensus within the cabinet on priorities; resolving conflict over policy jurisdiction and overlap between ministers; establishing the legislative agenda; and providing oversight of the public service's implementation of the policy agenda.[36] How the cabinet will be structured to meet these purposes is largely up to the premier to determine, as there is little legal or constitutional direction on these matters.[37] In Ontario's case only two cabinet structures—Treasury Board and Management Board—are required by statute. The inner cabinet (Policy and Priorities Board, or P&P), standing policy committees (which provide a coordinating role by broad policy field—social, economic, justice), and ad hoc policy committees (temporary bodies for discrete, high profile issues) are all optional in that they are not required by law.[38] The policy committees provide a forum for review and deliberation of policy issues by ministers.

The very existence of P&P indicates a hierarchy of decision-makers within the cabinet. This committee has existed since the Davis era. Chaired by the premier, P&P is composed of ministers with the most substantive portfolios and who tend to be the most trusted by the premier.[39] In its role as the gatekeeper to cabinet, this committee is a key source of the premier's power.

The critical role of cabinet committees is seen in the changing role of the cabinet secretary, who is not only head of the public service but also the deputy minister to the premier. The cabinet secretary's role has evolved from a largely administrative, indeed secretarial, role that involved collecting and distributing documents to ministers for their review, recording cabinet decisions (known as a cabinet minute), and apprising the premier on the administrative health of the government apparatus. The cabinet secretary's role now includes supporting the policy decision making of cabinet committees and cabinet, and advising the premier directly on policy matters.[40]

A number of factors contribute to shaping how a premier organizes the cabinet and whether the objective is to centralize power, share it, or both. These include the premier's personality, the political context, the relationship sought with ministers, and how he or she opts to organize the PO.[41] One key indicator is cabinet committee structure. One interpretation is that a large number of cabinet committees is indicative of a preference for a decentralized approach. A cabinet environment populated by a large number of committees means ministers have the opportunity to discuss and design policy before the premier has had a chance to consider the issue.[42] From the 1970s forward, we see a structure that includes a number of standing policy committees, several ad hoc committees, and a pre-eminent policy and priorities committee that determines what proposals move forward. The purpose of these committees is to efficiently divide up the immense volume of work confronting cabinet into manageable loads organized by policy field—economic, social, justice, and so on. This structure reflects the need for greater policy specialization at the centre of government as a result of the state's expanding role in the delivery of public services and the regulation of economic and other activities.[43] Signalling a remarkable degree of stability in the organization of the centre, the roles of the various cabinet committees have remained largely constant since COGP in 1969. A survey of the committee structure since 1985 provides evidence of modest structural change amid a general continuity.

Peterson's government did not fundamentally restructure the centre of government established by the COGP reforms. The total number of cabinet ministers averaged 26 during his premiership—rather larger than the 20 or so of the Davis era—and was marked by a consultative style. Conversely, Rae's premiership (1990–95), while initially consultative, became more centralized in response to increasing fiscal stress.[44]

The Harris premiership (1995–2002) was highly centralized through the first few years. The policy directions set in the election platform, expressing an aggressive cost-cutting and deregulation agenda that was unprecedented for Ontario, necessitated strong control from the centre. A streamlined, "built for speed" cabinet structure was established in the wake of the 1995 election. The CSR platform set the policy agenda. Consequently, the only real discussion points related to how to proceed with implementation.[45] The cabinet as a whole consisted of 19 ministers. This compared to the average of 25 ministers for Peterson and Rae. The elaborate ecology of policy committees and subcommittees was done away with. What remained were the cabinet, the policy and priorities board, the management board, and the legislation and regulations committee. Each committee had only six members to facilitate rapid decision making.[46] And, given the priority allocated to efficient decision making, there was less cabinet deliberation over policy.[47] The cabinet committee structure was modified in 1996 to include a cabinet committee on privatization and three subcommittees of policy and priorities—restructuring and local services, jobs and the economy, and federal/provincial issues. Harris opened up committee membership to allow for two parliamentary assistants to sit on each of the P&P subcommittees. Parliamentary assistants are not ministers, but rather MPPs who have been assigned responsibilities to assist ministers. In 1997 the structure was again modified with the addition of a short-lived cabinet committee on financial planning (four months) and a new P&P subcommittee for policy coordination to assist with the volume of policy. Thus, Harris's first term was dedicated to implementing a radical policy agenda. The very structure of cabinet was an expression of the ideological conviction of this government and its priorities to cut taxes, eliminate the deficit, and change the role of the state in Ontario's social and economic life. In 1999 standing policy committees again appeared, and an additional ad hoc committee was struck—"Superbuild"—to deal with infrastructure projects. However, the policy committees would again be suspended in the autumn of 2001, as the economy slowed and revenues to the treasury slid, leading Harris again to exert greater control over the policy process and constrict cabinet attention to a small number of initiatives.[48]

Ernie Eves's premiership would last 18 months after he replaced Harris (April 2002–October 2003). His most noteworthy innovation was to integrate caucus members into the work of cabinet by appointing five associate ministers, up from one under Harris. Associate ministers were responsible for making ministry-related announcements, managing stakeholders, and providing back up for the minister in the Legislature.[49] However, structural characteristics belie what was a "one-man" government. Indeed, Eves's P&P never met and his preference was to make decisions entirely outside the cabinet process.[50] The strategic source of power in Eves's PO, which enabled him to exclude ministers from key decisions, was the presence of former finance deputy minister Michael Gourley within the office. Eves would go so far as to bypass the finance minister and have the budget drafted in the PO.[51]

Dalton McGuinty returned to a more institutionalized cabinet model during his premiership (2003–13). His cabinets tended to consist of 25 to 26 ministers (though his first cabinet had only 23). Four standing policy committees were struck (economic affairs; federal, interprovincial, and municipal relations; education; and health and social services), plus one new committee responsible for community affairs. This committee was a catchall capturing community safety, Indigenous, environment, and justice issues. These committees stood alongside the treasury/management board and the legislation and regulations committee. Of course, a priorities and planning board (a renamed policy and priorities committee) stood at the apex of the committee system. While

Harris and, to a greater degree, Eves had made some effort to integrate caucus members into the cabinet process (despite the reality of Eves's one-man government), McGuinty went further than any previous premier in this respect. Parliamentary assistants as well as backbench caucus members were appointed to serve as chairs or as committee members. The chair of the Liberal caucus was appointed as a full member of the P&P. By 2006, nonministers held a majority of seats on four cabinet committees and chaired five of these. The prominent leadership roles of nonministers, in addition to the extent of backbench participation, were both unprecedented in Ontario's history. McGuinty's approach to cabinet building runs contrary to the thesis that a detailed election platform and a difficult fiscal or economic context would require a greater degree of centralization. Indeed, the McGuinty government was elected on a platform with clear priorities and confronted a $5.6 billion deficit, but the premier was evidently seriously interested in using the full cabinet system, with the participation of nonministers whether backbench MPPs or PAs, as a "deliberative forum."[52] Between 2007 and 2011, McGuinty's second term, some modest restructuring of the cabinet system took place. Two new ad hoc committees appeared: poverty reduction and Ontario's economic future. The number of policy committees was shrunk from five to three by eliminating community affairs and merging education with health and social services. These changes were in response to the recession of 2008, which significantly damaged Ontario's manufacturing sector, and the initiative of several prominent Liberal cabinet ministers who sought to reassert the party's progressive credentials.

Ministers' Offices and Political Staff

Every minister employs staff serving explicitly partisan purposes. Their work includes writing speeches, providing policy analysis and advice with a view to the politics surrounding a proposal, stakeholder relations, navigating relations with the Premier's Office and Cabinet Office, and liaising with the caucus and the minister's own electoral constituency.[53] In assisting ministers with both political and administrative responsibilities, political staff are required to engage extensively with the public service. In acting for their minister, they do carry considerable authority within the administrative apparatus.[54] The significant and growing number of partisan political staff working in ministers' offices, as well as in the Premier's Office, has been attributed to the American influence on Canadian politics.[55] The quality of the services provided by staff to their ministers is contested given they tend to be young, inexperienced, and often known more for their loyalty than their skills.[56] One substantive contribution political staff make is in their capacity to communicate to the public service their minister's political preferences and interests given that the public service may lack this political acuity or may need to remain uninvolved in such deliberation over political considerations.[57]

In the 1970s, Ontario Ministers' Offices (MOs) played a small role in the work of government and their staffing levels of one to no more than six staff reflected this. By 1985, with the Peterson Liberals in government, MOs employed 10 or more staff. The total number of MO staff throughout the Ontario government reached 157. And by 1990, the last year of Peterson's government, the total number rose to 292. The number of explicit MO-based policy positions also saw a notable expansion from 39 in 1985 to 61.

With yet another change in government in 1995, a decline in total staff positions in MO offices occurred (down from 292 in 1990 to 149 in 1995). In 2000, MO staffing levels rebounded to 211 positions across all MOs. Government-wide, MOs employed 10 or more staff. And the expansion in MOs continued with the McGuinty Liberals. The total number of MO staff in 2005 stood at 269 and the number of dedicated policy positions increased from more than 60 to over 80 positions. And as of 2012, with total MO staffing stabilized around 250 positions, the number of policy advisors expanded modestly to a total of 89 (up from 81). The two largest MOs were found in the finance ministry (20) and the health ministry (21).[58]

The number of MO staff throughout the Ontario government thus doubled between 1980 and 2012. This phenomenon is not unique to Ontario, as partisan political staff play an important role in all Westminster systems; however, cabinets in Canada "remain distinctive, if not unique, for the numbers and prominence of political staff and for their unabashed partisan tilt."[59] The motive behind this expansion (a tendency which begins in earnest with the Peterson premiership between 1985 and 1990) is to strengthen cabinet control over policy by increasing the intellectual capacity available to ministers in the process.[60] Political staff provide an alternative source of analysis and advice to ministers and thus contribute to shifting power and influence away from the public service toward the elected political arm of government.[61] This expansion of capacity and the consequent shifting of power toward Ministers' Offices, together with the expansion of the role of the centre of government, are said to constitute the emergence of a "new political governance."[62]

Deputy Ministers

Deputy ministers are akin to being the chief executive officers for a ministry. The duties of deputy ministers include operation of the ministry; provision of advice to the minister; and assurance of a nonpartisan, professional, ethical, and competent public service. The deputy minister's advisory role is explicitly acknowledged.[63] Deputy ministers are appointed by orders-in-council

(OIC). This means the premier, in consultation with the cabinet secretary, makes the appointment. Deputy ministers serve the elected government of the day whether they personally agree with the policy of that government or not. They provide their own advice based on the best analysis available to them and allow the premier or minister to arrive at their own conclusions. This "speaking truth to power" is the hallmark of the professional public service, though the integrity of this practice has been disputed as power has become more concentrated in the premier.

In the Davis era (1971–84), substantial latitude was granted to deputy ministers in the policy process.[64] The Liberal–NDP Accord provided a much larger policy role for the political arm of government than had previously been the case. The public service role was limited to policy implementation. For New Democrats, the senior public service was seen to be unsympathetic to their social democratic agenda.[65] Given the absence of "a strong and trusting relationship,"[66] it was impossible in many cases for deputy ministers to function as policy advisors. And Harris's "Common Sense Revolution" manifesto held serious implications for the senior public service. Just as the Liberal–NDP Accord shifted the role of the senior public service in the policy process, the CSR established the agenda and it was for the public service to implement this. Veteran public servant Rita Burak was ostensibly appointed cabinet secretary as an expression of confidence in the public service's professionalism. David Lindsay, Harris's former principal secretary explained the choice of Burak was intended to align the public service to the priorities of the Common Sense Revolution. Lindsay explained: "we gave her a free hand to do what she needed to do to put the civil service into the right position to implement this huge agenda. Rita quickly recommended a number of senior deputy ministers to take on a number of portfolios to help start implementing the agenda."[67] With Harris, the deputy's role as policy advisor continued to be limited and his or her attention was refocused toward management of resources and policy implementation.[68]

The competencies required of Ontario's deputy ministers under McGuinty suggest something of a rebalancing of executive roles and functions. This is particularly so with respect to the provision of policy advisory support to the minister, premier, and cabinet.[69] Thus, the McGuinty era saw a restoration of a collaborative relationship between the senior public service and the political leadership.

The Wynne Premiership

Kathleen Wynne replaced McGuinty as Liberal Party leader and premier in February 2013. From a political perspective, Wynne ran for the leadership as a progressive committed to repairing relations with key political allies and most notably teachers. The 2014 budget expressed Wynne's makeover of the Liberal Party as one of the "activist centre."[70] After two and a half years in the PO, from a structural perspective, there is more continuity than change in the Wynne premiership but there are clear indications of a greater focus on policy.

Staffing numbers are essentially similar to those of her predecessor, but building the policy capacity of the "centre" and MOs has clearly been an area of focus. Wynne's PO employed a markedly larger number of policy staff: 19, compared to 11 in McGuinty's. Overall MO staffing levels through the Wynne premiership have seen very modest increases of a hardly remarkable two or three positions. However, as with Wynne's PO, this modest increase is largely a function of expanding the number of dedicated policy staff in each office. Two in particular grew significantly. The Research and Innovation MO added 13 policy positions while the Ministry of Economic Development added six.

With respect to cabinet committees, several changes here express the Wynne commitment to govern from the activist centre but also to address the Ontario budget deficit. She resurrected the cabinet committee on poverty reduction which, with the onset of the recession, had quietly disappeared from view. This ostensibly demonstrated in policy machinery terms Wynne's progressive bona fides, especially with respect to social inclusion. But in 2014 the activist centre government confronted the difficult reality of a $12.5 billion deficit. To manage this, and perhaps in keeping with the theme of government activism, Wynne expanded the role of the Treasury Board. Traditionally, the Treasury Board was responsible for managing routine government expenses, directing ministries to find savings, and was itself directed by the Ministry of Finance.[71] However, Wynne reallocated several challenging files including public sector labour relations and Crown corporations away from the Ministry of Finance and placed these under the Treasury Board. Wynne then appointed Deputy Premier Deb Matthews, her closest ally, as the new Treasury Board president who would report directly to her. This sent a powerful signal that Wynne was serious about bringing public expenditures under control.[72] The paradox here was that Wynne's progressive activist centre would also have to implement austerity.

As it matured, the Wynne government continued to respond to exogenous pressures and crises with nuanced but important shifts in the focus, capacity, and institutional structures. In this case, Wynne's commitment to government activism to address inequality and economic change ran up against pressures to eliminate the deficit. The point is that the Premier's Office continues in this case to demonstrate that, ultimately, it is the place where the priorities are established and the means to achieve objectives determined.

Conclusion

Since the 1970s, every major party has cycled through Ontario's government. What has been constant is a trend to build an ever more robust and sophisticated centre of government. The capacities of the Premier's Office and the Cabinet Office have expanded significantly. This does suggest the emergence of premier-centric government, but given the expansion of political staff in minister's offices this is too blunt a conclusion. Instead, taken in sum, these developments suggest a significant strengthening of the political arm of government in general. The evidence is that the premier is without question the most powerful actor on the stage, but this power, considerable though it is, is not absolute, as ministers can mobilize their own resources and power bases. And, more importantly, the premier-dominated cabinet government is still fundamentally one that requires collegiality and collective action to be optimally effective. Even the highly centralized first years of the Harris premiership were still fundamentally collegial and even embraced the senior public service. But in this we can discern a shifting of roles. The most obvious is concerned with the role of the senior public service in policy formulation. The political arm of government has taken on a greater role in the formulation of policy while the public service has become more concerned with implementation. In part, this was precisely what the COGP wished to achieve in the 1970s. This is not to say that the public service is now excluded from policy work. Given the complexity of governing, that would be impossible. What it does suggest, however, is that strategic policy-setting has become the domain of the political executive.

Discussion Questions

1. What evidence can we draw upon to confirm or refute the thesis of the "presidentialization" of Ontario government and politics?
2. The politics-administrative dichotomy is a long-standing concept in public administration. What can be said about its application to our understanding of the Ontario centre of government?
3. A relatively new theoretical concept is concerned with the emergence of a new political governance paradigm where the political arm of government becomes monolithically dominant. What evidence is there to support this development in Ontario's case?
4. What are the distinctive features of Ontario's Premier's Office and Cabinet Office?
5. If the policy agenda is increasingly established by the election platform of the winning party, what roles can the senior public service play?

Notes

1 Graham White, *Cabinets and First Ministers* (Vancouver: UBC Press, 2005), 18.
2 Michael Howlett, "Modern Canadian Governance: Political-Administrative Styles and Executive Organization in Canada," in *Executive Styles in Canada: Cabinet Structures and Leadership Practices in Canadian Government*, ed. Luc Bernier, Keith Brownsey, and Michael Howlett (Toronto: University of Toronto Press and Institute of Public Administration of Canada, 2005), 7.
3 Christopher Dunn, "Premiers and Cabinets," in *Provinces: Canadian Provincial Politics*, 2nd ed., ed. Christopher Dunn (Toronto: University of Toronto Press, 2008), 231.
4 Peter Aucoin, "New Political Governance in Westminster Systems," *Governance* 25, no. 2 (2012): 177–99.
5 Herman Bakvis and Steven Wolinetz, "Canada: Executive Dominance and Presidentialization," in *The Presidentialization of Politics*, ed. Thomas Poguntke and Paul Webb (Oxford: Oxford University Press, 2009), 199.
6 White, *Cabinets and First Ministers*, 31.
7 Richard Loreto and Graham White, "The Premier and the Cabinet," in *The Government and Politics of Ontario*, 4th ed., ed. Graham White (Toronto: University of Toronto Press, 1990), 79–80.
8 Ted Glenn, "Politics, Personality, and History in Ontario's Administrative Style," in *Executive Styles in Canada: Cabinet Structures and Leadership Practices in Canadian Government*, ed. Luc Bernier, Keith Brownsey, and Michael Howlett (Toronto: University of Toronto Press, and Institute of Public Administration of Canada 2005), 166.
9 Herman Bakvis, "Prime Minister and Cabinet in Canada: An Autocracy in Need of Reform?" *Journal of Canadian Studies* 35, no. 4 (2001): 60–79.
10 Thomas Walkom, "How Eves' Empire Collapsed," *Toronto Star*, 2 November, 2003; Graham White, "Adapting the Westminster Model: Provincial and Territorial Cabinets in Canada," *Public Money and Management* 21, no. 2 (2001): 21.
11 Loreto and White, "The Premier and the Cabinet," 80.
12 White, *Cabinets and First Ministers*, 74–75.
13 Loreto and White, "The Premier and the Cabinet," 84.
14 Bryan Evans, "Capacity, Complexity, and Leadership: Secretaries to Cabinet and Ontario's Project of Modernization at the Centre," in *Searching for Leadership: Secretaries to Cabinet in Canada*, ed. Patrice Dutil (Toronto: University of Toronto Press and Institute of Public Administration of Canada, 2008), 122–23.
15 William Bromm, personal correspondence, 2013.
16 Patrice Dutil and Peter Constantinou, "The Office of Premier of Ontario 1945–2010: Who Really Advises?" *Canadian Parliamentary Review* 36, no. 1 (Spring 2013): 45.
17 Ontario Cabinet Office, *Results-Based Plan Briefing Book (2006–2007)*, 3, http://www.ontla.on.ca/library/repository/ser/267098/2006-2007.pdf
18 White, *Cabinets and First Ministers*, 84–85.
19 William Bromm, "Cabinet Office and the Government Decision Making Process" (PowerPoint presentation, Cabinet Office of Ontario, 26 March 2012).
20 Evans, "Capacity, Complexity, and Leadership," 131.
21 Dutil and Constantinou, "The Office of Premier of Ontario," 46.

22 Evans, "Capacity, Complexity, and Leadership," 139–40.

23 Ibid.

24 David R. Cameron and Graham White, *Cycling into Saigon: The Conservative Transition in Ontario* (Vancouver: UBC Press, 2000), 86.

25 Evans, "Capacity, Complexity, and Leadership," 142.

26 Policy Innovation and Leadership, Ontario Cabinet Office, "Results-Based Management: Implications for Policy Professionals" (PowerPoint presentation, Cabinet Office of Ontario, n.d.).

27 Ontario Civil Service Commission, *Annual Report 2004–2005* (Toronto: Queen's Printer, 2005), 2.

28 Ontario Civil Service Commission, *Annual Report*, 5.

29 Paul Thomas, "Governing from the Centre: Reconceptualizing the Role of the PM and Cabinet," *Policy Options* (December 2003–January 2004): 80–81.

30 Dunn, "Premiers and Cabinets," 215.

31 Ibid.

32 Ibid., 237.

33 White, *Cabinets and First Ministers*, 30.

34 Ibid., 47.

35 Lorne Sossin, "Defining Boundaries: The Constitutional Argument for Bureaucratic Independence and Its Implication for the Accountability of the Public Service," in *Restoring Accountability Research Studies*, vol. 2, *The Public Service and Transparency* (Ottawa: Public Works and Government Services Canada, 2006), 26.

36 Thomas, "Governing from the Centre," 80.

37 White, *Cabinets and First Ministers*, 33.

38 Bromm, "Cabinet Office and the Government Decision Making Process."

39 Natalie Desimini, "Centralization of Power in the Ontario Provincial Cabinets" (paper presented at the Canadian Political Science Association annual conference, Wilfrid Laurier University, Waterloo, ON, 2011), 6.

40 D. McArthur, "Policy Analysis in Provincial Governments in Canada: From PPBS to Network Management," in *Policy Analysis in Network Management*, ed. L. Dobuzinskis, M. Howlett, and D. Laycock (Toronto: University of Toronto Press, and Institute of Public Administration of Canada 2007), 11.

41 William Matheson, *The Prime Minister and Cabinet* (Toronto: Methuen, 1976), 5.

42 White, *Cabinets and First Ministers*, 5.

43 Loreto and White, "The Premier and the Cabinet," 87.

44 Thomas Walkom, *Rae Days: The Rise and Follies of the NDP* (Toronto: Key Porter Books, 1994), 68–69.

45 Glenn, "Politics, *Personality*, and History in Ontario's Administrative Style," 167.

46 Richard Loreto, "Making and Implementing Decisions: Issues of Public Administration in the Ontario Government," in *The Government and Politics of Ontario*, 5th ed., ed. Graham White (Toronto: University of Toronto Press, 1997), 101.

47 Cameron and White, *Cycling into Saigon*, 109.

48 Glenn, "Politics, Personality, and History in Ontario's Administrative Style," 167–68.

49 Ibid., 169.

50 Walkom, "How Eves' Empire Collapsed."

51 White, *Cabinets and First Ministers*, 76.
52 Glenn, "Politics, Personality, and History in Ontario's Administrative Style," 170.
53 White, *Cabinets and First Ministers*, 49.
54 Peter Aucoin, "Canada," in *Partisan Appointees and Public Servants: An International Analysis of the Role of the Political Advisor*, ed. Chris Eichbaum and Richard Shaw (Northhampton, UK: Edward Elgar, 2010), 64.
55 White, "Adapting the Westminster Model," 21.
56 Herman Bakvis, "Advising the Executive: Think Tanks, Consultants, Political Staff and Kitchen Cabinets," in *The Hollow Crown: Countervailing Trends in Core Executives*, ed. Patrick Weller, Herman Bakvis, and R.A.W. Rhodes (New York: St. Martin's Press, 1997), 21.
57 Bakvis, "Advising the Executive," 21.
58 MO staffing numbers obtained from Government of Ontario Telephone Directories, 1970 to 2012.
59 White, "Adapting the Westminster Mode," 21.
60 Conrad Winn, "Cabinet Control of the Public Service," *Canadian Public Policy* 2, no. 1 (1985): 126.
61 White, "Adapting the Westminster Mode," 21.
62 Aucoin, "Canada," 64.
63 Government of Ontario, Public Service of Ontario Act, 2006 (Toronto: Queen's Printer, 2006).
64 Evans, "Capacity, Complexity, and Leadership," 131.
65 Evert A. Lindquist and Graham White, "Streams, Springs and Stones: Ontario Public Service Reform in the 1980s and the 1990s," *Canadian Public Administration* 37, no. 2 (1994): 283.
66 Andre Cote, *Leadership in the Public Service of Canada* (Ottawa: Public Policy Forum, 2007), 10.
67 Evans, "Capacity, Complexity, and Leadership," 142–43.
68 Civil Service Commission, Ministry of Government Services, *Civil Service Commission Annual Report, 1995/96* (Toronto: Queen's Printer, 1996), 3.
69 Ministry of Government Services, Government of Ontario INFO-GO Service (Toronto: Ministry of Government Services), 1–2, http://www.infogo.gov.on.ca/infogo/searchDirectory.do?actionType=changeLocale
70 Robert Benzie, "Kathleen Wynne Tells Liberal Troops She'll Govern from 'Activist Centre,'" *Toronto Star*, 17 June 2014, http://www.thestar.com/news/queenspark/2014/06/17/kathleen_wynne_tells_liberal_troops_shell_govern_from_activist_centre.html
71 Government of Ontario, 2014 Mandate Letter: Treasury Board Secretariat, https://www.ontario.ca/page/2014-mandate-letter-treasury-board-secretariat
72 Adrian Morrow, "Six Things to Know about Ontario's New Government," *Globe and Mail*, 24 June 2014, http://www.theglobeandmail.com/news/politics/six-things-to-know-about-ontarios-new-government/article19306219/

7

Local Government and Politics in Ontario

DANIEL HENSTRA

A STUDY OF THE GOVERNMENT AND POLITICS OF ONTARIO would be incomplete without an analysis of local governments, whose decisions and actions have a significant impact on the provincial economy, environment, and quality of life. Local governments are the community-level arm of the political system, providing a mechanism to resolve public problems and facilitate collective action within a defined territorial jurisdiction. Empowered by provincial enabling legislation and vested with a democratic mandate from the electorate, local governments have authority to make and enforce binding rules of behaviour, levy taxes and fees to raise operating revenue, and decide on the range and quality of services to be provided to residents, businesses, and organizations in communities.

Local governments also play a crucial role as implementers of provincial policy. Bills passed in the Legislative Assembly often impose legal and financial obligations on local governments, who are expected to serve as administrative agents in carrying out directives from Queen's Park. Provincial laws and regulations affect local governments in many ways, including their physical boundaries, the degree of autonomy they enjoy in decision making and service delivery, and the fiscal resources they can draw upon to carry out their responsibilities. As explained below, all three of these aspects of Ontario's municipal system were dramatically altered in the late 1990s by the Progressive Conservative government under the leadership of Mike Harris, and the impacts are still being addressed.

This chapter begins by describing the structure of Ontario's local government system and the reforms implemented by the Harris Conservative government. It then examines the political leadership and administrative structure of municipal governments. The third section analyzes the authority and functional responsibilities of local governments and how these have evolved over time. Finance is the focus of the fourth section, including sources of local government revenue and general fiscal capacity. The last section examines the dynamics of provincial-municipal relations, highlighting both the ways in which provincial decisions affect municipalities and how local politics can obstruct the provincial government's plans.

Structure of Local Government

The term "local government" includes various types of municipalities, such as cities, towns, townships, and villages, which have corporate status under provincial law and are endowed with broad powers and responsibilities. It also includes a large number of agencies, boards, and commissions, such as conservation authorities, school boards, and public utilities commissions, which are created under provincial or municipal authority to serve specific governing functions in communities or regions.[1] The analysis in this chapter focuses primarily on the 444 municipal governments in Ontario at the time of writing.

Municipalities vary greatly in size, ranging from small, rural villages like Westport, with a population of about 650 people, to the dense urban metropolis of Toronto, which houses a population of more than 2.6 million, or nearly 8 per cent of Canadians. Most municipalities are small- to medium-sized communities, and only about 7 per cent have a population greater than 100,000. About one-third of municipalities are located in Northern Ontario (north of Lake Huron), which makes up nearly 90 per cent of the land area of Ontario, but contains only about 6 per cent of the total population.

About 40 per cent of Ontario municipalities are single-tier units with sole responsibility for funding and providing services to residents. They are typically geographically distinct (such as St. Mary's, Guelph, and Kingston) or were created through amalgamation of several smaller units, such as Kawartha Lakes, Hamilton, and Greater Sudbury. However, most municipalities are part of a two-tier structure, in which service responsibilities are divided between several lower-tier municipalities and a single upper-tier authority (8 regional governments and 22 counties) that delivers services to the lower-tier units and their residents. The division of responsibilities varies, but largely reflects an attempt to coordinate regional interests and capture economies of scale in service provision. That is, while lower-tier municipalities normally retain responsibility for services that are sensitive to the needs and demands of local residents (such as fire protection, recreation, and property standards), upper-tier units generally manage functions and services that can be delivered more efficiently and effectively at a regional scale, such as arterial roads, solid waste management, and strategic land-use planning.

In these two-tier arrangements, lower-tier municipalities are usually represented on the upper-tier council by their mayors and select councillors, but in some cases regional councillors are elected directly by voters. The warden or chair of the upper-tier council is normally elected internally by the members of the governing council, but is sometimes elected directly by the regional voters. For example, the Region of Waterloo comprises three urban municipalities and four rural townships, and is governed by a

16-member regional council. The council is composed of the mayors of the seven lower-tier municipalities, eight councillors elected by voters in the various member municipalities, and a regional chair, who is elected at large by all eligible voters within the regional boundaries.

Writing in 1997, David Siegel labelled the 1990s as the "age of restructuring," referring in part to a major structural overhaul of Ontario's municipal system initiated by the Harris government, which permanently changed the face of local government for many Ontario residents.[2] The Tories took office with a strong majority government, propelled by a popular campaign platform, the "Common Sense Revolution," which pledged to simplify governing processes, do away with "nonpriority" services, and generally reduce public spending.[3] Although structural reform was not a prominent pillar of the electoral mandate, while in office from 1995 to 2003 the Harris (and later Eves) government nearly halved the number of municipalities from 815 to 447, largely by amalgamating groups of communities.[4]

Guided by a set of principles rooted in neoconservative doctrine—fewer politicians, lower taxes, streamlined service delivery, less bureaucracy, and simplified lines of accountability—the Harris government introduced the Savings and Restructuring Act in 1996, which authorized municipalities to initiate voluntary restructuring agreements with neighbours to consolidate their government and service delivery functions.[5] In the event that voluntary negotiations failed, a commissioner could be appointed by the province to impose a restructuring plan from above. The first such instance occurred in 1997, when a provincially appointed commissioner issued a binding decision amalgamating the City of Chatham with Kent County and the 21 lower-tier municipalities within its jurisdiction.[6]

Regional governments were also targeted. In 1999 the provincial Legislature passed the Fewer Municipal Politicians Act, which eliminated the two-tier governance structures in Hamilton-Wentworth, Ottawa-Carleton, and Sudbury, and replaced them with single-tier, amalgamated cities.[7] The most striking case of structural reform during this period was the creation of the "megacity" of Toronto, formed through amalgamation of the upper-tier Municipality of Metropolitan Toronto with its six lower-tier municipalities.[8] The decision, which took effect in 1998, created a city more populous than six Canadian provinces, governed by an enormous council of 57 ward-based members (reduced to 44 in 2000), headed by a mayor elected at large. The City of Toronto is now the sixth largest government in Canada, with an operating budget of more than $9 billion and a workforce of approximately 50,000, including both direct employees and members of agencies, boards, and commissions.

At the time, the Harris government framed the amalgamation as a strategy to effect cost savings, increase efficiency, and simplify governance, but it appears none of these objectives were achieved.[9] Operating costs have risen, largely owing to the harmonization of wages and services after amalgamation, and governance is complicated by a large, cumbersome council whose members continue to perpetuate pre-consolidation rivalries between the central city and suburbs. Furthermore, the megacity amalgamation has not resolved the challenges of regional governance: although the Greater Toronto Area constitutes a single, continuous urban area and economy, there is no overarching government body to address region-wide issues such as economic development, growth management, and infrastructure investment.[10] The Government of Ontario has had to assume some of these responsibilities. For example, in 2006, regional transportation planning was assigned to a new provincial agency, the Greater Toronto Transportation Authority (renamed Metrolinx in 2007).

By the time the Liberal government under the leadership of Dalton McGuinty had taken office in 2003, the wave of restructuring was complete, and since that time there have been only two municipal amalgamations. Apart from some political campaigns to de-amalgamate municipalities merged during the earlier period,[11] the issue of municipal restructuring has had low salience on the provincial agenda.

Government and Administration

Local decision-making authority is exercised by the council, a body of officials elected for a four-year term. In some municipalities, members of council are elected at-large (by all eligible voters) to represent the entire community, while in others members are elected to represent residents from a particular ward (a subjurisdiction within the community). Primary duties of the council include approving an annual budget, setting policies to direct municipal operations, and overseeing the administration to ensure decisions and legal obligations are effectively discharged. The head of council, generally referred to as the mayor, reeve, or warden, is elected at-large to represent the municipality in official business, provide leadership to the council, and preside over municipal business as chief executive officer.

To some observers, mayors might appear to be powerful leaders. They are often the primary focus of local media attention, speaking on behalf of the council to explain decisions and new initiatives, and promoting priorities outlined in their election campaigns. Directly elected by all eligible voters in the community, mayors can also claim a sizeable constituency: in Ontario's 10 largest cities, for example, the mayor represents more voters than the prime minister and the premier, considering the population of federal and provincial electoral districts. However, the Municipal Act grants the mayor no formal powers, and the duties as chief executive officer are general and vague. Although mayors have some influence over the council agenda, their vote on decisions is weighted equally to those of other members. Unlike the prime minister and premier, who lead political parties and can use patronage to induce loyalty from the caucus, mayors must persuade independent councillors to support their position on issues, often without success.[12] In Toronto, for example, a proposal by Mayor Rob Ford to abandon an approved development plan and build an entertainment and shopping area on the Port Lands (a 400-acre plot on the edge of Lake Ontario) was stymied by councillors opposed to the idea.[13]

Some mayors have a higher profile than others, commanding public and media attention with their charisma, passion, or performance. For example, "Hurricane" Hazel McCallion of Mississauga was one of Canada's longest-serving mayors, winning all 12 mayoralty races in the city between 1978 and 2014. McCallion's reputation as a fiscal conservative was underpinned by her commitment to keeping the city debt-free, a pledge the council supported throughout her tenure.[14] A 2011 poll of residents in the 15 largest Canadian cities placed McCallion as the most popular mayor, with a 78 per cent approval rating.[15] Mayors of large cities typically garner more media scrutiny, particularly if their rhetoric or behaviour is newsworthy. Mayor Rob Ford of Toronto was perhaps the epitome of both: elected in 2010 on a pledge to "stop the gravy train" at city hall by scaling back departmental budgets and "focusing on the fundamentals," Ford's leadership was overshadowed by numerous allegations of scandalous behaviour.[16]

A municipality's daily operations are managed by appointed staff, who administer programs, implement policies, and provide expert policy advice to elected decision-makers. The size and organization of municipal administrations vary considerably, but at a minimum all Ontario municipalities are required to appoint a clerk, who is responsible for recording council decisions, keeping a record of bylaws and meeting minutes, and other duties outlined in the Municipal Act. In supervising staff, municipal councils in many communities are aided by a chief administrative officer (CAO), who occupies the highest appointed office in the administrative hierarchy. The CAO ensures political direction is reflected in the programs and activities of staff and, conversely, presents to the council the needs and interests of the various departments.[17]

Authority and Functions

Canada's constitution allocates no independent legal authority to local governments, but rather assigns exclusive jurisdiction over municipal institutions to the provinces. The nature of the provincial-municipal relationship is one of superior to subordinate: local governing authority is limited to powers specifically delegated by provincial statute and these can be radically altered with a simple act of the provincial Legislature.[18]

The general powers and duties of municipal governments are specified in the Municipal Act, which has been amended many times since its first iteration in 1849. Historically, municipal government functions were limited in scope, related largely to regulating disorderly behaviour and nuisance, preserving order, and supporting the production and maintenance of the built environment. Modern municipal governments continue to perform many of the functions necessary to facilitate economic development and growth, such as installing buried infrastructure, maintaining roads, and regulating construction standards by enforcing codes and guidelines. However, they also provide a diverse array of other services to residents and organizations, including:

- *protective services*, such as policing, firefighting, and emergency planning, which are intended to protect people and property from human and environmental threats;
- *transportation services*, including road construction and maintenance, public transit, and snow clearing, which facilitate movement of people and goods in the community;
- *environmental services*, such as waste collection, sanitary and storm water treatment, and recycling, which protect health and safety and contribute to environmental sustainability;
- *social services* to assist members of the community with personal and family needs, such as public health, child care, social housing, and immigrant settlement services; and
- *recreation and cultural services*, such as parks and libraries, which contribute to a vibrant community and enhance quality of life for residents.

The responsibilities of municipal governments changed considerably under the Harris government. As part of their "Common Sense Revolution" agenda, the Conservatives pledged to eliminate "waste and duplication" by "reducing government entanglement," giving rise to a massive "Local Services Realignment" in January 1997, which dramatically altered the scope of municipal duties.[19] Municipalities were assigned greater responsibility for public health, land ambulance, and social services, including an increase from 20 per cent to 50 per cent of the cost of social assistance, as well as the full cost of child care, long-term care, and social housing.[20] Many facilities, such as ferries and airports, were transferred to municipal care and control, and maintenance of infrastructure assets such as roads would no longer be subsidized through provincial grants. In return, the province assumed a larger share of the cost of education and stripped local school boards of their authority to levy education property taxes on households, which freed up tax room for municipalities. A large, unconditional grant, the Community Reinvestment Fund, was created to assist municipalities in paying for new service delivery responsibilities delegated through the Local Services Realignment. Although the process was nominally intended to be revenue neutral, municipal leaders decried it as "downloading" of the province's financial liabilities to local governments.

Nearly 10 years after the Local Services Realignment, the weight of the added responsibilities had taken a major toll on municipal budgets and demands were mounting for the province to address the imbalance between local government resources and responsibilities. These demands were most stridently asserted by the Association of Municipalities of Ontario (AMO), a nonprofit advocacy organization whose membership includes most of Ontario's municipalities. AMO launched a campaign in 2005 to draw attention to "the $3 billion gap"—the approximate cost to municipalities of "subsidizing" formerly provincial responsibilities, particularly health and social services. By this time, the McGuinty government had taken office, and it proved receptive to a reexamination of provincial and municipal responsibilities. Between 2004 and 2007, the province increased its share of public health funding from 50 to 75 per cent and pledged $300 million to support local land ambulance services. The provincial government also agreed to partner with AMO to undertake a more comprehensive analysis of the provincial-municipal relationship.

In December 2006, the Provincial-Municipal Fiscal and Service Delivery Review was launched, bringing together elected officials and senior public servants to review provincial-municipal arrangements with respect to financial resources and service delivery responsibilities, and to recommend improvements. In a 2008 agreement, the province pledged to gradually take over full funding of social assistance benefits, which the task force argued are best supported by province-wide revenues, to protect municipal budgets from uncertainty and volatility. The province also agreed to assume the costs of providing court security, which had long been borne by some municipalities (and not others) and were generally increasing. Provincial grant support to municipalities would be reduced to offset these costs, but once fully implemented the agreement is expected to bring a net benefit to municipalities of approximately $1.5 billion per year. In addition, a memorandum of understanding was signed with the Association of Municipalities of Ontario, which obligates the provincial government to consult with AMO on key policy issues that could affect municipal services or finances.

·Local Government Finance

Despite their many responsibilities, municipal governments operate with limited fiscal resources. The primary source of municipal revenue is the property tax, a levy on owners of real property (land and improvements), calculated based on the assessed value of the property multiplied by rates set by the municipal council, which typically vary by property class, such as residential, commercial, and industrial. A second important source of income for municipalities is user fees, which comprise about 20 per cent of total municipal revenue. The Municipal Act authorizes municipal governments to levy charges for a wide range of services, including, for example, licensing and permit fees, use-based charges for water and wastewater, and entrance fees for recreational facilities.[21]

Transfer payments from higher-level governments are a third source of municipal operating revenue. The primary provincial transfer payment program is the Ontario Municipal Partnership Fund, the broad objective of which is to equalize municipal fiscal capacity across the province. The federal government also offers funds to municipalities for targeted purposes. For example, as part of his government's "New Deal for Cities and Communities," Prime Minister Paul Martin signed an agreement in 2005 to share approximately $1.9 billion raised through the federal gas tax with municipalities in order to support investments in environmentally sustainable infrastructure.[22] The agreement was subsequently extended by the Harper government until 2015.

Since the mid-1990s, Ontario's municipal governments have become more reliant on own-source revenue—mainly property taxes and user charges—and less dependent on intergovernmental transfers. To some extent, this has served to increase the autonomy of municipal councils, in that they are less vulnerable to sudden changes in transfers, and have flexibility to adjust property tax rates and service fees to generate the revenue needed to fulfill their spending commitments. However, it also puts greater responsibility on local decision-makers, who face political resistance from residents when they attempt to increase property taxes or user fees. Moreover, fiscal sustainability remains a concern, especially in light of the impacts of the global recession of the late-2000s.[23] Contraction of economic activity had various negative impacts on local economies, ranging from higher unemployment due to the closure of manufacturing facilities to weaker property tax revenues as a result of more vacant properties and escalating arrears.[24] Concurrently, municipal spending on social services increased in response to greater demand for social assistance, public housing, and other forms of community support.[25]

Provincial-Municipal Relations

The major changes to municipal boundaries and duties described above illustrate two key aspects of provincial-municipal relations. First, local governments operate in an uncertain political environment, where shifts in provincial policy can dramatically alter their fiscal resources and the scope and range of their functional responsibilities. It is difficult to make plans with a multiyear time horizon because these could be undermined when a new provincial government takes office or an existing government realigns responsibilities in pursuit of its policy objectives. Second, the terms of the provincial-municipal relationship evolve over time, sometimes influenced by intergovernmental negotiation, but often as a result of changing provincial government interests.

In examining the intergovernmental relationship, Frances Frisken identified five prominent motivations for provincial governments to intervene in municipal affairs, and all of these factors are evident in Ontario's approach to local governments.[26] First, it is in the interests of the province to promote local economic growth as a means to create employment and generate revenue to pay for municipal services. In pursuit of this objective, Ontario has implemented a number of initiatives to assist local governments in ensuring their communities are "investment-ready." For instance, the Communities in Transition program was created in 2007 to provide support for projects aimed at diversifying local economies and attracting new business investment, such as business case development, feasibility studies, and marketing initiatives. The province has also made major investments in municipal infrastructure, through programs such as ReNew Ontario, a five-year, $30 billion investment plan initiated in 2005, which allocated funding to many municipal infrastructure projects, and the $450 million Municipal Infrastructure Investment Initiative, which funded dozens of municipal infrastructure renewal projects in 2008.

A second provincial policy objective is to encourage sustainable development and growth. Ontario's Planning Act empowers municipal governments to create an official plan, which sets out goals and policies concerning land use, and to establish zoning by-laws that regulate development. However, all municipal planning is required to be "consistent with" a Provincial Policy Statement, which articulates the provincial government's interests, including, for example, planning for future land use, ensuring a range of housing types and affordability, stewardship of natural heritage, water, and agricultural land, and protecting public health and safety by directing development away from hazardous areas.

Over the last decade, provincial officials focused greater attention on growth management in specific areas of Ontario. One such area is the Oak Ridges Moraine, an ecologically significant landform north of Lake Ontario, which contains prime agricultural land, stores large volumes of clean water, and provides habitat for a diverse range of plant and animal species. Because of its location at the northern edge of the sprawling Greater Toronto Area, pressure was mounting in the late 1990s to develop parts of the moraine, and this was vehemently opposed by advocacy groups that sought to preserve the lands in their natural state.[27] Extensive media coverage of the dispute compelled the Ontario government to introduce the Oak Ridges Moraine Conservation Act in 2001, which temporarily suspended all development. A conservation plan, promulgated in 2002, divided the moraine into four areas with increasingly stringent controls, such that only about 8 per cent of the land is now accessible for development.[28]

Third, the province seeks to strengthen the effectiveness and legitimacy of municipal governments as democratic decision-making bodies. Consistent with this objective, in 2000 the Government of Ontario passed the Direct Democracy through Municipal Referendums Act, which empowers local governments to refer important questions directly to voters at election time. In a 2010 referendum in Waterloo, for instance, a majority of voters indicated that the municipality should end the practice of adding fluoride to the water supply.[29] Other provincial initiatives target transparency and accountability. Section 239 of the Municipal Act specifies that all meetings of municipal councils and boards must be open to the public, except in limited circumstances, such as labour negotiations, when confidentiality is paramount. Complaints regarding municipal noncompliance can be referred to the Ontario ombudsman, an independent officer of the provincial Legislature who monitors accountability by providing oversight of the administration of government services.

A fourth rationale for provincial intervention in municipal affairs is to prevent or correct disparities in the cost and quality of services. One approach involves spending, whereby funds are transferred from the provincial treasury to municipal governments with weaker fiscal capacity or special community needs. The Ontario Municipal Partnership Fund (OMPF) is the province's main transfer payment to municipalities, which aims to assist municipalities with social program costs, support communities with limited property assessment due to lower property values, address challenges faced by northern and rural communities, and offset policing costs in rural communities. As an illustration, the OMPF provided $550 million to 388 municipalities across the province in 2014.[30]

Regulation is another provincial tool for ensuring parity in municipal service quality. Many municipal services, such as water distribution, fire protection, roads, public works, and so on, are subject to detailed standards set by provincial statute. For instance, Ontario's Fire Protection and Prevention Act and regulations require local governments to provide fire protection services, but also to perform a fire risk assessment, implement a program to encourage smoke alarm use, distribute fire safety public education materials, and submit to the Office of the Fire Commissioner an annual Compliance Self-Assessment Form reporting on their implementation of the legislated standards.

Lastly, the province seeks to uphold a minimum standard of living for all Ontarians and therefore imposes obligations on local governments to ensure services and benefits are available to support disadvantaged residents. For example, Ontario municipalities are responsible for funding and administering social housing—government-subsidized accommodations for low- and moderate-income households. Whereas in the 1990s, social housing construction was supported through federal and provincial funding programs, fiscal and administrative responsibility was transferred to municipalities in 2000 as part of the Harris government's Local Services Realignment plan. But after nearly a decade of local administration, concerns were raised about the availability and quality of social housing, including in a 2009 report of the Auditor General of Ontario, which identified a number of weaknesses in the province's oversight system for social housing.[31] The government responded with a new Long-Term Affordable Housing Strategy, which aimed to simplify the criteria for accessing affordable housing and streamline municipal reporting requirements. However, it also required municipal governments to prepare comprehensive, multiyear plans for housing and homelessness programs, and created a stringent accountability framework, complete with performance indicators.[32]

The Evolving Nature of Provincial-Municipal Relations

Municipal governments have more operational autonomy than they did in the late 1990s, as a function of modernized enabling legislation.[33] Historically the Municipal Act was restrictive, enumerating specific powers available to municipal governments, beyond which provincial permission was required. However, a revised version was adopted in 2001 with the objective of establishing a "permissive policy framework," whereby local governments enjoy broad discretion to pass by-laws in key functional areas that are important to community life, such as public utilities, parks, and culture and recreation.[34] This approach reflects a view of municipalities as responsible and accountable governments, which should have the freedom to take action deemed necessary or desirable for the public, constrained only by specific limits set out by the province.

Although they have been endowed with broader statutory authority, many municipal councils appear reluctant to fully exercise these new powers. David Siegel and Richard Tindal attribute this to a "culture of comfortable subordination,"[35] whereby municipal decision-makers have become accustomed to a limited role circumscribed by provincial controls. Shifting to a culture of "assertive maturity," they argue, will require local governments to map out a long-term vision for the community, incorporate the public in setting priorities, value and engage the professional expertise of staff, and aggressively pursue the municipality's interests with other levels of government.

Practically every policy decision taken at Queen's Park has some implication for local governments, and municipal councils protest aggressively when they perceive an unfair financial or regulatory burden on their community. Provincial politicians are generally sensitive to the impacts their decisions have on municipalities, but the Government of Ontario ultimately reserves the power to impose its will on local governments in pursuit of its policy objectives. In contrast to the acrimonious nature of the provincial-municipal relationship under Mike Harris, the tenor of intergovernmental relations in Ontario since the turn of the millennium has been generally positive and cooperative. The McGuinty government appeared to regard local governments as partners, and tried to build a relationship of trust and mutual respect, as evidenced by the memorandum of understanding with AMO, the Provincial-Municipal Fiscal and Service Delivery Review, and ongoing consultations on other provincial policy initiatives that could affect municipal finances and service delivery responsibilities. This approach has endured under the leadership of Premier Kathleen Wynne, who built relationships with municipal leaders in her previous role as minister of municipal affairs and housing. Nevertheless, as explained below, and as discussed in greater detail in Chapters 13 and 14, a number of Liberal government policy initiatives were complicated or undermined by significant opposition from local politicians and residents.

Local Resistance to Provincial Initiatives

Land-use decisions are some of the most contentious issues that local governments face, particularly when nearby residents mobilize in opposition to a proposed development. Freeways, low-income housing units, adult entertainment establishments, landfills, and many other potential land uses typically trigger complaints from people who oppose the proximity of these developments, arguing that they will have a negative impact on the value of their property or their quality of life. This phenomenon is commonly referred to as the NIMBY syndrome: Not In My Backyard. Often dramatized by the media, these situations pose a difficult choice for politicians. On the one hand, development generates revenue for the municipality in the form of fees, charges, and property taxes, which can be used to provide services to residents. On the other hand, municipal councils have a responsibility to protect local quality of life, and concerted, strenuous objection to land use changes sends a clear signal that a decision is unpopular.

Provincial plans can be effectively derailed by NIMBY opposition, as evidenced in the difficulty the McGuinty government faced in pursuit of its strategy to close coal-fired power plants and expand renewable energy production in the province. A key part of this strategy was to build a number of natural gas power plants, but these projects were fiercely resisted by local residents in some communities. Notably, strong opposition in the Toronto area suburbs of Oakville and Mississauga prompted the McGuinty government to abandon two power plants after construction had begun. As Anna Esselment discusses in Chapter 13, these decisions cost the provincial treasury hundreds of millions and gave the opposition parties potent ammunition with which to attack the government.

Proposals for major wind power developments also encountered NIMBY opposition, as local residents protested against the erection of enormous turbines. One such proposal, which involved the construction of 60 wind turbines in the shallow water of Lake Ontario off the Scarborough Bluffs, ignited a well-organized and vocal opposition campaign that included both local residents and politicians.[36] Similar battles pitting residents against wind farm proponents were waged in dozens of other communities across the province. Responding to public opinion, some local governments attempted to fight wind power developments by passing resolutions, restricting zoning, and imposing exorbitant fees.

In the face of this local opposition, Dalton McGuinty vowed that provincial decisions would supersede local bylaws and regulations designed to block green energy projects, so that "NIMBYism will no longer prevail."[37] Indeed, the province ultimately amended municipal planning powers, effectively removing local authority to regulate renewable energy production projects.[38] As this example illustrates, despite the more collegial tone of intergovernmental relations in Ontario, municipalities clearly remain "creatures of the province," whose resources and authority are subject to the changing policy priorities of the premier and cabinet. Although cooperation and consultation with local governments may be the norm, the provincial government will not hesitate to assert its authority to ensure municipal behaviour is in line with its policy interests.

Conclusion

Local governments are a vital element of Ontario's political system, providing a democratic means to authoritatively resolve community problems, a mechanism to finance and deliver services to people and property within defined jurisdictions, and an administrative network through which the provincial government can effectively implement its policy objectives. All of these roles have evolved over time, influenced by both the changing needs and demands of residents and the political priorities of successive provincial governments.

Since the late 1990s, Ontario's local governments have had to adapt to major changes in their operating environment, including a radical restructuring of the municipal system. An overhaul of provincial enabling legislation and adjustments to municipal revenue streams have conferred greater autonomy on local governments, while new responsibilities with respect to accountability and transparency have focused scrutiny on both the decision-making processes and the outcomes they bring about. Perhaps more than ever before, Ontario's local governments are publicly recognized by the provincial government as responsible and accountable governing bodies with a legitimate mandate to make decisions to serve the public interest. Questions remain as to whether this collegial, mutually respectful relationship will last, and the extent to which local governments will embrace and effectively harness their broadened sphere of discretion. Generally, however, local governments appear better-equipped to face the challenges of the twenty-first century.

Discussion Questions

1. Should the provincial government be legally required to consult local residents (e.g., through a referendum) before amalgamating two or more municipalities into one? Why or why not?
2. The chapter notes that mayors are granted no formal powers in the Municipal Act and possess the same authority as other members of council. In what ways can mayors influence municipal decision making?
3. The NIMBY problem is a serious obstacle to many important developments, including green energy projects. Under what conditions should the provincial government or a municipal council proceed with a development proposal, even if it is opposed by nearby residents?

4. Some argue that local governments are the most relevant and accessible to Canadians, because of their close proximity to residents and due to the immediacy of the issues they deal with, which often have significant and visible impacts on quality of life in the community. Do you agree with this assessment? What political issues have you gotten involved with in your community?

Notes

1   Dale Richmond and David Siegel, eds., *Agencies, Boards, and Commissions in Canadian Local Government* (Toronto: Institute of Public Administration of Canada, 1994).

2   David Siegel, "Local Government in Ontario," in *The Government and Politics of Ontario*, 5th ed., ed. Graham White (Toronto: University of Toronto Press, 1997), 150.

3   John Ibbitson, *Promised Land: Inside the Mike Harris Revolution* (Scarborough, ON: Prentice-Hall Canada, 1997).

4   David Siegel, "Municipal Reform in Ontario: Revolutionary Evolution," in *Municipal Reform in Canada: Reconfiguration, Re-Empowerment, and Rebalancing*, ed. Joseph Garcea and Edward C. LeSage Jr. (Don Mills, ON: Oxford University Press, 2005).

5   Terrence J. Downey and Robert J. Williams, "Provincial Agendas, Local Responses: The 'Common Sense' Restructuring of Ontario's Municipal Governments," *Canadian Public Administration* 41 (1998): 210–38.

6   Thomas R. Hollick and David Siegel, *Evolution, Revolution, Amalgamation: Restructuring in Three Ontario Municipalities* (London, ON: Department of Political Science, University of Western Ontario, 2001).

7   Andrew Sancton, *Merger Mania: The Assault on Local Government* (Montreal: McGill-Queen's University Press, 2000), 154–59.

8   Graham Todd, "Megacity: Globalization and Governance in Toronto," *Studies in Political Economy* 56 (1998): 193–216.

9   Harvey Schwartz, "Toronto Ten Years after Amalgamation," *Canadian Journal of Regional Science* 32 (2005): 483–94.

10 Andrew Sancton, "The Governance of Metropolitan Areas in Canada," *Public Administration and Development* 25 (2005): 317–27.

11 Natalie Alcoba and Megan O'Toole, "Councillor Wants Province to Allow Toronto De-Amalgamation," *National Post*, 26 September 2011; "Essex Council Endorses De-amalgamation," *Windsor Star*, 4 February 2008.

12 Andrew Sancton, "Mayors as Political Leaders," in *Leaders and Leadership in Canada*, ed. Maureen Mancuso, Richard G. Price, and Ronald Wagenberg (Don Mills, ON: Oxford University Press, 1994).

13 David Rider, "Ford Gives up Goal of Seizing Port Lands," *Toronto Star*, 20 September 2011.

14 Tom Urbaniak, *Her Worship: Hazel McCallion and the Development of Mississauga* (Toronto: University of Toronto Press, 2009).

15 Kathryn Blaze Carlson, "Hazel McCallion Is Canada's Most Popular Mayor," *National Post*, 24 October 2011.

16   "Toronto Mayor Rob Ford's Pattern of Behaviour Tells a Troubling Story," *Toronto Star*, 26 March 2013.

17   Thomas J. Plunkett, *City Management in Canada: The Role of the Chief Administrative Officer* (Toronto: Institute of Public Administration of Canada, 1992), 28–37.

18   Caroline Andrew, "Provincial-Municipal Relations; or Hyper-Fractionalized Quasi-Subordination Revisited," in *Canadian Metropolitics: Governing Our Cities*, ed. James Lightbody (Toronto: Copp Clark, 1995).

19   Katherine A. Graham and Susan D. Phillips, "'Who Does What' in Ontario: The Process of Provincial-Municipal Disentanglement," *Canadian Public Administration* 41 (1998): 175–209.

20   David Siegel, "Recent Changes in Provincial-Municipal Relations in Ontario: A New Era or a Missed Opportunity?" in *Municipal-Federal-Provincial Relations in Canada*, ed. Robert Young and Christian Leuprecht (Montreal: McGill-Queen's University Press, 2004).

21   Robert G. Doumani, "Municipal Revenue Sources: Ontario's Experience with User and Licence Fees," *Canadian Tax Journal* 50 (2002): 600–05.

22   Association of Municipalities of Ontario, *Municipal Funding Agreement for the Transfer of Federal Gas Tax Revenues Under the New Deal for Cities and Communities*, https://www.amo.on.ca/AMO-PDFs/Gas_Tax/Agreements_and_Allocations_GTF/GTF-Municipal-Funding-Agreement-2005.aspx

23   Gord Hume, "Municipal Time Bombs," *Municipal World* 121 (2011): 5–6; R. Michael Warren, "Ontario Municipalities Struggle with Cost of Essential Services," *Toronto Star*, 27 February 2012.

24   Robert Heuton, "Fiscal Austerity and Urban Innovation: Challenges Facing Canadian Cities," *Municipal World* 120 (2010): 27–29.

25   Tanya Talaga, "Recession's Bite Swells Welfare Rolls," *Toronto Star*, 20 March 2009.

26   Frances Frisken, "Jurisdictional and Political Constraints on Progressive Local Initiatives," in *The Politics of the City: A Canadian Perspective*, ed. Timothy L. Thomas (Scarborough, ON: ITP Nelson, 1997), 155–56.

27   Kevin Hanna and Steven Webber, "Incremental Planning and Land-Use Conflict in the Toronto Region's Oak Ridges Moraine," *Local Environment* 15 (2010): 169–83.

28   Ontario Ministry of Municipal Affairs and Housing, *Oak Ridges Moraine Conservation Plan*, http://www.mah.gov.on.ca/Page1707.aspx

29   Jeff Outhit, "Voters Say No to Fluoride," *Kitchener-Waterloo Record*, 25 October 2010.

30   Ontario Ministry of Finance, *Ontario Municipal Partnership Fund (OMPF) 2014*, http://www.fin.gov.on.ca/en/budget/ompf/2014/

31   Auditor General of Ontario, *Annual Report* (Toronto: Queen's Printer for Ontario, 2009).

32   Ontario Ministry of Municipal Affairs and Housing, *Ontario's Long-Term Affordable Housing Strategy: An Overview* (Toronto: Queen's Printer for Ontario, 2008).

33   David Siegel and C. Richard Tindal, "Changing the Municipal Culture: From Comfortable Subordination to Assertive Maturity—Part I," *Municipal World* 116 (2006): 37–40.

34   Joseph Garcea, "Modern Municipal Statutory Frameworks in Canada," *Revue Gouvernance* 1 (2004): 18–31.

35 David Siegel and C. Richard Tindal, "Changing the Municipal Culture: From Comfortable Subordination to Assertive Maturity—Part II," *Municipal World* 116 (2006): 13–17.

36 John Spears, "Offshore Wind Farm Stirs Up a Tempest," *Toronto Star*, 24 November 2008.

37 Leslie Ferenc, "McGuinty Vows to Stop Wind Farm NIMBYs," *Toronto Star*, 11 February 2009.

38 Paul Manning and Joanna Vince, "Municipalities and the Green Energy Act: Benefits, Burdens, and Loss of Power," *Municipal World* 120 (2010): 5–8.

8

Ontario and Contemporary Intergovernmental Relations: Still a Responsible Partner in Confederation?

JULIE M. SIMMONS

MANY CANADIANS, BOTH WITHIN THE Province of Ontario and in other regions, have historically perceived the province's political and economic interests as interchangeable with those of the federal government. Ontario's demographic weight (38 per cent of the Canadian population) and its centrality to the economic well-being of the country mean that Ontario is a formidable power in the making of economic, social, fiscal, and any other policy in Ottawa. Perhaps not surprisingly, at the same time as Ontario has been seen as a key orchestrator and prime beneficiary of federal policies, Ontarians have not been known for expressing so-called regionalist sentiments, and the Ontario government has seen its role as one of a statesperson and mediator in federal-provincial relations, promoting harmony rather than dissent and maintaining national political and economic stability. As a quid pro quo, Ontario governments have also seen it as their responsibility to share the province's wealth with "have-not" provincial governments through the federal equalization program. As Nelson Wiseman suggests, "Ontario is not known for regional grievances, for feeling ignored, taken for granted, shunted aside or shortchanged.... Ontarians have touted grandness rather than victimization."[1]

Yet, prior to the 2015 federal election, the positions of the Ontario and federal governments on a great many issues and policies diverged at almost every turn. The "long war" between Stephen Harper and Kathleen Wynne was both intense and public.[2] In 2013, the federal immigration minister called Ontario's decision to provide health care for refugee claimants (made after the federal government denied them health care) "scandalous" and "irresponsible."[3] On who was responsible for job losses in Ontario in the last decade and the general state of its economy, the two governments pointed to the other, disagreeing on what the Canada Job Grant program for skills training should look like. The two governments also clashed on inter-provincial trade, employment insurance, transit, and federal inaction on missing and murdered Indigenous women. Following the release of the 2014 federal budget, Wynne issued a 34-page list of "the 116 ways" the Conservative government in Ottawa "had shortchanged Ontario."[4] Her minister of finance, Charles

Sousa, publicly battled the federal finance minister, Joe Oliver, and argued in an editorial in the *Financial Post* that "the Federal government must stop pick-pocketing the people of this Province, and instead help invest in and protect the schools, hospitals, and public transit that Ontarians expect and deserve."[5] For its part, the federal government stuck to the narrative that the Ontario government had "no one to blame but themselves" for their troubles, and that "Ontario's spending mismanagement [was] a problem for the entire country."[6]

In launching her 2014 Ontario election campaign, Wynne focused on the prime minister, as opposed to the leaders of the other provincial parties, arguing that "the interests of the people of Ontario are at odds with the policies of Stephen Harper's government" and that the "federal government [was] doing more to hurt [Ontario's] economic recovery than to help."[7] The development of an Ontario Pension Plan and the federal government's unwillingness to "get out of Ontario's way" was a key pillar in her campaign.[8] In part a reflection of these public feuds, or perhaps because of them, Harper refused to meet with Wynne for over a year. Wynne made this lack of face time with the prime minister a public issue as well, forgoing the conventional confidentiality of federal-provincial diplomacy, and releasing to the media copies of her multiple written requests for a face-to-face meeting. While recent premiers of Ontario have spoken out about issues or candidates in federal elections, none has done so more than Wynne, who took to the campaign trail in Ontario alongside Justin Trudeau.[9]

While one might be tempted to point to the ideological differences between Harper and Wynne or to Harper's Western orientation as the main reason the two governments were so frequently at odds, there are a multitude of other examples from the Wynne era that seem rather un-Ontarian, in the sense that they involve not just Ontario's direct relationship with the federal government, but also measuring the federal government's treatment of Ontario against its treatment of other provinces. Consider the uncharacteristic fighting words in Ontario's 2013 fiscal update, which argued that Ontario's net contribution of $16 billion to the equalization program was "redistributed to other regions of Canada to subsidize programs and services that Ontarians themselves may not enjoy."[10] On the potential $60 billion mining project in Northern Ontario known as the Ring of Fire, Wynne argued that it was incumbent on the (reluctant) federal government to take on a partnership role in the project because "they have been full partners in other projects across the country," particularly in the oil and gas sector in Alberta and Newfoundland and Labrador.[11] Such comparisons prompted one national newspaper columnist to urge Ontario to "get back its pride" and play "a leading role among Canadian provinces" rather than a "finger-wagging" one.[12]

Has Ontario shed its identity—entrenched in the postwar period in constitutional deliberations and the development of the welfare state—as "big brother" of Confederation, or first among equals?[13] Is Ontario now pursuing its self-interest at the expense of the rest of the family of provinces? This chapter places these more recent actions in historical perspective and identifies the factors that account for this apparent disconnection. It then considers what the consequences might be of the "Ontario first" approach to federal-provincial relations, both in the short and long term. This chapter argues that it is not out of step for the Ontario government to assert an intergovernmental position that is distinct from that of Ottawa. Examples dating to the time of Confederation reveal a pattern of resisting federal attempts to adopt policies contrary to Ontario's interests. In the postwar period, however, a strong federal government and a unified Canada benefited Ontario's economy and Canada as a whole. Ontario's economy was the engine of the Canadian economy, primarily by design but partly owing to evolving social, technological, and global trade patterns. It is not surprising that during this period Ontario figured prominently as a broker of interests in federal-provincial constitutional deliberations, and as a willing participant in national programs redistributing wealth from the prosperous "centre" to the less well-off "periphery" of the country.

"Fair shares" federalism did not begin with Wynne, but was first introduced in the Ontario-federal intergovernmental dialogue in the 1990s. It was at that time that Ontario's traditional "*noblesse oblige patina*" gradually tarnished as east-west trade linkages between Ontario and other provinces gave way to north-south trade and greater North American integration in the post–1988 free trade era.[14] Irrespective of their political ideology, Ontario premiers have, since that time, aggressively argued for Ontario's "fair share" of federal revenues when facing burgeoning deficits (under Bob Rae), the federal government balancing its own budget through reduced transfers to the provinces (under Rae and Mike Harris), and declining fiscal capacity as a result of the particularly sluggish recovery of the American economy after the global recession of 2008 (under Dalton McGuinty). The Ontario economy is undergoing transformation, as the manufacturing sector declines and plays a secondary role in the national economy to natural resource extraction in Alberta, Saskatchewan, and Newfoundland and Labrador. The mismatch between current regional economic patterns in Canada and the mechanisms for regional redistribution of wealth across provinces underlies Ontario's assertion that it can no longer afford to be as generous a big brother. Perhaps it is no longer necessary.

In the last 25 years, Ontario governments have argued that "fairer treatment" for Ontario is in the interests of the country as a whole because "a strong Ontario means a Strong Canada."[15] But if Ontario political leaders come across as merely operating out of provincial interest, they run the risk of sharpening among other premiers and Canadians outside Ontario the view that Ontario is now merely the "whiner of Confederation,"[16] and the "vampire squid of fiscal federalism," leaving less for other provinces to feed on with every dollar it "sucks from federal veins."[17] If, on the other hand, Ontario can play a leadership role in contouring a new generation of federal-provincial fiscal arrangements, and in shaping new multilateral federal-provincial partnerships, Ontario's actions moving forward will be consistent with Ontario's traditional intergovernmental strategy of big brother, "play[ing] neither a purely provincial nor purely national role, but ... exist[ing] in the space between the two levels of government."[18]

Ontario Then: The National Policy and the Politics of Redistribution

John A. Macdonald's National Policy of 1879 is key to understanding Ontario's traditional intergovernmental role and why the present-day Ontario "fair shares" mantra seems so out of step. This policy was intended to create a strong manufacturing base in central Canada so that the country as a whole would be on an independent footing vis-à-vis the United States. It was a deliberate attempt to resist the forces of north-south trade and prop up east-west trade. With Canadian tariffs placed on most manufactured goods entering Canada, the nascent manufacturing sector located around the St. Lawrence and the Great Lakes in the Montreal–Windsor corridor could sell goods to Canadians at a price higher than it would obtain if American products were allowed to flood the Canadian market. At the same time, the raw materials from other countries required for the manufacturing sector were subject to reduced customs duties, lowering the cost of production in Canada. The creation of the railway linking the east and west facilitated the movement of manufactured goods within the country. The Crow's Nest Pass agreement of 1897 (in place until 1983) guaranteed a western Canadian market for the manufacturing sector in Central Canada. It distorted the western Canadian economy by reducing eastbound rates on the Canadian Pacific Railway for unprocessed grain products (encouraging farming) but not for processed products (discouraging manufacturing) and reducing westbound rates for certain manufactured goods (benefiting the Central Canadian economy). As a result, Ontario's economy became the engine of the country. In the post-Confederation era, the economies of Nova Scotia and New Brunswick also declined—owing partly to the change in marine technology from wooden sailing ships to steel steamships, but also because of the effect of federal freight rates. The nationalization of the banking system and its centralization in Ontario also negatively affected the Maritimes.

By the end of World War II, Ontario's economy remained at the centre of the country as a whole but was now considerably diversified, to the point that virtually every federal policy affected it. Is it any wonder that there is a wide perception that Ontario's interests have been one and the same as the federal government's interests? Is it any wonder that other regions, particularly the West, might have voiced what an unsympathetic observer might dismiss as regional whining, to end what a sympathetic observer might call the West's neocolonial status within the country?

Ontario premiers have traditionally sought to maintain the status quo rather than venture into new policy directions in their intergovernmental relations. This is not to say that there have not been clashes between Ontario and the federal government, or that Ontario premiers have merely managed intergovernmental relations "off the corner of their desks" as has historically been the case in some other provinces.[19] On the contrary, Oliver Mowat, premier from 1872 to 1896, often joined with his Quebec counterpart, Honoré Mercier in resisting Prime Minister John A. Macdonald's attempts to centralize power in Ottawa. Howard Ferguson (1923–30) and Mitchell Hepburn (1934–42) both had run-ins with the federal government over which order of government had constitutional jurisdiction to legislate. For example, Ferguson argued in favour of Quebec's right to develop hydroelectricity on the St. Lawrence River. With the Judicial Committee of the Privy Council (then the highest court of appeal) tending to favour a wide interpretation of provincial jurisdiction, and Ontario involved in a great many of these cases, Bryden reasons that "successive generations of Ontario premiers had some basis for considering themselves equal to the prime minister."[20]

The quid pro quo for the National Policy's centralization of manufacturing wealth in one part of the country has been Ottawa's redistribution of that wealth to other regions of the country through fiscal federalism, the financial arrangements between the federal and provincial governments.[21] This redistribution has been central to the development of the modern welfare state in Canada since World War II. In brief, revenues collected by the federal government fund initiatives in federal jurisdiction (e.g., national defence) and, through transfer payments to provinces, initiatives in areas of provincial jurisdiction. A key fiscal building block of the welfare state is the equalization program initiated in 1957: the federal government makes payments to select provincial governments so that the latter have "sufficient revenues to provide reasonably comparable levels of public services at reasonably comparable levels of taxation," as enshrined in the Constitution Act, 1982. While the funds come from the federal government, sometimes equalization is characterized as taking funds from one province and giving it to another. Equalization is an unconditional federal grant received by some provinces according to a complex formula which calculates the revenue generating capacity of each of the provinces. Ontario taxpayers have collectively always been the largest contributors to equalization, by virtue of their demographic weight and the strength of the Ontario economy that results in higher than average incomes in the province. Nevertheless, Ontario governments have generally supported the development of the welfare state across the country because, as Matthew Mendelsohn reasons, "forging a stronger, unified Canada was in the interests of the dominant, most prosperous player in the federation."[22]

Other federal funds are transferred to *all* provinces but are targeted to specific provincial policy areas (e.g., health care, postsecondary education, and social services) or are conditional upon provinces designing provincial programs in specified ways. For example, receipt of the Canada Health Transfer is, in theory, conditional upon compliance with the Canada Health Act. The amount of funding each province receives and the nature of the conditions—indeed, whether it is even legitimate for the federal government to impose conditions—are issues of intergovernmental debate. While provinces were largely supportive of the development of the modern welfare state following World War II, Ontario did frequently side with Quebec in resisting fiscal centralization and federal development of social programs like the Canada Pension Plan (1966) and Medicare (1968).[23] In Hugh Segal's words, "While Ontario has been a reliable ally in defence of the legitimacy of the confederal union, it is not, nor has it ever been, a willy-nilly hallelujah chorus for slapdash trigger-happy excess from any federal administration."[24]

Given the centrality of Ontario's manufacturing sector to the National Policy, the province's historical preference for the status quo, and its track record of challenging Ottawa in the early years following Confederation and in the era of the development of the welfare state, it is understandable that Ontario protested the National Oil Policy brought in by the federal Diefenbaker government in 1961. This policy forced those citizens living west of the Ottawa Valley to buy oil from Alberta, rather than on the international market where oil could be purchased less expensively. This policy had the effect of protecting the budding oil industry with an inflow of cash for further exploration, but at the expense of consumers in Ontario (and the western provinces).[25] At the same time, it is also understandable why the federal government (with its track record of shaping the contours of the national economy) and Alberta (having experienced the obstacles to manufacturing put in place though the Crow's Nest Pass agreement) would view this policy as entirely justified.

A further example of Ontario's resistance from this period is its dissatisfaction with the 1957 formula for equalization, which was intended to elevate other provinces to the standard of Ontario and British Columbia, then the two wealthiest provinces. The federal government considered the per capita value of three provincial tax bases (personal, corporate, and inheritance taxes) in those two provinces and made payments to the other provinces such that they would have the same per capita value. From Ontario's perspective this was too rich an equalization scheme. A major change five years later was to shift to equalizing to a national average (a less generous scheme), and to include 50 per cent of the revenues provinces generate from the sale of their natural resources as a fourth tax base.[26] The latter captured the growing wealth of Alberta, and rendered the province ineligible for equalization payments.[27]

Despite this pattern of Ontario's resistance to federal attempts to centralize controls, particularly in the development of the welfare state, Ontario's support for Ottawa's response to the oil crisis of the 1970s feeds the commonly held perception that Ontario is the prime beneficiary of the federal government's economic policies and a province in favour of a strong central government. John Ibbitson goes so far as to say that under Premier Bill Davis (1971–85), Ontario "ceased to be."[28] When the value of natural resource commodities changes, so too does the eligibility of the various provinces for equalization. When the federal government includes the provinces that are benefiting from high prices for their natural resources in the national standard of revenue-generating capacity (as is the case with a 10-province standard), the national standard rises. This rise requires that the federal government redistribute more funding to bring less well-off provinces to the national standard. In the late 1970s, when 50 per cent of the value of natural resources was included in the calculation of a province's revenue generating capacity and the price of oil surged dramatically during the OPEC crisis, the revenue generating capacity of Alberta was especially high, pushing up the national standard. Ontario, with its economy built on manufacturing, and without Alberta's natural resource wealth, actually found itself eligible to receive equalization from 1977 to 1982, a politically unacceptable circumstance for Ontario, the federal government, and the rest of the provinces. This effect was contrary to the spirit of equalization and would have been especially costly for the federal government. It is during this period that the best strategy for defending Ontario's interests was aligning with the federal government. While Ontario could not affect oil prices or provincial taxation revenues, it relied on the federal government to "correct" the disruption to Ontario's privileged economic position in the country. Looking to access the wealth that could be generated from taxing oil, Ottawa introduced the

National Energy Program (NEP) in 1980. Deeply unpopular in Alberta, the NEP centralized oil revenues; partially moved energy development into federal hands; sought to increase Canadian ownership of the oil and gas industry; and artificially kept the cost of oil for the domestic market below world prices.[29] Once again, federal policy levers seemed to have been set to the advantage of Ontario, and to the disadvantage of Alberta.

Ontario's decision not to accept the equalization payments for which it was eligible is in keeping with the National Policy/Equalization bargain. If Ontario, the traditional economic engine of the country, qualified for equalization, it was time to revisit the formula. In 1981, with the support of Ontario's Premier Davis, the federal government amended the formula with the "personal income override" so that any province with per capita personal income regularly above the national average (i.e., Ontario) would not be eligible.[30] A more permanent solution was put in place the following year. With oil revenues still high, Davis's suggestions for reworking the formula were focused on excluding natural resource revenue entirely. In other words, the federal government would equalize only nonresource revenues across provinces. Alberta's wealth now made the formula too generous, and federal taxes collected from Ontarians would still make up a substantial portion of the cash being redistributed to other provinces. Ultimately, however, in 1982 the federal government moved from the 10-province standard to one based on the average of five supposedly representative provinces (British Columbia, Saskatchewan, Manitoba, Ontario, and Quebec), excluding Alberta from the calculation, thereby ensuring that the wealth of Alberta would have limited direct bearing on equalization payments, and that the federal government would not find itself in the somewhat nonsensical situation of Ontario again qualifying for equalization payments. While this was not Ontario's preferred option, it was still in Ontario's interest relative to the status quo.

There might have been some doubt about the centrality of Ontario's manufacturing industry to the economy of Canada during the 1970s period of prosperity in Western Canada. But in the 1980s such doubt diminished, as the world price of oil collapsed, and, benefiting from a weak Canadian dollar vis-à-vis the American dollar, Ontario manufacturers enjoyed an export boom. This period of prosperity for the province postponed any serious confrontations between Ontario and the federal government on fiscal matters.

Ontario's support of the federal government extended beyond Trudeau's centralizing NEP to constitutional deliberations as well. Following the failed Quebec referendum on sovereignty-association in 1980, Trudeau continued his quest to "patriate" the Constitution, including a Charter of Rights and Freedoms, with an eye to securing provincial agreement. However, with most provinces concerned about the implications for provincial rights of a

Charter promoting individual rights, Trudeau eventually unilaterally asserted that provincial consent was unnecessary. Ontario, for its part lined up with Ottawa on the Charter of Rights, the nature of Canada's political community, bilingualism, and economic policy. It and New Brunswick were the only provinces that did not join the "gang of eight" challenging Trudeau's vision of a strong central government. When the Supreme Court of Canada ruled that "substantial" provincial consent was required, Trudeau was forced to return to the bargaining table. At that point Ontario resumed its historical position of neither a strictly provincial nor federal role, mediating among the parties at the table. Unfortunately, and significantly, premiers reached an agreement with the prime minister, excluding Quebec premier René Lévesque. But with Ontario's interests seemingly so closely aligned with federal interests, both with respect to the NEP and the patriation of the Constitution, it would be fair to say that this era was a departure from Ontario's earlier willingness to challenge the federal government.

Ontario in the Free Trade Era

Despite Ontario's economic boom in the 1980s, major changes to Ontario's economy were at play, which eventually broke the province's alignment with the federal government. They significantly augmented Ontario's willingness to voice its interests vis-à-vis the federal government and vis-à-vis the other provinces, and there is some evidence that they are also affecting Ontarians' understanding of themselves. The regional redistribution of national income and wealth—particularly through the federal equalization program, but also through other federal transfers to provinces for various provisions of the welfare state—came under increasing stress as protected markets established through the National Policy were giving way to more globalized ones governed by free trade agreements. Under these trade agreements, Ontario's economy has become more integrated with and dependent upon the economy of the United States. For example, in 1965 Canada signed the Auto Pact with the United States, removing tariffs on vehicles and auto parts crossing the border. Whereas before the Auto Pact there were a diversity of cars made by Ontario's auto industry and almost exclusively for the Canadian market, after the Auto Pact the Canadian and American auto industries were integrated, with the Ontario auto industry making fewer models, but with a much larger percentage now destined for the US market. The 1988 Canada-US Free Trade Agreement (FTA) and the 1994 North American Free Trade Agreement (NAFTA) further reoriented the Ontario economy away from an east-west trajectory toward a north-south trajectory. Contrary to the federal government of the day, Ontario's business community, and almost every other province, the Ontario government did not support the FTA or NAFTA, in part because of the economic vulnerability it believed the agreements would expose the province to given the volatility of international markets. Ontario's opposition can be interpreted as an attempt to protect manufacturing jobs that it rightly feared would migrate from Ontario to jurisdictions where workers earn lower wages. The opposition also had ideological underpinnings, with a Liberal premier in 1988 opposing a federal Conservative prime minister and an NDP premier in 1994 opposing an agreement developed under both Conservative and Liberal governments. But Ontario's opposition can also be viewed as defence of Ontario's position of economic privilege established by the old National Policy.[31]

In any case, the free trade era has reoriented the Ontario economy from east-west to north-south, removing the protected markets constructed through the National Policy. The vulnerability of the free trade environment meant that when a global recession hit in the early 1990s, Ontario's economy, now so entwined with the US economy, experienced a particularly deep recession. This era also coincides with the politics of fiscal restraint. There was a rising obsession with balancing budgets, eliminating deficits, and paying down debt. Beginning in the 1990s the federal government unilaterally reduced in various ways the overall amount of funding it delivered to provinces as a way to balance its own budget. The first major cut was the 1990 cap on Canada Assistance Plan payments (which in part funded provincial social assistance) to the "have" provinces of Ontario, British Columbia, and Alberta. Facing a recession, double digit unemployment, and an economy that did not rely in the same way as it once did on interprovincial trade, Ontario premier Bob Rae began the practice of calculating what Ontario put into the federation versus what it got out. This "balance-sheet federalism" calculating Ontario's fair share of transfers from Ottawa continued until the end of the Harper/Wynne era of federal-provincial relations. Rae's government commissioned 10 studies which calculated in great detail the benefits or lack thereof to Ontario of a full spectrum of federal-provincial fiscal arrangements.[32] Over the subsequent decades Ontario has consistently promoted per capita federal transfers outside of the equalization program. In other words, each province should receive from the federal government the same entitlement per person for immigration settlement, health care, postsecondary education, and so on. For example, the 2014 Ontario budget was full of references to the ways the federal government had shortchanged Ontario. Finance Minister Charles Sousa argued, "The federal government is indeed balancing its books on the backs of the hardworking people of this province. Since 2006, the federal government has taken more than 110 adverse unilateral actions against people and businesses across Ontario. In addition, each year, the share of the federal revenue raised in Ontario is significantly higher than the share of federal spending in Ontario. Our province contributes $11 billion more to the federal government than we receive in return—this represents about $850 per person in lost services."[33]

On the constitutional front, both premiers David Peterson (1985–90) and Rae (1990–95) resumed the Ontario tradition of presenting the province as playing neither a strictly federal nor provincial role, and instead brokering interests, particularly with an eye to accommodating Quebec. In the late 1980s Peterson exhausted vast political resources defending the Meech Lake Accord—the first major attempt to amend the Constitution to bring Quebec back into the constitutional fold following the patriation of the Constitution Act, 1982—even when there was considerable opposition to it among Ontarians.[34] Bob Rae played a leadership role in the Charlottetown negotiations that followed the failure of Meech Lake, advocating the position of federalists in Quebec, even when, at the outset of the negotiations, Quebec was not a participant. He also pursued the constitutional entrenchment of a "social charter" which would require the federal and provincial governments to provide medicare and minimum levels of housing, high quality primary and secondary school education, and other basic social needs.[35]

Even though he was decidedly to the right of his predecessor on the ideological spectrum, when Mike Harris became premier in 1995, he continued a similar path of "fair shares" federalism and a call for per capita transfers outside of equalization. He also continued the Ontario tradition of constructive engagement in intergovernmental negotiation. On the night the "no" side won by a very fine margin in the 1995 Quebec referendum, Harris offered support for continuing change, urging, "We have a collective duty to address how our federation might better serve all Canadians.... [A]long with Quebecers, Ontarians earnestly believe that the way the federation is managed must be substantially changed for the better."[36] However, during the Harris years, Ontario's role in intergovernmental deliberations pertaining to fiscal federalism and social policy shifted from one of working with the federal government to working with other provinces in the absence of any federal leadership.[37] In 1995 the federal government cut by one-third the value of the Canada Health and Social Transfer to provinces in an effort to balance its own budget, leaving provinces scrambling to provide the same quality and scope of postsecondary education, health care, and social services citizens expected. Ontario played a significant role in the work of the provincial/territorial Ministerial Council on Social Policy Renewal, which promoted the development of "national" policy crafted by premiers as opposed to federal policy imposed by Ottawa. This council also sought guarantees that provinces would never be surprised by a future similar cut to federal transfers. Ultimately, the federal government put forward a Social Union Framework Agreement, stemming the momentum behind the Ministerial Council on Social Policy Renewal. However, it is noteworthy that under Conservative leadership Ontario did not seek greater autonomy vis-à-vis the federal government for itself, but rather worked within new intergovernmental structures promoting interprovincial collaboration.

Like Harris, McGuinty sought interprovincial cooperation, particularly on the fiscal federalism front, establishing with his provincial counterparts the 2005 Advisory Panel of the Council of the Federation to make recommendations to equilibrate the "vertical fiscal imbalance." But during this era when all governments, including the federal government, were establishing their positions on the renegotiation of the equalization formula, Ontario also acted independently, and sometimes found itself isolated.[38] In 2005 Dalton McGuinty launched a campaign to close what his government called the $23-billion gap between what it calculated the province paid into the federation and what it got out, distinguishing in a very public way what it saw as the interests of Ontarians from the fiscal policies of the federal government. In 2008 McGuinty launched a website, fairness.ca, which sought to inform Ontarians, and presumably other Canadians, as well as those inside the federal government, of the billions of dollars Ontario was contributing to the federal equalization scheme. "It's our money," McGuinty was quoted as saying, inviting Canadians in Ontario to identify with their province and implying that Ontarians, not Canadians as a whole or the federal government, were the "owners" of this money: "Every once in a while, you've got to look after yourself, and we've got to do that in Ontario."[39] That same year, McGuinty supported, to the tune of $5 million, the creation of the Mowat Centre, an independent think tank housed at the University of Toronto. This centre commissions national and global research with a focus on the interests of Ontario, providing a counterpoint to organizations such as the Canada West Foundation, a Calgary-based think tank. The latter describes its role as "giv[ing] the people of British Columbia, Alberta, Saskatchewan and Manitoba a voice" in shaping the national agenda.[40] While Ontario has historically played the role of the reserved, stately broker of federal and provincial interests in many intergovernmental deliberations, the Mowat Centre is free to explicitly voice and promote policies in Ontario's interest. Thus, when we reflect overall on the position of the Rae, Harris, and McGuinty governments, the Wynne statements and tactics described at the outset of this chapter are in many ways not new, and demonstrate the continuation of an intergovernmental strategy by premiers of all parties driven not by ideology, but by a fundamentally reoriented north-south economy and by the context of fiscal restraint.

The New Ontario in an Era of Industrial Restructuring

Since 2009, Ontario has again found itself eligible for equalization. Unlike Pierre Trudeau, Stephen Harper did not reintroduce the "personal income override." The $347 million Ontario received as a "have-not" province in 2009–10 ballooned to $3.2 billion in 2012–13, before falling back to just under $2 billion in 2014–15 and most recently $2.4 billion in 2015–16.[41] In contrast to Bill Davis's support of the 1982 adjustment, Dalton McGuinty pleaded with the federal government *not* to change the equalization formula, likening the program to a national insurance scheme where "we are told we are only to be a contributor—and never a recipient." McGuinty argued, "It's our money.... For years, we made investments in other provinces so that they could grow stronger. Now what we're saying is we want to hold on to a bit more of that money."[42] Why did McGuinty take a position so dramatically different from Davis? The answer lies in the remarkable increases in the value of natural resources on the international market, the concentration of the royalties for those natural resources in specific provinces, and the implications of these increases for the calculation of equalization.

While the equalization formula has undergone many changes since 1957, a significant change took place in 2006. In brief, 50 per cent of the natural resource revenues were put back into the calculation of provincial capacity and the formula was based on an average of the fiscal capacity of all 10 provinces, rather than five. In these two respects, the formula is similar to the one that existed when Ontario became eligible for equalization in the Davis era. Also like the Davis era, in the last decade, until mid-2014, oil rose in value, with a barrel of oil fetching over $120 on the international market at its 2013 peak. But the distribution of "have" and "have-not" provinces had shifted considerably from that period in the early 1980s; provinces like Newfoundland and Labrador now had strong economies, and the West had become the economic engine of the country. Based on provincial per capita gross domestic product in 2014, one can cluster the provinces into two categories. Saskatchewan, Newfoundland and Labrador, and Alberta range from $63,345 per person (Newfoundland and Labrador) to $91,183 (Alberta). The other provinces range between $41,071 (Prince Edward Island) and $52,785 (Ontario).[43] In the last decade, Saskatchewan, Alberta, and Newfoundland have all enjoyed increased revenues from the sale of their natural resources at relatively high prices on the international market. Even with the more recent decline in oil prices, all are ineligible for payments according to the equalization formula. But another key difference from the Davis era is that there is no National Energy Policy allowing the federal government access to the revenues accrued from these natural resources. To pay equalization to the receiving provinces, the federal government relies primarily on regular tax revenues. Because Ontario's economy is not primarily based on natural resource extraction and is still strong, relatively speaking, the Ontario government argues that a disproportionate amount of revenue is collected by Ottawa from Ontario taxpayers to fund the equalization payments to other provinces. Under these circumstances, Ontario's acceptance of equalization payments has been one way to recoup some of the revenue exiting the province through federal taxation. It is also true that under these circumstances Ontario is still a net contributor to equalization, putting in more than it receives.

As Matthias Oschinski's chapter in this volume argues, Ontario's economy is undergoing a period of restructuring, and the province is not in a permanent state of decline. Similarly, Josh Hjartarson has argued that "a new Ontario is emerging, one that is at the centre of global networks of finance, trade, and commerce, with centres of global leadership in industries as diverse as food processing, asset management, infrastructure financing, business services and information technology."[44] Whether or not this is indeed the case, the point to be made here is that the National Policy–equalization equation of the 1950s no longer exists and this propels the Ontario mission to highlight how Ontario is "shortchanged." Since 1997, over a dozen free trade agreements have been negotiated or are pending, including several with South American countries and the Comprehensive Economic and Trade Agreement with the European Union. Ontario's manufacturing sector no longer has protected markets inside Canada, economic benefits are no longer concentrated in Central Canada, other provinces also have strong economies, even with a decline in oil prices, and yet still in place is the policy architecture created to remedy the provincial economic disparities emanating from the National Policy.

Is the Fair Shares/Ontario First Message Resonating?

In the free trade era, Ontario's intergovernmental relations have: (a) distinguished Ontario's interests from those of Ottawa; (b) emphasized an approach that highlights what, in dollar terms, Ontario puts into the federation compared to what it gets out; and (c) particularly in the McGuinty/Wynne years, included a call for major changes to the architecture of Canada's arrangements for income redistribution, including the equalization program. These measures could be interpreted as a return to the pre-1970s style of intergovernmentalism, in which Ontario was known for challenging Ottawa head-on. But what kind of results has "fair shares" federalism yielded Ontario?

Key cabinet ministers in the Conservative federal government did not attempt to mask their vitriol for the McGuinty and Wynne governments. The irony here is that key current and past federal cabinet ministers, including former finance minister Jim Flaherty, were part of the provincial Harris government that also touted fair shares federalism. Suffice to say, the 72 Ontario MPs, close to half of the Harper Conservative caucus, did not acknowledge Dalton McGuinty's request that they represent Ontario's interests (as the provincial Liberal government defined them) in matters of fiscal federalism.

There have been some noticeable "wins" for Ontario. Prime Minister Paul Martin did concede $6 billion to Ontario in 2005 through a variety of promises (some of which were not realized following his loss to Harper in 2006). In Harper's early days as prime minister he committed to per capita transfers for health care. When the global recession hit in 2009, Harper heeded the province's call not to balance his own budget by reducing transfers to provinces. The 2009 federal budget established the Federal Economic Development Agency (FEDDEV) for Southern Ontario to distribute $1 billion over five years. This agency can be seen as levelling the playing field, given that Southern Ontario was the only region in the country without such a "special needs scheme."[45]

At the same time, however, these actions can be interpreted primarily as driven by the federal Conservative government's own 2011 re-election interests in vote-rich Ontario, rather than as evidence that the discourse and pressure of fair shares federalism was resonating in Ottawa. On the key matter of health care transfers, Flaherty, without consultation with any province, announced in 2012 what amounted to a decline in federal support over the next 10 years. This kind of "hourglass federalism" in which "Ottawa starved the provinces in the sense that they have to divert discretionary spending from everywhere to feed the voracious appetite for medicare, so much so that citizens and cities were welcoming of any and all federal spending initiatives directed toward them," did not resolve Ontario's sense of unfair treatment.[46]

There is also little evidence in media discourse that the fair shares approach is resonating with Canadians as a whole; rather, Ontario is seen as pursuing an unjustified self-interest. Nor is it easy to find allies among the other provincial governments, in part because other provincial economies are not as diversified as Ontario's and thus they define their interests differently when it comes to sharing national wealth. Licia Corbella puts it less politely, identifying the fault line as oil. She describes Ontario in the *Calgary Herald* as an "ingrate" whose auto sector, in her view, was kept alive by Alberta's strong economy.[47] Perhaps more significantly, there is some glee in seeing Ontario, the prime beneficiary of the National Policy, as an "aging star athlete" struggling to "manage eroding abilities and avoid an embarrassing end."[48] There is some satisfaction in seeing "the flywheel of confederation, now officially a have-not province, sliding down all the league tables of achievement in education, job creation and personal income."[49]

There is also considerable scepticism that Ontario is truly suffering. In contrast to the GDP per capita measures above that show Ontario well below the energy-producing provinces in total income per person, the actual median family income for Ontarians in 2013 was $76,510, just shy of the national median of $76,550. Only Alberta, Saskatchewan, the Yukon, and the Northwest Territories had higher median family incomes.[50] It is no surprise, therefore, that one commentator observed in 2010 that Ontario's "poor man of Confederation" narrative was "not persuasive to Ontarians, let alone Albertans" as "there is a reason that immigrants flock to [Ontario's] southern metropolises—it's where the largest number of good jobs are found."[51] The message that outdated fiscal architecture is hurting Ontario appears to conflict with Ontario's simultaneous assertion that it has a vibrant, growing, "new" post-manufacturing economy.

Most intriguing is the changing receptiveness of Ontarians to the fair shares message. In 2005 McGuinty asserted that "Ontario remains—the heart of Canada.... No group identifies more closely with Canada than do Ontarians."[52] More recently, Martin Regg Cohn reasoned that "Ontarians are too quintessentially Canadian to hold a grudge against their federal government. Even when we're being pickpocketed, poked in the eye, shortchanged or double-crossed."[53] Indeed, polling data published by the Mowat Centre reveals that Ontarians, more than Canadians in any other region of the country, continue to identify with Canada more than their province. However, they are increasingly similar to other provinces when it comes to their evaluation of whether their region is treated fairly.[54] The report notes that in 2010 a majority (51 per cent) of Ontarians said that they were treated unfairly, up from 27 per cent in 2004. When compared to other provinces, Ontarians still stand out as less aggrieved. The West, Quebec, and the Atlantic provinces all hovered between a little less than 60 per cent and 75 per cent. Only 32 per cent of Ontarians reported that Ontario got less than its fair share of influence, compared to responses in the mid-60s for western provinces and mid-70s for Atlantic provinces. But, more so than in any other part of the country, Ontarians feel that their influence on important national decisions is decreasing. Regarding fiscal transfers, in 2001 just 37 per cent of Ontarians claimed the province received less than its fair share of federal dollars. In 2010 the figure was 63 per cent—roughly the same percentage as in the Atlantic and western provinces. It appears, then, that the fair shares message of Ontario's premiers just might be whittling away at Ontarians' traditional sense of identity. Ontarians are now more like Canadians in other provinces in their sense of dissatisfaction; they still identify firmly with Canada and, more than people in any other part of the country, they still feel they are treated fairly, but increasingly less so.

Time will tell whether the Liberal federal government elected in 2015 will be receptive to the Ontario government's fair shares mantra, or whether

Ontario will soften its fair shares focus. On the one hand, Kathleen Wynne's significant role in Justin Trudeau's Ontario campaign and the large Ontario contingent in the federal caucus suggest that Ottawa will be sympathetic. On the other, the national perception that Ontario is still a well-off province and the sluggishness of the Canadian economy in an era of lower prices for oil mean that Trudeau might have other, more immediate priorities.

Prior to hosting the premiers for the 2013 Council of the Federation meeting, Wynne asserted that "Ontarians are being shortchanged by outdated federal programs when we can least afford it.... Ontario is well positioned to build goodwill among the provinces by promoting evidence-based, principled reforms—a process I will lead as premier." The tenor of her finance minister's comments in July of 2014 also suggest a more country-wide approach. For example, in an article he authored in the *Financial Post* he argued that "deep and damaging cuts by the [then Conservative] federal government ... put all of our shared progress at risk."[55] The governments of Ontario and Quebec have also held joint cabinet meetings since Wynne became premier, stepping forward on climate change, interprovincial trade, and developing criteria for approving the Energy East pipeline. To the extent that Wynne succeeds in engaging her provincial counterparts and the new prime minister in an overhaul of the fiscal architecture for redistributing wealth in the federation, she will have succeeded in returning Ontario to its pre-Davis self: playing a leadership role within the federation, asserting an alternative vision to that of the federal government, all with an eye to the economic well-being of the federation as a whole. However, if Wynne fails to present a clear alternative vision for fiscal federalism that can be interpreted as not just in Ontario's interest, then Ontario will be that much further from its traditional position in intergovernmental relations.

Discussion Questions

1. How is Ontario traditionally perceived in intergovernmental relations?
2. How has Ontario's tenor in intergovernmental relations changed since the election of Bob Rae?
3. What are the economic factors that have contributed to the "fair shares" approach of Ontario governments?
4. If Ontario is a "have-not" province, why does it argue that it is not receiving its "fair share"?
5. How has the "fair shares" argument been perceived by (a) Ontarians, (b) the Harper federal government, and (c) other sources outside Ontario? Do you find this argument compelling?
6. Can Ontario still play its traditional role as broker of federal and provincial interests *and* pursue the "fair shares" strategy? Why or why not?

Notes

1   Nelson Wiseman, *In Search of Canadian Political Culture* (Vancouver: UBC Press, 2007), 187.
2   Tim Harper, "Harper-Wynne War Will Worsen," *Toronto* Star, 21 November 2014, A8.
3   Tim Harper, "Ontario, Ottawa in a Risky Game," *Toronto Star*, 27 January 2014, A4.
4   Robert Fisher, "Ontario Votes 2014: Kathleen Wynne Takes Aim at Ottawa, a Classic, Move," *CBC News*, 5 May 2014, www.cbc.ca/news/canada/toronto/ontario-votes-2014/ontario-votes-2014-kathleen-wynne-takes-aim-at-ottawa-a-classic-move-1.2631891
5   Charles Sousa, "Ontario Expects Fairness, Not Sad Rhetoric from Ottawa," *Financial Post*, 8 July 2014, http://business.financialpost.com/fp-comment/ontario-expects-fairness-not-sad-rhetoric-from-ottawa
6   Jim Flaherty cited in "Ontario's Fiscal Fairytale," *National Post*, 4 July 2014, A10.
7   David Reevely, "Interests of Ontario at Odds with Tories, Wynne Says: Fight with Harper's Government at Centre of Provincial Campaign," *Ottawa Citizen*, 9 May 2014, A2.
8   Kathleen Wynne, quoted in "Caught in the Crossfire," *Toronto Star*, 24 November 2014, A10.
9   For three federal elections in a row, Dalton McGuinty urged Ontarians to use an "Ontario filter" when voting, assessing which political party would best represent Ontario's interests.
10 Konrad Yakabuski, "Ontario Can No Longer Take One for the Team," *Globe and Mail*, 4 April 2013, http://www.theglobeandmail.com/opinion/ontario-can-no-longer-take-one-for-the-team/article10739658/
11 Robert Benzie, "Wynne, Harper Prepare for Tête-à-Tête," *Toronto Star*, 5 December 2013, A6.
12 Kelly McParland, "Ontario Needs Its Pride Back," *National Post*, 16 December 2014, A12.
13 See P.E. Bryden, *"A Justifiable Obsession": Conservative Ontario's Relations with Ottawa, 1943–1985* (Toronto: University of Toronto Press, 2013).
14 Hugh Segal, "The Evolution of Ontario's Confederal Stance in the Nineties: Ideology or Continuity?" in *Canada: The State of the Federation 2001: Canadian Political Culture(s) in Transition*, ed. Hamish Telford and Harvey Lazar (Montreal: McGill-Queen's University Press, 2002), 203. "Noblesse Oblige" translates as "Nobility Obliges."
15 Ontario Ministry of Finance, *Statement from Ontario Finance Minister Dwight Duncan at the Finance Ministers' Meeting*, 20 May 2008.
16 "McGuinty Fumes Over West's Success," *Regina Leader-Post*, 2 March 2012, A10.
17 Konrad Yakabuski, "How Ontario's Squeezing Other Have-Nots," *Globe and Mail*, 18 December 2014, A19.
18 P.E. Bryden, "Ontario Exceptionalism: Old Ideas in the New Ontario," in *Canada: The State of the Federation 2010: Shifting Power—The New Ontario and What It Means for Canada*, ed. Matthew Mendelsohn, Joshua Hjartarson, and James Pearce (Montreal: McGill-Queen's University Press, 2013), 41.

19 Hamish Telford, "BC as an Intergovernmental Relations Player: Still Punching Below Its Weight?" in *British Columbia Politics and Government*, ed. Michael Howlett, Dennis Pilon, and Tracy Summerville (Toronto: Emond Montgomery Publications, 2010).

20 Bryden, "Ontario Exceptionalism," 36.

21 Douglas M. Brown, "Fiscal Federalism: Maintaining a Balance?" in *Canadian Federalism: Performance, Effectiveness and Legitimacy*, 3rd ed., ed. Herman Bakvis and Grace Skogstad (Toronto: Oxford University Press, 2012), 118.

22 Matthew Mendelsohn, "Introduction: Accommodation of the New Ontario and Canada's New Narratives," in *Canada: The State of the Federation 2010: Shifting Power—The New Ontario and What It Means for Canada*, ed. Matthew Mendelsohn, Joshua Hjartarson, and James Pearce (Montreal: McGill-Queen's University Press, 2013), 5.

23 See P.E. Bryden, *"A Justifiable Obsession": Conservative Ontario's Relations with Ottawa, 1943–1985* (Toronto: University of Toronto Press, 2013).

24 Segal, "The Evolution of Ontario's Confederal Stance in the Nineties," 213.

25 Hugh Segal, *The Right Balance: Canada's Conservative Tradition* (Toronto: Douglas and McIntyre, 2011).

26 André Lecours and Daniel Béland, "Federalism and Fiscal Policy: The Politics of Equalization in Canada," *Publius* 40, no. 4 (2010): 569–96.

27 Alberta did, however, continue to receive equalization payments for several years after 1962 under a special guarantee provision.

28 John Ibbitson, *Loyal No More: Ontario's Struggle for a Separate Destiny* (Toronto: Harper Collins, 2001), 101.

29 David Cameron and Richard Simeon, "Ontario in Confederation: The Not-So-Friendly Giant," in *The Government and Politics of Ontario*, 5th ed., ed. Graham White (Toronto: University of Toronto Press, 1997), 158–85.

30 Thomas J. Courchene. "Fiscalamity! Ontario: From Heartland to Have-Not," *Policy Options* (June 2008), http://policyoptions.irpp.org/magazines/citizenship-and-immigration/fiscalamity-ontario-from-heartland-to-have-not/

31 Cameron and Simeon, "Ontario in Confederation."

32 Ibid.

33 Sousa, "Ontario Expects Fairness, Not Sad Rhetoric from Ottawa," http://business.financialpost.com/fp-comment/ontario-expects-fairness-not-sad-rhetoric-from-ottawa

34 Cameron and Simeon, "Ontario in Confederation."

35 See David P. Shugarman, "The Social Charter," in *Constitutional Politics: The Canadian Forum Book on Constitutional Proposals 1991–1992*, ed. Duncan Cameron and Miriam Smith (Toronto: James Lorimer and Company, 1992).

36 Cited in Segal, "The Evolution of Ontario's Confederal Stance in the Nineties," 213.

37 On this era of interprovincialism, see Peter Graefe and Julie M. Simmons, "Assessing the Collaboration That Was 'Collaborative Federalism' 1996–2006," *Canadian Political Science Review* 7 (2013): 25–36.

38 Matthew Mendelsohn, "Big Brother No More: Ontario's and Canada's Interests Are No Longer Identical," *Literary Review of Canada* (October 2010), http://reviewcanada.ca/magazine/2010/10/big-brother-no-more/

39 Lee Greenberg, "'Ontario Must Never Be Allowed to Collect Equalization': Federal Philosophy One of Worst Kept Secrets in Ottawa, McGuinty Says," *Ottawa Citizen*, 23 September 2008, A3.

40   Canada West Foundation, "About Us," http://cwf.ca/about-us/

41   Government of Canada, "Federal Support to Provinces and Territories," http://www.fin.gc.ca/fedprov/mtp-eng.asp#Ontario; Neil Reynolds, "In Ontario, 'Have Not' Means 'Have A Lot,'" *Globe and Mail*, 2 April 2012.

42   Greenberg, "Ontario Must Never Be Allowed to Collect Equalization," A3.

43   Government of Canada, "Provincial Economic Indicators," http://w03.international.gc.ca/Commerce_International/Province_Indicator-Indicateur.aspx?lang=eng

44   Josh Hjartarson, "Old Habits Die Hard: 'New' Ontario and the 'Old' Laurentian Consensus," in *Canada: The State of the Federation 2010: Canadian Political Culture(s) in Transition*, ed. Hamish Telford and Harvey Lazar (Montreal: McGill-Queen's University Press, 2002), 55.

45   Murray Campbell, "Harper and McGuinty on the Same Page—At Last," *Globe and Mail*, 29 January 2009, A8.

46   Thomas J. Courchene, "Alberta: The New Dominant Player in the Federation?" *Policy Options* (June 2007), http://policyoptions.irpp.org/magazines/nicolas-sarkozy-europe-2007/alberta-the-new-dominant-player-in-confederation/

47   Licia Corbella, "McGuinty Bites the Hand That Feeds Him," *Calgary Herald*, 29 February 2012. For more detail on this bailout, see Chapter 2 in this volume.

48   Don Butler, "The Times They Are a-Changin': Don Butler Looks at What This Week's Provincial and Federal Budgets Will Mean for Ontarians: It Seems the Day of Reckoning Is Here," *Ottawa Citizen*, 31 March 2012.

49   Robin V. Sears, "The Next Federal-Provincial Battles: This Time It's Different," *Policy Options* (May 2010), http://policyoptions.irpp.org/magazines/the-fault-lines-of-federalism/the-next-federal-provincial-battles-this-time-its-different/

50   Statistics Canada, "Median Total Income, by Family Type, by Province and Territory (All Census Families)," http://www.statcan.gc.ca/tables-tableaux/sum-som/l01/cst01/famil108a-eng.htm

51   Sears, "The Next Federal-Provincial Battles," http://policyoptions.irpp.org/magazines/the-fault-lines-of-federalism/the-next-federal-provincial-battles-this-time-its-different/

52   Cited in Robert Sibley, "Decline of the Empire: Once the Heartland of Confederation, Ontario's Influence in Canada Has Been Steadily Eroded," *Ottawa Citizen*, 29 September 2009, B1.

53   Martin Regg Cohn, "No Luck in Premier's Plight to Rally against Feds," *Toronto Star* 13 February 2014, A6.

54   Matthew Mendelsohn and J. Scott Matthews, *The New Ontario: The Shifting Attitudes of Ontarians toward the Federation* (Toronto: Mowat Centre for Policy Innovation, 2010).

55   Sousa, "Ontario Expects Fairness, Not Sad Rhetoric from Ottawa," http://business.financialpost.com/fp-comment/ontario-expects-fairness-not-sad-rhetoric-from-ottawa

PART 3

Politics

9

Media in Ontario Politics: The Press Gallery in the Twenty-First Century

TAMARA A. SMALL

T HIS CHAPTER FOCUSES ON THE PRESS GALLERY IN ONTARIO. Within Westminster parliamentary systems, the press gallery is a group of accredited journalists that cover the activities of Parliament. In thinking about politics and government in Ontario, why should we concern ourselves with such an institution? It is important to remember that like political parties, governments, and political organizations, the news media are political actors in democratic political systems. As Brian McNair points out, the news media "function both as transmitters of political communication which originates outside the media organisation itself, and as senders of political messages constructed by journalists."[1] Today, the news media consist of broadcasting (television and radio), newspapers, and online media outlets. The democratic importance of the press stems from the fact that most of what citizens know about politics comes from the news media. Few citizens engage directly with politics. Most citizens gain information about politics and form opinions about it by watching television news, listening to the radio, or reading newspapers. This information is crucial to democratic citizenship. Without information, citizens cannot effectively evaluate political options. The news media are a crucial source of political information. They are also watchdogs of the political system, scrutinizing the actions of politicians and policymakers and requiring them to account for decisions. The democratic importance of the media is entrenched in section 2 of the Charter of Rights and Freedoms. Moreover, the news media are important targets of political actors. Attaining positive coverage is a crucial goal of the government and opposition parties as well as other political organizations including interest groups. Therefore, the Ontario press gallery are "an essential part" of Ontario's political system,[2] and much of what we know about Ontario politics comes from their reporting and commentary.

Media consumption is directly related to political knowledge. Elisabeth Gidengil and colleagues have found that the more attention Canadians pay to the media, irrespective of media type, the more knowledgeable they are about politics.[3] Today, there are a multitude of options when it comes to news consumption. Technological changes, including cable, satellite, and digital technologies, have extended what is available to consumers. Rather than a few sources such as the *Globe and Mail* or CBC dominating the media landscape, news audiences are increasingly fragmented. Although the news habits of Canadians (and Ontarians) are changing due to technological developments, traditional and mainstream media organizations remain important. Indeed, when asked about daily news consumption, television news continues to dominate. Christopher Waddell found in a 2012 survey that 40 per cent of Canadian respondents watched television news every day. However, news on the Internet was becoming a serious competitor at 32 per cent, and only 20 per cent of Canadians read printed news daily.[4] Similar findings were found in Ontario during the 2011 provincial election. When asked how much attention they paid to news about the provincial election on various media, respondents paid most attention to television, followed by newspapers (on- and offline) and the Internet.[5] Waddell also found that almost 35 per cent of Canadian respondents often went directly to the website of a newspaper or television or radio network when searching for online news. Alternative news websites, such as the *Huffington Post*, were used regularly by only 7 per cent of respondents. Despite the Internet era, the traditional media as sources of news for Canadians continue to dominate, though how the news is delivered and consumed is changing.

While there is a considerable body of research on the news media at the federal level, there is less at the provincial. The work of Frederick Fletcher[6] defines our understanding of the media in Ontario politics, especially regarding the press gallery.[7] However, much has changed in the media environment since the publication of Fletcher's last piece in 1997; perhaps the most notable change to political communication is the arrival of the Internet. Another important and related change in Canada's media environment is media concentration. While this is not a new phenomenon, Canada has one of the highest levels of concentrations of media ownership in industrial countries.[8] Indeed, as of 2012, eight corporations owned the majority of Canada's media,[9] including many outlets in Ontario. Torstar, for instance, owns numerous papers including the *Toronto Star*, *Hamilton Spectator*, and *Metro* (the last a free daily with Toronto and Ottawa editions). Continuing on from the work of Fletcher, this chapter explores the media in Ontario politics with a focus on the press gallery in the twenty-first century. First, the chapter reflects on the current press gallery and how it goes about covering Ontario politics. It then goes on to explore the implications of changes to the media environment in which Ontario politics operates. The chapter is based on documents about the press gallery and interviews with four journalists currently covering Ontario politics: Maria Babbage (The Canadian Press), Robert Benzie (*The Toronto Star*), Christina Blizzard (*The Toronto Sun*), and Andrew Reeves (*QP Briefing*). In a number of ways, Ontarians are well served by the press gallery coverage of Queen's Park. However, we will also see that the diminishing size of the gallery raises a number of democratic concerns.

Press Gallery of the Legislative Assembly of Ontario

At Queen's Park, politics are covered by the Press Gallery of the Legislative Assembly of Ontario, which consists of accredited journalists and camera people from newspaper, magazine, broadcast, and Internet organizations. The press gallery reports on the activities of not only the Legislature and committees, but also the premier, the cabinet, and the public service. Many gallery members cover election campaigns in the province as well. The gallery operates as an independent organization within the Office of the Legislative Assembly. As noted, the press gallery is the central link between Ontarians and the government and Legislature, thereby serving a number of democratic functions. The interviewees from the press gallery are fully aware of this role; Maria Babbage, of The Canadian Press, puts it this way: "Our role is to hold the government to account and inform the public, in as understandable a way as possible, what happens here and how it will affect them."[10]

As part of their daily work, members of the gallery watch and report on legislative debates in the chamber, including oral question period, held each morning when the Legislature is sitting. According to Graham White, "Question period is arguably the most significant proceeding of the Ontario legislature."[11] As discussed in Chapter 5, one reason that question period is so essential stems from the principle of responsible government, which requires the government to maintain the support of the Legislature to govern. Oral questions permit opposition MPPs to scrutinize the actions of the executive, and question period thereby provides an accountability mechanism. In addition, question period attracts considerable attention of the news media, and consequently citizens who regularly watch or read the news.[12] Indeed, it has been estimated that 80 per cent of news stories on Ontario politics originate from question period.[13] Question period, in Ontario and elsewhere, makes for good television.[14] This said, the nature of question period and the amount of coverage it receives are of concern to many who worry about the potentially negative effects it has on citizens who watch their political leaders hurling insults and heckling one another each night on the evening news.

Another important aspect of the gallery's job is to interview political actors in media scrums or press conferences. Scrums, which can be either impromptu or organized in advance, occur when reporters from different media organizations surround a politician and ask questions. Scrums take place at the end of debates in the Legislature when politicians leave the chamber to return to their offices. Key targets include the premier, cabinet ministers, opposition leaders, and the shadow cabinet. For print journalists, scrums may serve as supplementary material for a story. For television reporters, the scrum may provide the image of the day.

The press gallery is not merely a group of reporters; it is a formal association with a constitution, elected executive, and accredited membership. Membership provides access to areas of the Legislature that are off limits to the general public. Accredited journalists have their own gallery on the south side of the chamber to watch debates. Members can access the library and the press gallery lounge, and active members have offices on the third floor of the Legislative Assembly. The gallery operates the media studio, where most press conferences are held. The media studio provides a "neutral location" for the government, the opposition, MPPs, and interest groups to communicate with the press gallery. The executive also represents the membership regarding their relationship with the Office of the Legislative Assembly. The Legislative Press Gallery is supported by the Press Gallery Coordinator. An employee of the Office of the Legislative Assembly, the Press Gallery Coordinator liaises between politicians and the media. Tasks include sending out emails to MPPs and gallery members regarding media events, maintaining the media studio, and providing some clerical assistance.

Press–Politician Relations in Ontario

Here, we explore the relationship between the press gallery and politicians at Queen's Park. Newsmaking is an ongoing power struggle between politicians and reporters.[15] Politicians seek "the delivery to voters of as full and unchallenged versions of their messages as possible,"[16] while reporters seek to control the framing and content of news stories. Until the 1960s, journalists and the government had a very "cosy relationship,"[17] where gallery members often had partisan ties, and some were even advisors to politicians. This changed, however, by the 1970s. While federally the relationship between the gallery and politicians has always been strained, this description has not and does not reflect the relations at Queen's Park.

From Pierre Trudeau onwards, relations between the Canadian Parliamentary Press Gallery (CPPG) and Canadian prime ministers have never been overly harmonious. However, shortly after the Conservative Party took office in 2006, relations between the CPPG and the Prime Minister's Office imploded. The communication staff ceased publicizing cabinet and caucus meeting times and barred the reporters from the corridor outside the cabinet room, which limited scrums.[18] They also began choosing which reporters could ask questions at press conferences based on a pre-assigned list. Finally, the party moved to using alternative communication channels to circumvent the CPPG.[19] However, relations between Prime Minister Justin Trudeau and the CPPG appear to be far less acrimonious in the first year of the Liberal government.

With few exceptions, such characterizations are not reflective of Queen's Park. According to *QP Briefing*'s Andrew Reeves, there is a very "open system" of press relations in Ontario.[20] Gallery members do not cite having access to the premier, cabinet ministers, opposition leaders, and backbenchers as a problem. Moreover, there are no limitations on who can ask questions in a scrum, and ministers continue to participate in them. Indeed, both Babbage and Reeves spoke of staffers from all three parties visiting the offices of reporters on a regular basis to inform them about what was occurring within the parties. For Babbage, such regular, personal interactions made possible by sharing the same building are important in the maintenance of a good relationship.

A positive relationship does not mean a cozy relationship. There will "always be tensions and there should be," says the *Toronto Star*'s Queen's Park Bureau Chief Robert Benzie.[21] For instance, in 2009, communication staff instituted a "five-foot buffer" during scrums with then-premier Dalton McGuinty. Reporters were asked to stand at least five feet from McGuinty when asking questions. The goal, according to the premier's aides, was to make the scrums "more civilized."[22] Not surprisingly, the gallery was less than impressed with this rule.[23] Occasionally the McGuinty Liberals planned "media avails a long way from Queen's Park,"[24] making it more difficult for the gallery to cover particular events. This said, for the most part, the interviewees accept this as part of the job.

Another factor in characterizing press–politician relations is the cycle of a government. Several of the interviewees point out that things were a bit more difficult near the end of McGuinty's tenure, while the Kathleen Wynne government was quite accessible to reporters in its "honeymoon" phase. Despite expected tensions and difficulties, the relationship between the Ontario press gallery and political parties is a good one. In Ontario, unlike the federal arena, the gallery does not feel that the government is attempting to thwart its ability to perform their public education and watchdog roles. As Reeves puts it, responses by politicians at Queen's Park "may not necessarily be what we want or what we are looking for or that satisf[y] the question that we asked. But at the very least calls don't go ignored, and there is no kind of unnecessary process to go through." Such a characterization could hardly describe what took place in Ottawa in the same period.

Table 9.1 Queen's Park Press Gallery (as of August 2015)

Active Members	Members	Vacant
Newspapers	17	1
Radio	5	0
Television	10	4
Total	32	5
Associate Members	22	0

Source: Press Gallery Coordinator.

Implications of a Diminishing Press Gallery in Ontario

Here, we take a closer look at the membership of the Legislative Press Gallery and explore the democratic implications of its current size and composition. As of August 2015, there were 32 active Ontario Press Gallery members (Table 9.1). According to their constitution, active members are journalists, photographers, camera persons and sound persons who cover Queen's Park on a permanent basis and require the use of gallery facilities to perform their work. These 32 active members represent a total of 18 different news organizations (Table 9.2). There were also 22 associate members, assigned to Queen's Park on a part-time basis.[25]

Given the importance of press galleries to political communication, there are some concerns about the size and the composition of the current gallery.[26] Indeed, when asked to characterize the press gallery in 2013, several of the interviewees, unprompted, noted the small size and declining membership as a key factor. Table 9.3 shows the size of the press gallery as reported by Fletcher. Since 1995, there is a notable decline in membership. Even if the current cohort was operating at full capacity, the gallery would still have

Table 9.2 News Organizations with Active Members in Queen's Park Press Gallery (as of August 2015)

Newspapers/Press Services	Radio	Television
Canadian Press (2)	CBC Radio (1)	CBC Television (1)
Toronto Star (4)	CFRB (2)	Global Television (1)
Globe and Mail (2)	680News (1)	CTV Ontario (1)
Toronto Sun (3)	Radio-Canada/CJBC (1)	CHCH (1)
Sing Tao Daily (1)		TVOntario (2)
QP Briefing (4)		CityTV (1)
National Post (1)		TFO (1)

Table 9.3 Queen's Park Press Gallery Membership

1975	40
1979	40
1984	37
1989	52
1995	52
2015	32 (5)

Source: Fletcher (1975, 1980, 1985, 1990, 1997) as detailed in note 27 below.

15 fewer members than it did in the 1990s. The number of vacancies remind us that high turnover has been and continues to be an issue in the Ontario press gallery.[27]

Perhaps the shrinking press gallery should not be a surprise. As noted earlier, the media environment is changing due to factors such as growth of digital technologies and greater concentration of media organizations. For instance, there is the so-called decline of newspapers. Internet growth has negatively affected newspapers by cutting into readership and advertising revenue,[28] resulting in layoffs and buyouts.[29] The decline should not be over-stated or interpreted as a decline in news consumption. Rather, consumers are eschewing the printed product and opting to get their news online. However, a majority of Canadians are unwilling to pay for online news,[30] and this contributes to substantial financial problems for media organizations. Given that newspapers have always dominated press gallery membership in Ontario, the decline of newspapers is an issue. It is not that Ontario politics has become less relevant to journalists; it is more likely that newsrooms are simply getting smaller.

This decline has a number of potential consequences for the quality and perhaps even the quantity of coverage of Ontario politics. First, with so few bureaus and so many bureaus with a single reporter, there may be a tendency for reportage to focus on the centre—the premier's office and the cabinet.[31] Given the importance of the premier and the cabinet to public affairs, it is not surprising that journalists would gravitate to them. However, some see the potential for reporters to look for different angles or to speak to back-bench MPPs decreasing. For instance, Jim Coyle writes, "MPPs will spend their entire term without seeing a notepad or microphone in their vicinity or their name in the paper."[32] However, one interviewee appears less concerned about this. Robert Benzie sees backbenchers as valuable sources, especially in a minority government: "I talk to MPPs from all three parties all the time because they want to tell me what is going on in their ridings. ... I like to talk to them because they like to talk to me." If coverage of MPPs is minimal, it is more plausible that this is a function of the limited role backbenchers play in Canadian politics (at both the provincial and federal levels) rather than of changes in the press gallery.

Another consequence is that smaller regional or local news outlets have almost completely disappeared from the press gallery. For instance, while there were 34 daily newspapers operating in the province in 2011,[33] only five have Queen's Park bureaus (Table 9.2). This means only 15 per cent of Ontario newspapers are represented in the gallery. There are several regional news organizations that were once a part of the press gallery but are no longer, including television stations such as CFPL (London) and CKCO (Kitchener) and newspapers such as the *London Free Press* and *Hamilton Spectator*. CHCH (Hamilton) is now the only regional member. Northern Ontario has no representation at all. Interestingly, the regional decline was identified by three of the interviewees without prompting when asked to characterize the current press gallery. Indeed, Benzie wonders whether "readers in other communities are getting the same level of coverage that they used to get."

Leslie De Meulles argues that this decline means that smaller news outlets may rely on communication materials created by MPPs, such as direct mail and press releases.[34] This is certainly of concern given that MPPs' communications are decidedly partisan and cannot serve as a proper replacement for neutral and objective journalism. However, the regional decline does not necessarily mean that regional papers and stations do not feature stories on Ontario politics. Many do. It is just that coverage of Queen's Park has been consolidated within media organizations. As noted, there is a high level of media concentration in Canada. Articles, editorials, and news footage written or produced by bureaus of the large news organizations may filter down to smaller sister organizations. Other newspapers may print articles written by The Canadian Press.

One implication of this consolidation could be that reportage has become Toronto-centric. Most of the major news organizations in the press gallery are now based in Ontario's largest city. Of this, *Toronto Star* reporter Jim Coyle has said, "I don't have a Hamilton perspective. I'm an east Toronto guy, working for a Toronto paper, and that's what I write about. The interests of Hamilton are not at the top of my mind most days when I'm writing."[35] Christina Blizzard offers a different perspective. A columnist with the *Toronto Sun*, Blizzard's articles appear in newspapers across the province. As such, she feels that Toronto-based reporters have been forced to branch out and pay attention to regional issues. She describes this as a "new awareness" within the gallery that other regions need to be served by their reporting. However,

Benzie feels that Queen's Park has always been "biased towards Toronto" given the number of Toronto-based MPPs and the city's population. But the issues addressed by the Assembly, such as health and education, are province-wide. Another concern about the diminishing size of the gallery related to the consolidation of media is the limited number of voices covering Ontario politics. As noted, Christina Blizzard's column or Canadian Press stories can be found in newspapers all over the province. The fact that one reporter writes for such a broad audience means that there are fewer perspectives on Ontario politics being written. Regardless of the quality of each story, there is limited diversity. For Kelly Blidook, this lack of voice does "not serve the ideals of democracy" well.[36]

Another observation gleaned from the composition of the Ontario press gallery is that it is mainly an English-language organization. Ontario is Canada's most diverse province. It boasts the largest francophone community in Canada outside of Quebec, with 4.8 per cent of the population according to the 2011 Census.[37] Indigenous peoples make up about 2 per cent of Ontario's population. Almost 30 per cent of Ontarians are foreign born while 26 per cent are visible minorities.[38] More than 140 languages and dialects are spoken in Toronto.[39] The landscape of ethnic media across Canada is extensive; in 2007 there were more than 250 ethnic newspapers, 40 television, and 60 Canadian mainstream radio stations that offered ethnically targeted programming,[40] and many are based in Canada's large cities such as Toronto. Nevertheless, this diversity is only minimally represented in the Ontario press gallery. *Sing Tao Daily*, a Chinese-language newspaper, is the only ethnic media organization with a full-time member. Some of the associate members represent Indigenous, Chinese, Indian, and Italian media organizations. Part-time members typically cover Queen's Park during special events such as the Speech from the Throne and/or the budget. While ethnic media offer a number of functions to subscribers and viewers, the National Ethnic Press and the Media Council of Canada highlight a key political role: the ethnic media help to introduce "democratic institutions and the new way of living."[41] As such, Ontario's diversity is not particularly well served by the current composition of the gallery.

It is not all bad news when it comes to the size and composition of the gallery. One notable change is the arrival of *Queen's Park Briefing* (*QP Briefing*) in 2011. This was a change not only in size, but also in the nature of reporting. Part of Torstar, *QP Briefing* is a daily subscription-based digital newsletter. Unlike traditional media outlets, *QP Briefing* targets a specialized audience within public and private organizations that deal regularly with the Ontario government. Its reporting delves into the "nitty-gritty"[42] of Queen's Park, including attending and reporting on all legislative committees, exploring issues that would not be of interest to the mass audiences of traditional news organizations. It has one of the largest bureaus in the gallery, with four active members—more than the *Globe and Mail* or The Canadian Press. While *QP Briefing* is a positive story, given that it speaks to a specialized audience, this highlights again how limited the press gallery is in providing broad-based news on Ontario politics.

In speaking of the size and composition of the press gallery in the late 1980s, White noted that "many members of the press gallery must cover virtually all aspects of Ontario government and politics: this allows little time for specialization, detailed research, or thoughtful analysis, let alone investigative journalism."[43] If this was the case, then the current small membership of the legislative press gallery is even more of a democratic concern. In addition to the issue that reporters must attempt to cover all aspects of Ontario politics, there are also concerns about the diversity of regional and ethnic voices in coverage about government and the Legislature. Moreover, there is a potential impact on the quantity of coverage of Ontario politics, with fewer stories being published or produced. While there is little doubt that the individual press gallery members are professional and diligent in their reportage of Queen's Park, as a whole, however, Ontario may not be as well served as it once was.

Mediums and the Media

Even though more Canadians get news from television than from other formats, including newspapers and the Internet,[44] newspapers dominate the coverage of Queen's Park, in terms of the strength of their bureaus (Table 9.2) as well as their ability to set the media agenda.[45] As Benzie puts it, newspapers "rule the roost" in Ontario compared to Ottawa, where television dominates reporting of the federal government. The *Toronto Star* is probably the most important media actor in Ontario. The *Star* is Canada's largest daily newspaper, reaching the largest audience in Ontario. In 2013, the paper edition had more than 1 million readers a day.[46] Indeed, the *Star*'s outreach surpasses most major television channels.[47] For instance, the Saturday edition of the paper reaches over 50,000 more people than CBC News Network does over the course of a week. The online edition of the *Star* is more popular than the *Globe and Mail* and the *National Post*. Moreover, the *Toronto Star* devotes more attention to provincial affairs than other papers. Overall, it has considerable agenda-setting abilities within the province.

There is only one television program covering Ontario politics: *Focus Ontario*. Appearing on Saturdays on Global TV, *Focus Ontario* is a half-hour public affairs show hosted by Alan Carter (an active member of the Press

Gallery). In 2006, TVOntario cancelled the long-running program *Studio 2*. The program included a Queen's Park segment called "4th Reading," which featured a panel of veteran Ontario politicians from the three major political parties who analyzed provincial politics. The cancellation of *Studio 2* caused a bit of controversy given that the program was quite popular, reaching about 1 million viewers a week.[48] To be sure, the loss of the program was a blow to province-wide discussion and analysis of Ontario politics. However, Ontario politics still is important on TVO. *Studio 2* was replaced by *The Agenda with Steve Paikin*, which has a more national focus, although host Paikin remains an active member of the Ontario gallery. As one of the most knowledge-able commentators on Ontario politics, Paikin has written two books on Ontario premiers and moderated the Ontario leaders' debates in 2007, 2011, and 2014. Also, when the Legislature is in session, TVOntario produces an online weekly show called *Queen's Park This Week*, which provides an executive summary of the issues debated in question period that week.

Proceedings of the Legislative Assembly are also aired on television through ONT.PARL, the Ontario Legislative Television Satellite Network. On the advice of the Ontario Commission of the Legislative Assembly, or Camp Commission, television cameras were allowed in the chamber in 1976. Fletcher found this had little notable impact on the coverage of Queen's Park.[49] In 1986, ONT.PARL was established. When the Legislature is in session, ONT.PARL provides daily coverage of the chamber's business, committee meetings, and important press conferences in both official languages. It is broadcast to many Ontarians across the province on cable and is also available within Queen's Park on a closed-circuit television system.

One big change to the media environment is the Internet and related digital technologies. In addition to ONT.PARL, the Legislative Assembly began webcasting its proceedings in 2008. Ontario was slower than the federal government in introducing parliamentary webcasting,[50] as the House of Commons introduced ParlVU in 2004. In Ontario, the opposition Progressive Conservatives initially suggested the idea in hopes of making politics more accessible, citing diminishing coverage of Ontario politics as an important factor.[51] The webcast provides live streaming of all proceedings plus all committee meetings held in Room 151. The site also provides an eight-day archive of question period.

Widespread adoption of the Internet has changed the political communication environment and rewritten the rules and conventions of newsmaking.[52] David Tewksbury and Jason Rittenberg suggest the Internet changes the relationship between news producers and audiences in a number of ways.[53] First, news organizations and journalists are now forced to interact with audiences in a way that did not exist in the era of broadcasting.

Second, audiences are no longer merely consumers of news but producers. Finally, audiences also now have greater control over the news. Whereas news organizations controlled the news agenda in the broadcasting era, audiences can choose "the sites, stories, posts and images they prefer."[54] This has dramatically changed the consumption of news. As noted earlier, there is some evidence of this as the Internet is an important source of news for Ontarians.

As we have seen, the Internet has allowed for the entry of new players into the press gallery. *QP Briefing* has no offline print component. Although not a part of the gallery, another digital media player is ontarionewswatch. com. In addition to aggregating news stories from outlets across the province, Ontario News Watch also produces original content by a small staff, and contributors include a former premier and former cabinet ministers.

The job of journalists has also changed because of digital technologies.[55] For journalists, the Internet "speeds it up and spreads it thin."[56] That is, journalists need to do more in less time. Fenton notes that reporters are no longer simply writing or producing stories for a single daily edition or program.[57] They are also writing for the online editions, using Twitter and, due to the quality of mobile technology, some journalists become videographers and photographers. We find evidence of this change in the current press gallery. Blizzard notes the "change to our jobs has been really, really significant, and we are probably doing 100% more work than we were doing before and we weren't really slackers before." Benzie concurs that due to website and social media such as Facebook and Twitter, "we have a whole new media to feed." Both Blizzard and Benzie suggest that the Internet, in some ways, is a return to the old days when newspapers had more than one edition and journalists would file a story twice a day; except now, journalists might file a story several times a day.

More specifically, Twitter is playing a large role for news organizations worldwide and in Ontario. In addition to the news organization they worked for, all but three (active) Ontario press gallery members operated a Twitter feed in 2015. More than 185,000 people follow at least one member of the gallery.[58] TVOntario's Steve Paikin leads with more than 65,900 followers. Other Queen's Park journalists and columnists with Twitter clout and influence are Jane Taber (*Globe and Mail*), Robert Benzie (*Toronto Star*), and Paul Bliss (CTV), who each have more than 10,000 followers. In addition to regular Ontarians, MPPs, political parties, municipalities, think tanks, and other journalists are followers of these accounts. Queen's Park tweets will also be found on the main news organization feeds and websites. These tweets have the potential to reach large numbers of Ontarians interested in politics.

According to Paul Farhi, journalists and news organizations have adopted Twitter because "its speed and brevity make it ideal for pushing out scoops and breaking news to Twitter-savvy readers."[59] Live-tweeting has become a commonplace practice within the gallery. Live-tweeting is the sequence of focused tweets around a specific event. Interviewees point out that legislative debates, press conferences, and scrums are now regularly live-tweeted at Queen's Park. The following is an example of live-tweeting by the *Globe and Mail's* Adam Radwanski of a speech by Liberal Finance Minister Charles Sousa at the Economic Club of Canada in April 2013:

> 12:21 pm Sousa's speech hints at scaling back corporate tax credits and more income testing for personal ones, notably the Clean Energy Benefit.
>
> 12:24 pm I wrote at more length on the income testing possibility a little while ago. m.theglobeandmail.com/news/politics/
>
> 12:31 pm Sousa has nothing if not a soothing way of speaking, which I suppose could come in handy for a Finance Minister.
>
> 12:49 pm FWIW, I'd argue the clean energy benefit should've been means tested all along. It actually disproportionately helps higher earners now.
>
> 12:56 pm Sounds like maybe Sousa is talking more about what happens with energy benefit once it expires in a couple years.
>
> 1:07 pm That was confusing. Under pressure, Sousa said 10% benefit will remain on hydro bills. Guessing he meant *some* hydro bills.

As we can see from the example, Twitter allows journalists to provide up-to-the-minute details and analysis on a political event. Also, the use of Twitter by reporters allows information to enter the public sphere that would not normally make the daily edition or the evening news broadcast; according to one, "You can get a lot [of] the trivia and notebooks items, those types of things you might not have written about in the past. In this way it's a good thing for the public; it's like a public service announcement. There's a lot more coverage of Queen's Park." Twitter may also help push Internet traffic to the websites of new organizations.[60] This is evident in the Radwanski example, where in the second tweet he links a related story from March 2013 on the *Globe's* website. Babbage notes at the "most basic level Twitter can be used to direct people to our stories online which is helpful to our news organizations because they want people clicking on the stories and reading them."

In summary, the Internet and particularly Twitter have changed how the reporters in the Ontario press gallery do their jobs. Perhaps Christina Blizzard sums it up best when she says, "How we do things now is we tweet, then we post to the Internet and then we write for the newspaper." In some ways, the Internet and Twitter might compensate for the declining size of the press gallery, for Ontarians now have more ways of getting more and different types of information about politics. As noted, online news websites are growing in popularity with Ontarians. While we know little about how Canadians use Twitter politically, American research shows that those who use social media as an outlet for political engagement are far more active in traditional realms of political participation than other Internet users.[61] This implies that social media does not dramatically change levels of the engagement though it is rather useful for political junkies. However, more research into the Canadian context is needed.

Conclusion

This chapter began highlighting the democratic role of the news media. In Frederick Fletcher's last analysis, his co-author Rose Sottile and he conclude on a positive note: "When provincial politics is not adequately covered, the democratic process suffers. Governments have less reason to be responsive to public needs and preferences. The governing party benefits greatly from the media neglect, since few Ontarians would know about government blunders without the media. Thus, the current higher levels of attention is to be welcomed."[62] What can we conclude this time around? Based on this analysis, there are some reasons to be optimistic about the news media within Ontario politics, but there are also some democratic concerns.

From the interviews with journalists, it is clear that Ontarians are well served by a highly professional and dedicated group of journalists and camera people at Queen's Park. The legislative press gallery is filled with individuals who are highly committed to their role as educators about Ontario politics and watchdogs on political actors. These journalists work hard, engaging with a number of media platforms to fulfil these roles. Second, Ontarians are well served by the positive relationship that the press gallery has with the politicians. To be sure, the relationship between the press and politicians should never be as cozy as it was in an earlier era described above. But unlike the federal arena, Queen's Park is a venue in which both the news media and politicians can attempt to influence the public agenda. Third, we see the Internet can have an enormous impact on the work of politicians, including those in the Ontario press gallery. Canadians, and accordingly Ontarians, are moving online for political news. The news media are meeting these needs by providing content in a variety of media. And those on social media are getting up-to-the-minute content and analysis of Ontario politics.

Changing dynamics including new technologies and media concentration have affected the size of the gallery and therefore the quantity and quality of news about Queen's Park. As we have seen, there is limited regional and ethnic participation in the gallery. We have to question how well regions outside of the Greater Toronto Area such as Northern Ontario and ethnic communities are being served by the overall coverage of Queen's Park. If information is central to democratic participation and the news media are one of the main purveyors of that information, the decline of the press gallery of Ontario is of concern.

Discussion Questions

1. What is the optimal size of the Press Gallery of Ontario?
2. Does it matter if the Press Gallery is not representative of Ontario's regional and ethnic diversity? Why or why not?
3. How have digital technologies, including social media, changed political communication in Ontario?
4. Have you ever watched ONT.PARL or the webcast of Queen's Park? Why or why not?
5. What type of relationship should a press gallery have with politicians?

Notes

1 Brian McNair, *An Introduction to Political Communication*, 3rd ed. (London: Routledge, 2007), 12.
2 Frederick J. Fletcher, "The Crucial and the Trivial: News Coverage of Provincial Politics," in *The Government and Politics of Ontario,* 4th ed., ed. Graham White (Toronto: Nelson Canada, 1990), 190.
3 Elisabeth Gidengil, André Blais, Neil Nevitte, and Richard Nadeau, *Citizens* (Vancouver, BC: UBC Press, 2004).
4 Christopher Waddell, "Engaging the Public through Social Media" (paper presented to the Democracy in the 21st Century Conference, Toronto, 2012).
5 William Cross, Jonathan Malloy, Tamara A. Small, and Laura Stephenson, *Fighting for Votes: Parties, the Media and Voters in an Ontario Election* (Vancouver: UBC Press, 2015).
6 Frederick. J. Fletcher, "Between Two Stools: News Coverage of Provincial Politics in Ontario," in *Government and Politics of Ontario*, ed. Donald C. MacDonald (Toronto: Macmillan Company of Canada, 1975), 248–69; Frederick. J. Fletcher, "The Crucial and the Trivial: News Coverage of Provincial Politics," in *The Government and Politics of Ontario*, 2nd ed., ed. Donald C. MacDonald (Toronto: Van Nostrand Reinhold, 1980), 245–71; Frederick J. Fletcher, "The Crucial and the Trivial: News Coverage of Provincial Politics," in *The Government and Politics of Ontario*, 3rd ed., ed. Donald C. MacDonald (Toronto: Nelson Canada, 1985), 192–218; Frederick J. Fletcher, "The Crucial and the Trivial," in *The Government and Politics of Ontario*, 4th ed., ed. Graham White (Toronto: Nelson Canada, 1990), 189–214; Frederick J. Fletcher and Rose Sottile, "Spinning Tales: Politics and News in Ontario," in *The Government and Politics of Ontario*, 5th ed., ed. Graham White (Toronto: University of Toronto Press, 1997), 236–67.

7   See Fred Cutler, "One Voter, Two First-Order Elections?" *Electoral Studies* 27, no. 3 (2008): 492–504; Kirsten Kozolanka, *The Power of Persuasion: The Politics of the New Right in Ontario* (Montreal: Black Rose Press, 2007); P.G. Watson and C. Greiffenhagen, "On Press Scrums: Some Preliminary Observations," in *Media, Policy and Interaction*, ed. Richard Fitzgerald and William Housely (London: Ashgate, 2009), 115–33; Tamara A. Small, "At the Races: The *Toronto Star*'s Coverage of the 2011 Ontario Election" (paper presented to the 2012 Annual Meeting of the Canadian Political Science Association, Edmonton, Alberta).

8   Paul Nesbitt-Larking, *Politics, Society and the Media: Canadian Perspectives* (Toronto: University of Toronto Press, 2001).

9   Dillan Theckedath and Terrence J. Thomas, *Media Ownership and Convergence in Canada* (Ottawa: Library of Parliament, 2012), http://publications.gc.ca/collections/collection_2012/bdp-lop/eb/2012-17-eng.pdf

10 Maria Babbage, personal interview, 3 April 2013.

11 Graham White, *The Ontario Legislature: A Political Analysis* (Toronto: University of Toronto Press, 1989).

12 Michel Bédard, *Question Period in the Canadian Parliament and Other Legislatures* (Ottawa: Library of Parliament, 2011), http://www.parl.gc.ca/Content/LOP/ResearchPublications/2011-88-e.htm#a10

13 White, *The Ontario Legislature.*

14 David Taras, *The Newsmakers: The Media's Influence on Canadian Politics* (Scarborough, ON: Nelson, 1990).

15 Ibid.

16 Jay G. Blumler and Dennis Kavanagh, "The Third Age of Political Communication: Influences and Features," *Political Communication* 16, no. 3 (1999): 205.

17 Fletcher and Sottile, "Spinning Tales," 241.

18 Global National, "Stephen Harper vs. The Press," 23 May 2006, http://www.canada.com/globaltv/national/story.html?id=89eafbaf-ddbe-45b6-aff9-f33ec9cb20a3

19 Ira Basen, "Stephen Harper's Press Gallery Take Down," 9 November 2006, http://rabble.ca/news/stephen-harpers-press-gallery-take-down

20 Andrew Reeves, personal interview, 9 April 2013.

21 Robert Benzie, personal interview, 8 April 2013.

22 Robert Benzie, "McGuinty Shuns Media Scrums; Premier Raises Eyebrows with Policy That Reporters Be 'At Least Five Feet' Away for Questions," *Toronto Star*, 12 February 2008.

23 Karen Howlett, "McGuinty to Reporters: I Need My Space," *Globe and Mail*, 12 February 2009.

24 Christina Blizzard, personal interview, 1 April 2013.

25 In May 2014, associate or part-time members of the Press Gallery included APTN-TV, the *Catholic Register*, CPAX, and Italicus.ca.

26 See Jim Coyle, "Vulnerable Press Loses Ground at Gallery," *The Hamilton Spectator*, 15 September 2008; Leslie De Meulles, "Provincial Unity Amidst a Diminishing Press Gallery," (paper presented to the 2010 Annual Meeting of the Canadian Political Science Association, Montreal, Quebec, 1–3 June 2010); Jonathan Ore, "Scrum and Gone," *Ryerson Review of Journalism* (2010), http://www.rrj.ca/scrum-and-gone

27 See White, *The Ontario Legislature*; Fletcher and Sottile, "Spinning Tales."

28 David Taras, *Power and Betrayal in the Canadian Media* (Toronto: University of Toronto, 2001).

29 Sunny Freeman, "Canada's Newspapers Push Paywalls, Cut Jobs as Ad Revenue Evaporates," *The Huffington Post*, 9 April 2013, http://www.huffingtonpost.ca/2013/05/09/newspaper-paywalls-job-cuts-ad-revenue_n_3243641.html

30 University of British Columbia (Public Affairs), Media Release, "Most Canadians Unwilling to Pay for News Online, Study Suggests," 21 April 2011, http://www.publicaffairs.ubc.ca/2011/04/12/most-canadians-unwilling-to-pay-for-news-online-study-suggests/

31 Coyle, "Vulnerable Press Loses Ground at Gallery," and Ore, "Scrum and Gone."

32 Coyle, "Vulnerable Press Loses Ground at Gallery."

33 Newspapers Canada, *2011 Daily Newspaper Circulation by Province*, http://www.newspaperscanada.ca/sites/default/files/2011%20Daily%20Newspaper%20Circulation%20by%20Province.pdf

34 De Meulles, "Provincial Unity Amidst a Diminishing Press Gallery."

35 Ore, "Scrum and Gone."

36 Kelly Blidook, "Choice and Content: Media Ownership and Democratic Ideals in Canada," *Canadian Political Science Review* 3, no. 2 (2009): 53.

37 Government of Ontario, *Portrait of the Francophone Community in Ontario*, http://www.ofa.gov.on.ca/en/franco.html

38 Statistics Canada, "Immigration and Ethnocultural Diversity in Canada," http://www12.statcan.gc.ca/nhs-enm/2011/as-sa/99-010-x/99-010-x2011001-eng.cfm

39 City of Toronto, *Toronto Facts—Diversity*, http://www1.toronto.ca/wps/portal/contentonly?vgnextoid=dbe867b42d853410VgnVCM10000071d60f89RCRD&vgnextchannel=57a12cc817453410VgnVCM10000071d60f89RCRD

40 Matthew Matsaganis, Vikki S. Katz, and Sandra J. Ball-Rokeach, *Understanding Ethnic Media: Producers, Consumers and Societies* (Thousand Oaks, CA: Sage Publications, 2011).

41 National Ethnic Press and Media Council of Canada, *Welcome*, http://nationalethnicpress.com/welcome/

42 Reeves, interview.

43 White, *The Ontario Legislature*.

44 Lauren McKeon, "How Do Canadians Get Their News?" *The Canadian Journalism Project*, 19 April 2011, http://j-source.ca/article/how-do-canadians-get-their-news

45 Fletcher, "The Crucial and the Trivial" (1990).

46 Toronto Star Marketing Research, *Newspaper Report* (July 2013), http://mediakit.thestar.ca/acrobat/20130904/TorontoStarHighlights_Ju12013.pdf

47 *The Star vs. Television*, http://mediakit.thestar.ca/acrobat/20130904/TorontoStar_Summary_July2013.pdf

48 Antonia Zerbisias, "Many Questions Unanswered in Strategic Rethink," *Toronto Star*, 30 June 2006.

49 Fletcher, "The Crucial and the Trivial" (1985).

50 Kenneth Kernaghan, "Making Political Connections: IT and Legislative Life," in *Digital State at the Leading Edge*, ed. Sandford Borins, Kenneth Kernaghan,

David Brown, Nick Bontis, Perri 6, and Fred Thompson (Toronto: University of Toronto Press, 2007), 224–52.

51   Canadian Press, "Ont. Liberals Support Webcasts of Legislature Debates," 22 April 2008, *CBCNEWS.ca*, http://www.cbc.ca/news/canada/toronto/story/2008/04/22/legislature-online.html

52   Stuart Allan, *Online News: Journalism and the Internet* (Berkshire, UK: Open University Press, 2006).

53   David Tewksbury and Jason Rittenberg, *News on the Internet: Information and Citizenship in the Twenty-first Century* (London: Oxford University Press, 2012).

54   Ibid., 13.

55   Barrie Gunter, *News and the Net* (London: Routledge, 2003).

56   Natalie Fenton, "News in the Digital Age," in *The Routledge Companion to News and Journalism Studies*, ed. Stuart Allen (London: Routledge, 2009), 561.

57   Ibid.

58   As of August 2015, there were 185,138 followers of active Press Gallery members with Twitter accounts. (Calculation by author.)

59   Paul Farhi, "The Twitter Explosion," *American Journalism Review* (2009), http://www.ajr.org/article.asp?id=4756

60   Ibid.

61   Aaron Smith, Kay Lehman Schlozman, Sidney Verba, and Henry Brady, "The Internet and Civic Engagement," *Pew Internet and American Life Project* (Pew Foundation, 2009), http://pewinternet.org/~/media//Files/Reports/2009/The%20Internet%20and%20Civic%20Engagement.pdf

62   Fletcher and Sottile, "Spinning Tales," 265–66.

10

Continuity and Change in Northern Ontario

GINA COMEAU

NORTHERN ONTARIO CONSISTS OF almost 90 per cent of the province's land area, yet is home to just over 6 per cent of its total population. According to the latest census data in 2011, there are 775,178 individuals living in Northern Ontario, with five major population centres located in North Bay, Sault Ste. Marie, Sudbury, Thunder Bay, and Timmins.[1] Given its vastness, several authors question whether speaking of Northern Ontario as one region can encompass the diversity of its various parts. While some researchers such as Michel Beaulieu prefer to divide the north into five distinct regions[2] and others prefer to divide it into two—northwest and northeast (see Rand Dyck's discussion of provincial regions in Chapter 3 of this book)—the fact remains that in legal terms there is one North. Whether one classifies Northern Ontario as one region or many, one of its unifying features is the heartland–hinterland dynamic, which has persisted since its creation and remains a recurring theme in Northern Ontario literature. While the assumptions that inform the heartland–hinterland binary are debatable, few authors would dispute that the politics of Northern Ontario differ from those of its southern neighbours. Any disagreement lays in the perceived degree of the distinction.

This chapter examines the politics and society of Northern Ontario, with particular attention to the elements of continuity and change. It is divided into four parts, the first of which provides a brief overview of the region's development by outlining the historical forces that have shaped Northern Ontario's politics and political culture. The second part provides a demographic profile of the region, followed by a third section on political culture and behaviour and finally a discussion of government policies and institutions. As a whole, this chapter argues that while Northern Ontario has witnessed significant changes in the last 20 years—particularly in comparison to the preceding 20—a number of issues and challenges remain that reflect the persistence of the heartland–hinterland dynamic. The most enduring feature of Northern Ontario politics is that it continues to be significantly different from that of Southern Ontario.

Historical Development

The history and politics of Northern Ontario are intrinsically linked to the development and exploitation of its natural resources.[3] It is in large part the extraction of natural resources from the North to serve the needs of the South that created the heartland–hinterland relationship between Northern and Southern Ontario.[4] In the heartland–hinterland relationship, the hinterland region is used to serve the needs of the heartland or metropolis, which in turn influences the hinterland's politics.[5] This theory owes its origins to Harold Innis's seminal work on the history of the Canadian economy. Innis's staples theory argues that the development and exportation of raw materials, such as fur, fish, and lumber, explain the development and settlement patterns of many communities and the regional character of the Canadian economy. The exportation of these raw materials from the hinterland (Canada) to the heartland (Britain) hindered Canada's ability to diversify its economy by creating an overreliance on primary resources and continued dependence on Britain.[6] Many authors have expanded on the heartland–hinterland thesis by applying it to the Canada–US relationship, and to the centre and periphery within Canada, which has led to a political analysis of subregions such as Northern Ontario.[7] For example, Geoffrey Weller builds upon the heartland–hinterland thesis to explain the impact of these development patterns on the politics of Northern Ontario.[8] He argues that the economics and politics of extraction (characterized by the politics of futility and handouts) led to the politics of frustration (radicalism and fringe movements) and the politics of parochialism (the politics of sublimation and dependency). The resulting politics of frustration are still evident today, albeit to a much lesser extent.

The vast majority of Northern Ontario communities can be categorized as resource communities and, similar to many other resource communities, they experience "boom-and-bust" cycles that reveal their vulnerability to external forces. The North was not originally developed for its natural resources but was intended as a transportation route to the western part of Canada. The provincial government subsequently attempted to develop the area first as an agricultural region and a market for the south. As H.V. Nelles explains, it took years for the government to realize the futility of its efforts to develop a new agricultural frontier: "Whenever the farmers of the southern part of the province demanded the opening up of more land in the north the lumbermen reminded them of the cold, inhospitable nature of the land and the government of the revenues that would be lost if such a course of action were followed. The Shield itself and the economic interests dependent upon it challenged a unitary, agrarian view of the environment."[9]

While the terrain proved too rugged to flourish as an agricultural region, it was rich in mineral deposits and other natural resources. It was thus only in the early 1900s that the exploitation of the environment through forestry and the mining industry truly became the driving force of economic growth in the region.[10]

Resource companies located outside the region largely undertook the extraction of northern resources. The region's infrastructure was developed to facilitate the exploitation and transportation of resources from North to South, which in turn impacted the development of many communities.[11] Government policies targeting the North were largely intended to encourage the exploitation of the region, referred to as "New Ontario," in order to benefit Southern Ontario.[12]

Weller argues that the politics of extraction and dependency have led to Northern alienation and the rise of fringe movements supporting greater autonomy.[13] The quest for greater autonomy has taken various forms throughout the years, with some seeking greater representation at Queen's Park and others calling for provincial status or union with Manitoba. The first of these movements for separation occurred shortly after Confederation in the 1870s and again in the early 1900s, periods when other new provinces were joining Confederation. In the 1940s and 1950s, Hubert Limerick tried to generate support for provincial status with the New Province League. In the 1970s, Ed Diebel championed the movement for separation, and the idea continues to recur in editorials and public discussion from time to time.[14] The politics of extraction also plays out in attempts by both regions, Northern and Southern Ontario, to extract benefits from each other. The North seeks "economic and social change" or concessions, often in the form of political handouts, and the southern part of the province attempts to extract resources from the north at the lowest possible cost.[15] This cycle contributes to a sense of alienation and frustration among the residents of Northern Ontario.

In addition to creating a sense of alienation, the politics of extraction significantly influence the demographics of the region, as detailed further in the next section. The exploitation and extraction of natural resources is ever more reliant on heavy machinery rather than intensive labour, with serious consequences in terms of population growth, immigration, age, and population distribution.[16] An economy dependent on natural resources tends to channel the flow of resources and wealth outside the region, limiting the number and diversity of job opportunities for youth and leaving the population highly dependent on external forces. These adverse implications of the politics of extraction are also found in other Canadian hinterlands, creating an increasing divide in employment and population rates.[17] In Northern

Ontario and other Canadian hinterland regions, external factors have created conditions that persist today, including unemployment and out-migration, with a devastating impact on resource economies.

While the politics of extraction shape the contemporary moment, they have a long history of producing alienation and discontent in Northern Ontario. Such sentiments were present during the investigatory phase of the provincial Royal Commission on the Northern Environment during the late 1970s and early 1980s. The commission was to examine both the positive and negative impacts of resource development on the environment and the people of Northern Ontario, and the politics of frustration are evident in its report: "beneath the many conflicts over resource development lies a wide-spread belief amongst northerners that they have precious little influence over the course of development. That belief is well-founded."[18] The importance of consulting northern populations and understanding the key differences between Northern and Southern Ontario were deemed key in quelling the evident dissatisfaction among Indigenous and non-Indigenous communities in Northern Ontario. The *Final Report and Recommendations* of the Royal Commission on the Northern Environment was submitted in 1985,[19] which recommended the development of institutional mechanisms to ensure the voices of the North were heard, as well as environmental and land use guidelines for sustainable development practices. Although a provincial commission report, it argued that both federal and provincial policies played a central role in reinforcing feelings of disaffection, and it detailed specific recommendations for both the federal and provincial governments in regard to consultation practices and education, treaty, and environmental negotiations with Northern Indigenous communities. But three decades later these concerns remain. Michel Beaulieu argues that provincial and federal policies have often been "adversarial, and steeped in attitudes of colonialism that regional concerns are secondary."[20] Such policy decisions have fuelled the alienation and discontent still prevalent in Northern Ontario, with a particularly devastating impact on many Indigenous communities.

Demographics

The demographic profile of Northern Ontario starkly differs from other regions in the province in terms of ethnicity, language, economic status, and population density. The most significant difference is in population density, measured by calculating the number of individuals living in a specific land area. According to the 2011 census, there were 775,178 individuals living in Northern Ontario—as mentioned earlier, this represents approximately 6 per cent of Ontario's total population living on close to 90 per cent of the province's land mass. The population density of Northern Ontario is thus only one person per square kilometre, compared to 119 people per square kilometre in Southern Ontario. There is also a significant difference in urbanization. While 89 per cent of Southern Ontarians live in urban areas, the comparable figure in the North is only 66 per cent. Thus while a majority of Northerners still live in cities and towns, there is a much greater percentage of individuals who live in rural and remote populations in the North.[21]

Suffice it to say that it is possible to discern a number of distinct demographic trends that differentiate Northern Ontario from the remainder of the province. According to Chris Southcott,[22] these include increasing youth out-migration (which is increasing at a faster rate than in previous decades), an aging population, and slow population growth, and estimates indicate that this trend will continue. Northerners are more likely than other Ontarians to be employed in natural resource industries such as forestry and mining; there is also a greater reliance on public sector employment.[23] Further, low levels of education and literacy persist, and while these are improving, the regional gap compared to the provincial average is growing rather than shrinking.[24] While some of these tendencies are apparent in other areas of the country such as Atlantic Canada, when one compares Northern to Southern Ontario, there is an increasing divide and intensifying inequalities between the two areas of the province. The North continues to depend on natural resources, rendering it extremely vulnerable to external forces. While other industries such as manufacturing in Southern Ontario are also vulnerable to external forces such as trade and globalization, natural resource economies tend to be more volatile and experience more frequent and extreme boom-and-bust cycles.

Of the various demographic trends that shape the politics of Northern Ontario, perhaps the most salient is the continual decrease in its population relative to that of the province as a whole. In 2001, the population of Northern Ontario constituted 7.4 per cent of the provincial population; by 2006, this figure had decreased to 6.5 per cent, and by 2011 again to 6 per cent.[25] Only four northern areas (Manitoulin, Parry Sound, Nipissing, and Greater Sudbury) experienced growth in the early 2000s, but the increases remained below the provincial average of 5.7 per cent and the national average of 5.9 per cent. The remaining northern areas witnessed a decrease in population while the southern part of the province has experienced continual growth almost everywhere except some rural and more remote areas, mainly in Eastern Ontario.[26]

Such significant variations between north and south carry over into the realm of language and ethnicity. Northern Ontario has fewer immigrants settling into the region than Southern Ontario, as the majority of immigrants to Ontario opt to settle in larger urban centres. Yet Northern Ontario is home to substantially larger francophone and Indigenous populations. One quarter of the province's francophone population resides in the region—in numerical terms, this amounted to 134,875 people in 2011[27]—as does 40 per cent of its Indigenous population, with close to 25 per cent of the area's population consisting of 98,000 Indigenous people. Despite different challenges, both minority populations face shared language and cultural barriers, albeit to varying degrees. Furthermore, they are each bearers of unique constitutional rights according to their recognized status in the Canadian polity. Both groups are also less likely to have a university degree or high school education, and both earn less than the provincial average, with a greater gap in income between northern francophone and Indigenous residents of the province, on the one hand, and their southern counterparts, on the other.[28] However, while these examples illustrate some similarities between the Indigenous and francophone populations of Northern Ontario, significant differences remain. While the Northern Ontario population is generally aging, the Indigenous population is getting younger. The opposite is true of the francophone population, which is older than the provincial average.[29]

Indigenous communities in remote areas often face a number of additional social issues, such as access to clean drinking water, access to affordable and nutritious food, higher suicide rates, and higher chronic and infectious disease rates, to name a few.[30] The majority of these issues are not new. They were noted by the provincial Royal Commission on the Northern Environment in 1985 and the federal Royal Commission on Aboriginal Peoples in 1996 and have been studied repeatedly by numerous experts. The media coverage of such issues provides immediate short-term awareness, but does not necessarily aid the long-term situation.[31] For example, in 2011, housing conditions in Attawapiskat made national headlines due to the dire living conditions found in the Northern Ontario First Nation's community. The community declared a state of emergency when many residents were found living in makeshift accommodations without water or electricity or in houses in states of serious disrepair. The response of the federal government—which involved a decision to send in emergency shelter and dispatch third-party management—was deemed insufficient by the community, with the courts laying the blame on bureaucratic problems in a subsequent judicial review in 2012.[32] More recently, in 2016, Attawapiskat and many other First Nation Communities across Canada, have faced a youth suicide crisis with Attawapiskat declaring a state of emergency.[33] While these are federal jurisdictional issues, they illustrate the unique challenges faced by isolated Indigenous communities. Authors such as Charania and colleagues have noted that improved collaboration, communication, and interpretation among federal, provincial, and First Nations communities could improve health care delivery in remote First Nations communities when a patient must receive services outside the community.[34] The federal Auditor General's 2015 spring report also identified interjurisdictional challenges as one of many factors negatively impacting health care delivery both within and outside First Nations communities. The Auditor General's report highlighted a series of major problems such as deficiencies in health and safety requirements, lack of proper training, and transportation issues.[35]

Political Culture and Political Behaviour

There are several ongoing debates regarding the nature of Ontario's political culture, as explored in Chapter 4 of this collection. Key to such debates are questions as to not only whether Ontario has a distinct political culture, but also whether Northern Ontario, in particular, has its own separate political culture. Nelson Wiseman, for example, distinguishes a specific provincial culture for Ontario but does not address the possible existence of regional subcultures.[36] However, authors such as Dyck, Weller, and Martin, among others, have argued that Northern Ontario has its own distinctive regional subculture. For Rand Dyck, the political culture of Northern Ontario is "a culture of alienation, dependence, handouts, and frustration, based on isolated settlements, distance from Toronto, poor communications, and inadequate services."[37] For Charles Martin, the political culture of Northern Ontario is similarly distinguished by its "feelings of dissatisfaction, dependency, and domination, as well as by parochialism and pragmatism."[38]

This distinct political culture manifests itself in what Weller has labelled the "politics of disaffection." The politics of disaffection are a reflection of the profound discontent triggered by neglect at Queen's Park, isolation from and exploitation by the South, a lack of political representation, inequalities of wealth, and underfunded basic services such as health and education. The politics of disaffection manifest themselves in a number of ways, including distinct voting patterns. Particularly notable is a tradition of protest voting evident in NDP support; while Liberal and Conservative fortunes may rise and fall considerably, the NDP is regularly a strong presence in Northern voting and consistently competitive in almost every Northern riding. There are also signs of a radical undercurrent in strong support for workers' movements. The politics of dissatisfaction are further expressed in minority politics, with both francophones and Indigenous people constituting important segments of the population for whom issues of service and accessibility are magnified. As noted, statistical measurements of levels of employment, income, and education indicate that francophone and particularly Indigenous communities continue to receive inferior services in comparison to the Northern Ontario average, which in turn pales in comparison to Southern Ontario averages. The politics of disaffection for these groups are often expressed in different ways and arenas but constitute an important part of Northern Ontario's politics.

Given such widespread disillusionment, perhaps it is not surprising that there have been regular calls for internal secession since the late 1800s, as mentioned above, either for separate provincial status or for the northwestern part of the province to join Manitoba. The latter option is principally fuelled by two factors: first, the closer proximity to Manitoba's capital, and second, a greater influence in the smaller Legislature. As Di Matteo and colleagues note, using 2006 formulas, the merger of Northwestern Ontario and Manitoba could signify a 16 per cent increase in the number of seats, thereby increasing the weight of the former's voice in the Legislature.[39] For many secessionists, the desire to separate is often expressed in a number of recurring themes. Tim Nieguth identifies six themes in the Northern Ontario separatist discourse: "neglect, adverse effects, heartland mentality, distinct identity, representation and self-determination."[40] Many Northerners express discontent at their continual battle for services easily obtained in the southern part of the province. The lack of political power and issues of representation are a continuous struggle given the dwindling population of Northern Ontario. While the North is actually somewhat overrepresented with 10 electoral districts federally and 11 provincially, when its share of the Ontario population would only warrant eight,[41] it is still heavily outweighed in provincial politics, comprising less than a tenth of the Legislature.

Northern Ontario mirrors the overall stability of the Ontario three-party system but expresses itself somewhat differently than the South in relation to party standings.[42] Historically, there were two voting tendencies in Northern Ontario. While Northerners tended to vote for the party in power at both the provincial and federal levels—hoping that this would lead to political assistance—there was also a strong undercurrent of radical politics illustrated by solid support for the NDP. Weller suggests that the trend to vote with the ruling party was broken in 1995,[43] and recent electoral outcomes seem to support this argument, at least provincially. In 1995, the North maintained support for the NDP when the Conservatives were elected, and in three of the last five elections, Northern Ontario as a region did not give a majority of seats to the party elected to power. The last four provincial elections (2003, 2007, 2011, and 2014) have seen a steady increase in NDP support (both specifically in the North and generally in the province) and in 2011 and 2014 the North elected more NDP members than Liberals, despite the latter's overall victory. However, in the 2014 election, second place went to a Liberal candidate in all but one riding where the NDP member was elected, and a Liberal candidate obtained second place in the ridings where a Progressive Conservative candidate was elected. It should also be noted that in almost all cases, Conservative wins are located in the areas closest to Southern Ontario. Surprisingly, there was limited evidence of protest voting in the 2015 provincial by-election in Sudbury despite public controversy after Kathleen Wynne appointed NDP MP Glenn Thibeault as the Liberal provincial candidate over a strong local candidate. Allegations of bribery and the premier imposing a candidate on the northern riding led to a number of resignations within the local Liberal party executive and a criminal investigation.[44]

Dynamics at the federal level are somewhat different and more volatile, with all three parties rising and falling in popularity, and the NDP not always in second place regardless of a Liberal or Conservative win, as was commonly the case before. In the 1997, 2000, and 2004 federal elections, Northern Ontarians voted primarily for the Liberal party in power, which they did again in 2015; however, from 2006 to 2011, the Conservatives in power never managed to win more than four of the 10 federal seats. The NDP won seven federal seats in 2008 and six in 2011, but fell to two seats in 2015 while the Liberals leaped from zero in 2011 to seven in 2015. Again, the dual trends of supporting the party in power and a strong NDP protest vote are both evident.

Government Policy and Institutions in Northern Ontario

For years, the source of much discontent in Northern Ontario was the piecemeal approach of both the provincial and federal governments to addressing the problems of the North. These efforts were often criticized for failing to create a strategy based on long-term planning rather than ad hoc measures to appease discontent in northern communities. Weller argued that policy development in the North not only failed to incorporate any long-term vision but also lacked co-ordination among the different levels of government and local organizations.[45] The end result was that development efforts occurred in metaphorical silos. Recent policy initiatives indicate longer term planning in federal government initiatives, which might somewhat temporarily appease discontent in the area. However, it is the government of Ontario—with its jurisdictional responsibility for Northern Ontario's primary industries of mining, forestry, and tourism—that can significantly alter Northern Ontario's political economy.

At the federal level, some authors argue that significant changes have occurred, with greater foresight in planning and increased communication among governmental agencies and a considerable change in the political context of economic development in Northern Ontario. For decades, authors have noted the need to work collaboratively in the field of economic development by rejecting the silo approach typical of governmental agencies. Recent attempts in the field of economic development reflect a changing multiple-level governance environment in which actors seek to work cooperatively to coordinate regional economic development efforts.[46] The Federal Economic Development Initiative for Northern Ontario (FedNor), established in 1987, has come a long way in its attempts to adapt its model of policy implementation to its changing external environment. The creation of FedNor represented an attempt to develop programs with an inclusive regional focus in a departure from previous top-down approaches.[47] It emphasizes economic development through partnerships between levels of government, First Nations communities, non-governmental organizations, and the private sector.[48]

The field of health care is plagued by many of the same problems that have traditionally faced the field of economic development. Attracting and retaining physicians was long a particular concern.[49] The lack of training opportunities was noted as problematic by many authors, with young Northern Ontarians moving to more central locations for training and then not returning to the North. The creation of a new Northern Ontario School of Medicine (NOSM) in 2005, a joint initiative between Lakehead University in Thunder Bay and Laurentian University in Sudbury has helped to alleviate the lack of training opportunities in the field of health. In addition, to address the physician shortage in the North, NOSM has also taken a different approach than other medical schools in Canada by requiring an eight-month community clerkship in Northern Ontario.

In previous decades, there was also a tendency to develop short-term strategies in an attempt to alleviate the political disaffection of Northern Ontarians. In recent years, however, there has been a shift in government policies, actions, and programs. The 2011 provincial Growth Plan for Northern Ontario established a framework for the next 25 years structured around six themes: economy, people, communities, infrastructure, environment, and Indigenous peoples. While the policy goals included within the plan are quite commendable, there are few result measurement indicators developed to assess both the plan and progress to date, and this makes it highly challenging.[50]

Recent mining discoveries also seem to reflect previous patterns that shape the politics of extraction. The Ring of Fire, an area located in Northern Ontario that is rich in chromite, nickel, copper, and platinum was discovered in 2008. From a government standpoint, the Ring of Fire is one of the most significant mining development projects Ontario has seen in close to a century, with estimates of its worth up to $60 billion.[51] From an Indigenous standpoint, there are important jurisdictional and environmental issues that need to be resolved prior to any development, and from a corporate standpoint, there are a number of infrastructural issues. The area is approximately 300 kilometres from the nearest railroad or highway and 500 kilometres north of Thunder Bay, which raises a host of questions as to how the minerals will be transported.

Many First Nations communities view the potential development of the Ring of Fire with mixed feelings. While it could provide employment and a boost to the local economy, there are also environmental and cultural costs. The concern extends to areas like Sudbury, a potential location for an ore processing plant.[52] For Northern Ontario as a whole, there is certainly the potential for job creation, but there is also the prospect of the region yet again serving as a development hub for the South, thus raising the spectre of a resurgence of the politics of extraction. In response to some of the concerns raised by First Nations communities and environmentalists, and with a view to improving communication between the affected parties, the provincial government established the Ring of Fire Secretariat in the Ministry of Northern Development and Mines, with a role of consulting and collaborating with Indigenous communities, industry, and other levels of government.

There are a few signs that, under the leadership of Kathleen Wynne, Northern Ontario features more prominently in government policy than it did under previous governments. The Wynne government established a Cabinet Committee on Northern Ontario (CCNO) to address the various economic challenges in the North and committed $1 billion in the 2014 provincial budget toward infrastructure in the Ring of Fire area, but thus far there have been few concrete actions related to the development and extraction of mining resources located in the Ring of Fire.

Ironically, the government is willing to entertain discussions to improve transportation for the North, yet recent decisions not linked to the extraction of resources appear to have gone the opposite way. The provincial government's decision to privatize the Ontario Northland Transportation Commission (ONTC) in 2012 angered many Northerners, as it seemed to confirm perceptions that their concerns were subordinate to those of the province's southern residents. Requests to further investigate the divestment of the ONTC were realized with the provincial auditor's report in December 2013. The report held the Liberal government accountable for the misinformation, asserting that it failed to properly communicate the implications of the divestment and citing a lack of communication between the ONTC and the Ministry of Northern Development and Mines.[53] Shortly before the release of the report, the language of divestment had been changed to transformation. The fate of the ONTC remains unclear at the time of writing, but the report's findings will probably not improve perceptions that regional concerns are secondary. Such government decisions reinforce the politics of disaffection and the idea that services taken for granted in Southern Ontario are not obtained without a fight, a typical pattern in the heartland–hinterland relationship. Interestingly, at the end of April 2014, a few days prior to the 2014 provincial election call, the provincial government announced its commitment to invest $1 billion to develop a transportation corridor. While this could be seen as a way to regain support from the North, one could also argue that it is consistent with policy decisions relating to the politics of extraction.

The politics of disaffection are also expressed through municipal organizations. The Federation of Northern Ontario Municipalities (FONUM), which represents the northeastern municipalities, has in recent years asked the provincial government to desist from ignoring the concerns of northern municipalities. Two other organizations provide a forum for northern mayors: the coalition of Northern Ontario Large Urban Mayors (NOLUM) and the Northwestern Ontario Municipal Association (NOMA). A 2005 study sponsored by all three groups, *Creating Our Future: A New Vision for Northern Ontario*,[54] outlined a number of issues facing the North, such as a declining population, mortality and hospitalization rates, and transportation issues, to name but a few.

Conclusion

In the last 20 years, Northern Ontario has witnessed significant structural, political, and economic change. Progress has been made on a number of fronts in the form of improvements to infrastructure, the creation of the NOSM, the organization of a cabinet committee, and the installment of a 25-year growth plan. Nevertheless, the socio-demographic trend remains the same, with a population that is both declining and aging as well as ongoing out-migration remaining characteristic of many hinterland economies. Significant inequalities between Northern and Southern Ontario continue to exist with regards to population growth, education, and health services. The federal and provincial governments have attempted to address a number of these issues for decades, some more successfully than others.

The economic cycles of boom and bust persist as the region continues to rely heavily on natural resources. Decisions related to infrastructure are somewhat reminiscent of earlier policies, with government action occurring principally around the exploitation of natural resources. Since the discovery of the Ring of Fire, the provincial government has created a Ring of Fire

Secretariat, a northern cabinet committee, and promises of investment in infrastructure to improve access to resources. Yet the feelings of alienation persist, albeit to a lesser extent than in previous decades, and while there continues to be discussion of secession, mobilization efforts are few to non-existent.[55] The prevalence of alienation is arguably understandable given the key distinctions that remain between the politics and policies of Northern and Southern Ontario.

The politics of disaffection are still evident in Northern Ontario, with recent trends indicating an increase in protest voting. There are still elements of secessionist discourse, and even if not strong, they point, among other things, to continued discontent with the lack of representation at both the provincial and federal levels of government. Relatedly, many northern communities feel ignored by key decision-makers as civil responses to the privatization of the NOTC reveal. Municipalities also often complain of the lack of consultation and of being ignored by the provincial government.

Recent decades point to some change in Northern Ontario both in how the politics of disaffection manifest themselves as well as in terms of issues of governance and policy orientation. Even the recent changes in voting patterns, with greater support for the NDP provincially, continue to reflect hinterland politics, and the most significant changes in governance and policy orientation are primarily at the federal level, which has a lesser impact on the dynamics of the heartland–hinterland relationship. The provincial government's requirement to work closely with Indigenous communities and to consider environmental factors in developing the Ring of Fire may help diminish some of the negative aspects traditionally related to the politics of extraction. One thing that remains certain is that the politics of Northern Ontario continue to distinguish themselves from those of Southern Ontario. Until important structural changes are made to Northern Ontario's political economy, the effects of the heartland–hinterland relationship will continue to manifest themselves, albeit to a lesser extent than in the past given some of the positive changes of recent decades.

Discussion Questions

1. Do you agree that Northern Ontario politics are distinct from the rest of the province, and if so, in what ways?
2. How has the hinterland–heartland dynamic shaped Northern Ontario over time, and is it likely to continue in the future?
3. How do the politics of alienation and disaffection shape voting and political activity in Northern Ontario?

4. Is new and expanded economic development the best solution to meet the needs of Indigenous communities in Northern Ontario? Why or why not?

5. Would Northern Ontario be better off becoming a province of its own? Explain.

Notes

1   Statistics Canada subdivides the population of Northern Ontario into two regions: Northeast with a population of 551,144 and Northwest with a population of 224,034, for a total of 775,178. Statistics Canada, http://www12.statcan.ca/census-recensement/2011/dp-pd/hlt-fst/pd-pl/Table-Tableau.cfm?LANG=Eng&T=1402&PR=35&S=51&O=A&RPP=25

2   Michel S. Beaulieu, "A Historic Overview of Policies Affecting Non-Aboriginal Development in Northwestern Ontario, 1900–1990," in *Governance in Northern Ontario: Economic Development and Policy Making*, ed. Charles Conteh and Bob Segsworth (Toronto: IPAC and University of Toronto Press, 2013).

3   Chris Southcott, *The North in Numbers: A Demographic Analysis of Social and Economic Change in Northern Ontario* (Thunder Bay: Centre for Northern Studies, 2007), 4.

4   For a more detailed description of the development of the North as a hinterland and the relevant literature, see Geoffrey R. Weller, "Hinterland Politics: The Case of Northwestern Ontario," *Canadian Journal of Political Science* 10, no. 4 (1977): 440–70.

5   Ibid., 731.

6   For a more detailed overview of Innis's staples theory, see Harold Innis, *The Fur Trade in Canada* (Toronto: University of Toronto Press, 1999). The original text was published in 1930 but this edition provides a new introduction outlining the impact of Innis's work. The staples theory has fallen into disuse in recent decades but some of the work inspired by this seminal text continues to influence.

7   For example, Kari Levitt, *Silent Surrender* (Toronto: Macmillan Publishing, 1970).

8   In this first instance, Weller, "Hinterland Politics," examines Northwestern Ontario but in subsequent studies he examines the politics of Northern Ontario as a whole. In later texts, Weller does not always specifically refer to the metropolis–hinterland relationship. He does continue to argue that the resulting politics continue to influence both the policies and politics of Northern Ontario and its relationship with Southern Ontario. See Geoffrey R. Weller, "Managing Canada's North: The Case of the Provincial North," *Canadian Public Administration* 27, no. 2 (1984): 197–209, and Geoffrey R. Weller, "Politics and Policy in the North," in *The Government and Politics of Ontario*, 5th ed., ed. Graham White (Toronto: University of Toronto Press, 1997).

9   H.V. Nelles, *The Politics of Development: Forests, Mines and Hydro-Electric Power in Ontario, 1849–1941*, 2nd ed. (Montreal: McGill-Queen's University Press, 2005), 45.

10 It should be noted that for the first few decades of the twentieth century, there were still intermittent government efforts to develop the North as an agricultural frontier. For a detailed historical account of the development of natural resources in the North, see Nelles, *The Politics of Development*, 42–62.

11 Beaulieu, "A Historic Overview," 97.

12 Beaulieu, "A Historic Overview," 96. See also Tim Nieguth, "We Are Left with No Other Alternative: Legitimating Internal Secession," *Space and Polity* 13, no. 2 (2009): 141–57.

13 Weller, "Hinterland Politics."

14 Weller, "Politics and Policy in the North."

15 For more information on the history of these movements, see Di Matteo, Livio, J.C. Herbert Emery, and Ryan English, "Is It Better to Live in a Basement, an Attic or to Get Your Own Place? Analyzing the Costs and Benefits of Institutional Change for Northwestern Ontario," *Canadian Public Policy* 32, no. 2 (2006): 173–96.

16 See ibid., 735–37, for a detailed analysis of how the politics of extraction have influenced the demographics of Northern Ontario. Note that this article specifically deals with Northwestern Ontario but the argument is also applied to a lesser extent to the whole of Northern Ontario in the various editions of Weller, "Politics and Policy in the North."

17 Michael D. Ray, R.H. Lamarche, and Maurice Beaudin, "Economic Growth and Restructuring in Canada's Heartland and Hinterland: From Shift-Share to Multifactor Partitioning," *The Canadian Geographer* 56, no. 3 (2012): 296–317.

18 Ontario Royal Commission on the Northern Environment, *Final Report and Recommendations* (Toronto: Ontario Ministry of the Attorney General, 1985), 2, https://archive.org/stream/finalreponorenviron00onta/finalreponorenviron00onta_djvu.txt

19 Ibid.

20 Beaulieu, "A Historic Overview," 94.

21 Ontario Ministry of Northern Development and Mines (OMNDM), *Northern Ontario: A Profile* (Toronto: Queen's Printer for Ontario, 2012).

22 Chris Southcott, "Regional Economic Development and Socio-economic Change in Northern Ontario," in *Governance in Northern Ontario: Economic Development and Policy Making*, ed. Charles Conteh and Robert Segsworth (Toronto: Institute of Public Administration of Canada, 2013).

23 Southcott, *The North in Numbers*, 9.

24 For example, Southcott's 2007 study indicated that 44 per cent fewer Northern Ontarians had a university education than Southern Ontarians. *The North in Numbers*, 176.

25 OMNDM, *Northern Ontario: A Profile*. Further decline is predicted in the Northern Ontario population; see Ontario Population Projections Update, 2015–2041 (Toronto: Queen's Printer for Ontario, 2016), www.fin.gov.on.ca/en/economy/demographics/projections/projections2015-2041.pdf

26 Ibid.

27 Ontario Ministry of Francophone Affairs, *Data Based on the Inclusive Definition of Francophone (IDF) from the 2011 Census*, http://www.ofa.gov.on.ca.3pdns.korax.net/en/franco-stats.html

28 It should be noted that the trend is shifting for francophones, for whom average income is changing. It is higher in certain parts of the province but is currently lower in the northeastern part of the province and higher in the northwestern part of the province.

29 Ontario Ministry of Francophone Affairs, *Data Based on the Inclusive Definition of Francophone (IDF) from the 2011 Census.*

30 Shinjini Pal, Francois Haman, and Michael A. Robidoux, "The Costs of Local Food Procurement in Two Northern Indigenous Communities in Canada," *Food and Foodways* 21, no. 2 (2013): 132–52.

31 These stories also tend to frame Indigenous communities in a negative manner or as problems rather than as communities with rights. For more on the media portrayal of Indigenous communities in Canada, see Augie Fleras, *The Media Gaze: Representations of Diversity in Canada* (Vancouver: UBC Press, 2011).

32 Meagan Fitzpatrick, "Attawapiskat Handed Victory by Federal Court: Judicial Review Says a 3rd Party Manager Was 'Unreasonable' Fix to Housing Crisis," *CBC News*, 1 August 2012; Gloria Galloway, "Ottawa's Response to Attawapiskat Emergency 'Unreasonable,' Court Rules," *Globe and Mail*, 1 August 2012.

33 Globe and Mail and The Canadian Press, "Four Things to Help Understand the Suicide Crisis," *Globe and Mail*, 8 July 2016, http://www.theglobeandmail.com/news/national/attawapiskat-four-things-to-help-understand-the-suicidecrisis/article29583059/

34 Nadia Charania, Don Wowan, and Leonard J.S. Tsuji, "Health Care Delivery in Remote Isolated First Nations Communities in Canada," *The International Journal of Technology, Knowledge, and Society* 8, no. 5 (2013): 71–84.

35 Office of the Auditor General of Canada, *Report 4: Access to Health Services for Remote First Nations Communities* (Ottawa: Minister of Public Works and Government Services. 2015).

36 Nelson Wiseman, *In Search of Canadian Political Culture* (Vancouver: UBC Press, 2007).

37 Rand Dyck, *Provincial Politics in Canada: Toward the Turn of the Century* (Scarborough: Prentice Hall Canada, 1995), 311.

38 Charles Martin, "The Politics of Northern Ontario: An Analysis of the Political Divergences at the Provincial Periphery" (MA thesis, McGill University, 1999).

39 Di Matteo et al., "Is It Better to Live in a Basement …," provide a brief historical overview of these movements and also outline the various advantages and disadvantages relating to union with Manitoba, provincial status, and regional government options.

40 Tim Nieguth, "We Are Left with No Other Alternative: Legitimating Internal Secession in Northern Ontario," *Space and Polity* 13, no. 2 (2009): 141–57.

41 CBC News, "Northern Ontario Keeps Its 10 Federal Ridings," 1 October 2013, http://www.cbc.ca/news/canada/sudbury/northern-ontario-keeps-its-10-federal-ridings-1.1874615

42 See Chapter 11 in this volume for an expansion on Ontario's political parties and party system.

43 Weller, "Politics and Policy in the North."

44 Carol Mulligan, "Investigating Sudbury Scandal Not So Simple," *Sudbury Star*, 27 June 2015.

45 Weller, "Politics and Policy in the North."

46 Charles Conteh, "Policy Implementation in Multilevel Environments: Economic Development in Northern Ontario," *Canadian Public Administration* 54, no. 1 (2011): 121–42.

47 Ibid. Conteh also outlines the differences in autonomy between FedNor and other federal development agencies in Canada.

48 Ibid.

49 Raymond Pong, "Strategies to Overcome Physician Shortages in Northern Ontario: A Study of Policy Implementation over 35 Years," *Human Resources for Health* 6, no. 24 (2008), http://www.human-resources-health.com/content/6/1/24

50 Bob Segworth provides a number of recommendations to rectify the plan's shortcomings in "Results Measurement and Economic Development in Northern Ontario," in *Governance in Northern Ontario: Economic Development and Policy Making*, ed. Charles Conteh and Bob Segsworth (Toronto: IPAC and University of Toronto Press, 2013), 58–75.

51 Ontario Ministry of Northern Development and Mines, "Ring of Fire Secretariat," www.mndm.gov.on.ca/en/ring-fire-secretariat

52 Carol Mulligan, "Wildlands League Wants Freeze on Ring of Fire Development," *Sudbury Star*, 17 October 2013.

53 Office of the Auditor General of Ontario, *Divestment of Ontario Northland Transportation Commission: Special Report* (Toronto, 2013), http://www.auditor.on.ca/en/content/specialreports/specialreports/ONTC_en.pdf

54 Northern Ontario Large Urban Mayors, Northwestern Ontario Municipal Association and Federation of Northern Ontario Municipalities, *Creating Our Future: A New Vision for Northern Ontario* (March 2005), http://www.greatersudbury.ca/content/div_mayor/documents/CreatingOurFuture_March29-05.pdf

55 Di Matteo et al., "Is It Better to Live in a Basement ...," 191.

11

Political Parties and the Party System in Ontario

JONATHAN MALLOY

POLITICAL PARTIES PLAY A CRUCIAL ROLE in politics and governance. They act as transmitters of ideas and channel many of the forces and people that allow modern and complex political systems to function. Parties are independent entities that may come and go over time. Yet they are also deeply embedded in the institutions of the state, and it is hardly possible to imagine legislatures and elections operating without them. Furthermore, parties are not only instruments through which democracy functions; they also serve as overall barometers of democratic health and political culture. And while they normally exist in competition with each other, together they form *party systems* that also change and adapt over time. Overall, political parties play an essential but often overlooked role in complex political societies like Ontario. Indeed, Ontario political parties may be particularly taken for granted because of their remarkable staying power.

This chapter examines Ontario's political parties, with particular attention to some of the more unique aspects of the Ontario party system. Most important is the system's remarkable durability. The same three parties—the Liberals, Progressive Conservatives, and New Democrats—have dominated the Ontario political landscape for decades. While there have been adjustments in their relative standings, including the one-time leap of the NDP into government in 1990, the parties themselves have proved remarkably resilient. They have fended off all newcomers; neither have two parties managed to squeeze a third into obscurity. We should also note the unusual Progressive Conservative dynasty of 1943–85, another example of remarkable durability which set the tone of Ontario politics for many years and continues to have a legacy. And while Ontario saw a rapid rotation of governing parties in the 1980s and 1990s, it is also significant that after a stormy decade, the system settled back into more traditional patterns.

Party organizations and the institutions surrounding them have also seen little change. Until very recently, Ontario saw few significant reforms in party and candidate finance in recent years; neither, with rare exceptions, have Ontario parties been known for innovation or novelty. While the 1990 Progressive Conservative leadership race featured one of the first all-member leadership votes in Canada, as recently as 2013 the Ontario Liberal Party held a traditional multi-ballot delegate convention, in an age when nearly all major Canadian parties had long moved to various forms of direct member voting for leaders. This was partly due to its hasty circumstances, but was also an indicator of the stability and institutional conservatism of Ontario parties.

The overall question of this chapter is why Ontario parties and the party system have remained so stable. It begins with an overview of the party system as a whole, including questions of why the system has seen little change. It then contrasts Ontario parties with their federal counterparts, and looks in more detail at the evolution of each of the three major parties. The chapter concludes with the question of whether the stability of Ontario parties is a symbol of democratic health, or a sign of staleness and atrophy.

Party Systems

Party systems can be understood in several ways. In the simplest terms, they involve the number of parties and changes over time. As mentioned, Ontario has had the same major parties for many years. But beyond numbers, the concept also refers to how parties are arranged against each other—ideologically, regionally, or otherwise, and the effects of this arrangement on ideas, policies, and discourse. Do parties clearly polarize over clear and distinct perspectives, or are party positions more shifting and malleable with each election? To what extent are they rooted in ongoing social cleavages between distinct groups in society? Do they clearly draw support from distinct regional and geographic bases? Finally, party systems can be understood in terms of institutional arrangements and relationships, including how they are organized, use technology, raise money, and are themselves embedded in the legislative and executive institutions of governance.

The Ontario party system shares its origins with the national system, given their common development in the pre-Confederation Province of Canada and the loose groupings in the early days of responsible government. In 1867, both the Parliament of Canada and the Ontario Legislative Assembly started off with the same two closely linked parties, the Liberals and the Conservatives, with heavy overlap between provincial and federal levels.[1] Individuals could sit in both chambers simultaneously until 1872—and in 1867, provincial and federal elections were even held simultaneously.[2] Indeed, the first two Ontario premiers, John Sandfield Macdonald and Edward Blake, also held seats in the House of Commons. Over time, though, the parties became more clearly distinct, especially with Oliver Mowat's construction of a highly organized and dominant provincial Liberal machine that contrasted with Conservative primacy at the federal level. Ideologically, though, the federal and provincial parties shared similar distinctions, with the Conservatives more ardently pro-Empire and gradually more estranged from French Canadians; for example, it was the Ontario Conservatives that introduced the controversial Regulation 17, which restricted the teaching of French in Ontario schools in 1913.

The federal and provincial systems diverged at the end of World War I, a time of social unrest with new populist and socialist parties arising across the country. While federally the western Progressives temporarily became the second largest party before dwindling away, the United Farmers of Ontario swept into power in 1919 with a narrow minority (while a separate Labour Party became the fourth party in the Legislature with 11 seats). The unfortunately named UFO was as "unprepared for victory"[3] as the New Democrats 70 years later and fell into disarray, with some elements eventually joining the Ontario branch of the new Cooperative Commonwealth Federation (CCF) that formed in Canada in the early 1930s and elected its first Ontario MLA in 1934. While winning no seats in 1937, the CCF surged in 1943 to become the official opposition with 34 seats, only four fewer than the governing Progressive Conservatives (renamed across Canada from "Conservatives" in 1942).

But since the disruptions of 1919–43, Ontario has seen the same three main players (with the CCF transforming into the NDP across Canada in 1961), with changes only in their order of precedence. No other party has won a legislative seat since 1951 (the dwindling Labour-Progressives, representing the outlawed Communist Party of Canada, held two seats in the postwar era) and only one independent MPP has been elected since the 1930s—former New Democrat Peter North in 1995. The CCF/NDP's fortunes have been the most elastic, falling to a low of two seats in the early 1950s but rising steadily to come within one seat of tying the second-place Liberals in 1971 and becoming the official opposition from 1975 to 1977. Throughout this period the Progressive Conservatives formed the government, providing another remarkable dimension of stability. Their reign ended in 1985 at the hands of an unusual Liberal-NDP accord, and the PCs slid to third place in 1987 and again in 1990, the year of the unexpected NDP victory.

Since 1995, the Liberals and PCs have maintained their status as the two major parties while the NDP has remained consistently in third place. And as noted, no other party has managed to break into the Legislature since the demise of the Labour-Progressives in the 1950s. The Green Party of Ontario has a modest presence but unlike its federal counterpart has never held a legislative seat; it garnered 8 per cent of the vote in 2007, fell back to 3 per cent in 2011, and rose modestly to 5 per cent in 2014. Other minor parties like the Libertarians, Family Coalition, Freedom, and Communist parties are familiar perennials but consistently marginal in Ontario elections, along with even smaller parties.

Outside of Atlantic Canada,[4] no other Canadian party system has seen more stability than Ontario's. The national party system was similar to Ontario's up to 1993, but it diverged into a series of splits, mergers, and new parties in the 1990s and early 2000s. It then saw the 2011 surge of the NDP to second place ahead of the Liberals and the election of the first Green Party MP, before falling back into an Ontario-style pattern for the major parties again in 2015. Nova Scotia has developed a robust three-party system resembling Ontario's, but only in the early 2000s and with more dramatic rises and falls; Manitoba had a similar three-party array in the late 1980s, but it has dwindled back to a traditional PC-NDP rivalry; and Quebec's two-party rivalry between the Liberals and Parti Québécois, consolidated in the 1970s, was challenged by the rise of the Action Démocratique du Québec (ADQ) in 2007 and then the Coalition Avenir Québec (CAQ) in 2012. British Columbia and Saskatchewan, while both long-standing two-party systems, each saw one of their two major parties replaced in the 1990s and early 2000s (Social Credit was replaced by the Liberals in BC, and the Progressive Conservatives were supplanted by the Saskatchewan Party in Saskatchewan). Finally, while Alberta saw a 44-year Progressive Conservative dynasty beginning in 1971—breaking the Ontario PC record of 42 years—this was upset with the election of an NDP government in 2015, consistent with the province's unique pattern of long periods of one-party dominance followed by rapid disruption, much as when the Alberta PCs displaced Social Credit in 1971.

The Ontario party system is thus exceptionally stable in terms of party names and standings. But how stable is it in other ways—such as ideologically or regionally? Are party policies and supporters consistent? Here again we see a high level of stability, though with some variance over time. The parties have generally held consistent positions in relation to each other, but the relative salience of ideology has varied in the parties. This will be explored further in the next section, but we can quickly note that since the 1980s the Progressive Conservative Party has lurched back and forth between the centre and right, the Liberals have made more modest swings between the centre and left, and the NDP, while traditionally following in the footsteps of its more consistently left-wing federal counterpart rather than the more centrist regimes found in Western Canada and Nova Scotia, underwent a sudden pragmatic conversion during their brief stint in power. While party positions may converge at times (such as in 2007 when little differed between the Liberals and PCs) and sharply diverge at other moments (such as the 1995 PC "Common Sense Revolution" sharply opposed by the other two parties), Ontario voters generally seem to have little difficulty classifying the three major parties and determining where they stand relative to each other.

Regionally, Ontario parties have been somewhat less consistent in their centres of support. In the mid-twentieth century, one could speak of "Tory Toronto" both federally and provincially, but the Progressive Conservative's hold on the city dwindled in the 1980s, and the party has failed to win a single general election seat in the City of Toronto since 1999, despite some by-election victories. In turn, Southwestern Ontario was historically Liberal "Clear Grit" territory and remained a party stronghold in the 1970s when Liberal fortunes were at a low point. But this base slowly dwindled, with the Liberals losing nearly all their rural seats west of Toronto in 2011 and again in 2014 (though they retained some mixed urban-rural seats such as Brant). The NDP, again similar to its federal counterparts, finds strength in the two extremes of the province—densely populated core urban areas, especially in Toronto and Hamilton, and the sprawling, sparsely populated ridings of Northern Ontario. The North in general has been a Liberal-NDP battle-ground; while the Progressive Conservatives did well in the region up into the 1980s, they have not won any seats further north than Muskoka-Parry Sound and Nipissing (North Bay) since then. The Liberals have traditionally done well in northern cities while the NDP is strongest in the more remote areas.

Urban, suburban, and rural variations in party support are also very clear. As mentioned, the NDP primarily wins seats at the two extremes, while in recent decades the Progressive Conservatives have done better in rural areas and the Liberals in cities, a pattern particularly evident in the 2011 and 2014 elections. But suburbs, especially in the Greater Toronto Area, are most significant for Ontario elections, with the Liberals and PCs battling for supremacy and the NDP rarely a significant factor. The GTA suburbs were key to both Mike Harris's Conservative victory of 1995 and the subsequent Liberal victories of Dalton McGuinty and Kathleen Wynne. A particularly interesting contrast is the failure of the provincial Progressive Conservatives to emulate the onetime success of their federal Conservative counterparts in the GTA. In the spring 2011 federal election, Stephen Harper's federal Conservatives broke through in traditionally Liberal-held areas of Bramp-ton, Mississauga, and the outer boroughs of the City of Toronto, propelling him to a national majority. Yet, in the provincial election later that year, Tim Hudak's Progressive Conservatives did not emulate this federal success and won only a single Toronto-area seat in 2011 (Thornhill). The 2014 election saw further setbacks for the Ontario PCs, who lost outer GTA seats like Halton and Burlington (and it should be noted that the federal Conserva-tives lost many of the above seats in the 2015 election).

A final way of understanding party systems is through the institutional configurations that surround and support the party system, such as the electoral system, finance and spending regulations, and the election machinery itself. Ontario has had the same single-member-plurality electoral system since Confederation. However, in the early 2000s it joined several other provinces in seriously considering a change. Following a pledge by the Liberals in the 2003 election, an independent citizens' assembly was created to consider alternative systems, closely following a similar initiative in British Columbia. The assembly recommended a change to the mixed-member proportional system used in New Zealand, but this was roundly defeated by two-thirds of voters in a provincial referendum held with the 2007 election. (In contrast, BC voters came very close to approving a change to a single-transferable vote system.) Significantly for our discussion here on political parties, the NDP and Green parties officially endorsed changing to mixed-member proportional, likely to increase their seats in future. However, the Liberals and Conservatives, who were generally served well by the current system, took no official position and/or gave mixed signals.[5] After the referendum defeat, some reform proponents argued that the Liberals, supported implicitly by the Progressive Conservatives, had deliberately thwarted the chances of reform by leaving little time or resources for public education and awareness of the proposals. Regardless of these charges, stability again trumped change in this supporting aspect of the Ontario party system.

Another area of stability is the relative lack of change in Ontario party financing laws. General disclosure laws and spending limits were established in 1975[6] in a trend widely seen in Canada and the United States, but there was little subsequent change. Federal laws were considerably overhauled in the mid-2000s—banning corporate and union donations, restricting individual donations, and establishing a system of public financing (later dismantled), while Quebec banned corporate and union donations to parties in the 1970s. But Ontario party financing remained relatively wide open, with the two major parties continuing to depend on corporate and large individual donations, while unions directed support to both the Liberals and New Democrats along with additional "third-party" election spending campaigns of their own. Finally, in the spring of 2016, following media revelations about the extent of its own aggressive fundraising, the Wynne government introduced legislation to restrict donations and fundraising actiuity in Ontario politics.

The internal affairs of Ontario parties are similarly unremarkable—slow to change and generally insignificant. As Robert MacDermid documents, party memberships—while difficult to track—are low, as is local fundraising and general constituency association activity.[7] Ontario parties also have shown little interest in institutional innovation. One notable exception was the 1990 Progressive Conservative leadership election, one of the first in Canada to rely on direct voting by all party members.[8] This was an innovative idea at a very low point in the party, and was followed by further innovations in policy consultations and development that led to the dynamic and controversial "Common Sense Revolution" by the Harris government in 1995. But this was exceptional and did not lead to a long-term dynamic culture of innovation in the party. The innate institutional conservatism of Ontario parties is most evident when the parties are confronted with unexpected disruptions. The policy superficiality and amateurism of the NDP became rudely evident when it was thrown unprepared into power in 1990, and as noted earlier the Liberals relied on a nearly obsolescent model of leadership selection in 2013 when Dalton McGuinty suddenly resigned as leader. In short, even the institutional aspects of the Ontario party system remain highly stable, durable, and arguably a bit stale.

Explaining the Lack of Change

Why has the Ontario party system been so stable, and in particular why has it had the same three parties, without even brief interlopers, for so many decades? This is difficult to answer, in part because Canadian party systems have long posed a puzzle in comparison to other countries. A chief issue is the unusual historic dominance at the federal level by a centrist party (the Liberals), something not found in similar countries like Britain or Australia where centrist parties have been more marginal and squeezed between dominant left and right parties. Richard Johnston thus classifies the federal Canadian party system as one of "polarized pluralism."[9] This of course applies equally to Ontario, where the Liberals have always been a significant party, even during the long PC dynasty and the party's temporary drop to third place in the 1970s. But the Ontario party system provides an additional puzzle, since there is no "fractionalization"[10] and growth of new parties, unlike the churning at the federal level since 1993 or occasional shakeups and disruptions in most other provinces.

One of the chief reasons for changes in party systems is that existing parties fail to offer sufficient choice for voters, and so new parties arise to fill the gap. This leads to two outcomes: either the new parties push out or minimize existing parties, or the existing parties adapt to the external threat and ultimately absorb or beat back the newcomers. The first outcome is best seen in Western Canada; as we saw above, British Columbia, Alberta, and Saskatchewan have all seen new parties arise, and sometimes decline, to produce three historically distinct systems. An example of the second outcome is in Quebec. Since the late 1970s Quebec has had two main parties, the Liberal Party and the Parti Québécois (which supplanted the earlier Union Nationale, which last won seats in 1976). But various smaller parties have occasionally surged to win seats before dwindling over time. In 1989, the English-language-rights Equality Party won four seats, but had no further electoral success. The ADQ held a single seat in the 1990s, and then surged to form the official opposition after the 2007 election, ahead of the PQ. The party then slipped back to third place in the 2008 election and eventually dwindled. In 2012 another party, the CAQ, won a significant number of seats, with a slight increase in 2014; Québec Solidaire has also won a small number of seats in recent elections. But in the long run it is not clear that these newcomers will be able to supplant either the Liberals or the PQ, given their past ability to withstand challenges. The federal system may be seen as an example of both outcomes. In 1993 the Progressive Conservatives were reduced to a small rump with the rise of Reform and the Bloc Québécois. But the PCs and Reform eventually reconciled into a new Conservative Party, while the Bloc Québécois was greatly reduced by the NDP surge of 2011. The NDP surge was then reversed by the Liberal 2015 victory, so that after two decades of disruption the system was largely back to what it looked like in the 1980s (though with an ongoing Bloc and Green presence).

In contrast, the Ontario party system has seen neither of the above outcomes and appears able to accommodate change within itself and keep out new players entirely. The rapid rotation of governing parties in Ontario in the 1980s and 1990s, especially the abrupt rise and fall of the NDP, suggests that Ontario voters were indeed restless but found sufficient choice within the existing system. While the federal system split as a consequence of catalysts like Preston Manning and renewed Quebec nationalism, potential threats to the Ontario system have dissipated or been absorbed. An example of such absorption is the Progressive Conservative co-optation of Randy Hillier—leader of a right-wing populist group, the Ontario Landowners Association—into running as a PC candidate in 2007.

A final possible reason for party system change is internal collapse of a party due to infighting and/or widespread corruption, such as the BC Social Credit or Saskatchewan Progressive Conservative parties in the 1990s, or the breakdown of the federal Liberal Party in the 2000s due to the Jean Chrétien–Paul Martin rivalry and the sponsorship scandal. Again, each of the major Ontario parties has remained strong and resilient; the most significant internal party crisis was probably the soul-searching dilemmas of Bob Rae's NDP when in power, discussed in the next section.

Federal–Provincial Contrasts

Broad similarities between the federal and Ontario party systems are evident. However, another intriguing aspect is how Ontario and Canada almost always have opposing parties in power. In the 70 years from 1946 to 2016, the same party governed both jurisdictions for a total of less than 12 years (the Liberals from 2003 to 2006 and again beginning in 2015, and the Conservatives in 1984–85, 1979–80, and 1957–63).

This remarkable alternating pattern is especially interesting given the continuing similarities and informal overlap between the parties. The NDP is organizationally integrated as a theoretically single overall party, and while the Ontario Liberal and PC parties are entirely separate entities from the federal parties of similar names, there are considerable informal ties and affinities, especially at election time.[11] In addition, since the 1990s Ontario electoral districts have been identical to federal ridings (except in the North), which should further encourage convergence. While some Canadian provincial parties are substantively different from the federal parties of the same name (e.g., the Quebec and BC Liberal parties are not associated with the federal Liberal Party) or occasionally estranged (such as the relationship between Stephen Harper's Conservatives and the Newfoundland and Labrador Progressive Conservatives under Danny Williams in the late 2000s), Ontario and federal parties usually have good relations, if sometimes arm's-length formally. Politicians occasionally move from the provincial to federal level, such as George Drew in the 1940s and Sheila Copps in the 1980s, and most notably three Harris government ministers (John Baird, Tony Clement, and Jim Flaherty) in the 2000s, along with lower-profile individuals like the NDP's David Christopherson, but overall, this is not particularly common. The reverse is even more unusual, though Bob Rae in 1982 and Patrick Brown in 2015 both left the House of Commons to assume provincial party leaderships.

While some of the pattern may be explained by contrasting national versus provincial voting patterns (i.e., changes in governing parties may be partly explained by national swings rather than flip-flopping provincial voters), Ontario voters do display an affinity for selecting different parties at virtually the same time. As noted there were differing Conservative results in 2011. In that year, the federal Conservatives won all six Mississauga seats and made inroads into suburban Toronto proper; yet all those seats were retained by the provincial Liberals five months later. This alternation of federal and provincial governing parties in Ontario has long fascinated observers but has never been fully explained.

These differences have created very different legacies for the federal and provincial parties. While the federal Liberal Party dominated Canadian politics for much of the twentieth century, with the phrase "the natural governing party" encapsulated in Whitaker's 1977 *The Government Party*,[12] the federal Progressive Conservatives were notable for infighting and self-destruction, as noted in George Perlin's *The Tory Syndrome*.[13] But the situations were reversed in Ontario. The 42-year Progressive Conservative dynasty made it the natural governing party, in some ways even more skillful than the federal Liberals, while the provincial Liberals of this era were less known for infighting than for a remarkable continued irrelevance and inability to capture public attention. Given its formal integration and perennial opposition status, the NDP has a more common history between the federal and provincial wings, of course with the exception of the Rae government in Ontario in the 1990s.

The Parties in Flux

The above discussion has focused on the Ontario party system as a whole. In the next section, the chapter outlines the individual evolution of each of the three Ontario political parties. As suggested, while the system has been exceptionally stable, the parties themselves have undergone somewhat more substantial change over time.

The Ontario Progressive Conservative Party

Despite ending in 1985, the 42-year Progressive Conservative dynasty remains a keystone for understanding Ontario politics. Unlike other political dynasties in Canada, such as the mid-century federal Liberals or the Alberta PCs, the Ontario PCs maintained a remarkable institutional steadiness that is itself perhaps a metaphor for Ontario political culture as a whole.[14] The party passed power through four successive leaders (and one interim), without a defeat and retooling as the federal Liberals had undergone in 1957. Nor was it shaped by one or two dominant personalities, like the Alberta PC leaders Peter Lougheed and Ralph Klein. Instead, it was the party itself that dominated in a competitive system. Jonathan Manthorpe described it well in his 1974 book, *The Power and the Tories*:

> The Ontario Conservatives ... have somehow avoided the most deadening fault of dynasties: the arrogant assumption of the right to rule. As each election comes round, the Tories whip themselves into a kind of Dervish dance of despair; the aim of the mad whirling is to convince themselves that

they are going to be beaten. The result is the salutary one that they seldom take an election result for granted until the votes are counted.[15]

The dynasty displayed an overwhelming sense of pragmatism, with little passion or evident ideology. This was undoubtedly helped by the economic bounty of the postwar boom, making government a test of "managing prosperity."[16] But also notable was the ability of the party to adapt to social change in Ontario, especially the vast growth of suburbs and increasing ethnic diversity. As noted above, the party had strong representation in Toronto right up into the 1980s, a viable Northern Ontario presence—battling the NDP in labour strongholds like Sudbury—and they dominated the growing suburbs of the Golden Horseshoe. And while the Ontario PCs did not make inroads into multicultural communities like Italian- and Portuguese-Canadians to the extent of the federal Liberals, they avoided the image of anglophile nostalgia and rural traditionalism found in the federal Conservatives of the same period.

Substituting managerialism for populism and passion, the dynasty was sustained by a sophisticated and often elitist cadre that became known as "the Big Blue Machine." Perhaps most interesting is how many of the key party players did not sit in the Legislature, preferring more lucrative professions like the law and advertising while still heavily influencing the party and government. The most important governing decisions were often made in informal groups, often not even in government offices, in a way that would be unheard of today. When Bill Davis was premier (1971–85), the most critical decision-making meeting was a Tuesday morning breakfast group at the Park Plaza Hotel (with funds paid for by the PC Party), attended by senior members of the Premier's Office, party officials, the theoretically non-partisan cabinet secretary E.E. Stewart, and select cabinet ministers.[17] And across the province, the dynasty was closely tuned to local elites—business owners, municipal politicians, and others who kept the party apprised of developments and oversaw the dwindling bounty of patronage.

Most important of all were the skilled leadership transitions that renewed the party once a decade and allowed it to keep pace with social change in Ontario. George Drew, premier from 1943 to 1948, was closely identified with Anglo-Saxon "Tory Toronto" (though he was originally from Guelph). Leslie Frost (1949–61) was known as "Old Man Ontario" and famously remarked that he took his cues from what he heard in the barber's chair in his hometown of Lindsay. But the party had a remarkable ability to stay comfortably in the middle of a changing province. John Robarts (1961–71) captured the *Zeitgeist* of the technocratic 1960s by calling himself a "management man."[18] Bill Davis's (1971–85) more equiv-ocal image (famously captured in his phrase "bland works") was perhaps more suited for the ambiguity of the 1970s, and Davis's very hometown of Brampton was transformed during his time in politics from a small centre to a deeply urbanized and increasingly racially diverse satellite of Toronto. Looking at this model of renewal through smooth succession, it is easy to see how the party stumbled with the choice of Frank Miller in 1985—from the rural Muskoka riding and two years *older* than Davis. This does not tell the whole story of the dynasty's fall—the party was caught by the controversial funding of Catholic high schools, the Liberals set a new tone under David Peterson, and Tory energies had switched to the new national Mulroney government. But it emphasizes how even in 1985, the Ontario PCs were not roundly rejected by the province. Their dynasty ended not with a bang but with a drawn-out whimper.

The PC dynasty may be long gone, but it continued to set the tone for much of the party, including its adaptability to changing conditions, a wary relationship with ideology, and an occasional elitist arrogance, but also a natural and close fit with the business of governing, best seen in its smooth takeover of power in 1995.[19] The party's essential pragmatism was particu-larly evident in the leadership of John Tory (2004–09) who had difficulty distinguishing his positions from Dalton McGuinty. On the other hand, Tory's views stayed relatively consistent, while both his predecessor and suc-cessor were more opportunistic. Ernie Eves, briefly leader and premier in 2002–03 was highly pliant, lurching from the centre to the right in a bid to retain power. Tim Hudak in his initial years as leader avoided ideological commitments (at one point declaring himself to be neither a Red Tory nor Blue, but instead "Purple"),[20] and was considerably more moderate in the 2011 election than in the 2014 race when he adopted an aggressive right-wing platform. But even Mike Harris (1990–2002), the dominant figure of the post-dynasty party, was arguably more pragmatist than ideologue. While some around Harris (like party president Tom Long) were more clearly intellectually committed to small-government libertarianism, it is probably more accurate to say that Harris followed his dynastic predecessors by grasp-ing the *Zeitgeist* of the age, in which citizens had little faith in government. While not afraid of confrontation in the implementation of the "Common Sense Revolution," in a different era Harris might have led a quite different government and party. Hudak's 2014 shift can be seen as a similarly oppor-tunistic move, though one that clearly did not catch fire with voters. Patrick Brown was elected leader in 2015 despite giving very little clear sense of his ideological views, suggesting opportunism remains a key value in the Ontario PC Party.

The Ontario Liberal Party

The Ontario Liberal Party dominated the province in the late nineteenth century under Oliver Mowat, but was missing in action for much of the twentieth century. The exception was the stormy premiership of Mitchell Hepburn (1934–42), perhaps the most colourful premier in Ontario history, who presided over a government that defies easy classification. After sliding into disarray under Hepburn and being supplanted by the PCs in 1943, the party played a perennial secondary (and for a time in the 1970s, tertiary) role. Only one of its leaders from the era is at all memorable—Robert Nixon, the son of an earlier premier and later a key minister under David Peterson—and the party served as an affable but rarely threatening foil for the PC dynasty.

More recently, the party has been notable for resembling its federal counterpart, governing vaguely in the centre, tacking left when necessary, with occasional tendencies toward arrogant complacency. This resurrection began in 1982 with the election of leader David Peterson, who underwent a remarkable cosmetic transformation, shedding thick glasses and adopting a red tie as his signature image. Peterson's trim appearance and urbanized—but not too urban—"Yuppie Premier" image fit much better with the Ontario of the 1980s than did the above-described Frank Miller's; though the party positions were not very different, their styles contrasted sharply. The PCs won a narrow minority in the 1985 election, but Peterson soon reached an "accord" with the NDP that dislodged the PC dynasty and brought in the first change of power since 1943. This 1985–87 government was activist and comfortably centre-left, bringing in key reforms like pay equity; following the expiry of the two-year accord, Peterson called a new election and won a landslide majority. Lacking the prod of the NDP, the new Liberal government was more centrist but still very popular, and appeared ready for a long stretch of centrist government much like the earlier PC dynasty.

However, anticipating poor economic conditions ahead, Peterson called an early election in 1990, only to find a backlash against his obvious opportunism. This merged with a much deeper anti-elite mood, leading to the surprising NDP victory of 1990. After recovering from the shock, the Liberals elected the first female party leader in Ontario, Lyn McLeod, and prepared a suitably centrist platform for its expected restoration in 1995—only to be supplanted in the final weeks of the election by Mike Harris's Conservatives. The party began again by electing the unknown Dalton McGuinty as leader, and McGuinty's eventual victory in 2003 was similar to Peterson's in 1985—an earnest new Liberal against a tired and clumsy PC dynasty. In its initial years the McGuinty government governed comfortably from the centre-left with largesse for all and especially public sector workers; as the economy and fiscal conditions soured, its attempts to cut back led to conflict, and its arrogance led it to cancel gas plants and ignore various spending scandals. This burden eventually became too much and led to McGuinty's political demise in 2012. However, the party demonstrated a previously unseen resilience with the election of Kathleen Wynne as leader and her majority victory in 2014, echoing the earlier ability of the PC dynasty to renew itself though a change in leadership. While this success was due partly to errors and weaknesses in the other parties, Wynne clearly demonstrated the ability to keep the party in the pragmatic centre while the other parties struggled to compete.

The Ontario New Democrats

While the Ontario NDP has shared a close resemblance to the federal New Democrats, especially long periods of third-party status, there have been some important variations, most obviously the unexpected victory of 1990. There was also the earlier heyday of the 1940s noted above; the provincial CCF came within four seats of forming the government in 1943, forming the official opposition that year and again in 1948 (and again in 1975 and 1987). Yet generally the provincial and federal parties have followed similar strategies. In the 1950s the provincial CCF, like the federal party, was marginal in numbers but spoke with an outsized voice, especially under long-time party leader Donald C. MacDonald (1953–70). The transformation of the national CCF to the NDP in 1961 meant a new Ontario NDP as well and, again like the federal party, it found influence through minority governments. In 1975 the party under Stephen Lewis surpassed the Liberals into second place in the Legislature while the PCs were held to a minority government. The resulting 1975–77 government was notable for progressive legislation such as rent control; another successful opportunity arose with the 1985 accord with the Liberals, though the NDP was quickly discarded once the two-year accord expired.

The 1990 election of a New Democratic majority government under Bob Rae remains a pivotal and mixed moment for the party a quarter of a century later. Woefully unprepared in both policies and personnel, the NDP government lurched through several phases, with watershed moments as it first drove up the deficit but also discarded plans to introduce public auto insurance as in Manitoba and British Columbia and eventually imposed new conditions on public sector unions against their will (see discussion in Chapter 16).[21] For many in the party, the unknown question was, and still is, whether the party gave away a "miracle"[22] by not pursuing a more strident ideological agenda in power. Indeed, the Ontario NDP remains noticeably ambivalent about its governing legacy, and not just because of Bob Rae's later defection to the federal Liberals. The Rae government often appears erased entirely from party history, and it is more comfortable for the party to recall its success with minority governments than its own stint in power.

Under leader Andrea Horwath, the party has even more closely followed the federal lead, particularly that of late federal leader Jack Layton who downplayed ideology and class conflict in favour of middle-class appeals and consumer breaks. For example, in the 2011 provincial election, the NDP promised to freeze transit fees, but said much less about the need for new transportation infrastructure. Horwath also quickly moved after the election to exploit the Liberal minority status, positioning the NDP to again play its traditional role of extracting concessions from embattled minority governments. However, this calculation was overplayed in 2014, leading Kathleen Wynne to call an election after the NDP refused to support the Liberal budget. While the NDP modestly gained four seats, the drop in PC support meant the Liberals won a majority and could keep the NDP back on the outside.

Conclusion

This chapter has explored the key features of Ontario political parties and the party system, especially their durability and ability to absorb change within themselves. But this comes at a cost of atrophy and staleness. Ontario parties have largely kept to their traditional ways, as has the institutional framework surrounding them, and there are only limited examples of innovation and imagination among them. They are essential instruments of democracy in the province; they animate the Legislature and, at least for the Liberals and Conservatives, ease naturally into governing. But their own democratic health is questionable. They show little aptitude for ideas that endure beyond the next election date; nor do they engage citizens and societal forces beyond their small bands of loyalists. The Liberals and PCs seem to be built primarily for governing, where they demonstrate a reasonable amount of pragmatic success. But neither display truly enduring ideological traditions and principles. The NDP badly botched its one stint in government—though the reasons remain contested—and remains distinctly ambivalent in its vision and the salience of its ideological principles. In short, even by the modest standards of Canadian political parties generally, Ontario parties are weak as democratic vehicles, and serve primarily as election machines at the disposal of their leaders.

There is little prospect for change on the horizon. As is continually evident, the Ontario party system is highly stable, and the upsets of the 1980s and 1990s had little long-term effect. While governments may come and go, the same three players seem both destined to remain and able to fend off all interlopers. Neither is there much hope that Ontario parties will suddenly become laboratories of innovation and dynamism. Instead, Ontario political parties will likely continue to adjust incrementally and keep pace with change in the province—but following, and rarely leading.

Discussion Questions

1. Ontario has had the same three major political parties for many years. Is this better understood as a sign of healthy stability or of political stagnation? Why?
2. Do Ontario political parties have strong and enduring core values, or are they willing to say almost anything to get elected? What evidence is available?
3. Are changes to party and election finance rules likely to have a significant impact on politics in Ontario?
4. To what extent is the divide between rural and urban voting patterns in Ontario elections a concern for democracy and public policy?
5. Was the 2007 rejection of the MMP electoral system a missed opportunity for Ontario? Why or why not?

Notes

1 S.J.R. Noel, *Patrons, Clients, Brokers: Ontario Society and Politics, 1791–1896* (Toronto: University of Toronto Press, 1990).
2 Ibid., 213.
3 Randall White, *Ontario 1610–1985: A Political and Economic History* (Toronto: Dundurn Press, 1985), 214.
4 The Liberals and Conservatives have been the dominant parties in New Brunswick, Newfoundland and Labrador, and Prince Edward Island since each province joined Confederation, though the NDP has developed a marginal presence in the first two. New Brunswick also saw a brief interloper, the Confederation of Regions party, in the early 1990s. Nova Scotia is distinct from the other Atlantic provinces with a significant NDP presence since the 1990s and all three parties holding government in recent years.
5 As an example of mixed signals: "Toward the end of the campaign [PC leader] John Tory stated that he would vote against the proposal, but his PC Party did not take an official position," in *Ontario's Referendum on Proportional Representation: Why Citizens Said No*, ed. Brian Tanguay and Laura Stephenson (Montreal: Institute for Research on Public Policy, 2009), 14.
6 David Johnson, "The Ontario Party and Campaign Finance System: Initiative and Challenge," in *Provincial Party and Election Finance in Canada*, ed. F. Leslie Seidle (Toronto: Dundurn Press, 1991).

7   Robert MacDermid, "Ontario Political Parties in the Neo-Liberal Age" (paper presented to the annual meetings of the Canadian Political Science Association, 29 May 2009), https://www.cpsa-acsp.ca/papers-2009/MacDermid.pdf

8   Peter Woolstencroft, "'Tories Kick Machine to Bits': Leadership Selection and the Ontario Progressive Conservative Party," in *Leaders and Parties in Canadian Politics: Experiences of the Provinces*, ed. Ken Carty, Lynda Erickson, and Donald Blake (Toronto: HBJ-Holt, 1992).

9   Richard Johnston, "Polarized Pluralism in the Canadian Party System," *Canadian Journal of Political Science* 41 (2008): 815–34.

10 Ibid., 817.

11 Anna Esselment, "Fighting Elections: Cross-Level Political Party Integration in Canada," *Canadian Journal of Political Science* 43, no. 4 (2010): 871–92; Scott Pruysers, "Two Political Worlds? Reconsidering Party Integration in Canada" (PhD diss., Carleton University, 2015).

12 Reginald Whitaker, *The Government Party: The Liberals in Power, 1935–57* (Toronto: University of Toronto Press, 1977).

13 George Perlin, *The Tory Syndrome: Leadership Politics in the Progressive Conservative Party* (Montreal: McGill-Queen's University Press, 1980).

14 John P. Wilson, "Ontario: The Red Tory Province," in *The Government and Politics of Ontario*, 2nd ed., ed. Donald C. MacDonald (Toronto: Van Nostrand Reinhold, 1980), 208–26.

15 Jonathan Manthorpe, *The Power and the Tories: Ontario Politics—1943 to the Present* (Toronto: Macmillan of Canada, 1974), 8.

16 Sid Noel, "The Ontario Political Culture: An Interpretation," in *Government and Politics of Ontario*, 5th ed., ed. Graham White (Toronto: University of Toronto Press, 1997), 49–68.

17 Claire Hoy, *Bill Davis: A Biography* (Toronto: Methuen, 1985), 4–6. Hoy reports that "when the breakfast routine first began … there were no cabinet ministers," but when Toronto lawyer Eddie Goodman joined in 1975, "he insisted that cabinet ministers be included."

18 Steve Paikin, *Public Triumph, Private Tragedy: The Double Life of John P. Robarts* (Toronto: Viking Canada, 2005).

19 David Cameron and Graham White, *Cycling into Saigon: The Conservative Transition in Ontario* (Vancouver: UBC Press, 2000).

20 Antonella Artuso, "Hudak Launches Party's Election Platform," *Simcoe Reformer*, 30 May 2011, http://www.simcoereformer.ca/2011/05/30/hudak-launches-partys-election-platform

21 Thomas Walkom, *Rae Days: The Rise and Follies of the NDP* (Toronto: Key Porter, 1994); Patrick Monahan, *Storming the Pink Palace: The NDP in Power: A Cautionary Tale* (Toronto: Lester and Orpen Dennys, 1995).

22 George Ehring and Wayne Roberts, *Giving Away a Miracle: Lost Dreams, Broken Promises and the Ontario NDP* (Oakville, ON: Mosaic Press, 1993).

12

A Path Well Travelled or Hope on the Horizon? Women, Gender, and Politics in Ontario

CHERYL N. COLLIER

O**N II FEBRUARY 2013, KATHLEEN WYNNE** made history twice in Ontario, becoming the province's first woman premier *and* the first openly gay premier in Canada. A Canadian Press-Harris/Decima national survey released shortly after Wynne won the Liberal leadership convention found that 70 per cent of Canadians saw her appointment as "a significant breakthrough for women in politics."[1] This was despite the fact that Ontario was somewhat late to the party, joining five other jurisdictions that already had sitting women premiers that year: British Columbia, Alberta, Quebec, Newfoundland and Labrador, and Nunavut. Wynne herself noted that while gender parity had finally been reached (however briefly)[2] among provincial premiers, more needed to be done to see the same result in provincial, territorial, and federal legislatures where representation ranged from 15 to just over 30 per cent. "There is a catchup that needs to happen," she remarked. "I hope that as we see female leadership across the country, we will see more representation in those legislatures and in Parliament."[3]

When we take stock of the state of women, gender, and politics in Canada's most populous province, it is important to heed Wynne's cautious observations. Although some progress has been made by breaking the glass ceiling in the Premier's Office and in electing a record number of women to the Ontario Legislature in 2014 (35.5 per cent), ceilings still remain firmly in place in other provincial areas of representational and appointed office. And there is a growing trend under neoliberalism and post-neoliberalism to largely ignore a gender lens that addresses women's inequality in the provincial policy arena. While there are important distinctions in the openness of different Ontario parties in their commitment levels to gender issues, a focus on gender continues to remain largely absent from wider policy debates, even though support for feminism and gender equality has historically been high in public opinion polls in the province (60.5 per cent as "very or quite sympathetic towards feminism" in one 2000 survey).[4]

This chapter will explore these themes and evaluate the changes and continuities regarding women, gender, and politics in Ontario since I last wrote about the topic in 1997.[5] This chapter continues the original approach of evaluating both the numeric (or descriptive) representation of women in elected and appointed political office alongside a consideration of more substantive forms of representation demonstrated through public policy results. In addition, I will attempt to assess the level of intersectionality that is achieved numerically, keeping in mind the constraints of space (and available data) that will limit these efforts. As Brenda O'Neill noted in 2006, there are an unlimited number of ways in which one can compare and assess the state of women between (or within) the provinces.[6] This is compounded by the fact that there are no specific policies that we can tag as specifically "women's policies" or "women's issues" as "few policy areas [if any] do not have gendered effects."[7] However, the link between women's numeric presence in politics and their ability to influence attention to gender equality issues remains persuasive and deserves continued attention, particularly as women struggle toward the ever-elusive goal of gender parity in most representational arenas. Moreover, the chapter assesses substantive representation to gender equality policy in the areas of pay equity, child care, and violence against women and the ways in which the provincial state addresses these debates through discursive frames.

Analytical Approach

Karen Celis and Sarah Childs remind us of the dominance of research on women's substantive and descriptive/numeric representation inside gender and politics research internationally over the past decade. The case for increasing the numbers of women in elected and appointed political office is based on the assumption that women will represent "women's issues, needs and wants" even if these are not monolithically homogeneous or in many cases easy to identify.[8] Women have worked toward full representational equality via gender parity in legislative assemblies but this goal has not been reached in jurisdictions such as Ontario that do not employ a quota system to ensure 50/50 representation between men and women. Thus, researchers have used lenses such as critical mass theory to understand the impact of a substantial minority of women legislators on political power structures.[9] However, a sustained lack of progress in the numbers of women in Canadian legislatures has recently prompted researchers such as Sylvia Bashevkin to question whether women can exercise enough influence when they remain in a token minority position over time. Drawing on Rosabeth Mass Kanter's study of male/female interaction in business corporations, Bashevkin suggests that the plateau of women's representation in the Canadian House of Commons at around 20 to 25 per cent for the past two decades has made it easier to marginalize women's voices. Thus, women's representation is skewed, rendering elected women to serve as "symbolic 'stand-ins for all women'" without real power or influence in political circles.[10]

Whether or not women have been able to reach a level of critical mass or are more akin to the skewed group described by Bashevkin is important to consider when evaluating the progress in women's numeric/descriptive representation in Ontario. We must also use an intersectional lens to consider the promotion of diverse women to elected and appointed office as part of the complexity of women's representation in Ontario. As Ontario has become more diverse ethnically and culturally, it is arguably more important to consider intersectionality in women's descriptive representation. Intersectionality as a concept recognizes that women's oppression and interests are shaped by their complex diversity, not just that they are women, and that this diversity impacts them in ways that are "simultaneous and interacting."[11]

Alongside this, the chapter assesses whether or not women have achieved substantive policy gains from the provincial state. As mentioned, it is difficult to identify specific public policy issues as being "women's issues" as women hold a variety of interests that are impacted by their class, race, sexual orientation, location, age, ethnicity, and so on. However, the chapter measures provincial policy in three areas often tied to women's goals of greater societal equality: child care, violence against women, and pay equity. In order to assess the level of substantive responses in these policy areas, the chapter briefly analyzes the attention and commitment to these policy areas over the past two decades. In addition, it assesses the type of discourse used by the state to better understand how these policy areas are framed.

Attention to discourse and framing has increased in women and politics research in a neoliberal/post-neoliberal era as governments have, in many cases, moved away from investments in the welfare state in order to reduce the size, cost, and influence of government activity. As women rely more than men on social policy investments to address issues of systemic inequality, they are disproportionately affected by these neoliberal trends. In addition, as some governments have made decisions to reinvest in certain areas of social policy in what some authors describe as post-neoliberalism or the social investment state, women and politics researchers have noticed a trend toward a de-gendering of policy language and focus. As Jane Jenson notes, women are "written out" of public policy debates in areas traditionally associated with gender equality, such as child care.[12] It is important to assess the presence or absence of these trends in Ontario, as well as the extent to which different parties may or may not embrace them in their policy responses in areas of women's equality. This chapter does this in the second section while evaluating women's substantive impact on provincial public policy.

Ontario Women's Numeric/Descriptive Representation in Elected Office

The obvious place to begin is an assessment of how well women have done in gaining access to the Ontario Legislature since being awarded the right to stand and hold elected office in 1917. The Royal Commission on the Status of Women in the 1960s, the 1984 Toronto-based Committee for '94, and more recently the non-profit multi-partisan Canada-wide group Equal Voice, have worked to achieve gender parity in Canadian and Ontario legislatures, yet as is evident in Table 12.1, the goal of 50 per cent representation of women in the Ontario Legislature has still not been achieved.

Table 12.1   Women Elected by Each Party, 1945–2014

Election Year	Progressive Conservatives	CCF/ NDP	Liberals	Total # (%)
1945	0*	0	0	0 (0)
1948	0*	1	0	1 (1)
1951	0*	0	0	0 (0)
1955	0*	0	0	0 (0)
1959	0*	0	0	0 (0)
1963	1*	0	0	1 (1)
1967	1*	1	0	2 (2)
1971	1*	0	0	1 (1)
1975	3*	2	1	6 (5)
1977	3*	2	1	6 (5)
1981	4*	1	1	6 (5)
1985	3	3	3*	9 (7)
1987	1	3	16*	20 (15)
1990	3	19*	6	28 (21)
1995	11*	4	4	19 (15)
1999	9*	6	3	18 (17)
2003	3	2	17*	22 (21)
2007	7	3	19*	29 (27)
2011	8	7	15*	30 (28)
2014	6	11	21*	38 (35)

* indicates governing party.

Sources: Cheryl Collier, "Judging Women's Political Success in the 1990s," in *The Government and Politics of Ontario*, 5th ed., ed. Graham White (Toronto: University of Toronto Press, 1997); Elections Ontario data.

It wasn't until the late 1980s that women were able to reach double digits in representation at Queen's Park, and even though there was progression to the level of 21 per cent in 1990, we see regression in 1995 back to 1987 levels (15 per cent), illustrating that increases in numbers of women certainly do not follow a linear model. Progress did resume in subsequent elections reaching a new high in Ontario with 35 per cent female representation in the Legislature in 2014. This is the first time that women have reached a level above 30 per cent representation in provincial history. While it is possible that this marks the beginning of a trend toward a critical mass (30–35 per cent), it is too early to tell whether or not this can be sustained over time as progress has dipped depending on which party holds power. Notably, Ontario still falls short of gender parity and the pace of improvement and potential for regression do not suggest parity will be reached any time soon.[13]

When we look even closer at Table 12.1, it is apparent that the type of party that wins an election matters when it comes to the numbers of women at Queen's Park. Notably, both dips below the 20 per cent range since 1990 happened under Progressive Conservative regimes. Since parties are the gatekeepers to elected office in Ontario, including controlling access to the nomination and selection process, it is important to further uncover differences in commitment levels to women's representation among the parties and to assess efforts by the parties to increase numbers of women nominees and candidates in turn.

Figure 12.1 shows the number of women in each party in the Ontario Legislature by election year as a percentage of the entire party caucus elected that year. As we can see, there are stark differences between the parties beginning in the early 1980s when parties began to implement some programs to assist women's participation in formal politics, in part in response to lobbying from feminist groups. We also see that the NDP consistently has the highest percentages of women inside of its party caucuses than either the Liberals or the PCs, with the Liberals performing slightly better than the PCs in most years. Some of the reasoning behind this is reflected in the data in Table 12.2. In this table we see more distinctions between the parties in the number of women that they run as candidates for election across the province. Again there is a significant difference between the percentages of women run by the PCs (the highest being in 2014 at 27 per cent) compared to the Liberals and NDP who have both grown their numbers to close to 40 per cent (Liberals in 2011) or over 40 per cent (NDP in 1987 and 2014). Disturbingly, these gains have also not been linear, with each party showing years when its percentage of women candidates fell compared to the previous election. Thus, party commitment to running women candidates, while improved, is not sustained with effective internal policies. Similarly, when

Figure 12.1 Female Percentages in Party Caucuses, 1945–2014

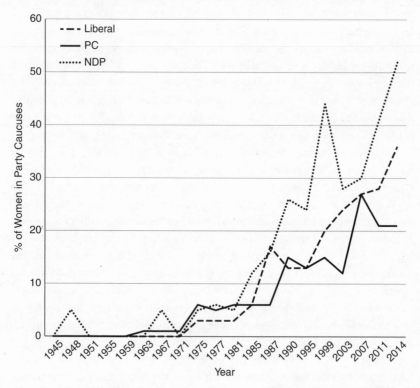

Sources: Cheryl Collier, "Judging Women's Political Success in the 1990s," in *The Government and Politics of Ontario*, 5th ed., ed. Graham White (Toronto: University of Toronto Press, 1997); Elections Ontario data.

Table 12.2 Women Candidates by Party—percentage (number)

Year	PCs % (n)	NDP % (n)	Liberals % (n)	Total n
1987	18 (23)	35 (45)	21 (27)	95
1990	15 (19)	30 (39)	21 (26)	84
1995	15 (19)	29 (37)	24 (31)	87
1999	17 (18)	31 (32)	18 (19)	69
2003	20 (19)	33 (32)	22 (21)	75
2007	22 (24)	39 (42)	35 (38)	104 (126 with 22 Green Party)
2011	22 (24)	35 (38)	39 (42)	104 (130 with 26 Green Party)
2014	25 (27)	41 (44)	34 (37)	108 (145 with 37 Green Party)

Sources: Graham P. Murray Research Limited, Working Paper, "Women MPPs at Queen's Park, 1981 through 2010"; Elections Ontario data.

we look at the programs put in place to increase the numbers of women involved in the internal workings of Ontario political parties, we again see a mixed and fleeting effort overall.

The Conservatives are the least committed. In 2007, in response to a challenge to all parties by Equal Voice Canada to increase the number of women candidates,[14] PC leader John Tory pledged that one-third of his candidates would be women, but there was nothing put in place inside the party to facilitate this goal. The PCs encourage two-fifths of the members on internal "Special Party Committees" to be women and two-fifths to be men, however, this is not mandated. The party used to have a PC Women's Association that served as a volunteer arm of the party. That association has disappeared from the party's online website in 2015. It also used to help fund women candidates' campaigns with the national PC Ellen Fairclough Fund, but this fund was discontinued once the federal Progressive Conservatives joined the Canadian Alliance to form the new Conservative Party of Canada in 2004.

The Ontario Liberal Party has an active Women's Liberal Commission (OWLC) with a stated "aim ... to bring equal representation of women in the Ontario Legislature by encouraging their active participation in the Liberal Party, strengthening women's presence and helping them grow as activists."[15] However, as with the Conservatives, this "policy" does not include any quotas or specific targets. Also in 2007, Liberal Premier Dalton McGuinty pledged that 50 per cent of candidates "in ridings not held by Liberal members would be women." In many cases this meant that those ridings were not safe Liberal seats and could be construed as "unwinnable" for a Liberal candidate, thus ensuring that those women had a slim chance of success if nominated. Despite this pledge, which would have added 35 women to run alongside the sitting 17 women Liberal MPPs, the party fell short that year. Unlike the PCs the Liberal Party still maintains a special women's fund named after Margaret Campbell, the first Liberal MPP elected in Ontario, to offer financial support to female candidates. Arguably, the presence of the OWLC and the Campbell fund helps explain the improved success rates of Liberal women's representation compared to their PC colleagues, particularly in the 2014 election.

Finally, the Ontario NDP has a similar party-based Women's Committee with a mandate to "encourage women's participation in the political process" and to "break down barriers and dispel stereotypes" related to women.[15] Like the Liberals, the ONDP has a female candidate support fund named after the first woman CCF/NDP MPP (and MP), Agnes Macphail. In addition, it has an affirmative action nomination policy in its party constitution which was extended to cover not only women, but also visible minorities, people with disabilities, and Indigenous nominations. The party sets a gender parity target for its candidates at each election but because there are no set quotas attached to the target, the party has yet to reach this goal.

Despite the lack of sustained success in attracting electoral candidates to the parties beyond the 20–30 per cent range, women have been able to win the leadership in Ontario in two out of three of the competitive parties. In 1992, the Liberals became the first party to select a female leader: Lyn McLeod. McLeod served as Liberal leader from 1992 to 1996 until she was succeeded by Dalton McGuinty. She led the party in one election in 1995, losing to the Mike Harris Conservatives and their "Common Sense Revolution." After McGuinty resigned in late 2012, the Liberal leadership convention held in early 2013 actually came down to a choice between the two front runners, both women—Kathleen Wynne and Sandra Pupatello. Pupatello noted the significance of not only Wynne's election as the first women premier in Ontario, but also of the choice on the final ballot. "From the beginning," she said, "we had the boys on the run."[16]

It is important, however, to not overstate the significance of this choice. Research by Bashevkin suggests that parties in trouble electorally are usually more open to choosing a woman leader. Subsequently, the chances are higher that those women who are ostensibly put in charge of "uncompetitive parties" will fail in upcoming elections. Thus women leaders can be assumed to be the reason for failure and this decreases the likelihood that parties would choose female leaders when the stakes are higher and they view the party as very competitive in upcoming electoral contests.[17] Notably, Wynne was able to successfully defend her position as premier in the 2014 election bringing the Liberals a majority mandate. The majority win was not predicted by media pundits and many later credited it more to a failure of the opposition NDP and PC campaigns than as a ringing endorsement of the Liberals. Nevertheless, Wynne was able to hold onto her job, whereas many of her female premier colleagues across the country were not so lucky.[18]

The NDP is the other party that selected a woman as leader in the province. Andrea Horwath won the job in 2009, replacing long-time leader Howard Hampton. Hampton had just led the NDP to another poor showing in the polls in the 2007 election and the party was seen as being in a perpetually weak state following the defeat of the Rae NDP in 1995. Horwath was chosen to breathe new life into the NDP and improved the party's fortunes in the 2011 election, nearly doubling its seat total and raising its share of the popular vote to its more traditional 20 per cent. This success demonstrated the potential for a strong female to turn the party around when it was in a weak state. Horwath's NDP wasn't as successful in the 2014 election, however, losing one seat and angering many inside the party who suggested she forced the election at the wrong time. Horwath was able to survive a subsequent leadership review and remained party leader at time of writing.

The presence of female leaders in the centre and centre-left Liberal and NDP provincial parties, alongside women's electoral success and institutional party supports in the same parties, demonstrates the openness of those parties to gender equality compared to the right-wing Progressive Conservatives. It also helps us understand the reason why progress in electoral mirror representation is not linear but instead depends on the party in power at the time. Despite the stated party commitments, however, progress in electoral office remains slow and in cases of female leadership, arguably fleeting. Also notable is the fact that none of the female party leaders were visible minority women. As mentioned, Wynne is the first openly gay premier to be elected in Canada and she did not hide her sexual orientation during her run for the Liberal leadership. This is a significant milestone in Canadian politics but it remains to be seen if this is a token recognition or one that truly begins to break down barriers for sexually diverse politicians. The next section examines numeric representation in appointed office to further test these trends.

Ontario Women's Numeric/Descriptive Representation in Appointed Office

Beyond the Premier's Office, the location of power in Ontario's executive-dominated Westminster Legislature is at the cabinet table. In order to assess how much power and influence women could potentially exert, it is important to examine how many women have been appointed to cabinet posts. Table 12.3 shows the irregular pattern of progress of women as a percentage of cabinet ministers in Ontario since 1970. The high point of representation was in 1990 when 44 per cent of the governing NDP cabinet were women. Many of these women, including Evelyn Gigantes, Marion Boyd, and Francis Lankin, were strong feminist activists who had a marked impact on policy results during their time around the cabinet table.[20] Arguably this substantial minority, which approached gender parity, was a good example of women constituting a critical mass.

Unfortunately, this milestone appears to be an anomaly compared to previous and subsequent years in the Ontario cabinet. Table 12.3 shows that after the NDP was defeated, the PCs more than halved women's cabinet representation during its tenure in office to 20 per cent. Once the Liberals assumed office in 2003, things did not improve immediately as women's cabinet representation remained at 20 per cent. After the 2007 election the Liberal party began to increase women's representation to first 32 per cent and then to 39 per cent in 2010. But by 2011, female cabinet representation slumped back to 27 per cent, showing the lack of commitment to steady

Table 12.3 Women Cabinet Ministers in Ontario, 1970–2014[19]

Year	Party Government	Number	%
1970	PC	0/22	0
1972★	PC	1/23	4
1974★	PC	1/24	4
1975★	PC	3/26	11.5
1976★	PC	3/26	11.5
1978★	PC	3/26	11.5
1981	PC	2/26	8
1985	PC	2/28	7
1985	Liberal	2/23	9
1987	Liberal	4/26	15
1990	NDP	11/25	44
1995	PC	4/20	20
1999	PC	5/25	20
2003	Liberal	5/25	20
2007	Liberal	9/28	32
2010	Liberal	11/28	39
2011	Liberal	6/22	27
2013	Liberal	8/27	29
2014	Liberal	8/27	29
2016	Liberal	12/30	40

Note years marked with asterisk ★ when 100% of women elected to the governing party were promoted to cabinet.

Source: Data compiled by author.

progression in representation. Even when Kathleen Wynne was promoted to the Premier's Office in 2013, there was no real marked improvement in women's cabinet representation until a cabinet shuffle in 2016 with the Liberals falling in the polls. Wynne increased the cabinet size to 27 (from 22 in 2011), but women's representation remained virtually unchanged at 29 per cent and stayed at this level through to 2015. In 2016, Wynne increased cabinet to a new high of 30 members, 12 of which were women. This was a milestone for the Liberals at 40 per cent but still did not match the NDP high in 1990 nor the 50 per cent gender parity of the federal Liberals under new Prime Minister Justin Trudeau.[21]

Although we do not have comparative data to years prior to 2003, it is also important to assess the numbers of diverse women and men over the past five Liberal cabinets. In 2007, one visible minority woman (Margarett

Best) was promoted to cabinet as a junior minister of health promotion. Best remained in cabinet in 2011 as minister of consumer services, but was demoted by Wynne to a parliamentary assistant post in education in 2013.[22] The only other minority woman (representing diversity in sexual orientation) included in cabinet was Wynne herself. She was first promoted to cabinet in 2003 and has remained there ever since, holding the education, chair of cabinet, municipal affairs and housing, Aboriginal affairs, and agriculture portfolios. Currently, she is the minister of intergovernmental affairs alongside holding the job of premier. In 2013, there were four visible minorities in Wynne's cabinet (14 per cent), all male.[23] In 2014, Wynne increased this number to five but two of these visible minority ministers were women and both held junior posts—Mitzie Hunter who was associate finance minister responsible for pensions, and Dipika Damerla who was associate minister of health, long-term care, and wellness. The 2016 cabinet shuffle saw Hunter promoted to the education portfolio along with the addition of one more visible minority woman minister, Indira Naidoo-Harris, who replaced Hunter at the associate minister of finance post. Thus six visible minority ministers made up 20 per cent of the new Liberal cabinet.

The demotion of Best to the role of parliamentary assistant, a minor office outside of cabinet, prompts a closer look at the number of women and visible minorities appointed to parliamentary assistantships. In 2013 the government had 20 parliamentary assistants, of which six were women (30 per cent). Interestingly, five of these women were visible minority women. In addition there were three visible minority males, meaning that visible minorities constituted 40 per cent of parliamentary assistants—much higher than in cabinet. In 2015 the number of parliamentary assistants was larger—30, reflecting the larger Liberal caucus after the 2014 election—and 12 were women (40 per cent), higher than two years earlier. However, the representation of visible minorities dropped—nine in total, or 30 per cent, with four being visible minority women. Unfortunately, parliamentary assistants are much less powerful at Queen's Park than their senior cabinet colleagues, and indeed nearly all government MPPs held parliamentary assistantships in 2015.

Finally, it is important to look at the number of women appointed to elite levels of the bureaucracy as well as inside the ranks of political staffers who hold key positions aiding the governing party. Table 12.4 compares the number of women deputy ministers and assistant deputy ministers appointed in 2013 to data collected in the late 1990s. What is striking here is the fact that women have not sustained the higher levels of representation reached at the DM or ADM levels in the 1990s. This is likely a direct result of the 1995 decision by the Harris Tories to repeal the Employment Equity Act. The act did much to increase the pool of qualified female bureaucrats

Table 12.4 Women Deputy Ministers and Assistant Deputy Ministers[24]

Year	Deputy Ministers % (N)	Assistant Deputy Ministers % (N)
1995	40 (8/20)	42 (38/90)
1996	40 (8/20)	43 (39/90)
2013	28 (8/28)	40 (57/141)

Sources: Cheryl Collier, "Judging Women's Political Success in the 1990s," in *The Government and Politics of Ontario*, 5th ed., ed. Graham White (Toronto: University of Toronto Press, 1997); Government of Ontario Phone Directory 2013.

and encouraged their consideration for promotion alongside qualified males, yet it appears that without it, women's bureaucratic representation, particularly at the deputy minister level, has suffered. Women DMs fell from a high of 40 per cent in 1995–96 to the 2013 level of 28 per cent. The story was a bit better for ADMs, which only decreased slightly from 43 per cent in 1996 to the current level of 40 per cent. Finally, the Secretary of Cabinet position, the most senior public service position and a close advisor to the premier, was held by a male, Peter Wallace, in 2013 (although after Rita Burak—the first woman Secretary of Cabinet—left the post in 2000, one other woman was appointed by Dalton McGuinty—Shelly Jamieson in 2007). After Wynne's re-election in 2014, she named another male, Steve Orsini, as Wallace's successor.[25] Finally, the most senior political advisors (not career public servants) to Premier Wynne between 2013 and 2015 were also male (Tom Teahen as chief of staff and Andrew Bevan as principal secretary). Of course these are snapshots in time and could very well change in the future; but for now the representation at the top of the Ontario Public Service and in the ranks of key political staff is more male-dominated than it was in 1995–96.

Substantive Representation of Women in Ontario

While tracking the number of women appointed to elected and appointed office is an important measurement of women's representation in provincial politics, it is also essential to examine how the provincial state "acts for" women. In this way we can begin to link numbers with results and can assess a government's overall commitment levels to women's equality issues. In this section, I examine the bureaucratic department in place to address women's interests and issues—the Ontario Women's Directorate. I also assess three areas of public policy that are closely associated with women's equality goals: child care, violence against women, and pay equity. Finally, I will look briefly at the 2013 and 2014 Throne Speeches to assess present attention to gender issues.

In 1997, the Mike Harris Conservative government had just eliminated one of two bureaucratic departments put in place to address women's equality—the Ontario Advisory Council on Women's Issues. The OACWI had served as an evaluative body that advised the government of the day on ways it could improve public policy to better address women's equality issues. As well, it consulted regularly with women's groups and kept open the lines of communication between the women's movement and the minister responsible for women's issues. In the 1990s, particularly after the Harris Tories took office in 1995, the government was less interested in consulting with women's groups and thus the OACWI was eliminated.[26]

Thereafter, the role of addressing women's issues inside of government and of advising the minister fell to the lone office for women left in the Ontario bureaucracy—the Ontario Women's Directorate. The OWD was historically more involved in developing women's policy than the OACWI. After the OACWI disappeared, the OWD took on more of an advising and outreach role, although much of its entire mandate suffered as its budget and staff component was cut over time (even after the OACWI was gone). In 1995, the OWD had a staff of about 85 and a budget of about $18 million (down from $24 million under the previous NDP regime). By 1996, the OWD was moving away from a policy role. Instead, gender policy was spread out over many existing departments (labour, health, human resources) and given less attention.

Despite the change in regime after the McGuinty Liberals were elected in 2003, things did not improve for the OWD. It took the lead on violence against women policy and implemented the Liberal's Domestic Violence Action Plan and its more recent Action Plan to Stop Sexual Violence and Harassment, but it ceased to be an active advisor to the minister responsible on *new* gender equality policy. Notably, its budget continued to be reduced from 1995 levels, reaching a low of $12.4 million in 2004–05. The most recent available numbers for 2007–08 saw an increase to $17.3 million, but this still registered below the 1995 spending levels (at a time when the Harris Tories were slashing social policy expenditures).

Substantive Gender Equality Policy

During the 1990s, there was a marked difference between commitment levels of different Ontario party governments to women's issues such as child care, violence against women, and pay equity. The Bob Rae NDP government with a strong critical mass of feminist women cabinet ministers has been touted as perhaps the most open to gender equality than any other government in provincial history.[27] By contrast, the Harris Tories and their

"Common Sense Revolution" made sustained and deep cuts to women's policy areas, including cuts to child care spaces and child care workers' salaries, elimination of second stage shelter funding for victims of violence against women, and abolishing the proxy method of comparison for pay equity cases and capping pay equity payouts.[28] The Harris Tories saw women as "special interests" and strongly resisted calls for improvements in these policy areas, preferring instead to cut back on progress made under the previous NDP government.

On the pay equity file, the SEIU Local 204 union challenged the Harris pay equity changes in court and in 1997 these changes were overruled for contravening the Pay Equity Act (1987). Even though both Mike Harris and subsequent premier Ernie Eves promised to abide by the court decision and to fully ensure the payout of retroactive pay equity claims, the government dragged its heels on ensuring subsequent settlements beyond those inside the provincial public service owing for 1995–98. The lack of compliance on the part of the Tory government prompted another court challenge, this one via the Charter of Rights and Freedoms, in 2001. The Charter challenge was settled in 2003 resulting in payments of $414 million to 100,000 women over three years.

Once the Liberal government took office and the payment of proxy-based claims had been settled in the courts, the issue of proper funding for the Pay Equity Commission (which enforces the Pay Equity Act) continued to be a problem. The Harris Tories cut the Pay Equity Commission budget by 46 per cent in the 1997 budget, drastically reducing the effectiveness of the commission from its previous years under the NDP. When the Liberals took office in 2003, it continued to cut the commission's budget by a further 20 per cent. In 2006, there were 32 employees at the commission and only 15 review officers to cover the entire province. By contrast, in 1992 there were 86 employees and 28 review officers. In 2014, the Liberal government made an election promise to "develop a wage gap strategy to close Ontario's gender pay gap," which saw women on average earn 31.5 per cent less than men in the province. But to date, no details have been announced besides a commitment to public consultation, nor has a significant change been made to the Pay Equity Commission.[29]

The story of child care and violence against women under the Liberals was not as negative as that of pay equity. After the Tories left office, the Liberals reinstated funding and increased government attention to both files in a marked improvement from the Harris years. However, compared to the NDP years, post-2003 was not as fruitful for child care or violence against women policy. Notably, some positive movement on both files appeared to be on the horizon in 2015, but it is too soon to tell how sustained the moves will be as the Liberals still struggle with significant budgetary pressures related to its promise to balance the provincial books. As well, the Liberal government began to gender-neutralize both policy areas, moving the focus away from women in many instances.

The federal government provided child care funding to the provinces in 2000 under the Early Childhood Development Agreement but left the door open to the provinces to decide what to spend the money on. The Harris Tories used it for everything it could associate with "early childhood development" except for increasing child care spaces. In 2003, the federal government announced more targeted funding for early learning and child care for children under six under the Multilateral Agreement on Early Learning and Child Care but still allowed provincial flexibility in using the funds. The McGuinty Liberals directed some of this money to new child care spaces under its Best Start Plan, signifying the first time new money was made available for space creation since the 1990s in the province. The Liberal Best Start plan also included a promise to create and extend full-day junior and senior kindergarten across the province to be rolled out over a five- to six-year period between 2010 and 2015–16.

When the federal government ended its commitment to child care funding in 2009, the Ontario Liberals in turn tempered their efforts toward child care space creation. After the McGuinty Liberals won a minority government in 2011 and had to rely on NDP support to pass its budget, this approach to child care again changed. One of the NDP's demands for support was the creation of a child care stabilization fund to address what the industry estimated was a nearly $300-million per year shortfall. The Liberal/NDP budget deal saw just under $250 million earmarked for child care spaces over the next three-and-a-half years. While this was short of the advocacy targets, it was welcomed and demonstrated the distinction among the parties once again, with the NDP being more open to increasing government commitment to the child care policy file. By 2012, the Liberals had announced they would change the funding formula for child care and give municipalities more flexibility in how they delivered child care locally. In 2014, the Liberals promised a much-needed $1-per-hour wage enhancement for child care workers in the budget (some made as little as $13 per hour), which was welcomed by advocates but seen as more of a bandage instead of the desired workplace strategy for the regulated child care sector.[30]

On violence against women, the Liberals appeared to be more proactive after taking office in 2003, enacting a $60-million Domestic Violence Action Plan at the end of 2004. The plan was supposed to increase funding to shelters and sexual assault centres as well as increase collaboration with anti-violence front-line workers. However, initial funding was provided on a one-time basis instead of for ongoing sustainability, and in 2005 shelter staff were directed by Sandra Pupatello, then minister responsible for women's issues, to essentially find their own money thereafter. Even though spending on anti-violence increased over the previous government, the overall percentage of provincial spending remained largely steady through 2007.[31] In 2011, the Liberals launched their Sexual Violence Action Plan to target sexual assault issues more specifically and to encourage better responses from law enforcement agencies. Developed in consultation with provincial sexual assault and anti-violence groups, the plan committed $15 million over four years for education, prevention, training, and awareness programs.[32] The focus on sexual assault was strengthened in 2015 with the three-year action plan entitled It's Never Okay, including a public awareness campaign, new funding for sexual assault centres, as well as changes to the sexual assault provisions of the Limitations Act and a review of provisions in the Criminal Code to improve the treatment of survivors. Advocates were optimistic about these commitments and vowed to monitor the province's movement on this file closely throughout the three-year implementation period.[33]

While actual policy gains in both child care and violence against women appear to be improved but mixed since the Liberals took office in 2003, there was a notable change in framing of both issues that followed neoliberal and post-neoliberal trends to de-gender each policy arena. Policy debates on child care centred on the educational needs of the child and not on the equality focus for women as it had in the past. For violence against women, the mere mention of "women" was often removed from policy debates, opting for more gender-neutral frames of "domestic" or "family" violence and to address the problem of violence against men as well as women. This shift over time was noted in an examination of government documents on early learning and the rollout of full-day kindergarten as well as the government Action Plans on Domestic Violence and Sexual Assault. This de-gendering of very gendered policy areas has the potential to further dilute a commitment toward gender equality inside of government agendas and to weaken the influence of feminist actors both inside and outside of the government as a result.[34] The newest Action Plan on Sexual Violence initially appears to restore a more gendered lens to at least the sexual assault policy agenda with its focus on "rape culture" and use of the word "misogyny," which suggests there may be an improvement under a female premier leading a majority government with a higher proportion of women in its caucus. However, a look at the 2013 and 2014 Throne Speeches illustrates more of the past gender neutrality.

It is interesting to note the lack of gender attention in the Throne Speeches delivered by the Liberal government of Kathleen Wynne in 2013 and 2014.[35] Other than mentioning that she was the "first female premier" in the province in both speeches and then referencing the "election of more women to this chamber than in any Ontario Parliament before it" in 2014, the speeches are devoid of any mention of policy to address women's inequality, gender, or diversity policy (save for a reference to increasing the numbers of men and women with disabilities in the workforce in 2013 and mention of the promise to increase child care workers' salaries in 2014). They both address commitments to improve the lives of First Nations' children, the francophone community, and the strength of Ontario's diverse population, but all are cast in vague and gender-neutral language. The cores of the speeches centre instead on economic issues such as "trade," "productivity," "infrastructure," and a vague promise to "lead from the activist centre" in 2014.

Conclusion

While this chapter would certainly be remiss not to address the milestone of Wynne's promotion to the Premier's Office in Ontario, it would be erroneous to assume that this is a "significant breakthrough for women in politics" on its own. Instead, the direction of women's representation, both numeric and substantive, has seen some progress and some regression since the 1990s which, save for the more recent increase in elected women MPPs in 2014, seemed to suggest stalled gains overall for women in the province. Only time will tell whether or not the more recent gains can be sustained and there is hope for women's equality agenda in the province or whether we are back on the road well-travelled where women's issues are still seen as secondary and a gender lens is largely absent from public policy debates, including in areas often identified as "women's issues."

What has remained constant since 1997 is the strong impact that provincial parties have in the willingness to see and to address gender equality issues. Centre and centre-left parties are more open to gender equality than right-wing ones, with the centre-left NDP performing better in its commitment to affirmative action in numeric representation in elected and appointed office, particularly at the cabinet table. The NDP also continued to positively impact the policy agenda for women through its influence on the minority governing Liberals, even when the Liberals appeared to have embraced a post-neoliberal, gender-neutral approach to traditional "women's" issues like child care and violence against women. The Liberal Party's unwillingness to support pay equity enforcement also raises questions about its commitment to gender equality, even under a progressive female premier, although positive movements on the sexual assault file leave the door open for change in this area over the next years. If the party in power continues to impact a government's commitment to gender issues as much as it appears to have over the past two decades, women in Ontario should be wary of a potential right turn at Queen's Park in the future. The present incarnation of the Ontario Progressive Conservative party may not embrace the "Common Sense Revolution's" years of austerity and attacks to social programs, but its weak to non-existent commitment to women does not bode well for gender equality policy if it is returned to power in the near future.

As this chapter has shown, it is also extremely difficult to collect data on the intersectionality of women's representation both numerically and substantively. What is apparent in the small amounts of data presented here is that diverse women have an even tougher climb to attain proper representation at Queen's Park. Although they form small pockets of appointed office, diverse men and women are not well represented at the cabinet table or in policy circles. Even more than gender representation, attention to intersectionality is clearly skewed and marginalized. It remains to be seen whether Ontario parties will be convinced in the years to come to address these representational failures more consistently and systematically than is presently the case. Until then, we are unlikely to see many more "significant breakthroughs" for women, gender, and diversity in Ontario.

Discussion Questions

1. All three Ontario parties have held power since the 1990s. How open has each been to the promotion of women to elected and appointed office?
2. What's the difference between women's numeric and substantive representation? How easy is it to link both of these concepts together?
3. Ontario has its first openly gay female premier. How does this impact her approach to governing, if at all?
4. Do you think Ontario finally has a critical mass of women in elected office? What changes do you think will occur as a result of this, if any at all?
5. In your opinion, what has to occur for Ontario women to reach gender parity in appointed and elected office?

Notes

1 Maria Babbage, "Women in Canada Politics: Kathleen Wynne's Premier Win a Breakthrough?" The Canadian Press, 11 February 2013, http://www.huffingtonpost.ca/2013/02/11/wynne-women-politics-canada-premier_n_2662863.html

2   While Wynne was able to hold onto her job as Ontario premier following the 2014 election, other female premiers were not so fortunate. Pauline Marois (Quebec), Kathy Dunderdale (Newfoundland and Labrador), Eva Ariak (Nunavut), and Allison Redford (Alberta) were all replaced by male premiers. In 2016, women only held three of the 10 provincial and none of the three territorial leadership positions (Wynne in Ontario, Christy Clark in British Columbia, and Rachel Notley in Alberta).

3   Babbage, "Women in Canada Politics."

4   Data from the 2000 Canada Election Study in Brenda O'Neill, "Women's Status across the Canadian Provinces, 1999–2002: Exploring Differences and Possible Explanations," in *Provinces: Canadian Provincial Politics*, 2nd ed., ed. Christopher Dunn (Toronto: University of Toronto Press, 2006), 451.

5   Cheryl Collier, "Judging Women's Political Success in the 1990s," in *The Government and Politics of Ontario*, 5th ed., ed. Graham White (Toronto: University of Toronto Press, 1997), 268–83.

6   O'Neill, "Women's Status across the Canadian Provinces."

7   Collier, "Judging Women's Political Success in the 1990s," 268.

8   Karen Celis and Sarah Childs, "The Substantive Representation of Women: What to Do with Conservative Claims?" *Political Studies* 60 (2012): 213.

9   See Drude Dahlerup, "From a Small to a Large Minority: Women in Scandinavian Politics," *Scandinavian Political Studies* 11, no. 4 (1988): 283–87.

10   Sylvia Bashevkin, "Women's Representation in the House of Commons: A Stalemate?" *Canadian Parliamentary Review* (2011): 20.

11   Leah Bassel, "Intersectional Politics at the Boundaries of the Nation State," *Ethnicities* 10, no. 2 (2010): 155.

12   Jane Jenson, "Writing Gender Out: The Continuing Effects of the Social Investment Perspective," in *Women and Public Policy in Canada: Neo-liberalism and After?* ed. Alexandra Dobrowolsky (Don Mills: Oxford University Press, 2009).

13   No historic data are available on the number of visible minority or other diverse categories of women elected to the Ontario Legislature over time.

14   "Commissions," Ontario Liberal Party, http://www.ontarioliberal.ca/OurTeam/WhoWeAre/Commissions.aspx

15   "Committees," Ontario New Democratic Party, http://www.ontariondp.ca/committes

16   Adrian Morrow and Karen Howlett, "Wynne Makes History as First Openly Gay Premier in Canada," *Globe and Mail*, 26 January 2013.

17   Sylvia Bashevkin, "'Stage' versus 'Actor': Barriers to Women's Federal Party Leadership," in *Opening Doors Wider: Women's Political Engagement in Canada*, ed. Sylvia Bashevkin (Vancouver: UBC Press, 2009), 121.

18   See note 2 above.

19   Note that Table 12.3 does not include every cabinet shuffle that occurred between 1970 and 2000, but does include those in which the numbers of women or percentages of women in cabinet changed, along with shuffles that occurred as a result of changes in government.

20   See Collier, "Judging Women's Political Success in the 1990s"; and Lesley Byrne, "Making a Difference When the Doors Are Open: Women in the Ontario NDP Cabinet, 1990–95," in *Opening Doors Wider: Women's Political Engagement in Canada*, ed. Sylvia Bashevkin (Vancouver: UBC Press, 2009).

21   Robert Benzie and Rob Ferguson, "Struggling Wynne Shuffles Cabinet, Adds
      7 New Ministers," The Star.com, 13 June 2016, https://www.thestar.com/
      news/queenspark/2016/06/13/struggling-wynne-shuffles-cabinet-adds-7-
      new-ministers.html
22   Best reportedly had health problems and this may help explain the demotion,
      although this is speculative.
23   No historic data are available on the representation of visible minorities in cabinet.
24   This table was compiled by the author and reflects a snapshot in time as these
      positions change at various time points over the course of a government's
      tenure. Note the total N reflects numbers of different people holding office, not
      the positions themselves as some ADMs and a few DMs actually held multiple
      portfolios.
25   Wallace was extremely critical of the Liberals' fiscal plans during his tenure as
      cabinet secretary and played a key role in bringing attention to the destruction
      of key documents in the gas plant scandal inside of former premier McGuinty's
      office—both of which explain his exit from the cabinet secretary position.
26   Collier, "Judging Women's Political Success in the 1990s."
27   See Collier, "Judging Women's Political Success in the 1990s"; Byrne, "Making
      a Difference When the Doors Are Open."
28   "History—Ontario," Equal Pay Coalition, http://www.equalpaycoalition.org/
      history/ontario/
29   Ibid.
30   Ontario Coalition for Better Child Care, "OCBCC Welcomes Action on Child
      Care Wages, But Questions Remain and More Support Needed," http://www.
      childcareontario.org/ocbcc_welcomes_action_on_child_care_wages_but_
      question_remain_and_more_support_needed
31   Cheryl Collier, "Violence Against Women or Violence Against 'People'?
      Neoliberalism, 'Post-Neoliberalism' and Anti-violence Policy in Ontario and
      British Columbia," in Women and Public Policy in Canada: Neoliberalism and After?
      ed. Alexandra Dobrowolsky (Toronto: Oxford University Press, 2009), 175–76.
32   Government of Ontario, "Changing Attitudes, Changing Lives: Ontario's
      Sexual Violence Action Plan," March 2011, http://ywcacanada.ca/data/
      research_docs/00000380.pdf
33   Government of Ontario, "It's Never Okay: An Action Plan to Combat Sexual
      Violence and Harassment," March 2015, http://www.ontario.ca/document/
      action-plan-stop-sexual-violence-and-harassment
34   For more on this study and its implications see Cheryl Collier, "Feminist and
      Gender Neutral Frames in Contemporary Child Care and Anti-Violence
      Policy Debates in Canada," Politics and Gender 8 no. 3 (2012): 283–303.
35   Government of Ontario, "Speech from the Throne: The Way Forward," 19
      February 2013, http://news.ontario.ca/opo/en/2013/02/the-way-forward-1.
      html; Government of Ontario, "Speech from the Throne: Building Ontario Up,"
      3 July 3 2014, http://news.ontario.ca/opo/en/2014/07/building-ontario-up-
      speech-from-the-throne.html

13

An Inside Look at the Ontario Liberals in Power

ANNA ESSELMENT

O N 2 OCTOBER 2003, DALTON MCGUINTY and the Ontario Liberals ended the Conservative "Common Sense Revolution" that had swept Ontario eight years earlier. Ontarians had decided to chart a new course under the Liberals, who offered a kinder, gentler government from its predecessors. The 2003 victory was the first of four for the Liberals. Dalton McGuinty led the party to another majority in 2007 and a minority in 2011, a feat previously achieved only by Oliver Mowat in the late 1800s. In somewhat of a surprise, the Liberals regained their majority status in the 2014 election, this time under new leader Kathleen Wynne.

During his almost 10 years as Premier, Dalton McGuinty oversaw the implementation of policy changes in key fields of importance to the government: children's education, health care, and the environment. There is little doubt the former premier will be able to point out his policy legacies. At the same time, the Ontario Liberals faced a number of scandals and a shifting economy that challenged the government's ability to fulfill its commitments. To this point, little has been written about Premier McGuinty's tenure in power. This chapter is devoted to an examination of key aspects of his administration. A retrospective analysis shows that, while the McGuinty government was adept at implementing big policy visions for the province, in its dogged pursuit to do so, it consistently tripped over local politics. There is a saying that all politics is local and, by the 2014 election, it appeared as though Liberal fortunes in Ontario were expiring. However, a change in leadership, an apology for past mistakes, and mediocre performances by the opposition parties resulted in both Liberal renewal at Queen's Park and the possible cementing of a new dynasty in Ontario politics.

Dalton McGuinty: From Underdog to Ontario's Premier

Dalton James Patrick McGuinty Jr. was first elected in 1990 in the riding of Ottawa South. His father, Dalton McGuinty Sr., held the riding from 1987 until his death in 1990. As the eldest son of 10 siblings, there was some sense of duty attached to the younger McGuinty's decision to run in his father's place.[1] A second (more practical if possibly apocryphal) reason was the shared name: it was already printed on his father's stockpiled election signs. McGuinty won the riding in the 1990 election and again during the 1995 campaign. When Liberal leader Lyn McLeod resigned shortly after the party's 1995 loss, McGuinty angled for the top job.

Dalton McGuinty was not considered a front-runner in the 1996 Liberal leadership. Most observers expected Gerard Kennedy—a charismatic politician who had headed the Daily Bread Food Bank in Toronto—to win over the convention delegates. If not Kennedy, then perhaps victory would be claimed by Dwight Duncan, an ambitious and savvy member from Windsor, Ontario. To the surprise of many, McGuinty's organizers kept him on the ballot, weaving him from fourth place to first after five rounds of voting. In the early morning of 1 December 1996, Dalton McGuinty was chosen the new Liberal leader and, with that, the leader of the Official Opposition at Queen's Park.

Taking over the reins of the Ontario Liberal Party in 1996 was no easy task. The party had expected to win the 1995 election, but instead lost to the Progressive Conservatives under Mike Harris and their "Common Sense Revolution." The revolution created discord in Ontario, with the government pitted against teachers, welfare recipients, and labour unions.[2] The politics of division was an effective weapon wielded by the Harris Conservatives and scores of voters put their faith in what a "Common Sense Revolution" could bring to Ontario.

Considering the animosity between some large groups of Ontarians (teachers in particular) and the PC government, Ontario Liberals were hopeful that the 1999 campaign would swing their way. Despite an increase for the Liberals in both popular vote and seat share,[3] the Conservatives maintained their hold on Queen's Park. The 1999 loss was hard on McGuinty and his party. The Tories had unleashed devastating commercials suggesting the Liberal leader was "not up to the job" and the Liberal campaign team's response gained little traction with Ontarians. After the election, a few disgruntled insiders who blamed McGuinty for the 1999 election debacle initiated a "Dump Dalton" campaign. They were convinced the party would be better off without him as leader.[4] McGuinty and his office quickly quashed the internal dissention and this move cemented part of his leadership style. While he readily acknowledged there was room for self-improvement, he wanted commitment and loyalty from his team: his MPPs, his staff, and the staff at the Ontario Liberal Party offices.

Between the 1999 and 2003 elections, several changes were made to better position McGuinty and the Ontario Liberals in a fight against the Progressive Conservatives. First, the party brought in well-known consultant David Axelrod (later a key strategist to Barack Obama in 2008 and 2012) to help improve McGuinty's public speaking style (which had been criticized as stiff and scripted) and appearance, to assist McGuinty and his team on developing key messages that would resonate with Ontarians, and to advise on aspects of campaign strategy.[5]

Second, a restructuring of the Leader's Office at Queen's Park brought in several new outsiders to occupy key positions. Particular emphasis would be placed on developing strong policies, and by the end of 2001 serious work had already started on the campaign platform. Policy analysts in the Leader's Office, together with MPPs and the larger party membership, developed proposals for the 2003 platform; these were then divided into five themes and printed in booklet form. Borrowing the strategy that had successfully launched the "Common Sense Revolution," McGuinty decided to release the party's platform incrementally in advance of the 2003 election. Each fully costed "theme" was launched separately, with a month or two between releases. This gave the media, stakeholders, and the public time to familiarize themselves with the Liberal commitments.

Third, McGuinty's office also wanted to ensure that the leader would be ready for the cut and thrust of the campaign, and so debate preparations also began a year before the election. The 1999 leaders' debate had not gone well for McGuinty—he was attacked by his opponents, he occasionally fumbled for answers, and at one point froze completely.[6] The goal was to erase any doubt in voters' minds that McGuinty was not "up to the job"—McGuinty had to look, act, and sound like a leader.

Finally, the assembled campaign team for 2003 was a capable group. Not only did McGuinty have smart operators who had learned much from their experience in 1999, but he was also able to draw on key strategists who had worked for former prime minister Jean Chrétien.[7] These individuals were well heeled in the craft of electioneering, with skills such as preparing for the leader's tour, war room tactics, effective political communication, and managing the press. It was a successful blend of talent. On 2 October 2003, the Ontario Liberals claimed victory, winning 72 seats in the Assembly—the leadership candidate underdog from 1996 was now the Premier of Ontario.

Ontario Liberals in Government: Deficit Shock and "It's the Right Thing to Do"

The euphoria of triumph was quickly deflated when the new government inspected the province's books more closely. In advance of the 2003 election, the opposition parties were aware that the province was likely facing a $2.3 billion deficit.[8] The Liberals had been careful to take that deficit into consideration when putting together their election platform. Less than a month after winning, a government-appointed auditor revealed that the previous Conservative government had not been entirely forthcoming about the province's finances: the $2.3 billion deficit was actually $5.6 billion.[9] The drastically different fiscal situation put a number of Liberal plans in peril—the first order of business would be to find a way to reduce the deficit.

The revised budget numbers, and what the new government would have to do about them, fit into what would become the overarching Liberal narrative—a Liberal government and its premier would always choose "the right thing to do"[10] for the province. This mantra was evident leading up to the election: for Ontario Liberals the right thing included (among others) more nurses, better primary education, investments in universities, and a greener environment. But with an altered economic landscape, a good governance imperative meant the "right" choices for the province could involve taking a longer view of Liberal platform commitments and implementing policies that would (from the government's perspective) help the province in the future even if they were deeply unpopular with the public. This position was an about-face from the modus operandi of the previous Conservative government. Particularly for former PC premier Mike Harris, the electoral imperative of "doing what we said we were going to do" was the driving force behind most of the political executive's decision making.[11] The Ontario Liberals, on the other hand, proved willing to bend and break political promises as circumstances required. Both parties faced some degree of public backlash for their actions; their justifications to Ontarians for doing so, however, were quite different ("we said we would" versus "it's the right thing to do").

The charge that Dalton McGuinty was, at best, a flip flopper and, at worst, a liar, was levelled just months into his first term when the government's first budget imposed a health premium.[12] During the 2003 campaign the Liberal leader had signed a pledge vowing not to impose any new taxes.[13] While deliberately labelled a premium, few were fooled that the extra money taken from the paycheques of Ontarians was not a new tax. The McGuinty government made the argument that the health premium was simply "the right thing to do"—Ontarians could either invest more into their health care system or public services would suffer to help balance the books. Two factors helped the Liberals survive the negative politics brought on by the health premium. First, they imposed that tax early in their first year of governing. The Liberals gambled that fallout from the new levy would be long forgotten by the 2007 election. Second, borrowing from the example of Tony Blair and "New Labour" in the UK, the Liberals were careful to measure the outcomes in their health care investments. In 2006, the government boasted that wait times had already been reduced in areas of high demand such as

MRI scans, hip and knee replacements, cancer care, and heart surgery.[14] Over the next six years, wait times were also reduced in other areas, such as emergency rooms, and the government made efforts to communicate these results to Ontarians, demonstrating that the added investment in health care was having a positive effect.[15]

The "it's the right thing to do" philosophy permeated other policy areas as well. The 2008 decision to bail out the Ontario auto sector was premised as being the responsible decision.[16] Harmonizing the GST with the provincial sales tax in 2010 was met with some resistance since it meant another rise in taxes, but the Liberal government insisted that the short-term pain brought on by harmonization would be beneficial to Ontario's economy in the long run.[17] Similarly, the McGuinty government framed the right of high school students to name their gay rights advocacy groups whatever they wanted as an issue of respect and fairness, despite the opposition from Catholic school boards.[18] The Liberals deliberately chose to frame numerous unpopular decisions as the "right" ones since it gave them a cushioning to defend their actions. When combined with some of the Liberal government's legacy policy pieces, it is not surprising that McGuinty took on the moniker "Premier Dad" early in his tenure.

The Liberal Legacies under "Premier Dad"

A decade of leadership provides ample time to create legacy policies. While the Liberal government fumbled a number of political issues, Premier McGuinty was clear on the few big items he wanted to get right: education, health care, and the environment.

In education, the Liberal government made major investments in the early years of primary school.[19] The first priority was to create a hard cap of just 20 students in public school classrooms from Junior Kindergarten to Grade 3. For the Liberals, smaller class sizes meant better learning opportunities since educators could spend more time teaching the curriculum and less on classroom management. The Liberals also wanted to improve the test scores of Ontario children and amended the curriculum to focus more directly on literacy and numeracy. As a result, reports from the OECD suggest that Ontario students improved their performance on standardized tests between 2003 and 2010.[20]

The key piece in education, however, was the introduction and implementation of full-day, every-day junior and senior kindergarten in Ontario schools. Based on research that suggested young children become better learners the earlier they start school, the program was to roll out over five years beginning in September 2010. Full-day kindergarten for four- and five- year-olds was widely popular with parents, and early evidence has suggested it is having a positive impact on learning outcomes for children.[21] However, with a price tag of $1.5 billion, the cost of the program raised some eyebrows, particularly as Liberals struggled with a $16 billion deficit in 2012. The opposition Progressive Conservative Party vowed to halt the continued rollout of full-day learning until the deficit was eliminated.[22] This was also the recommendation of the Drummond Report, produced by an expert panel tasked by the Ontario government to suggest ways in which the Liberals could balance the province's books.[23] In its response to the Drummond Report, the McGuinty government assured Ontario parents that the popular full-day kindergarten program would be considered sacrosanct and the government would pursue its planned implementation. However, the government would consider an increase in classroom caps from 20 to 23 students to help tighten spending.[24]

Health care was a second policy area in which the Liberals were determined to make improvements. Armed with revenue from the health premium, the government set about to hire more nurses, reduce wait times in key areas, ensure more families had family doctors (usually as part of a "family health team"), and improve the nature of home care in the province. On nurses and wait times, the government had a measure of success. Thousands of nurses were hired to staff hospitals and other health care sectors. As noted earlier, the government was also able to measure wait times for certain procedures and could report significant reductions by the end of their second term in power. Access to family doctors was also ameliorated; numbers of medical professionals agreed to take part in the family health teams (FHTs) the Liberals had envisioned. These teams involved family doctors, nurses, nurse practitioners, and other health professionals working together to provide care to patients. The Liberals created over 200 FHTs, providing 2.1 million Ontarians who did not have one before 2003 with a family doctor.[25] Other areas such as birth screening, new publicly funded vaccines for babies, and lower drug prices were all touted as successful government policies in the field of health care. Improving senior care (both at home and in nursing homes) did not fare as well. The growing number of seniors in Ontario requiring health services and the expense required to provide care for this group meant slower-paced improvements. Instead, the Liberals hoped that their emphasis on health promotion and illness prevention would eventually ease the demand on the health care system by helping Ontarians stay healthier in general. Acting much like a concerned father, McGuinty, along with his cabinet, implemented a province-wide smoking ban in public places, banned junk food from primary and secondary schools, and required more physical activity in the education curriculum.[26]

But with these health care pieces in place coupled with stagnating economic growth, it is unsurprising that the health care budget continued to grow under the Liberal watch. In the 2012–13 budget, health care comprised $48.4 billion (or 41.8 per cent) of total government expenditures. Education was the second biggest expense, at $23.9 billion (or 20.6 per cent) of total expenditures.[27] As Don Drummond noted in his report to the Ontario government, if health care spending continued at its current rate of growth (about 5.5 per cent a year since 2008), it would soon comprise well over half the total budget for the province.[28] The issue of health care cost and its ultimate sustainability is a complex conundrum that has both domestic and intergovernmental dimensions, and budget growth in this area is not isolated to Ontario but is a concern for provinces across Canada.[29]

The environment is a third area where the McGuinty government wanted to make an impact, and it is a policy field where successes also bred failures. Two points are particularly relevant here: the Greenbelt and green energy power. Created two years after the Liberals took power, the Greenbelt is an area of permanently protected green space, including farms, watersheds, wetlands, rivers, small lakes, and forests totalling 1.8 million acres around the Golden Horseshoe Area of Ontario. While it is not without challenges from developers in the province, environmentalists have praised the creation of the Greenbelt and its role in preserving fragile ecosystems in the heart of Southern Ontario.[30] It has also been lauded for its role in promoting healthy living, particularly for its numerous hiking trails and the promotion of locally grown food by Ontario farmers within the belt.

Green energy (or, more broadly, alternative sources of energy—see Chapter 14 in this volume for a full treatment of the issue) is a secondary policy field where the Liberals strived to make gains. The commitment to more sustainable and eco-friendly ways of generating power was evident in the 2003 platform promise to shut down Ontario's five coal-fired plants by the end of the government's first term. The Liberals grossly overestimated their ability to get other clean and renewable power-generating sources online; the initial 2007 deadline was moved to 2009, but the province's remaining coal-fired plants at Nanticoke (in Haldimand County) and Sarnia remained open until the end of 2013.[31] The promise of thousands of new jobs in the green energy sector propelled the government forward on nuclear, solar, wind, and natural gas power; the government has estimated more than 20,000 jobs are connected to this new energy sector, particularly with the addition of 17 new natural-gas-fired generating stations. The successful pursuit of alternative sources of power has made Ontario a leading jurisdiction in clean power generation,[32] although this particular legacy has brought on its share of civic dissent with which the government has had to contend, and which is discussed in the next section.

Notable Scandals from a Decade in Power: From Broken Promises to Gas Plant Cancellations

History will judge whether the McGuinty government got the big policies "right." But like all governments in power for extended periods, policy advancements are often accompanied by pitfalls along the way, and the McGuinty Liberals faced their share of criticism for action or inaction. The short- and long-term effects of these scandals marred the reputation of the premier and that of his government, and posed a real threat to the party's hold on power.

The first challenge for the Ontario Liberals was their penchant for breaking promises. It may seem counterintuitive, but reneging on pledges can be characterized as a good governance imperative. Governments who refuse to alter their decisions based on changing evidence are often doomed to make bad choices. For citizens who expect parties to uphold their election platforms, the Liberals were a disappointment from the outset. Within months of taking office, Premier McGuinty and his cabinet had gone back on their "no new taxes" campaign promise and imposed the health premium, costing some Ontarians upwards of $900 annually. The Liberals had also made a firm commitment to cancel a planned development of 6,600 houses on the Oak Ridges Moraine, an environmentally sensitive area near Richmond Hill slated to be part of the new Greenbelt. Just two weeks after the election, the government announced that the legal rights within the developers' contract precluded any cancellation of the development, disappointing many environmental activists and Liberal voters in the area.[33]

The development of homes on the Oak Ridges Moraine was a stark contrast to a forced stoppage of new housing construction in Caledonia, Ontario, where a tense standoff between First Nations' groups (who claimed the tract of land where the construction of new homes had already started) and residents, police forces, and the government itself, began in late 2005 and, at the time of writing, was yet to be resolved. The inability of the provincial government (or the federal cabinet for that matter) to effectively resolve the dispute[34] remained a sore point for many Ontarians living in Haldimand County.[35] (For more on the Caledonia dispute, see Chapter 15.)

The Liberals also faced other challenges. The government's second term witnessed the cabinet resignation of health minister David Caplan in 2009 over the soaring costs of developing and implementing electronic health records in the province.[36] Problems with the eHealth initiative (which started in 2000 under the previous government) were uncovered by the provincial auditor, who pointed out deficiencies in oversight by the government, the extensive use of consultants hired without proper procurement processes in place, and the 1 billion of taxpayer dollars that had been invested into the project with very little to show for it.[37] David Caplan did not stand for re-election in 2011.

Trials and tribulations in the second term continued with the introduction and implementation of the HST in the 2009 budget.[38] While unpopular among some members of the general public, the support of the federal Conservative cabinet and most business groups in the province helped shield the government from major fallout. Accompanying the boost by businesses was the government's strategy to offset the initial sting of the new harmonized tax by providing Ontarians with rebate cheques over the course of a year.[39] The opposition parties were quick to point out that the government was attempting to buy the support of Ontarians with their own money. For McGuinty, any avenue that allayed concerns about the added cost of the HST to Ontario residents was worth pursuing, and part of the government's strategy was to give Ontarians two years to become accustomed to the tax before the next election. The government's success at this is questionable: the Conservative labelling of McGuinty as the "Tax Man" in the 2011 campaign likely had some traction with the public and contributed to the party's tumble to minority status.

The ORNGE Air Ambulance fiasco came to light after the 2011 election, but the problems developed during the government's second term. Coupled with the eHealth scandal, both incidents appeared to establish a pattern of a government lacking any serious oversight capacity of their agencies. Established in 2006, the provincial government spent more than $730 million over five years to operate the air ambulance service.[40] An employee with ORNGE blew the whistle on the agency in 2008; a full investigation into ORNGE by the provincial auditor did not occur until 2011–12. The auditor's special report on the matter noted a clear lack of transparency and accountability by ORNGE to the Liberal government and a lax system of oversight of the agency by the government itself, which resulted in many questionable financial decisions by the corporation.[41] The Ministry of Health took over ORNGE in January 2012, fired the executives, replaced the board of directors, and began the process of dismantling the for-profit companies started by the former ORNGE CEO.[42] While it appeared that the minister of health was taking charge of the situation, the fact remained that under the Liberals' watch another substantial portion of taxpayer dollars had gone to waste. The story for the opposition was clear: the McGuinty Liberals were bad managers and could not be trusted with the public's money.

The inability to "manage" was also evident in the government's handling of local politics, particularly in the areas of wind turbines and the location of gas plants. Second-term hiccups continued with the investments the Liberals were making in wind energy as part of the government's plan to expand into clean, renewable sources of power. The government underestimated how this policy area would impact local politics. There was little consultation with the primarily rural communities about where many of the wind turbines would be located. Different groups mounted protests to the government's plan: homeowners, who felt their property values would sink (and their landscapes would be destroyed) if turbines were located too close to their homes or cottages; environmental activists, who worried about the effect of the turbines on migrating birds; citizens' groups, who worried about the health impacts of living near turbines; and farmers, who tended to have divided opinions about wind energy, since permitting the erection of a turbine on a farm provided valuable extra income.[43] The anger rural Ontarians felt toward the government over wind energy was effectively demonstrated in the 2011 election. Seven Liberal-held seats in rural areas (including those of three cabinet ministers vying for re-election) fell to the Tories, contributing to the loss of a Liberal majority in the Legislature.[44]

The challenge of local politics was not isolated to rural and small-town Ontario. In the run-up to the 2011 campaign, the Liberals were also knee-deep in politics over a proposed gas-fired plant in Mississauga, having already cancelled a similar project in Oakville amidst local pressure.[45] The decision to scrap the planned Oakville plant was made in February 2011; according to former finance minister Dwight Duncan, the relocation of the proposed Mississauga plant occurred only days before the 6 October provincial election, making it an obvious political decision to the benefit of five local Liberal MPPs.[46] The Liberals suggested the cost of the cancellation was $190 million; a special report by the provincial auditor pegged the cost at $275 million.[47] The Legislature's investigation into the fiasco resulted in accusations of a cover-up, and in fall 2012 the opposition parties filed a contempt motion against both the government and personally against the minister of energy, Chris Bentley, for failing to produce, in their entirety, documents related to the gas plant decision. The Liberals were challenged to move out from under the shadow of this political scandal—Chris Bentley, a respected member of the cabinet and Legislature since his election in 2003, announced his resignation from the Legislature effective 14 February 2013.

The new premier, Kathleen Wynne, continued to be dogged by the controversy, especially since the provincial auditor estimated the total costs for both cancellations at almost $1 billion.[48] Compounding the issue were allegations that political staff in the Premier's Office erased sensitive emails regarding the scandal, and as of 2015 these matters were still under investigation.[49] The scandal surrounding the gas plant decision found its way into the 2014 election, and Kathleen Wynne deftly worked around the issue by effectively distancing herself from the issue and by offering a direct apology to voters during the leaders' debate. Through some skill and more luck for Premier Wynne, voter blame for the cost of the gas plant scandal was left squarely at McGuinty's feet and did not appear to impact the results on election day.

The Old McGuinty Government and the New Wynne Government: Rearview Reflections and the Challenge Ahead

A review of McGuinty's tenure as premier of Ontario reveals, as it would for most leaders, a mix of strengths and weaknesses. The Ontario Liberals certainly had big visions and expectations of their desired policy changes. The government would invest in children and their education, health care would be transformed to improve access and quality, the environment would become a priority, and the province's finances would remain balanced. Unlike the preceding Progressive Conservative government, the Liberals tried to avoid polarizing confrontations, and were much less inclined to identify scapegoats on which to place blame for the province's ills.

For the government's first two terms, this strategy was largely successful because the government felt strongly about maintaining the support of its electoral base. Teachers, nurses, and other public sector unions were respected and, arguably, treated well by the government as it moved forward with implementing aspects of its platform. But when confronted by the global recession and the particularly hard impact it had on Ontario's manufacturing sector, the government had less room in which to manoeuver to keep its core supporters content. Revenue generation was limited—the Liberals had imposed a premium in 2004 and, only five years later, again asked Ontarians to pay a little more with the HST; the shrinking manufacturing base meant less income in both personal and corporate taxes. The third term was particularly hard with regard to the province's finances—the Drummond Report was dire in its prediction that the province had to drastically reform its spending pattern to resolve its financial woes.

In order to save legacy programs such as full-day kindergarten, the Liberals decided that reeling in expenses would have to start with the public sector, thus far a dependable ally during elections. After two years of signalling the need for salary restraint in the broader public service (the 2010 budget was obvious in its theme of compensation and the public service,)[50] and while still singing the Liberal refrain of doing the right thing, the government requested that teachers agree to a salary freeze and a reduction of benefits. The plan was to secure a contract from the teachers, and then make similar requests of the public service, universities, and doctors, among others. The government hoped that teachers would recognize how favourable the past eight years had been for them, particularly if they contrasted their experience under the Mike Harris regime; in return, the Liberals were now requesting some cooperation on compensation restraint. For the most part, the response by the teachers to the government was outright rejection;[51] the teachers' unions also believed that *they* had been quite good for the government and were undeserving of being singled out. The lack of agreement and an escalation of animosity between the two sides meant the imposition of a contract in early January 2013. The fallout between the teachers and the government was significant, resulting in rallies, marches, protests, and the withdrawal of extracurricular activities from public elementary and high schools.

It was in this climate in October 2012 (teacher protests, questions swirling about the cost of cancelled gas plants, wind turbine politics, and declining economic growth), that Premier McGuinty—after 16 years as leader of the Liberal Party—announced his resignation. It came as a shock to many in his caucus, his party, and among his loyal staffers, especially since he had won almost 86 per cent support at a party leadership review the month before.[52] The resignation was accompanied by a request to the Lieutenant-Governor to prorogue the Assembly, which effectively suspended the Legislature's investigation into the political decision behind the gas plant cancellation.

Three months later, Kathleen Wynne, the MPP from Don Valley West, won the Liberal leadership race in a delegate-style convention held in Toronto. As premier, Wynne attempted to bring a different approach to the job than McGuinty had. First, she appreciated the minority situation in which the government found itself after the 2011 election. McGuinty had two terms at the head of a majority government where government initiatives moved forward regardless of the position of opposition parties in the Assembly; when faced with a minority government, McGuinty was less adept at adapting his approach.[53] Wynne was far more conciliatory and, after winning the party leadership, immediately reached out to opposition leaders Tim Hudak and Andrea Horwath to emphasize her willingness to work with them on different issues. Wynne also made gains with the province's teachers; as a former Toronto school board member, the new premier was well acquainted with both the union and school board leadership. Within three months, the government had reached a deal with teachers that returned some of the benefits that were at issue in the contract imposed in January 2013, although the move was met with sharp criticism that the government essentially bought their way out of trouble with core supporters.[54]

Second, Wynne understood that she could not disown the previous decade of Liberals in power. There were a number of policy areas that the Wynne government continued to champion—a greener environment, better primary education, and a reinvigorated (if expensive) health system. In the months before the 2014 election, however, Wynne also acknowledged previous political mistakes, such as the gas plant cancellations, and apologized to voters who, apparently, were in a forgiving mood.[55]

Third, both before and after the successful 2014 election, Wynne wasted little time moving forward on issues that would distinguish her leadership from her predecessor's. Aside from achieving labour peace with teachers, tackling transportation and gridlock in the province was the government's next major policy piece.[56] For an MPP from Toronto and a former minister for transportation and municipal affairs, this is perhaps an unsurprising policy direction to take. Two other items are also noteworthy. One is the creation of an Ontario Retirement Pension Plan (ORPP). Premier Wynne was determined to enhance retirement savings for Ontarians, something that McGuinty never initiated during his time in office, and went ahead with this proposal despite admonishments by the federal Conservative government of Stephen Harper that it simply imposed a new "tax" on residents of Ontario.[57] (The subsequent Trudeau government elected in October 2015 was far more supportive.) The second policy item that differentiates Wynne from McGuinty is the update to the Ontario health and physical education curriculum that included new guidelines regarding sex education. McGuinty's government proposed similar changes to the curriculum in 2010, but quickly backed away when religious and other groups protested.[58] The Wynne government proceeded with the changes in 2015 in spite of similar backlash, and launched an ad campaign to dispel myths about what Ontario children would be taught in schools. Wynne's willingness to take on Stephen Harper over his objections to the ORPP and to push back against niche communities that opposed the teaching of sexual education in public schools demonstrated a renewed energy in the Liberal government.

With some opportunities ahead, the Ontario Liberals still face numerous challenges. The primary barrier is that the province is facing a structural deficit—it is unlikely the traditional manufacturing sector will return to the same level it was before the 2008 recession. This means a major hole for the province's revenues; it also slows the prospect for a strong economic recovery. This problem is compounded when we consider the government's numerous long-term spending commitments such as financial assistance for postsecondary students (OSAP), green energy investments, full-day kindergarten programs, and senior care. Premier Wynne, like McGuinty before her, prefers government intervention over austerity measures to grow the economy, so the fiscal challenges are great. The party's re-election success in 2018 will depend on a deft ability to pursue the government's ambitious agenda within a constrained budgetary reality.

Conclusion

By the time of his resignation in October 2012, Premier McGuinty and the Ontario Liberal Party had fulfilled a number of their grand policy visions for the province. By doing what it considered was right, the government was able to raise the necessary funds to ensure Ontario embraced early child-hood education, clean energy production, and some health care reform. But two realities haunted the Liberal time in government. Their first was the old adage that all politics is local. Wind turbines and the gas plant cancellations serve as examples where the Liberals foundered on the small politics that often permeate ambitious policy visions. The second was the advent of economic hardship; the 2008 crash affected key manufacturing sectors in the province and challenged the ability of the Liberals to maintain good relations with their core supporters in a period of necessary austerity.

The electoral fortunes of new premier Kathleen Wynne have been tested and the notion of a Liberal dynasty in Ontario is not that farfetched. The 2014 victory, however, is perhaps attributed less to Ontarians' enchantment with Wynne and the Liberals and more to the unpalatable options presented by the Progressive Conservatives and New Democrats. Both opposition parties appeared ill prepared for the campaign and neither inspired much confidence in voters. If either one hopes to unseat the Liberals, this will obviously have to change.

It is too soon to tell how history will judge Dalton McGuinty's time as premier. Some will point to legacy policies, others will focus on egregious missteps. It is inevitable that nine years at the centre of government will result in a mix of both. If nothing else, the tenure of the Liberals under "Premier Dad" has sparked some thought about whether "doing what you said you were going to do" is better or worse than doing what is thought to be right at the time. These are very different positions in politics with varied implications for government. For now, Ontarians have rewarded the Liberals and forgiven their mistakes. How the Wynne government builds on the McGuinty years and guides the province through economy instability will be two key factors determining the fate of the Ontario Liberals at the apex of power.

Discussion Questions

1.   Do you agree that the Ontario Liberals created "legacy policies"? Are there other policies that you think define the Liberal time in power?

2. In your view, what is more important for a government: to "do what it said it was going to do" or to "do the right thing" despite the potential public backlash for breaking campaign promises? Why?

3. Was Dalton McGuinty's 2012 suspension of the Legislative Assembly a legitimate use of the power of prorogation? Why or why not?

4. Do you think Kathleen Wynne successfully distinguished her own premiership apart from McGuinty's? If so, how? If not, why not?

5. What do you foresee to be the biggest policy challenges facing the Ontario government over the next five years? How can they be addressed?

Notes

1 Jim Coyle, *The Quiet Evolution: How Dalton McGuinty Changed Ontario—and Why He Resigned* (Toronto: Toronto Star Newspapers, 2012), 37.

2 John Ibbitson, *Promised Land: Inside the Mike Harris Revolution* (Toronto: Penguin Canada, 1999).

3 The Liberal seat count improved from 30 in 1995 to 35 in 1999 and was proportionately an even larger increase given that total seats in the Assembly were reduced by 27 in 1996 under the Fewer Politicians Act. The party's popular vote went up almost 9 per cent to 39.9 per cent in 1999.

4 Coyle, *The Quiet Evolution*, 59–60.

5 Robert Benzie and Rob Ferguson, "McGuinty and Obama Share Strategist," *Toronto Star*, 14 January 2008, http://www.thestar.com/news/world/2008/01/14/mcguinty_and_obama_share_strategist.html

6 *CBC Digital Archives*, "McGuinty Attacked! 1999 Debate a Disaster for Liberal," http://www.cbc.ca/archives/entry/mcguinty-attacked-1999-debate-a-disaster-for-liberal

7 Anna Esselment, "Fighting Elections: Cross-Level Political Party Integration in Ontario," *Canadian Journal of Political Science* 43, no. 4 (2010): 871–92.

8 The 2003 budget was purportedly "balanced," but it showed government plans to sell off $2.3 billion in assets as part of achieving a balanced budget. The Liberals and NDP assumed that meant the province was facing a deficit of that amount if no assets were sold. See Ontario Ministry of Finance, *2003 Ontario Budget 2003*, https://www.poltext.org/sites/poltext.org/files/discours/ON/ON_2003_B_37_04.pdf

9 CBC News, "Ontario Liberals Inherit $5.6 Billion Deficit," 29 October 2003, http://www.cbc.ca/news/canada/story/2003/10/29/ont_deficit031029.html

10 See Dalton McGuinty, "Remarks to the Economic Club of Toronto," 30 October 2003, http://news.ontario.ca/opo/en/2003/10/remarks-by-dalton-mcguinty-premier-of-ontario-to-the-economic-club-of-toronto.html; and see Karen Howlett, "Be Fearless in Face of Wage Freeze Furor," *Globe and Mail*, 29 September 2012, http://www.theglobeandmail.com/news/politics/be-fearless-in-face-of-wage-freeze-furor-mcguinty-urges-ontario-liberals/article4577326/

11 David Pond, "Imposing a Neo-Liberal Theory of Representation on the Westminster Model: A Canadian Case," *The Journal of Legislative Studies* 11, no. 2 (2005): 170–93.

244   ESSELMENT

12   Ontario Ministry of Finance, *2004 Ontario Budget Highlights*, 18 May 2004, http://booksnow1.scholarsportal.info/ebooks/ebooks2/ogdc/2014-02-21/1/243827/243827.pdf

13   CTV News, "McGuinty Vows Again Not to Raise Ontario Taxes," 11 September 2007, http://toronto.ctvnews.ca/mcguinty-vows-again-not-to-raise-ontario-taxes-1.255938

14   News.ontario.ca, "McGuinty Government Reducing Health Care Wait Times," 18 May 2006, http://news.ontario.ca/archive/en/2006/05/18/McGuinty-Government-Reducing-Health-Care-Wait-Times.html

15   Rob Ferguson, "Ontario ER Wait Times Down," *Toronto Star*, 31 October 2012, http://www.thestar.com/news/canada/2012/10/31/ontario_er_wait_times_down_12_hours_since_2009_dalton_mcguinty_says.html; Ontario Ministry of Health and Long-Term Care, "Ontario a Leader in Reducing Wait Times," 20 June 2012, https://news.ontario.ca/mohltc/en/2012/12/ontario-continues-to-lead-canada-in-wait-times.html

16   CBC News, "Canada, Ontario Announce $4 Billion Auto Aid Package," 20 December 2008, http://www.cbc.ca/news/canada/story/2008/12/20/auto-package.html

17   Richard J. Brennan, "Dalton McGuinty Defends HST," *Toronto Star*, 7 May 2010, http://www.thestar.com/news/canada/2010/05/07/dalton_mcguinty_defends_hst.html

18   The Canadian Press, "Premier Defends 'Gay-Straight Alliance' in Catholic Schools," 29 May 2012, http://toronto.ctvnews.ca/premier-defends-gay-straight-alliance-in-catholic-schools-1.833011

19   Between 2003–04 and 2007–08, the government had invested over $1 billion in operating and capital costs to achieve their 20-student cap in the early grades. See Nancy Naylor, "Implementing Primary Class Size Caps in Ontario" (paper presented to the American Educational Research Association Annual Conference, Chicago, 11 April 2007), http://www.edu.gov.on.ca/eng/research/PCS.pdf

20   Ontario Ministry of Education, "Ontario Students in the Top Ten in the World for Reading," 7 December 2010, http://news.ontario.ca/edu/en/2010/12/ontario-students-in-the-top-10-in-the-world-for-reading.html

21   Kate Hammer, "All Day Kindergarten Gets High Marks in Ontario," *Globe and Mail*, 20 March 2012, http://www.theglobeandmail.com/news/national/all-day-kindergarten-gets-high-marks-in-ontario/article534960/

22   Adrian Morrow, "Ontario Tories Would Halt Roll-Out of All-Day Kindergarten," 24 January 2013, http://www.theglobeandmail.com/news/national/education/ontario-tories-would-halt-roll-out-of-all-day-kindergarten-hudak-says/article7780594/

23   Ontario Ministry of Finance, *Commission on the Reform of Ontario's Public Services*, February 2012, http://www.fin.gov.on.ca/en/reformcommission/chapters/ch6.html#ch6-e. Don Drummond, the chair of the commission, was the former chief economist at the TD Bank.

24   Robert Benzie, "Drummond Report: New Roadmap for Ontario," 15 February 2012, http://www.thestar.com/news/canada/2012/02/15/drummond_report_new_roadmap_for_ontario_includes_higher_hydro_bills_larger_school_classes.html

25   Government of Ontario, *Progress Report 2012: Health Care,* http://www.gov. on.ca/en/initiatives/progressreport2012/ONT05_040345.html

26   *Globe and Mail,* "Ontario to Ban Trans Fats from School Cafeterias," 4 December 2007, http://www.theglobeandmail.com/news/national/ontario-to-ban-trans-fats-from-school-cafeterias/article25677027/

27   Ontario Ministry of Finance, *2012 Ontario Budget,* Chart 2.28, http://www.fin. gov.on.ca/en/budget/ontariobudgets/2012/ch2g.html#c2_secG_chart28

28   Ontario, *Commission on the Reform of Ontario's Public Services.*

29   Jeffrey Simpson, *Chronic Condition: Why Canada's Health Care System Needs to Be Dragged into the 21st Century* (Toronto: Penguin, 2012).

30   David Suzuki Foundation, *Ontario's Wealth, Canada's Future: Appreciating the Value of the Greenbelt's Eco-Services,* September 2008, http://davidsuzuki.org/ publications/reports/2008/ontarios-wealth-canadas-future-appreciating-the-value-of-the-greenbelts-eco-serv/

31   Ontario, Office of the Premier, "McGuinty Government Closing Coal Plants Earlier, Growing Greenbelt," 10 January 2013, http://news.ontario.ca/opo/ en/2013/01/cleaner-air-and-more-green-space-for-ontarians-to-enjoy.html

32   Keith Schneider, "How Ontario Is Putting an End to Coal-Burning Power Plants," *Yale Environment 360,* 2 April 2013, Yale School of Forestry and Environmental Studies, Yale University, http://e360.yale.edu/feature/ how_ontario_is_putting_an_end_to_coal-burning_power_plants/2635/

33   Richard Mackie, "McGuinty Backpedals on Vow," *Globe and Mail,* 6 November 2003, http://www.greenbeltontario.org/pages/globenov62003.htm

34   The jurisdictional complexities vis-à-vis Indigenous issues (particularly land claims) often result in provincial and federal governments passing the buck (and the blame) where they can. See Colin Perkel, "McGuinty Points Finger at Ottawa," *Brantford Expositor,* 15 September 2007, http://www. brantfordexpositor.ca/2007/09/15/mcguinty-points-finger-at-ottawa-opposition-leaders-say-liberals-failed-caledonia-blame-game. It is also likely the Harris government's bungled handling of the deadly 1995 Ipperwash stand-off impacted the response of the McGuinty government in Caledonia.

35   CBC News, "Caledonia Land Claim," November 2006, http://www.cbc.ca/ news2/background/caledonia-landclaim/

36   CBC News, "EHealth Scandal a $1 billion Waste: Auditor," October 2009, http:// www.cbc.ca/news/canada/toronto/story/2009/10/07/ehealth-auditor.html

37   Ontario, Office of the Auditor-General, *Special Report: Ontario's Electronic Health Records Initiatives,* October 2009, https://www.oanhss.org/oanhssdocs/ Issue_Positions/External_Resources/Oct2009-Auditor_General_EHealth_ Records_Initiative.pdf

38   Ontario Ministry of Finance, *2009 Ontario Budget,* http://books2.scholarsportal. info/viewdoc.html?id=415624

39   CBC News, "Ontario HST Cheques Are in the Mail," 8 June 2010, http:// www.cbc.ca/news/canada/toronto/story/2010/06/08/ont-hst-rebate-cheques-100608.html

40   Ontario, Office of the Auditor General, *Special Report: ORNGE Air Ambulance and Related Services,* March 2012, 17–18, http://www.auditor.on.ca/en/ content/specialreports/specialreports/ornge_web_en.pdf

41   Office of the Auditor General, *Special Report.*

42   Kevin Donovan and Rob Ferguson, "ORNGE Air Ambulance Service Now Run by Deputy Minister," *Toronto Star*, 11 January 2012, http://www.thestar.com/news/canada/2012/01/11/ornge_air_ambulance_service_now_run_by_ontario_deputy_minister.html

43   There are approximately 800 wind turbines generating power in Ontario.

44   John Wilkinson, Carol Mitchell, Leona Dombrowsky, and Maria Van Bommell lost their bids for re-election. The PCs also took the seats of retiring Liberal MPPs Steven Peters and Pat Hoy, as well as that belonging to Bruce Crozier, who passed away before the election. The Liberals lost seats in other areas of the province as well, but the rural thumping was particularly evident.

45   Jim Coyle, "MPP Kevin Flynn Takes on Gas Plant," *Toronto Star*, 1 April 2012, http://www.thestar.com/news/canada/2010/04/02/coyle_mpp_kevin_flynn_takes_on_oakville_gas_plant.html; Michael Talbot, "Profile: Charles Sousa Vows to Be the 'Jobs Premier,'" *680 News*, 22 January 2013, http://www.680news.com/2013/01/22/profile-charles-sousa-vows-to-be-the-jobs-premier-2/

46   CBC News, "Government Cancelled GTA Power Plant as Election Neared," 19 July 2012, http://www.cbc.ca/news/canada/toronto/story/2012/07/19/toornto-power-plant.html

47   Ontario, Office of the Auditor General, *Special Report: Mississauga Power Plant Cancellation Costs*, April 2013, http://www.auditor.on.ca/en/content/specialreports/specialreports/mississaugapower_en.pdf

48   CBC News, "Wynne Faces Questions about Gas Plant Cancellation Costs," 16 April 2013, http://www.cbc.ca/news/canada/toronto/story/2013/04/16/ontario-mississauga-gas-plant-report-wynne-response.html; see also Adrian Morrow and Karen Howlett, "Ontario Liberals' Gas Plant Cancellations," *Globe and Mail*, 8 October 2013, http://www.theglobeandmail.com/news/politics/ontario-liberals-gas-plant-cancellations-cost-1-billion-auditor/article14744879/.

49   Adrian Morrow and Karen Howlett, "Police Say McGuinty's Chief of Staff 'Double Deleted' Gas Plant Emails," *Globe and Mail*, 6 February 2015, http://www.theglobeandmail.com/news/national/opp-say-mcguintys-chief-of-staff-double-deleted-gas-plant-e-mails/article22851460/

50   Ontario Ministry of Finance, *Ontario Budget 2010*.

51   The English Catholic teachers' group and the French Language teachers negotiated a contract with the government in July, 2012 (see CBC News, "Liberals Strike Historic Wage-Freeze Deal," 5 July 2012, http://www.cbc.ca/news/canada/toronto/story/2012/07/05/toronto-oecta-contract.html). It was essentially the content of that contract that was imposed on the public elementary and secondary teachers in January 2013.

52   CBC News, "Ontario's McGuinty Surprises with Resignation, Prorogation," 15 October 2012, http://www.cbc.ca/news/canada/toronto/story/2012/10/15/toronto-mississauga-gas-plant.html

53   McGuinty attempted to achieve a majority post-2011 when Elizabeth Witmer, a long-time MPP for Waterloo, resigned her seat in order to accept the government's invitation to become chair of the Workplace Safety and Insurance Board. The Liberals failed to win Witmer's former riding in a fall 2012 by-election and their minority status remained.

54   Kate Hammer and Caroline Alphonso, "Ontario Sick Days Deal Softens Blow," *Globe and Mail*, 2 April 2013, http://www.theglobeandmail.com/news/national/education/ontario-sick-days-deal-softens-blow-to-younger-teachers/article10667008/

55   Adrian Morrow, "Ontario Premier Kathleen Wynne Apologizes for Cancelled Gas Plants," *Globe and Mail*, 14 May 2013, http://www.theglobeandmail.com/news/politics/ontario-premier-kathleen-wynne-apologizes-for-cancelled-gas-plants/article11926079/

56   Robert Benzie, "Transit Funding: Ontario Needs $2 Billion A Year, Kathleen Wynne Says," *Toronto Star*, 17 April 2013, http://www.thestar.com/news/queenspark/2013/04/17/transit_funding_ontario_needs_2_billion_a_year_premier_kathleen_wynne_says.html

57   Keith Leslie, "Harper Tories to Wynne Liberals: Don't Expect Any Co-operation from Us on the Ontario Pension Plan," *Canadian Press*, 17 July 2015, http://news.nationalpost.com/news/canada/canadian-politics/harper-tories-to-wynne-liberals-dont-expect-any-co-operation-from-us-on-the-ontario-pension-plan

58   Karen Howlett and Kate Hammer, "McGuinty Backs Down on Frank Sex Ed," *Globe and Mail*, 22 April 2010, http://www.theglobeandmail.com/news/politics/mcguinty-backs-down-on-frank-sex-ed/article4315992/

PART 4

Policy

14

Environmental Policy in Ontario: Greening the Province from the Dynasty to Wynne

MARK WINFIELD*

Introduction

The literature on environmental policymaking at the provincial level in Canada is relatively sparse, having only really emerged in relation to forest policy in British Columbia.[1] This is despite the increasingly dominant role played by provincial governments in environmental and energy policy formulation and implementation over the past 20 years. The combination of the Liberal Chrétien government's surrender of the federal leadership role in the setting of national environmental standards and the environmental assessment of major projects through the 1998 harmonization accord,[2] and the Conservative Harper government's hostility to climate change and other environmental issues, meant that the centre of energy and environmental policy leadership and innovation has shifted to the subnational level.[3] Ontario has been at the centre of this phenomenon.

Historically, Ontario has tended to be a leader among Canada's provinces in environmental policy. The province was the site of Canada's first comprehensive environmental protection statute, the Environmental Protection Act adopted in 1971, and its first environmental assessment statute, enacted in 1975.[4] The province also played a central role in the near universal implementation of municipal sewage treatment on the Canadian side of the Great Lakes in the 1970s and 1980s; led initiatives, along with Quebec, on acid rain control in the 1980s; and was among the key actors on regulatory requirements for the cleanup of water pollution from the pulp and paper sector in the 1990s. Ontario is home to Canada's only comprehensive Environmental Bill of Rights, adopted in 1994.[5] The past decade saw the province provide the model for the protection of drinking water safety in Canada and the implementation of a phase-out of coal-fired electricity. The coal phase-out is by far the most significant action by any Canadian government to date to reduce greenhouse gas (GHG) emissions. The 2009 Green Energy and Green Economy Act (GEGEA) arguably represented the most serious attempt seen so far by a provincial government in Canada to integrate economic and environmental strategy.

At the same time, the province was the site of the May 2000 Walkerton disaster, the worst drinking-water contamination episode in modern Canadian history, and a number of other major environmental disasters, including the 1990 Hagersville tire fire[6] and the 1997 Plastimet polyvinyl chloride fire in Hamilton.[7] Ontario also gave rise to Mike Harris's neoliberal "Common Sense Revolution" that provided the model for much of the Harper federal government's regressive approach to environmental matters.[8] The GEGEA notwithstanding, Ontario's electricity system remains an archetypical "hard" path system with a significantly increased reliance on nuclear energy over the past decade. The province's position of subnational policy leadership on climate change has now been largely abandoned, while in Northern Ontario a near free-for-all of mining development is being accompanied by the weakening of the province's institutional capacity around natural resources management.

This chapter seeks to explore the reasons for these contradictions, where Ontario has historically been a leader in environmental policy among the Canadian provinces, but also a centre of regressive movement. The chapter builds on the author's earlier work on Ontario environmental policy and politics,[9] assessing the later stages of the McGuinty government's approach to environmental, energy, and natural resources policy and the implications of the January 2012 report of the Commission on the Reform of Ontario's Public Services (the Drummond Report).[10] Finally, the chapter reflects on the approach taken by the Wynne government.

Analytical Approach

In attempting to understand the drivers of the province's environmental policy behaviour through the modern (i.e., the post–World War II and particularly post-1970) period, the author found it helpful to employ a modified version of the institutional-ideological policy model used by Bruce Doern and Glenn Toner in their landmark 1982 study on the National Energy Program.[11] The approach is based on an analytical framework of four basic categories of variables: the institutional context within which policy is being made; the underlying normative assumptions about both the role of the state in general and the specific policy issues in question; the physical and economic conditions defining the context in which policy debates occur; and the roles of non-state actors and forces, such as interest groups, public opinion, and the media.[12]

In institutional terms, the combination of cabinet parliamentary systems of government and the strong jurisdictional position of provinces on natural resources, energy, environmental, and land-use matters[13] implies a very high level of policy autonomy on the part of the provincial government in these areas. In practice the federal government emerges largely as a weak factor in the Ontario environmental policy story. Its role has been limited to some occasional regulatory nudging along with providing financing and subsidies, particularly for reducing municipal and industrial pollution of the Great Lakes, acid rain control, and improving air quality in Southern Ontario. Stephen Harper's federal government emerged as an important driver of pre-emptive action on the part of the province with respect to climate change policy. The Conservative government's initial moves, before its effective abandonment of attempts at substantive action to reduce Canada's greenhouse gas emissions, suggested a federal approach that would significantly burden Ontario's manufacturing sector relative to the oil and gas sector in Western Canada.[14]

The growing body of judicial interpretation of the implications of the recognition of Aboriginal and Treaty Rights in the Constitution Act, 1982, has emerged as an increasingly important change to the institutional landscape for environment and natural resources management in Canada. The establishment, over the past decade, of a "duty to consult" on the part of the federal and/or provincial Crown where the rights, interests, or claims of title of Indigenous people may be affected[15] is particularly significant in this regard. Its consequences for Ontario remain far from fully understood or resolved, but a detailed exploration of these questions is beyond the scope of this chapter.

The changing structure of Ontario's economy since the mid-1970s, particularly the decline of manufacturing and resource extraction and processing relative to service and knowledge-based activities, has significantly altered the focus of environmental policy debates. Until the mid-1990s industrial air and water pollution and waste management issues around the Great Lakes dominated. Since then, questions related to urban sprawl and transportation have moved to the fore, particularly in the region now known as the Greater Golden Horseshoe (GGH),[16] which, along with the Ottawa region, has emerged as the centre of growth in terms of population and the service and knowledge-based sectors.[17] With respect to energy, the structural changes in Ontario's economy have produced a succession of crises in electricity policy as long-standing assumptions about continued growth in electricity demand, flowing from an expanding industrial sector, have collapsed.

Although the institutional framework and economic circumstances within which successive Ontario governments have operated provide key contextual elements to the story, they do not fully explain the behaviour of different governments on environmental issues. Rather, the key drivers in terms of understanding government behaviour in Ontario regarding the environment lie within the other two categories of variables. The first relates to societal factors and forces—specifically, the public salience of environmental issues as apparent in public opinion polling and the level of media and legislative opposition attention given to environmental issues. It has been long recognized that governments increase their levels of activity in the environmental field when public concern is high, and that policy activity is likely to stall or even reverse when concern is low.[18] It is also generally recognized, as shown in Figure 14.1, that levels of public concern for environmental issues are cyclical, and are characterized by relatively short periods of high concern and longer periods of relatively low concern. In Ontario there have been three major periods of high concern: from the late-1960s to the mid-1970s; from the mid-1980s to the early-1990s; and from 2004 to 2008, with each peak being terminated by a major economic downturn.

The second key variable relates to the government of the day's normative assumptions about the role of the state. In Ontario's case, these assumptions can be broadly organized into three categories. *Managerial/facilitative* governments tend to focus on measures that they perceive as being necessary to facilitate economic growth and development (understood in conventional terms of industrialization, resource extraction and processing, and

Figure 14.1 Level of Public Concern for the Environment in Ontario, 1972–2012

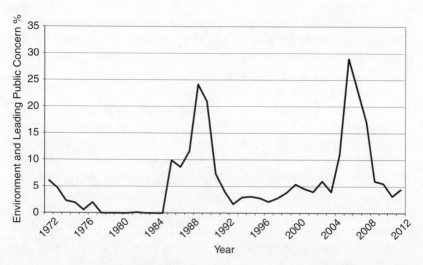

Sources: M. Winfield, *Blue-Green Province: The Environment and the Political Economy of Ontario* (Vancouver: UBC Press, 2012), Appendix 2; and Nanos Research, "Ontario PCs and Liberals Tied," 23 August 2012, http://www.nanosresearch.com/sites/default/files/POLONT-F12-T547.pdf.

urbanization), but they do not seek to expand the role of the state beyond these roles unless politically or practically necessary. The managerial/facilitative governance model was exemplified by the Progressive Conservative dynasty and, to a considerable degree, during the McGuinty period as well. Alternatively, *activist/progressive* governments envision a more directive role for the state in shaping the province's economy and society. Such an approach was evident during the Peterson minority period and during the first half of the Rae government. Finally *neoliberal* governments seek to minimize state interference with the market, as epitomized by the Harris "evolution."[19]

The combination of public salience of environmental issues and the normative orientation of the government of the day provides the strongest predictor of a government's likely behaviour toward environmental issues. As shown in Figure 14.2, all six potential combinations of public concern and government orientation have been seen in the postwar era in Ontario. At one end of the spectrum the combination of low public salience and a neoliberal government produced the major environmental policy retrenchments of the "Common Sense Revolution." At the other end, the combination of high levels of public attention and relatively activist governments resulted in periods of high policy activity and innovation, exemplified by the Liberal Peterson minority period and the first half of the NDP Rae government.

In Ontario the dominant combination has been one of relatively low public salience of environmental issues and facilitative and managerially oriented governments. The result has tended to be patterns of incremental policy progress, with an emphasis on achieving a balance between progressive and conventional themes. Such an approach became particularly pronounced under McGuinty. In electricity policy, for example, the 2009 Green Energy and Green Economy Act, with its focus on the development of renewable energy resources like wind and solar, paralleled a quiet but steady increase in the province's reliance on nuclear power,[20] a technology associated with very significant environmental, health, and economic risks,[21] and the pursuit of both nuclear new build and refurbishments of existing nuclear facilities. Similarly, the creation of the GGH Greenbelt and major reforms to the land-use planning process adopted in 2005 and 2006 were carefully designed to not disrupt low-density sprawling developments that were already planned and to leave considerable scope for such developments into the future.[22]

The McGuinty Legacy

The arrival of the first McGuinty government, which came to office following the October 2003 election, marked a distinct break with the

Figure 14.2 Ontario Environmental Policy Matrix: Government Orientation and Public Salience of Environmental Issues

Public Salience of Environmental Issues	Activist/Progressive	Managerial/Facilitative	Neo-Liberal
High	*Policy Outputs* High policy activity. Major new initiatives. Exploration of environment-economy relationship. Disruption of traditionally dominant policy relationships. *Examples* Peterson (Accord period) Rae (part I)	*Policy Outputs* Bipolar–high profile environmental initiatives matched with major countervailing moves in conventional directions. Policy driven by political management as opposed to reflection on conventional economic model. *Examples* Davis (1st mandate) Peterson (Majority) McGuinty (1st mandate)	*Policy Outputs* Reactive. High profile, but one-off initiatives. Maintenance of core policy path. *Examples* Harris post-Walkerton Eves Harper minority (Federal)
Low	*Policy Outputs* *Examples* Rae (part II) Wynne?	*Policy Outputs* Incremental, responses to crises (physical or political). Mitigation of impacts of conventional economic development models. *Examples* The "Dynasty" Davis (1975–84) McGuinty (2nd and 3rd mandates) Wynne?	*Policy Outputs* Retrenchment. Environment unimportant. Reinforcement of traditionally dominant policy relationships. *Examples* Miller The "Common Sense Revolution" Harper majority (Federal)

Government Orientation

Source: Adapted from M. Winfield, *Blue-Green Province: The Environment and the Political Economy of Ontario* (Vancouver: UBC Press, 2012), 190, Figure 8.1.

environmental policy directions of the Harris "Common Sense Revolution." The "revolution" had been characterized by a retrenchment unprecedented in the modern history of the province with respect to environmental and natural resources law and public policy, and the budgets of environmental and natural resources agencies.[23] In addition, a wide range of environmental responsibilities were downloaded to municipal governments, with little opportunity for preparation and minimal provincial financial support. A good deal of the succeeding Progressive Conservative government's efforts, led by former Harris finance minister Ernie Eves, were spent dealing with the consequences of these decisions. This was especially true in the electricity sector,[24] and in drinking water protection in the aftermath of the May 2000 Walkerton drinking water disaster, in which seven people died and nearly 3,000 became seriously ill.[25]

The new Liberal government came to office in part based on a platform that proposed a major re-engagement by the province on environmental issues. There was a particular focus on land-use and infrastructure planning in Southern Ontario and implementing recommendations from the inquiry that followed the Walkerton disaster. Concerns over the health impacts of air pollution from coal-fired electricity plants led to a commitment to phase-out these facilities by 2007. There were also promises to strengthen environmental law enforcement and the regulatory controls on the management of hazardous wastes.[26]

In practice the McGuinty government's first mandate would be marked by a reversal of the deregulatory directions of the Progressive Conservatives, and major initiatives in all of these areas, although always in context of the balance noted above. The phase-out of coal-fired electricity would, for example, be deferred, and while the government did re-engage around energy efficiency and renewable energy, it also made it clear that nuclear energy would remain the centrepiece of the province's electricity system.[27] The Liberal approach was electorally successful, as they retained a majority through the 2007 provincial election during a period of relatively high public concern over environmental issues. However, actual progress on environmental sustainability was more doubtful, given the one-step forward, one-step backwards character of the results of the strategy of balance. Rather, the gains and losses tended to cancel each other out, with the result that the actual shifts from the status quo were less than they might initially appear.

The defining event of the second McGuinty government, and in many ways the watershed for the McGuinty era, was the fall 2008 economic downturn. The recession severely affected the province's manufacturing sector, which had already been in a relative long-term decline. The province lost 250,000 jobs between fall 2008 and spring 2009, found itself facing a potential deficit in the $20-billion range,[28] and then was classified, for the first time, as a "have-not" province for the purposes of the federal equalization program.[29]

Consistent with its overall approach, the government's initial response was to move in two apparently contradictory directions. On the one hand, following the lead of the incoming Obama administration in the United States, the government began to explore the potential to make positive linkages between environmental and economic policy, particularly with respect to the development of renewable energy sources like wind and solar. The centrepiece of this dimension of the government's response, the 2009 Green Energy and Green Economy Act (GEGEA), provided for the establishment of a Feed-in-Tariff (FIT) program similar to those adopted in Denmark, Germany, and Spain. Under such programs renewable energy developers are paid a fixed rate for any electricity they generate, and they are guaranteed access to the electricity grid for their output.

FIT programs are intended to promote the rapid deployment of renewable energy sources. In Ontario's case this was seen as important not only in terms of helping to facilitate the phase-out of coal-fired electricity, but also to jump-start the development of renewable energy technology manufacturing and services industries, similar to those which had emerged in Germany and Denmark as a result of their FIT programs. The emergence of such industries was seen as a potential replacement for the traditional manufacturing activities that were in decline.[30] Local content requirements were established for projects participating in the FIT program to help support these goals, and a major agreement was signed with the Korean manufacturing giant Samsung at the beginning of 2010 as a means of securing rapid and large-scale investments in renewable energy technology manufacturing capability.[31]

The Peterson and, particularly, Rae governments had discussed the potential for integrating environmental and economic strategies. The work of the Ontario Round Table on the Environment and Economy, a multistakeholder body established in 1989 under Peterson to explore the integration of environmental and economic policy before its disbandment early in the first Harris government, had been especially noteworthy in this regard.[32] However, little progress had been made in putting such concepts into practice. In this context, the GEGEA, which the government stated would provide the foundation for the investment of $29 billion in renewable energy development over the following 20 years,[33] represented by far the most serious effort by any Ontario government in integrating the goals of environmental sustainability and economic prosperity.

The second dimension of the McGuinty government's response to the economic situation took a very different direction. Its foundation was an Open for Business initiative, led by the Ministry of Economic Development and Trade. Although driven more by desperation to resuscitate the province's failing manufacturing economy than ideological commitment, the initiative revived many of the themes of the regulatory reform aspects of the Harris "revolution." As part of the initiative, an Ontario Regulatory Policy was adopted in April 2010. The policy reintroduced the cost-benefit tests of the Harris-era Regulatory Impact and Competitiveness Test. A review of all leg-islation, regulations, and policy documents for opportunities to "update, sim-plify, consolidate or revoke"[34] was initiated at the same time.

The Ministry of the Environment, for its part, began to pursue proposals for the reform of its approvals process following exactly the same model that had been proposed during the Harris years prior to the Walkerton disaster. Under this model the ministry would no longer actively review most appli-cations for environmental approvals. Rather, proponents would simply assert their compliance with the required practices and procedures by "registering" with the ministry before proceeding with their proposed activities. Among other things, the process, which began to be implemented in the fall of 2011, eliminated the rights of members of the public, established 15 years earlier through the Environmental Bill of Rights, to notice of and the opportunity to comment on proposed approvals before they were granted, and of the chance to appeal approvals to the Environmental Review Tribunal.[35] Simi-lar reforms, also expanding on themes first articulated during the "Com-mon Sense Revolution," began to be pursued by the Ministry of Natural Resources at the same time.[36]

The contradictions between the directions of the GEGEA, with its "eco-logical modernist"[37] vision of advanced green services and technologies as the foundation of the economy, and the race to the bottom character of the "Open for Business" strategy, highlighted the government's increasing uncer-tainty about its economic vision. A report from the University of Toronto's Martin Prosperity Institute recommending that the province's future eco-nomic strategy focus on creative and knowledge based sectors rather than manufacturing and resource extraction was given a high-profile welcome by the government.[38] At the same time, a Northern Ontario Growth Plan[39] and successive budgets pronounced mineral development, particularly the proposed Ring of Fire chromite mining project in the province's fragile and largely undisturbed northern boreal forest region, as the foundation of Northern Ontario's economic future.[40]

The Final McGuinty Mandate

The run-up to the October 2011 provincial election was defined by a strong and long-standing lead in the polls for Tim Hudak's Progressive

Conservatives. The PC lead was driven in part by unhappiness in rural Ontario over wind energy developments flowing from the GEGEA[41] and the source water protection requirements flowing from the implementation of the Walkerton Inquiry's recommendations. However, a host of wider issues, including the introduction of the harmonized sales tax, were also at work. In the end the government survived the election, emerging one seat short of a majority. The government's surprising success was seen to be the combined product of a very solid campaign on the part of the Liberals and a series of errors and misfortunes on the part of the PC camp. Hudak's threats to repeal the GEGEA, along with the misfortunes of City of Toronto mayor Rob Ford's administration, propelled younger, progressive, and urban voters looking to block a PC victory away from the NDP and Greens and toward the Liberals. The Green vote in particular collapsed dramatically relative to the 2007 election.[42]

Having unexpectedly won a "major minority," McGuinty's government seemed at something of a loss to know what to do with it. Considerable stock was placed in the ability of the forthcoming report of the Commission on the Reform of Ontario's Public Services, chaired by former TD Bank Chief Economist Don Drummond, to provide the required direction for a third mandate. The commission's report, delivered in January 2012, responded in part by noting that its efforts had been hampered by the government's own lack of any long-term vision for the province's economy and society.[43] With respect to the environment, energy, and natural resources, the report introduced little new analysis or thought. Rather, it largely confirmed the government's existing directions, particularly with respect to the reform of the environmental approvals process and the adoption of an Integrated Power System Plan based on the directions laid out in the government's December 2010 Long-Term Energy Plan.[44]

The Liberals' 2011 election platform had been very thin on new commitments related to the environment, energy, or natural resources. Its principal environmental element had been a vague proposal to expand the GGH Greenbelt, an option recycled from the party's 2007 document. To the extent that there was an environmental agenda for the third term, it focused on a proposed Great Lakes Protection Act that was notable only for its lack of meaningful content.[45] A Local Food Act was also proposed, although it was similarly short of substance.[46] Despite assurances of an ongoing commitment to green energy in the government's post-election Speech from the Throne, the GEGEA FIT program was subject to a moratorium on new applications immediately following the election while the program underwent a scheduled review. The review was completed in March 2012. It concluded that the program should continue, and potentially be expanded, subject to reductions in the rates paid for some types of FIT projects and a strengthening of the mechanisms to favour projects that were initiated or supported at the community level.[47] However, the moratorium on new applications remained in place until December 2012. Even then it was only opened for a short (two month) window for up to 200 megawatts of new small (less than 500 kilowatts) projects. Among other things, the more than year-long moratorium on new projects had a strong negative effect on the emerging renewable energy sector whose development was one of the central purposes of the legislation.[48]

The government's wavering on its flagship green energy commitment was driven by a number of factors. There were continuing internal tensions over the actual direction of the government's electricity strategy. The green energy strategy had been accompanied by repeated assurances that nuclear power would remain the centrepiece of the system. These assurances continued even after the government's efforts to solicit bids for two new build reactors produced a $26-billion price tag, more than three times the original estimates.[49] Efforts to refurbish the province's existing nuclear reactors had produced multibillion-dollar cost-overruns and multi-year delays,[50] while the federal government's June 2011 sale of Atomic Energy of Canada (AECL) eliminated the possibility that the federal government would underwrite the risks of cost-overruns and delays on future nuclear projects. The government's reaction to the March 2011 Fukushima nuclear disaster in Japan was simply to provide assurances of the safety of Ontario's reactor fleet.[51]

As a consequence of both the 2008 downturn and deeper structural changes taking place in the province's economy, electricity demand turned out to be declining rather than growing, as the government had predicted.[52] As a result, the ongoing commitment to nuclear meant that there was less space in the electricity system for other sources of supply, particularly new renewable energy sources. Concerns over the alleged costs of the green energy strategy[53] had already prompted the province to introduce an Ontario Clean Energy Benefit, effectively reducing residential electricity bills by 10 per cent, at an estimated cost in excess of $1 billion per year.[54]

In addition, the green energy strategy had produced some unexpected and surprisingly well-organized local opposition to wind energy projects around the province.[55] Although the GEGEA streamlined the approval process for renewable energy projects in part to circumvent this opposition, the government ultimately adopted a series of relatively restrictive rules on siting of wind turbines requiring, among other things, setbacks of over 500 metres from residential buildings. This was followed in February 2011 by an outright moratorium on offshore wind projects, an option which had been authorized by the province three years earlier, and for which there were incentives built into the structure of the FIT program.[56] There have been strong accusations that the decision was driven by concerns over local opposition to off-shore wind projects in Liberal-held ridings in the run-up to the 2011 election.[57]

A proposed gas-fired electricity plant in Oakville had been cancelled in October 2010 in the face of strong local opposition in the Liberal-held riding.[58] Then, in the midst of the 2011 election campaign, a decision was made to relocate a similar proposed plant in another Liberal-held riding in Mississauga.[59] It would emerge in the aftermath of the election that the cancellation of the plants, for which contracts had been signed between the province's power authority and the proponents, would approach $600 million.[60] The legislative opposition's pursuit of the issue, in the context of the minority Legislature produced by the October 2011 election, would be central to Premier Dalton McGuinty's October 2012 decision to prorogue the Legislature and announce his intention to resign.[61]

The Wynne Government

The McGuinty government began its mandate grounded in a rejection of the environmental dimensions of the "Common Sense Revolution," particularly the failure to deal with air quality issues in Southern Ontario and the Walkerton disaster. The new government arrived with a relatively ambitious environmental agenda and undertook a series of major initiatives, especially during its first term in office. The 2005–06 land-use planning reforms and the phase-out of coal-fired electricity stand out as particularly important achievements in this context.

In contrast, by the end of the McGuinty era, the Liberal government seemed to have no environmental agenda at all. Its high profile commitments to green energy were wavering and any serious commitment to action on climate change abandoned. Despite the return of Jim Bradley—the Peterson-era architect who transformed the Ministry of the Environment into a major policy actor—to the environment portfolio, the ministry's activities continued to focus on the Open for Business reform of environmental approvals and regulations. At the same time, a single-minded focus on clearing all possible obstacles to the Ring of Fire mineral development in Northeastern Ontario defined the government's approach to matters in the North.

The February 2013 Liberal leadership convention to select McGuinty's successor came down to a contest between former education, transportation, and municipal affairs minister Kathleen Wynne and former economic development minister Sandra Pupatello. Wynne was seen to represent the progressive side of the Ontario Liberal Party, while Pupatello, the architect of the Open for Business strategy, reflected its more conservative, business-oriented dimensions. Wynne would ultimately emerge as the winner of the Liberal Party leadership and premiership.

Although Wynne's victory was generally welcomed in environmental circles over Pupatello's, the initial direction of the new premier's government on environmental matters was uncertain. Wynne's leadership platform had included a number of specific environmental components, although many carried over commitments and ideas from the McGuinty era. These included completing the coal-phase-out by the end of 2014, continuing investments in public transit, and reintroducing the Local Food and Great Lakes Protection Acts. There were also references to improving the efficiency of water and waste-water infrastructures, and enhancing energy conservation and recycling rates.[62]

At the same time, reflecting the controversies over wind energy development, both Wynne's leadership platform[63] and initial February 2013 Speech from the Throne emphasized increased municipal autonomy and local control over the siting of green energy infrastructure. In Northern Ontario the emphasis in both the leadership platform[64] and Speech from the Throne was on the continued prioritization of the Ring of Fire mining development.

Investments in transportation infrastructure, particularly public transit, in the GTA and Hamilton emerged as a major theme during the new premier's initial period in office. Premier Wynne gave a positive and high-profile welcome to a series of potential capital financing measures proposed by Metrolinx, including increases in the HST, regional fuel taxes, and parking levies,[65] noting that "the reality is we need more money than we've got in the provincial treasury in order to build transit."[66] The emphasis on the need for additional revenues drew support from the business community,[67] and seemed to position the Wynne government away from the provincial PCs, NDP, Toronto Mayor Rob Ford,[68] and the federal Conservative government,[69] all of whom opposed the call for additional revenue measures. Initial polling analyses suggested the public could be accepting of additional charges if the revenues were committed to transit expansion,[70] potentially setting the question up as the defining issue for a provincial election campaign.[71] However, by the fall of 2013 the government seemed to be in retreat on the transit funding issue, passing the question to an expert panel.[72]

In addition, long-anticipated legislation to curb the increasing incidence of Strategic Lawsuits Against Public Participation (SLAPPs) in the province[73] was introduced, but not adopted, just before the Legislature rose in June 2013.[74] Legislation to implement extensive changes to the funding structure for municipal recycling programs was introduced at the same time.[75]

Less progressive directions began to emerge around energy, particularly electricity. The Oakville and Mississauga natural-gas-fired power plant cancellation issue continued to dog the new government.[76] A major retreat from the McGuinty government's high-profile green energy initiatives began to materialize in the late spring of 2013. In May the termination of the FIT program for large projects (greater than 500 kilowatts) in favour of competitive bidding processes was announced. At the same time there was a commitment of the remaining 900 megawatts of grid capacity space available until 2018 for renewable energy projects to the smaller renewable energy projects. However, even such projects were now to be subject to requirements for municipal participation, a difficult hurdle for smaller developers to meet given the potential transaction costs involved. There were no indications of any commitments to additional renewable energy supplies beyond 2018.[77]

Major decisions remained to be made over the construction of new nuclear facilities and the refurbishment of existing facilities, options that entail levels of economic risk dwarfing those associated with the gas plant cancellations. Initial comments from Wynne's energy minister, Bob Chiarelli, suggested that the government would maintain its commitment to a system that was at least 50 per cent nuclear.[78] Later, reflecting the reality of falling electricity demand, and the province's previous track record of massive cost overruns and delays with nuclear plant construction and refurbishment projects,[79] the minister indicated that it was reconsidering the proposed new build nuclear project at Darlington.[80] However, the province continued to press ahead with a proposed multibillion-dollar[81] refurbishment of the existing Darlington plant and a "life-extension" of the Pickering B plant.

The 2014 Election and the Wynne Majority

The June 2014 election resulted in an unexpected majority government for Premier Wynne's Liberals.[82] Despite a focus on energy and electricity issues in the run-up to the election, environmental questions were not perceived as having a major impact on the outcome. Indeed, with the exception of the Greens, who presented a range of new ideas in their platform around energy, climate change, transit, the protection of prime farmland, and governance issues,[83] the major party platforms were notable for their silence on the environment.[84] The Liberals were the only one of the three major parties to say anything at all about climate change, and even they simply reiterated their existing commitment to their 2020 targets for reducing green house gas emissions. There was an almost across-the-board silence on basic environmental issues like air and water quality, waste management, the protection of biological diversity, parks and protected areas, and endangered species. The only exception again was the Liberals, who referenced a strategy to protect bees and other pollinators from pesticides and financial incentives for controlling farm run-off and improving sewage and stormwater management.

The Liberals were similarly the only party to make reference to supporting "smarter" growth and expanding the Greenbelt, while the New Democrats were notable for their failure to say anything on issues related to urban development, other than transit, altogether. Even more surprising was the silence of the New Democrats on the nuclear question and their implicit rejection of further significant efforts at renewable energy development, offering nothing more than a proposal for a revolving loan fund for household-level solar installations.

In the end, the NDP's very thin environmental platform, and more general "pocketbook populist" approach to the election, in combination with the PC's emphasis on "reducing regulatory burdens" and cutting government expenditures, may have played a significant role in the election outcome. Specifically, it may have pushed younger, urban progressive voters in the direction of the Liberals as the least unattractive option in an unappealing field, contributing to their dominance of urban ridings in the GGH. Gains in these ridings provided the foundation for the Liberal's election victory.[85]

The Wynne government's post-election energy and environmental agenda has been defined by three issues. The pre-election pull-back from further significant renewable energy development has continued, as has the government's commitment to the refurbishment of the Darlington and Bruce nuclear facilities. This has been despite considerable evidence that hydro-electricity imports from Quebec could offer a cost-effective alternative, particularly in light of Quebec's substantial electricity surpluses and weakening US markets for electricity exports.[86]

The government's tepid approach to the potential to expand its electricity relationship with Quebec has been particularly surprising given the emergence of the action on climate change as the major environmental theme of the Wynne majority government. The government has collaborated closely with Quebec Liberal Premier Couillard to emphasize the need for a transition to a low-carbon economy through the Council of the Federation.[87] In February 2015 the province released a discussion paper indicating its intention to put a price on carbon, potentially in conjunction with Quebec's existing cap and trade system for greenhouse gas emissions.[88]

Finally, with respect to the need for major investments in public transit, the government decided not to proceed with the new revenue tools, widely discussed during the initial phase of the Wynne government. Instead, the government's April 2015 budget announced its intention to sell a portion of Hydro One Networks, one of the provincially owned successor companies to Ontario Hydro, and to use the proceeds to capitalize transit investments. Hydro One owns and manages the province's high-voltage transmission grid, and also provides electricity distribution services in rural areas.

The decision was subject to considerable criticism as a revenue and financing strategy. The existing public ownership structure provides a very steady and reliable revenue stream to the province, which could be used to support borrowing for transit investments. Policy concerns have also been raised given the natural monopoly inherent in the transmission and rural distribution infrastructure, central role of that infrastructure in the evolution of the electricity system toward a smart grid, its importance in the integration of renewable energy sources into the electricity grid, and Hydro One's role in the delivery of residential, commercial, and industrial energy efficiency programming in areas not served by municipal local distribution companies.[89]

More broadly, Ontario continues to face a range of biophysical, economic, and policy challenges related to the environment, energy, and natural resource management which have yet to be addressed by the renewed Wynne government. The 2005–06 reforms to the land-use planning process did appear to be having positive effects on the promotion of more compact, mixed-use and transit serviceable urban development patterns inside the GGH Greenbelt. However, the situation beyond the Greenbelt is much less promising, and the patterns of low-density, automobile-dependent development on high-value agricultural and natural heritage lands have continued, if not accelerated. In some cases, such as in southern Simcoe County, this has happened with the effective approval of the province.[90]

The prominence of classical industrial pollution issues has declined in Ontario as the province has transitioned from a manufacturing-based economy to one more grounded in service and knowledge-based activities. However, long-standing problems with the regulation of industrial air pollution remain, particularly the management of the cumulative effects of multiple sources in areas of intense industrial activity, as highlighted by the situation of the Aamjiwnaang First Nation in Sarnia's Chemical Valley.[91] These problems are likely to be reinforced under the direction of the province's Open for Business reforms to the environmental approvals process.[92]

In Northern Ontario, the 2010 Far North Act failed to provide a meaningful planning framework for the accommodation of Indigenous, environmental, and mining interests in the northern boreal region.[93] At the same time, the province's capacity to deal with resulting conflicts is in decline, especially in terms of the loss of field and scientific capacity at the Ministry of Natural Resources. Regulations adopted under the province's 2007 Endangered Species Act at the end of May 2013 provided effective exemptions from the act's requirements for a range of industries and projects, including forestry, Ring of Fire mine projects, transmission lines, wind power, mineral exploration, drainage works, hydroelectric generating facilities, subdivisions, condominiums, pipelines, waste management projects, transit, and gravel pits and quarries.[94]

The Wynne government had shown some more activist inclinations than its predecessor, particularly around climate change. At the same time, however, it engaged a major retrenchment on the McGuinty government's commitments on green energy and continued to move ahead with the industry-oriented reform of regulatory requirements and approvals processes at the Ministries of the Environment and Natural Resources. A more coherent and progressive agenda is still needed to address the environmental challenges facing the province, particularly those related to energy and climate change, development in the boreal north, industrial pollution, and urban growth in the Greater Golden Horseshoe. It remains an open question how and when such an agenda, capable of more fully advancing the sustainability of Ontario's environment, economy, and society, will emerge.

Discussion Questions

1. How has the public salience of environmental issues in Ontario risen and fallen over time? How would you characterize present and future trends?
2. What have been the dominant environmental issues in Ontario at different points in history?
3. Do you agree that Ontario governments have overall sought to achieve a balance between progressive and conventional approaches to environmental issues? Is a balanced approach sufficient to address challenges like climate change and advancing sustainability?
4. What has been the relationship between environmental policy and economic policy in Ontario politics?
5. Have the McGuinty and Wynne governments primarily been leaders or followers in environmental policy? Why?

Notes

* The author thanks Master of Environmental Studies student Sarah Goldstein for her assistance with the preparation of this chapter.

1 See, for example, J. Wilson, *Talk and Log Wilderness Politics in British Columbia 1965–1996* (Vancouver: UBC Press, 1998); B. Cashore, G. Hoberg, M. Howlett, J. Rayner, and J. Wilson, *In Search of Sustainability: British Columbia Forest Policy in the 1990s* (Vancouver: UBC Press, 2001).

2   M. Winfield, "Environmental Policy and Federalism," in *Canadian Federalism: Performance, Effectiveness and Legitimacy*, ed. H. Bakvis and G. Skogstad (Toronto: Oxford University Press, 2002), 124–37.

3   See, for example, D. VanNijnatten, "The North American Context: Canadian Environmental Policy and the Continental Push," in *Canadian Environmental Policy and Politics*, 3rd ed., ed. D.L. VanNijnatten and R. Boardman (Toronto: Oxford University Press, 2009), 92–108; M. Winfield and D. MacDonald, "Federalism and Canadian Climate Change Policy," in *Canadian Federalism: Performance, Effectiveness and Legitimacy*, 3rd ed., ed. H. Bakvis and G. Skogstad (Toronto: Oxford University Press, 2012), 241–60.

4   Environmental Assessment Act, R.S.O. 1990, c E-18.

5   Environmental Bill of Rights, 1993 S.O. 1993, c-28.

6   See J.R. Mawhinney, *The Hagersville Tire Fire, February 12 to 28, 1990* (Ottawa: National Research Council, Institute for Research in Construction, 1990).

7   On the Plastimet fire, see Office of the Fire Marshal, *Protecting the Public and the Environment by Improving Fire Safety at Ontario's Recycling and Waste Handling Facilities* (Toronto: Ministry of the Solicitor General and Correctional Services, 1997).

8   For an overview of the Harper government's approach to environmental matters, see M. Winfield, "The Environment, 'Responsible Resource Development' and Evidence Based Policy-Making in Canada," Working Paper, Sustainable Energy Initiative, Faculty of Environmental Studies, York University, http://sei.info.yorku.ca/files/2012/12/TheEnvironment.pdf

9   M. Winfield, *Blue-Green Province: The Environment and the Political Economy of Ontario* (Vancouver: UBC Press, 2012).

10   Commission on the Reform of Ontario's Public Services, *Report* (Toronto: Ontario Ministry of Finance, 2012).

11   G. Bruce Doern and Glen Toner, *The Politics of Energy: The Development and Implementation of the National Energy Program* (Toronto: Methuen, 1985); see also L. Pal, "The Accidental Theorist," in *Policy: From Ideas to Implementation*, ed. G. Toner, L.A. Pal, and M.J. Prince (Montreal: McGill-Queen's University Press, 2010), 39–58.

12   For a detailed discussion of this approach, see Winfield, *Blue-Green Province*, 3–9.

13   J. Benidickon, *Environmental Law*, 3rd ed. (Toronto: Irwin Law, 2009), 30–51.

14   I. Rice, "Ontario's Low-Carbon Transition: The Role of a Provincial Cap-and-Trade Program" (MA research paper, York University, 2011).

15   See D. Newman, *The Duty to Consult: New Relationships with Aboriginal Peoples* (Saskatoon, SK: Purich Publishing, 2009).

16   Bounded approximately by Kitchener-Waterloo in the west, Peterborough in the east, Barrie to the north and Fort Erie to the south.

17   M.B. Matthew, R. Simpson, A. Lorius, D. MacLeod, and A. Sjogren, *The Growth Outlook for the Greater Golden Horseshoe* (Toronto: Hemson Consulting, 2005), http://www.hemson.com/wp-content/uploads/2016/03/GrowthOutlookForGGH-17Jan2005.pdf

18   See, for example, A. Downs, "Up and Down with Ecology: The Issue Attention Cycle," *The Public Interest* 28, no. 38 (1972): 50; K. Harrison, "Retreat from Regulation: Evolution of the Canadian Environmental Regulatory Regime," in *Changing the Rules: Canadian Regulatory Regimes and Institutions*, ed. G.B. Doern, M. Hill, M. Prince, and R. Schultz (Toronto: University of Toronto Press, 1999), 122–43.

19 See Winfield, *Blue-Green Province*, 6–7.

20 As of 2003, nuclear energy constituted 42 per cent of the province's electricity output; as of 2012, it constituted 56.4 per cent of its output. See Ministry of Energy, *Ontario's Long-Term Energy Plan* (Toronto: Queen's Printer for Ontario, 2010), 18, Figure 5; and Independent Electricity System Operator (IESO), "Supply Overview," http://www.ieso.ca/Pages/Power-Data/Supply.aspx

21 On the sustainability of nuclear energy, see M. Winfield, R.B. Gibson, R.T. Markvart, K. Gaudreau, and J. Taylor, "Implications of Sustainability Assessment for Electricity System Design: The Case of the Ontario Power Authority's Integrated Power System Plan," *Energy Policy* 38 (2010): 4115–26.

22 See T. Coombs, *Neptis Commentary on the Draft Greenbelt Plan* (Toronto: Neptis Foundation, 2005). See also L.A. Sandberg, G.R. Wekerle, and L. Gilbert, *The Oak Ridges Moraine Battles: Development, Sprawl, and Nature Conservation in the Toronto Region* (Toronto: University of Toronto Press, 2013).

23 Relative to the NDP's final 1994–95 budget, by 1997–98 the Ministry of the Environment's operating budget had been reduced by 50 per cent (from $286 million to $142 million). By the end of March 1998, the Ministry of the Environment's total staff was reduced by 32 per cent (from 2,208 to 1,494) relative to its situation as of 31 March 1995. The MNR saw equally dramatic reductions, with its complement declining by 30 per cent (from 6,639 to 4,643) from 31 March 1995 in relation to the same date in 1998.

24 See J. Swift and K. Stewart, *Hydro: The Decline and Fall of Ontario's Electric Empire* (Toronto: Between the Lines, 2004). See also Winfield, *Blue-Green Province*, 134–41.

25 The Hon. D. O'Connor, *Report of the Walkerton Inquiry Part I: The Events of May 2000 and Related Issues* (Toronto: Queen's Printer, 2002).

26 Ontario Liberal Party, *Growing Strong Communities: The Ontario Liberal Plan for Clean, Safe Communities That Work* (Toronto: Ontario Liberal Party 2003).

27 The Hon. D. Duncan, Minister of Energy, *Directive to OPA re: Integrated Power System Plan*, 13 June 2006; Government of Ontario, *Ontario's Long-Term Energy Plan* (Toronto: Queen's Printer, 2010).

28 Ministry of Finance, *2010 Ontario Budget*, Chapter II, Table 1, http://www.fin.gov.on.ca/en/budget/ontariobudgets/2010/ch2a.html#c2_secA_ontarioFinances

29 K. Howlett and K. Carmichael, "Struggling Ontario Joins Have-Not Ranks," *Globe and Mail*, 4 November 2008.

30 R. Pollin and H. Garrett-Peltier, *Building the Green Economy: Employment Effects of Green Energy Investments for Ontario* (Toronto: Green Energy Act Alliance, WWF-Canada, Blue-Green Canada, 2009).

31 Canwest News Service, "Ontario Signs Green Energy Deal with Samsung Team," *Financial Post*, 21 January 2010.

32 Ontario Round Table on the Environment and Economy, *Restructuring for Sustainability* (Toronto: Queen's Printer, 1992).

33 Ministry of Energy, *Ontario's Long-Term Energy Plan*, Figure 13.

34 "Open for Business and the Ministry of the Environment," slide presentation to Regulation 419 Stakeholders, Public Health Units, First Nations, Environmental Non-Governmental Organizations, 11 January 2011.

35 R. Nadarajah, M. Carter-Witney, and E. Macdonald, *Modernizing Environmental Approvals: EBR Registry No. 010–9143* (Toronto: Canadian Environmental

Law Association, Canadian Institute for Environmental Law and Policy, and EcoJustice, 2010).

36   Ontario Ministry of Finance, "Ministry of Natural Resources Transformation," *2012 Ontario Budget*, "Chapter I: Transforming Public Services," http://www. fin.gov.on.ca/en/budget/ontariobudgets/2012/ch1.html#c1_ministryONRT

37   On "ecological modernization," see J. Dryzek, *The Politics of the Earth: Environmental Discourses*, 3rd ed. (Oxford: Oxford University Press, 2013), 165–84.

38   E. Church, "Ontario Needs Better Brain Trust, Report Says," *Globe and Mail*, 5 February 2009, and J. Wells, "Ontariowe," *Globe and Mail*, 21 March 2009, referring to R.L. Martin and R. Florida, *Ontario in the Creative Age* (Toronto: Martin Prosperity Institute, 2009).

39   Ontario Growth Secretariat, *Growth Plan for Northern Ontario* (Toronto: Ministry of Energy and Infrastructure, 2011).

40   Ministry of Finance, *2010 Ontario Budget*, "Chapter I: Ontario's Plan for Prosperity Section A: Jobs and Growth," http://www.fin.gov.on.ca/en/budget/ ontariobudgets/2010/ch1a.html#c1_secA_jobCreation

41   Recent analyses of the 2011 election outcome has suggested that the impact of the wind energy issue on the Liberal Party's electoral fortunes in rural Ontario has been overstated. See L.C. Stokes, "The Politics of Renewable Energy Policies: The Case of Feed-in Tariffs in Ontario, Canada," *Energy Policy* 56: 490–500.

42   In 2007 the Greens received 355,000 votes (8 per cent of the popular vote). In 2011 they received 127,000 votes (less than 3 per cent of the popular vote).

43   Commission on the Reform of Ontario's Public Services *Report*, 302, Recommendation 11–1.

44   Commission on the Reform of Ontario's Public Services, *Report*, Chapter 12, "Infrastructure, Real Estate and Electricity," Chapter 13, "Environment and Natural Resources," and Chapter 16, "Operating and Back-Office Operations," http://www.fin.gov.on.ca/en/reformcommission/. See also M. Winfield, "The Drummond Report and the Environment, Energy, Natural Resources and Public Safety in Ontario," February 2012, http://marksw.blog.yorku.ca/2012/02/15/ the-drummond-report-and-its-implications-for-the-environment-energy-policy-natural-resources-management-and-public-safety-in-ontario/

45   See Great Lakes Protection Act Alliance, "Letter to MPPs Re: Bill 6—the Great Lakes Protection Act," 7 March 2013, http://s.cela.ca/files/GLPAA-ltr-to-Ont-MPPs.pdf

46   See Sustain Ontario, "Good Food Policies," http://sustainontario.com/ initiatives/policies

47   F. Amin, *Ontario's Feed-in Tariff Program: Two-Year Review Report* (Toronto: Queen's Printer, 2012), http://www.energy.gov.on.ca/en/files/2011/10/FIT-Review-Report-en.pdf. On the debates over the development of wind energy in rural Ontario, see Chapter 14 of this volume. See also M. Winfield, P. Mulvihill, and J. Etcheverry, "Strategic Environmental Assessment and Advanced Renewable Energy in Ontario: Moving Forward or Blowing in the Wind?" *Journal of Environmental Assessment Policy and Management* 15, no. 2 (2013): 1–19. There are arguments that the negative impacts on wind turbine development on the Liberal's electoral fortunes have been greatly overstated. See Stokes "The Politics of Renewable Energy Policies."

48 See, for example, T. Hamilton, "Ontario Teaches World How Not to Run a FIT Program," *Toronto Star*, 5 October 2012. On the GEGEA as an economic development strategy, see M. Winfield, with Nageen Rehman, Mariana Eret, Dawn Strifler, and Paul Cockburn, "Understanding the Economic Impact of Renewable Energy Initiatives: Assessing Ontario's Experience in a Comparative Context," Working Paper, Sustainable Energy Initiative, Faculty of Environmental Studies, York University, 2013, http://sei.info.yorku.ca/files/2012/12/Green-Jobs-and-Renewable-Energy-July-28-20131.pdf

49 T. Hamilton, "$26B Cost Killed Nuclear Bid," *Toronto Star*, 14 July 2009.

50 See Ontario Clean Air Alliance, *The Darlington Re-Build Consumer Protection Plan* (Toronto: Ontario Clean Air Alliance Research, 2010).

51 The Hon. B. Duguid, Minister of Energy, quoted in Linda Nguyen, "Ontario Says It's Full Steam Ahead on Nuclear Projects," ipolitics, 18 March 2011, http://www.ipolitics.ca/2011/03/18/ontario-says-its-full-steam-ahead-on-nuclear-projects/

52 Independent Electricity System Operator (IESO), *18-Month Outlook: From December 2012 to May 2014,* page iv, Table 1, http://www.ieso.ca/imoweb/pubs/marketReports/18Month_ODF_2012nov.pdf

53 See, for example, T. Weis and P.J. Partington, *Behind the Switch: Pricing Ontario Electricity Options* (Drayton Valley: Pembina Institute, 2011), http://www.pembina.org/pub/2238; B. Dachis and J.Carr, *Zapped: The High Cost of Ontario's Renewable Electricity Subsidies* (Toronto: C.D. Howe Institute, 2011), https://www.cdhowe.org/why-ontarios-expensive-electricity-subsidies-should-be-zapped/13570

54 Environmental Commissioner of Ontario, *Managing a Complex Energy System* (Toronto: ECO, 2011).

55 See, for example, http://ontario-wind-resistance.org/

56 Winfield et al., "Strategic Environmental Assessment and Advanced Renewable Energy in Ontario."

57 See, for example, J. Spears, "Wind Moratorium Driven by Election, Court Told," *Toronto Star*, 23 March 2013.

58 J. Jenkins and A. Artuso, "Cancelled Oakville Gas Plant to Be Moved to Napanee," *St. Catharines Standard*, 24 September 2012.

59 CBC News, "Liberals Halt Mississauga Power Plant: Gas-Powered Plant Will Be Relocated," 24 September 2011, http://www.cbc.ca/news/canada/toronto/story/2011/09/24/tor-election-power-plant.html

60 A. Artuso, "Gas Plant Cancellations Cost $585 Million: Ontario Power Authority," *Toronto Sun*, 30 April 2013.

61 K. Howlett, A. Morrow, and P. Waldie, "Ontario Premier Dalton McGuinty Resigns," *Globe and Mail*, 15 October 2012.

62 KathleenWynne.ca, "Protect the Environment," accessed 25 March 2013.

63 KathleenWynne.ca, "Enable Communities to Prosper," accessed 25 March 2013.

64 KathleenWynne.ca, "Strengthen Northern Ontario," accessed 25 March 2013.

65 Metrolinx, *Investing in Our Region, Investing in Our Future* (Toronto: Metrolinx, 2013).

66 A. Morrow, "New Taxes and Tolls Vital for Transit and Road Ambitions, Wynne Says," *Globe and Mail*, 26 March 2013.

67   O. Moore, "Business Calls for Taxes and Fees to Expand Transit," *Globe and Mail*, 18 March 2013.

68   Morrow, "New Taxes and Tolls Vital."

69   R. Benzie and T. Kalinowski," Federal Finance Minister Jim Flaherty Rejects HST Hike to Fund Public Transit in Ontario," *Toronto Star*, 30 May 2013.

70   T. Kalinowski, "Poll Finds Commuters Ready to Pay," *Toronto Star*, 2 March 2013.

71   M. Cohn, "Kathleen Wynne's High-Stakes Gamble to Unblock Gridlock," *Toronto Star*, 3 April 2013.

72   A. Morrow, "Toronto Subway-Route Debate Stalls as Wynne Refers Funding Plan for Study," *Globe and Mail*, 18 September 2013.

73   SLAPPs are lawsuits, based on meritless claims of defamation, intended to silence individual or organizational critics of the plaintiff's behaviour by burdening them with the cost of a legal defense until they abandon their criticism. See R. Nadarajah and H. Wilkins, *Breaking the Silence: The Urgent Need for Anti-SLAPP Legislation in Ontario* (Toronto: CELA and EcoJustice, 2010), http://www.cela.ca/publications/breaking-silence-urgent-need-anti-slapp-legislation-ontario. For a recent example of an alleged SLAPP in Ontario, see R. Aulakh, "Quebec Forestry Firm Sues Greenpeace for $7M," *Toronto Star*, 25 June 2013.

74   See Bill 83, An Act to amend the Courts of Justice Act, the Libel and Slander Act and the Statutory Powers Procedure Act in order to protect expression on matters of public interest 2013, First Reading, 4 June 2013.

75   See Bill 91, Waste Reduction Act, 2013, First Reading, 6 June 2013.

76   A. Morrow, "Ontario Premier Kathleen Wynne Apologizes for Cancelled Gas Plants," *Globe and Mail*, 14 May 2013.

77   Ontario Ministry of Energy, "Ontario Working with Communities to Secure Clean Energy Future," News Release, 30 May 2013.

78   J. Spears, "Ontario's Long-Term Energy Plan Gets Short-Term Tweak," *Toronto Star*, 16 April 2013.

79   See S.P. Stensil, *Better Never than Late: The Climate Fall-Out of Ontario's Nuclear Electricity Plan* (Toronto: Greenpeace Canada, 2008), 11–22.

80   J. Spears, "Ontario Considering Nuclear Slowdown, Minister Says," *Toronto Star*, 9 May 2013.

81   Estimates of the project's cost run from $6 to $35 billion. See Ontario Power Generation, http://www.opg.com/power/nuclear/refurbishment/dn_factsheets.asp, and Ontario Clean Air Alliance, http://www.cleanairalliance.org/files/active/0/NuclearHandout_v5.pdf

82   The Liberals emerged with 58 seats (a gain of 10 seats), the PCs 28 (a loss of nine seats), and the NDP 21 (no change).

83   Green Party of Ontario, *2014 Election Platform* (Toronto: Green Party of Ontario, 2014).

84   For a summary of the major environment and energy related elements of the major party platforms, see M. Winfield, "Energy, the Environment and the Ontario 2014 Election: The Platforms vs What Needs to Happen" (May 2014), http://marksw.blog.yorku.ca/2014/05/30/energy-the-environment-and-the-ontario-2014-election-the-platforms-vs-what-needs-to-happen-may-2014/

85   M. Winfield, "The 2014 Ontario Election Outcome: The Electoral Politics of Economic Transitions," *Toronto Star*, 16 June 2014.

86　See, for example, J. Gaede, *Ontario, Quebec, Electricity and Climate Change: Advancing the Dialogue—Summary Report* (Toronto: Sustainable Energy Initiative, York University, and Montreal: HEC Montreal, 2015).

87　See The Council of the Federation, "Canadian Energy Strategy," 29 August 2014.

88　Ministry of Environment and Climate Change, *Re: EBR Posting 012–3452 Ontario Climate Change Discussion Paper* (Toronto: Queen's Printer, 2015).

89　M.R. Cohn, "Why Kathleen Wynne's Hydro One Sell-off Is a Sellout: Cohn," *Toronto Star*, 18 May 2015.

90　R. Tomalty and B. Komorowski, *Inside and Out: Sustaining Ontario's Greenbelt* (Toronto: Friends of the Greenbelt Foundation, 2011).

91　P. White, "Chemical Valley Health Issues Prompt Lawsuit against Queen's Park," *Globe and Mail*, 1 November 2010.

92　R. Nadarajah, M. Carter-Witney, and E. Macdonald, *Modernizing Environmental Approvals: EBR Registry No. 010–9143* (Toronto: Canadian Environmental Law Association, Canadian Institute for Environmental Law and Policy, and Ecojustice.ca, 2010), http://www.cela.ca/sites/cela.ca/files/720.ModernizingApprovalsProcess.pdf

93　See Environmental Commission of Ontario, "Far North Act, 2010," *2010/11 Annual Report* (Toronto: Environmental Commissioner of Ontario), http://www.ecoissues.ca/index.php/Far_North_Act,_2010

94　Ontario Regulation 176/13. See also Wildlands League, "Ontario Guts Endangered Species Protections," Media Release, 3 June 2013.

15

Ontario's Multiple Identities: Politics and Policy in a Diverse Province

MYER SIEMIATYCKI

POPULATION DIVERSITY IS AMONG ONTARIO'S most distinctive and defining political characteristics today. A province once regarded as a bastion of British homogeneity is now among the world's most diverse ethnic, racial, religious, and linguistic societies. Ontario has the largest Indigenous population of any Canadian province. It is home to over half of all immigrants and visible minorities in Canada, and its residents belong to over 200 different ethnic groups. As Canadian demographer David Foot has observed, a province's population profile will shape its politics. "The policies, programs, and priorities of Canadian provincial governments," Foot declares, "are inevitably influenced by the demographic compositions of the peoples within their jurisdictions."[1]

This chapter explores the connection between population, politics, and policy in Ontario. Global experience reminds us that demographic differences can generate a variety of political outcomes. Along a continuum of possibilities, in some cases diversity can produce a politics of inclusion and harmony; elsewhere, it can yield exclusion and hatred. Much is at stake in how diversity becomes politically manifested.

Iris Marion Young has drawn attention to the "politics of difference" as a defining challenge for diverse societies. She questions how differing identities are to live together when their interaction is often shaped by prevailing "structures of domination," leaving some groups privileged and others deprived. Young proposes that diverse societies are best served by "politics [that] lays down institutional and ideological means for recognizing and affirming diverse social groups by giving political representation to these groups, and celebrating their distinctive characteristics and cultures."[2] This chapter explores the "politics of difference" in Ontario through the lenses of history, demography, political representation, and policy. The reader may consider how closely Ontario comes to achieving Iris Marion Young's goal of "justice and the politics of difference."

Ontario's History of Diversity

Despite evidence to the contrary, Ontario has often been described and understood as a demographic monolith—a bastion of British ancestry and attachment. Ontario's official motto declares "Loyal She Began, Loyal She Remains." It conveys the view that the province was founded and forever defined by the Loyalists who fled the newly independent United States in the late eighteenth century to remain devoted British subjects in what remained of the British Empire in North America after the American Revolution. Fast-forward more than a century, and the leading civics text in Canada declared in 1926: "If Quebec is French, Ontario is British; and the two stand side by side in everlasting contrast."[3] Until recent decades, Ontario was presumed to be entirely and forever British in its population make-up.

Several cautionary implications arise from these descriptions of Ontario as a monolithic British transplant. First, it is unlikely that any social or political characteristic that can be identified at a given time will be "everlasting." Societies and their politics are not static; they can change dramatically over time. Ontario is no longer recognizable or described as uniformly British.

Second, it never was accurate to describe Ontario as homogenous. Population diversity has always been a defining characteristic of the province. Ontario's human history stretches back thousands of years before the arrival of the Loyalists. Evidence of Indigenous settlement in the Great Lakes area reaches back some 11,000 years. One thousand years ago, Native peoples in Southern Ontario had established villages of several hundred people, supported by agriculture and hunting. By the 1400s, Southern Ontario's Indigenous population was estimated as being between 60,000 and 65,000, with village populations reaching 3,000. By way of comparison, Toronto would not reach this population size until the late 1820s—40 years after the first arrival of the Loyalists.[4]

Ontario's Indigenous population was itself highly diverse, belonging to a variety of tribes, bands, and linguistic groups. Europeans arrived in the area during the 1600s, prompted by a variety of goals, including expansion of empire, territorial acquisition, economic gain, and religious missionary zeal. By the late 1700s, historian Peter Baskerville contends that Natives and Europeans saw their interaction differently. While Native leaders "envisioned a country within which Native peoples and Europeans could coexist, the British envisioned a colony increasingly fixed by finite borders and exclusivist notions of belonging."[5] This would mean a secondary, marginalized place for Ontario's Indigenous population in the land they had so long had to themselves. It also accounts for the mindset that would adopt a provincial motto erasing thousands of years of Indigenous history in Ontario.

More tangibly, Indigenous peoples were territorially displaced by a series of land treaties dating back to the late 1700s. A series of nine treaties between the British and various Native groups, including the Mississaugas and Iroquois, resulted in huge swathes of territory being taken over by the

British. Much of these lands would be ceded to the Loyalists and subsequent immigrants from Britain, with one-seventh of all land in townships set aside to support Protestant clergy and churches. Essentially, then, Protestantism was affirmed early on as Ontario's official government-supported religion.[6]

The past is not a disconnected time zone from our own. Several centuries later these events continue to have contemporary policy relevance. The Mississauga Natives of New Credit have now asserted land claim on much of the territory of present-day Toronto, claiming this was land wrongly appropriated from their ancestors. And, as we will see, other religions have subsequently made claims of their own for government recognition and support. Some policy issues arising from diversity have deep roots, indeed.

For over two centuries now, Ontario's population growth has been fuelled by immigration. Diversity and differences have always been manifested, along with new policies attuned to identities of difference.

The Loyalists of the late eighteenth century can be regarded as Ontario's and Canada's first refugees, fleeing fears of persecution for having supported the losing (British) side of the American War of Independence. No refugee or immigrant group has ever been better received in this province and country. Loyalists received free land and a new colony all for themselves, carved out of Quebec in 1791 by the British colonial power. Upper Canada was to be a Protestant, British, English-speaking place differentiated from French, Catholic Quebec. Originally named Upper Canada and later Canada West, it would be renamed Ontario when Confederation established Canada as a country in 1867. The British rewarded the Loyalists by creating for them a new jurisdiction where their identity would dominate. Interestingly, then, Ontario owes its existence to an act of "separation" from Quebec.

Put another way, it was a remarkable display of the "politics of difference" that created Ontario as a distinct, separate political jurisdiction in 1791. With the arrival of some 14,000 Loyalists from the United States into what was then the western part of the colony of Quebec, the British decided they deserved their own political jurisdiction in which a British ethnic population would not be outnumbered by French. Of course, no subsequent immigrant group arriving to Ontario in far greater numbers has ever been given their own political jurisdiction. The creation of Ontario as a distinct geopolitical unit is a reminder of the privileged status accorded to British ethnic ancestry in the province's past.

In the decades to follow, Ontario's population skyrocketed from 14,000 in 1791 to 455,000 in 1841 to over 1.5 million in 1867. These were the years known as "The Great Migration," when unprecedented numbers of people left Britain for Ontario. However, the British were hardly a uniform group themselves. Differences of ethnicity (English, Irish, Scots) and religion (Protestant and Catholic) fuelled fierce rivalries often erupting in full-fledged street riots. English Protestants stood atop Ontario's social hierarchy, with Irish Catholics on the lowest rung. An inventory of riots in Canadian cities from 1820 to 1850 reveals that many occurred in Ontario and would today be characterized as pitched ethnic and religious mob brawls. At least 17 different Ontario cities experienced such riots (typically pitting Protestants against Catholics), including Cornwall, Ottawa, Kingston, Toronto, Hamilton, Stratford, and Amherstburg.[7] Celebrating diversity was not a highly regarded value in nineteenth-century Ontario.

Since Confederation, Ontario has experienced three notable waves of immigration: the periods 1900 to 1914, the late 1940s to mid-1960s, and the period since the mid-1990s. Each era brought ever-more diverse newcomer arrivals. The early twentieth century brought continental Europeans in addition to British immigrants. During the mid-twentieth century, Southern and Eastern Europeans predominated. And, in recent decades, Asians have been predominant.

If Ontario was beginning afresh in search of a new provincial motto, it could do worse than "Indigenous She Began, Global She Became." Next, I sketch a portrait of Ontario's diversity.

Ontario's Diversity Today

Few political jurisdictions anywhere can match Ontario's multilayered diversity.[8] Ontario's population has a higher share of immigrants than the world's leading immigration-receiving countries. In 2011, the most recent year for which we have census data, 28.5 per cent of the province's 12.6 million population was foreign-born. This is greater than the ratio in Australia (26.8 per cent), the rest of Canada (15.7 per cent), and the United States (12.9 per cent). Impressively, the 2011 Canadian census revealed that Ontario was home to more than half (53.3 per cent) of all immigrants in Canada, well above its 38.5 per cent of national population. Immigration has transformed Ontario into a multicultural, multiracial, multireligious, and multilingual kaleidoscope.

Ontario is home to over half (52.3 per cent) of all visible minorities in Canada, who account for more than a quarter (25.9 per cent) of the province's population. The term "visible minority" is Canada's official terminology for persons who are non-Indigenous and non-white. The three largest visible minority groups in Ontario as identified by Statistics Canada are South Asians (965,985—7.6 per cent of the total Ontario population), Chinese (629,140—5.0 per cent of the total population), and blacks (539,210—4.3 per cent of the total population).

The 2011 census further demonstrated that more Indigenous people live in Ontario than in any other province. They number 441,395 by ethnic ancestry, accounting for 3.5 per cent of the province's population. Together, then, visible minorities and Indigenous people account for close to one in every three Ontarians.

As a magnet for global migration, Ontario's population is particularly rich in ethnic diversity. As noted earlier, the 2011 census identified over 200 different ethnic origins among Ontario residents. Respondents could cite a single or multiple ancestries in their background. Twenty-five different ethnic communities in Ontario recorded populations above the 100,000 mark. The 10 largest are Canadian (2,946,095), English (2,925,660), Scottish (2,080,545), Irish (2,069,110), French (1,363,370), German (1,154,550), Italian (883,990), Chinese (713,245), East Indian (678,465), and Dutch (508,565).

Derivative of their ethnic diversity, Ontarians speak many different languages. The top 10 non-official mother-tongue languages among Ontarians, reflecting both mid-twentieth century and more recent immigration waves, are Italian, Chinese, Cantonese, Spanish, Punjabi, Tagalog, Portuguese, Arabic, German, and Urdu. Interestingly, the vast majority of Ontarians (97.6 per cent) self-identify as able to speak English or French. French was the first non-Indigenous language spoken in Ontario, and the province's francophone population now stands at 611,500 (4.8 per cent of the population).

Finally, religion is a notable marker of diversity and change in Ontario. Roman Catholics are by far the largest religious group in Ontario. They account for 31.2 per cent of Ontario's population, followed by the United Church at 7.5 per cent and Anglicans at 6.1 per cent. This is a dramatic departure from much of Ontario's history when it stood out as a bastion of Protestantism, often wary of Roman Catholic influence. Waves of migration over the past 60 years from Catholic countries, combined with a decline in Protestantism, have now made Roman Catholicism Ontario's largest faith community. The fastest growing faith communities today are non-Christian—Muslim, Hindu, Sikh, and Buddhist. Together they account for 10.2 per cent of provincial population, just under 1.3 million persons.

It is evident from this section's overview of Ontario's demographics that the province is a tapestry of multilayered diversity. There is no such person as "the typical Ontarian." Rather, what defines the province's population is its remarkable range of birthplaces, ethnic and racial identities, mother tongues, and religions. Governing Ontario today requires attentiveness to the population's multiple identities. The remainder of the chapter explores how this diversity is manifested in Ontario politics and public policy.

Elected in Ontario: Diversity Representation

Is the diversity of Ontario's population reflected in the profile of our elected officials? Before attempting to answer the question, let us first consider why it warrants attention. Who we elect as our political leaders has important political, policy, and symbolic implications. Members of the provincial Legislature (MPPs) are our lawmakers, our policymakers, the "face and voice" of our provincial government. Political scientists have long maintained that the profile of our political leadership reflects basic power relations in society. Thus, Jerome Black and Aleem Lakhani contend that analyzing the ethnoracial composition of our elected institutions "may index the equality of access the system provides into the corridors of power."[9] Put another way, who is elected and who has a seat at the decision-making table can significantly influence what issues governments address and the decisions they make.

Today in Ontario there is a stark "diversity gap" between the province's demographic profile and its elected representatives.[10] This is particularly evident in the case of Indigenous people, immigrants, and visible minorities, when we compare their share of population to their share of seats held in the provincial Legislature. (Women are also under-represented among Ontario's elected officials, a subject discussed in Chapters 5 and 12.)

As we have seen, close to 450,000 Ontarians claim Indigenous ancestry. Yet there is no Indigenous MPP among the current 107 elected Members of Provincial Parliament. Indeed, only one Indigenous person has ever been elected to the Ontario Legislature—Peter North, who served two terms from 1990 to 1999 representing a rural Southern Ontario riding. So while Indigenous parliamentarians have at times played key roles in rallying and championing Indigenous causes in other provinces (e.g., Elijah Harper[11] of Manitoba in 1990), Queen's Park has never been such a platform for Ontario's Indigenous population.

The composition of Ontario's 40th Legislature, elected in 2011, highlights how severe the province's "diversity gap" has become. First, we profile the demographics of politicians elected that year, followed by the results of the most recent 2014 Ontario provincial election. Twice as many immigrant origin politicians would have needed to be elected in 2011 for their number of MPPs to match the province's foreign-born population share. In 2011 immigrants comprised 28.5 per cent of Ontario's population, but they accounted for only 14 per cent of all members elected that year. Of the 15 foreign-born MPPs, India and Italy were the most frequent birthplaces, each accounting for three MPPs. Ontarians of Indian and Italian ancestry have been most successful among minority ethnoracial groups in gaining elected office. Among the shared characteristics accounting for their electoral success are high residential concentration making them sizable blocs within certain constituencies, robust social capital reflected in a range of community institutions, strong sense of collective identity, and extensive homeland/ancestral traditions of democratic electoral politics.

Visible minority representation in the Ontario Legislature was equally problematic. Table 15.1 below compares Ontario's visible minority population in 2011 to their share of seats won in the provincial election that same year. As Table 15.1 reveals, Ontario would also have needed to elect twice as many visible minority MPPs in 2011 for their share of seats (12.15 per cent) to match their share of population (25.9 per cent). This shortfall is captured by the 0.48 proportionality ratio for all visible minorities, second row from the bottom right in the table. (If a group is underrepresented relative to population, its proportionality ratio is under 1; if a group is overrepresented, the ratio is over 1.)

The election of visible minority MPPs in 2011 reflected some interesting clustering trends. First, Table 15.1 reveals great disparities across different visible minority subgroups. Six subgroups with a combined population over 830,000 had no member of their community elected (Arab, Filipino, Japanese, Korean, Latin American, and South East Asian). The large Chinese and black communities in Ontario were significantly underrepresented as well. The most electorally successful group by far were South Asians, accounting for eight of 13 visible minorities elected. Yet even the South Asian proportionality ratio failed to match its share of provincial population. Second, visible minority MPPs were overwhelmingly (12 of 13) found in the Greater Toronto Area (GTA), with one from Ottawa. And third, the political party affiliation of visible minority MPPs is striking: 12 of 13 belonged to the Liberal Party (which won the election), with one from the NDP. This is despite the fact that the main parties ran practically the same number of visible minority candidates in 2011: New Democrats (19), Liberals, and Conservatives (18 each).

These electoral patterns, in turn, reflect some important underlying dynamics in the "politics of difference" in Ontario. First, visible minority MPPs are overwhelmingly elected in constituencies with high concentrations of visible minority residents and voters. Outside such constituencies, visible minorities are highly unlikely to secure party nomination to run for office. Across Ontario, in the 2011 election, 70 of 107 constituencies featured no visible minority candidate. Conversely, in seven GTA constituencies, all candidates of the three main parties were visible minorities. And in five GTA constituencies two of the three main parties had a visible minority

Table 15.1 Elected MPP Representation by Visible Minority Groups, 2011 Ontario Election

Visible Minority Group	Population	Per cent of Population	Elected MPPs	Percentage of MPPs	Proportionality Ratio
Arab	151,640	1.2	0	0.00	0.00
Black	539,210	4.3	2	1.87	0.43
Chinese	629,140	5.0	2	1.87	0.37
Filipino	275,385	2.2	0	0.00	0.00
Japanese	29,090	0.2	0	0.00	0.00
Korean	78,290	0.6	0	0.00	0.00
Latin American	172,560	1.4	0	0.00	0.00
South Asian	965,985	7.6	8	7.48	0.98
South East Asian	137,875	1.1	0	0.00	0.00
West Asian	122,530	1.0	1	0.93	0.93
Visible Minority, n.i.e.*	81,125	0.6	0	0.00	0.00
Multiple Visible Minority	96,735	0.8	0	0.00	0.00
All Visible Minorities	3,279,565	25.9	13	12.15	0.48
Not Visible Minority	9,372,225	74.1	94	87.85	1.19

* n.i.e.: not identified elsewhere in another subcategory

Source: Author's calculation, and Statistics Canada, National Household Survey, 2011.

candidate. Thus, over half (54 per cent) of all visible minority candidates in the 2011 election were confined to barely one-tenth (11 per cent) of all constituencies in the province. This raises the question of whether political parties regard constituencies as "colour coded," largely confining visible minority candidates to areas where a single minority community predominates and will be presented with candidates of that origin.

Second, the overwhelming Liberal Party affiliation of visible minority MPPs in Ontario suggests there is no fixed partisan "ethnic vote" in Ontario. It had become fashionable to presume a convergence of values between the federal Conservative Party of Stephen Harper and recent immigrant, visible minority communities. The suggestion was that these voters had an affinity for Conservative pro-business and "traditional" family values. Yet, in Ontario as we have seen, not one of the 13 visible minority MPPs elected provincially in 2011 was a Conservative. (Nor, we will see, did Conservative leader Tim Hudak's appeal to visible minority constituencies succeed in the 2014 election.) It may be more apt to suggest that minorities and recent immigrants strove to be included in the political mainstream, with a distinct preference for landing with the winning side.

The most recent 2014 Ontario provincial election saw a significant increase of visible minorities elected: rising from 13 to 17 MPPs. Still however, another 11 needed to be elected for visible minorities in the Legislature to match their share of the province's overall population. Ontario's "diversity gap" remains large. Other key patterns identified earlier for visible minority representation among elected MPPs also still prevail in the 41st Legislature elected in 2014. Almost all current visible minority MPPs, 16 of 17, represent constituencies in the Greater Toronto Area (the other again in Ottawa), and almost all, 16 of 17, belong to the election-winning Liberal Party (the other once more to the NDP); and again South Asians comprise the largest number of elected visible minorities, holding 10 of the 17 seats.

So far, we have focused on the profile of elected MPPs. Yet, as an earlier chapter explains, in Ontario's parliamentary system it is the premier and cabinet members who wield particular authority. What does the profile of Ontario's past premiers and recent cabinets reveal about the "politics of difference" in Ontario?

Ontario has had 25 premiers since 1867—all have been Caucasians (whites) of British ethnic ancestry, and all have been Christian: 23 Protestant, and two Catholic. Premier Kathleen Wynne is Ontario's first female premier and first openly gay premier.

Ontario's first visible minority cabinet minister (Liberal Alvin Curling) was appointed in 1985. Since then, the visible minority share of provincial population has climbed steadily from 13 per cent in 1991, to 19 per cent in 2001, to 26 per cent in 2011. Mindful of this growing population, no Ontario premier since 1985 has constructed a cabinet without visible minority representation. Their number has grown incrementally. For a period, under Premier Dalton McGuinty in the early 2000s, the practice had been to appoint one cabinet minister from each of the three largest visible minority communities: South Asian, Chinese, and black. This could be interpreted in different ways. It could be taken as evidence these minority communities had "arrived," and their significant numbers in Ontario required cabinet representation. Or it could be interpreted as crass tokenism by governments seeking minority community support. More recently, Premier Kathleen Wynne expanded visible minority membership in her cabinet, appointing six to her 27-member cabinet following the 2014 election. Interestingly, then, visible minority members accounted for a higher proportion of Premier Wynne's cabinet (22.2 per cent) than their share of seats in the Legislature as a whole (15.8 per cent). The record number of visible minorities in Premier Wynne's cabinet reflects the strong electoral support of visible minorities for the Ontario Liberal Party. As we have seen, 16 of 17 visible minorities in the Legislature are Liberals, and these MPPs accounted for 27.5 per cent of the provincial Liberal caucus available to Premier Wynne for cabinet selection. Ongoing support from these communities is clearly vital to the future of the Ontario Liberal Party, and their inclusion in cabinet is intended to signal the Party's responsiveness to these communities.

Franco-Ontarians are another group with a distinct record of cabinet membership. As we have seen, Ontario has a sizable francophone population, concentrated in eastern, northern, and southwestern pockets of the province. Over the past 12 Ontario Parliaments, stretching back to 1975, only one featured a cabinet without a Franco-Ontarian member. All three main political parties, when in office, recognized the significance of this community seeing (and hearing!) itself represented in cabinet.

Still, the overall profile that emerges from Ontario's Legislature is a significant underrepresentation of the province's diverse demographics. Indigenous people, immigrants, and visible minorities are not elected commensurate with their share of the population. This should be of public policy concern. A Legislature better reflecting its diverse citizenry would have a number of virtues. These include drawing members from a broader talent pool; increasing the capacity to express a broader range of experiences and issues; strengthening the Legislature's democratic legitimacy; establishing role models of political leadership in diverse communities; and signalling the inclusion of all communities in the shared project of leading Ontario.

A number of measures have been proposed to advance more diverse representation among elected officials. These include introducing proportional representation electoral provisions, which typically yield more diverse out-comes; better equalizing the average population size of constituencies, so that immigrant and visible minority areas have a fair and larger number of ridings; and greater commitment from political parties to nominating more candidates from underrepresented groups, particularly in ridings vacated by incumbents. To date, the Ontario NDP is one of the few political parties to adopt a specific target for candidate diversity. While not mandatory, the party aims to have 50 per cent of its candidates belong to underrepresented groups (including women, visible minorities, Indigenous people, disabled persons, gays, lesbians, francophones, and youth). Meanwhile Ontario's political lead-ership profile in both the provincial Legislature and cabinet continues to lag behind the province's extraordinary, diverse demography. Nor should we expect this "diversity gap" to somehow be automatically overcome over time. Indigenous underrepresentation in elected office reminds us that time itself is not the great equalizer.

Diversity Policy Issues

Demographic diversity inevitably raises distinct policy issues. Political juris-dictions with a heterogeneous population confront policy questions that are largely absent in more homogenous places. Jurisdictions first populated by Indigenous persons have a legacy of colonialism and First Peoples' claims to address. Add to this Ontario's intense diversity of ethnicity, race, reli-gion, and language derived from centuries of immigration, and we should expect "identity politics" to manifest themselves in the province's political and policy agenda.

Many different issues in Ontario politics do indeed flow from the province's diverse demographics. To briefly illustrate from a single policy field—immigration—we can identify a number of recent new issues and policies that have come to the fore. In 2005 the Canada-Ontario Immigra-tion Agreement was signed providing the province with enhanced funding and influence over newcomer services. In 2006 Ontario moved to address the economic adversities facing recent immigrants by pioneering a new approach to newcomer credential recognition with its Fair Access to Regu-lated Professions Act. And, in 2013, the City of Toronto called on the prov-ince to modify its Municipal Elections Act to extend municipal voting rights to close to 400,000 immigrant permanent residents of the city who have not yet acquired Canadian citizenship. Clearly, diversity impacts the province's political agenda.

In the limited scope of this chapter, it is impossible to identify or discuss all examples of this dynamic. Accordingly, several instances can be highlighted where conflicting claims regarding group rights have been particularly contentious and significant. These have ranged from Indigenous claims to ancestral lands, disagreements over public funding of religious schools, and attempts to have sharia law recognized as a basis for resolving some legal disputes. Each reflects a central challenge in the "politics of difference": how should a particular group's claim for recognition and fairness be handled? Ontario's response has not always been consistent or just.

Indigenous Policy

"Aboriginal affairs," Jonathan Malloy has written, "have always been com-paratively low on the Ontario political agenda."[12] The general disregard of Indigenous issues by Ontario provincial governments certainly cannot be attributed to an absence of matters worthy of attention. As Lorenzo Cheru-bini and colleagues have written: "The contemporary realities of Aboriginal peoples are arguably the greatest single social justice issue in Canada today."[13] Indeed, Indigenous adversities across a host of experiences, including pov-erty, health, housing, employment, and imprisonment, are widely recognized.

Political scientists recognize that public policy includes both the action and inaction of government in response to issues or problems. For dec-ades, even centuries, inaction has certainly been the predominant Ontario government response to Indigenous issues. Rand Dyck's assessment of the matter toward the end of the twentieth century remains apt today: "Little progress has been made on Native land claims in the province, or indeed on other aboriginal demands."[14] Explaining why successive Ontario govern-ments have not been more responsive helps us understand important politi-cal and policy realities. Any interest group's capacity to have government address its concerns depends above all on that group's power. This can be electoral power (ability to influence election outcomes through voting or financial donations), economic power (e.g., investment and job creation), or social power (the broader social support for the group beyond its own members).

Despite its significant numbers, Ontario's Indigenous community has lacked political leverage. While Ontario has Canada's largest Indigenous population, Aboriginals account for only 3.5 per cent of the province's pop-ulation, and they are not a sufficiently large segment of any single constitu-ency's population to be able to sway its election result. This lack of numeric strength at the constituency level also helps to explain why only one politi-cian of Indigenous origin has ever been elected to the Legislature. In turn, that has hindered the emergence of an Indigenous advocate and champion in the Legislature. Further disadvantaging the Indigenous community's

influence on policy are its elevated poverty levels and the negative, discriminatory public attitudes prevailing toward it. A recent report on urban Indigenous people in Ontario found that almost four in five surveyed (78 per cent)
identified racism as a problem Indigenous people face in Ontario cities.[15]

A notable development in Indigenous affairs since the 1990s has been
the adoption of more militant direct-action tactics by Indigenous people
striving to influence government policy. In 1990, Natives near Thunder Bay
pressing for on-reserve improvements blocked the CNR rail mainline carrying signs declaring Let's Get Canada Back on the Right Track.[16] Five years
later in Southwestern Ontario, members of a local Indian band occupied
Ipperwash Provincial Park in opposition to planned development on traditional burial grounds. Events ended tragically with provincial police shooting unarmed protester Dudley George dead.

Many ripples flowed from this event, including the conviction of an OPP
officer in the shooting and allegations that the Conservative premier of the
day Mike Harris had called for forceful police action. Liberal Premier Dalton
McGuinty subsequently established a provincial inquiry into the events at
Ipperwash, and his government ultimately returned Ipperwash Provincial
Park to Indigenous control. As the Ipperwash Inquiry's final report forcefully
declared, Indigenous occupations were a symptom of Indigenous frustration over long-neglected concerns, typically related to the use, control, and
ownership of land.

More recently, Indigenous occupations and protests have continued and
magnified. In 2006, hundreds of First Nations protesters occupied land in
the Southern Ontario community of Caledonia to prevent construction
of a new suburban subdivision on land the Six Nations regarded as legally
their own. Violence periodically flared, as Natives protested their land rights
were being violated, and many town residents complained the provincial
government and police were failing to defend law and order when protesters blockaded major local roads.[17] To this day the standoff continues: no
new suburban homes have been built, and ownership of the land remains
unresolved.

Finally, another Ontario Indigenous protest in 2012–13 contributed to
mobilizing the widest pan-Canadian Native protest movement in decades.
In late 2012, Chief Theresa Spence of the Northern Ontario Attawapiskat
reserve launched a hunger strike on the outskirts of Parliament in Ottawa
to draw attention to adverse conditions facing her community. (Since the
federal government holds jurisdiction over Native reserves, it and not the
provincial government was the target of Chief Spence's action.) Stretching for weeks into 2013, the hunger strike received wide media attention
and contributed to the launch of the nationwide Idle No More protests by

Indigenous people that same year, calling for wholesale advances in Native rights and self-government. Few tangible strides have been made, and recurring accounts of crises such as youth distress, poor housing, and substandard services reflect the ongoing inadequacy of government policy toward Indigenous communities.

Religion and School Funding

Among Ontario's most enduring and contentious policy challenges has been the question of whether faith-based schools should receive government funding. The issue dates back to before Confederation, when the new country's creation hung in the balance on whether satisfactory school funding arrangements could be made. At issue in 1867 was whether the religious minorities in Ontario (Catholics) and in Quebec (Protestants) would have their schools funded once education was established as a provincial jurisdiction under the terms of Confederation. A compromise was struck and enshrined in the constitution, guaranteeing the minority Catholics of Ontario and the minority Protestants of Quebec that, going forward, their level of school funding could not drop below the level existing prior to 1867. In Ontario, this has meant that Catholics have a constitutional guarantee of their own denominational separate school system.

From 1867 to the 1980s, the prime friction point in Ontario denominational education policy was the determined effort by Catholics to secure funding on a par with the public school system. Before 1867, governments only funded schools through the elementary years, so that was the extent of guaranteed funding to the Catholic system. But over the course of the twentieth century, funding to the public school system was extended through to secondary high schools. Meanwhile, Catholic parents with children in Catholic high schools had to pay tuition fees for their secondary education. Years of lobbying for parity funding with the public school system finally paid off in the mid-1980s when Conservative Premier Bill Davis extended separate school funding through to the end of high school.

By this time, the influx of global immigration into Ontario was well underway. Ontario was now home to sizable and rapidly growing non-Christian populations. Since the 1980s, coalitions of Muslims, Sikhs, Hindus, along with the longer-established Jewish community have been pressing for public funding of their religious schools. They have taken their cause to the courts, to the provincial political arena, and even to international tribunals. To date, their efforts have failed on all fronts.

In the 1990s, both the Ontario Court of Appeal and the Supreme Court of Canada ruled that it was constitutional for Ontario to fund Catholic schools but not other religious schools. Frustrated by these rulings, an Ontario parent went so far as to complain to the United Nations Human Rights Commission that Ontario was discriminating against non-Christian religions by refusing to fund their schools as they did Catholic schools. In 2005 the UN body issued a report condemning Ontario for practising religious discrimination and calling on the province to fund other religious schools. Such UN declarations are not binding, and no Ontario government has chosen to follow the UN's urging.

The issue dominated Ontario's 2007 election campaign, after Conservative Party leader John Tory announced his support for funding non-Catholic religious schools if elected. Opinion polls showed Ontarians strongly opposed to such a move, and the Conservative Party's overwhelming defeat in the 2007 Ontario election is partly attributed to the unpopularity of its commitment on faith-based schooling. John Tory supported faith-based funding on grounds of religious fairness and respect for diverse religions. A majority of Ontarians, however, feared that such funding would weaken public schools as sites of multicultural diversity and integration. Interestingly, then, both sides of the issue championed multicultural diversity as their goal but disagreed on how schooling could best promote it.

Ontario's policy today on faith-based schooling is unique in Canada. Five provinces provide some form of funding to all religious schools; four offer no funding to any faith-based schools. By contrast, Ontario provides full funding to Catholic schools but does not provide funding to any other religious schools. This discrepancy, we have seen, is a product of our history, of the constitutional guarantee given to the province's Catholic minority in 1867.

It is unlikely that the current Ontario policy will remain unchallenged. Steep tuition fees for minority religious schools will prompt non-Christian parents to keep up the pressure. And the discrepancy of supporting one faith group but not others continues to invite criticism. Unresolved, as Dawn Zinga notes, is "how best to accommodate the needs of all of its students within the context of a pluralistic and multicultural society."[18] Ontario could advance religious equality either by removing funding for Catholic schools or by extending such funding to other religious schools. The first option is electorally high risk with Catholics now constituting the largest religious group in the province. The second option proved unpopular in the 2007 election, and would be hugely costly for the financially strapped province. Ontario's policy of funding only the schools of one religious group is a reminder that sometimes inconsistent policy can be driven by its own irresistible logic.

On another recent policy issue involving religious rights, however, Ontario decided on a "one size fits all" solution, treating all religions the same. Next, then, is a discussion of Ontario's debate over sharia law.

Ontario's Sharia Law Debate

During 2004 and 2005 a spirited debate played out in Ontario over the use of Islamic law to settle family law disputes in the province. The issue reflected and manifested the complexities of policymaking in a diverse society. Back in 1991 Ontario passed the Arbitration Act allowing private disputes to be settled by arbitration rather than turning to the more costly and time-consuming courts of law. The act required both parties in the dispute to agree to resolve their differences through arbitration, and it made the resulting arbitration rulings legally binding.

Several religious groups (Jewish, Christian, and Ismaili Muslim) saw opportunity in the Arbitration Act and established arbitration tribunals to adjudicate cases based on their distinct religious principles. Cases involving family and business law were most typically brought forward for arbitration. In 2003 a retired Muslim lawyer, Syed Ali, announced plans to offer arbitration services in family disputes following sharia principles.

Jewish, Christian, and Ismaili arbitration had generated no public attention, let alone controversy. By contrast, the proposal to adjudicate cases based on sharia law unleashed a firestorm described by legal scholar Natasha Bakht as a "moral panic,"[19] and by *Toronto Star* columnist Haroon Siddiqui as "fear-mongering that Muslim barbarians are knocking on the gates of Ontario."[20]

Syed Ali and his supporters defended their request on two grounds: equal treatment with other religions, and respect for multiculturalism and the significance of religion to some communities. Critics of the proposal emphasized what they identified as the patriarchal, male-dominant values of sharia that would disadvantage women. "The sharia debate," Anna Korteweg has noted, "was at its core a debate on group rights."[21] Multiculturalism or women's rights—which should take pre-eminence?

Opinions were divided and multilayered. For some Muslims the issues were Ontario society's respect for their tradition and their right to equal recognition with other religions under the Arbitration Act. But the Muslim community was by no means united on the issue. Many, led by women Muslim leaders, charged that community pressure would oblige Muslim women to accept arbitration over court of law adjudication, and then sharia principles would disadvantage them. Opinion in the broader society of Ontario was also divided. Some critics condemned sharia as barbaric, "un-Canadian" and hostile to women. By contrast Canada's self-styled "National Newspaper," the *Globe and Mail*, editorialized in support of sharia-based tribunals declaring that "the Islamic tribunal may yet send a message that Muslims can be who they are and still be as Canadian as anyone else."[22]

This debate reminds us that policy demands in the name of a distinct group can divide both the group itself and the broader society. These are challenging issues for government to address. The Ontario Liberal government of Premier McGuinty took a classic first step in addressing the controversy. It commissioned a report on the subject by a respected, credible analyst—Marion Boyd, who was a lawyer, a former NDP Attorney General of Ontario, and a champion of women's rights. Boyd's report of late 2004 supported arbitration based on Islamic legal principles. She did not accept the view that sharia was inherently at odds with human rights or with Canada's Charter of Rights and Freedoms. At the same time, however, she argued that measures should be taken to safeguard individual rights and women's rights in any faith-based arbitration. This could be done, Boyd stated, by assuring that arbitrators were well trained and accountable and based their rulings on both religious and Canadian legal principles.

Controversy did not abate with the release of Boyd's report. Closure came later in 2005 when Premier McGuinty made a double announcement: there would be no sharia-based tribunals in Ontario, and furthermore, no faith-based arbitration of any denomination would be permitted under the Arbitration Act. Henceforth, the premier declared, there would be "one law for all Ontarians."[23] Saying no to Muslims, then, also meant saying no to all other religious groups. The previously existing Jewish and Christian tribunals were now disbanded. To have preserved them while rejecting Islamic tribunals would inevitably have raised charges of religious discrimination and intolerance.

Interestingly, then, Ontario has adopted different policies on faith-based education and faith-based arbitration. The school funding issue examined earlier bears the constitutional legacy of guaranteed support for Catholic schools. No such constitutional requirement exists related to arbitration, and here Ontario has opted for a one-size-fits-all policy of keeping religion out of the law. In both instances Ontario policy rejected conferring distinct recognition and resources on religious minorities as far as it constitutionally could. Secularism would appear to be Ontario's "official religion."

Conclusion

Ontario has an unfinished diversity agenda. The face of its elected political leadership does not reflect its demographic mosaic. Equitable treatment of First Peoples remains to be achieved. The place and recognition of religion in a secular society remains unresolved. Space constraints of this chapter have made it impossible to explore other current challenges such as developing more robust mechanisms to overcome unequal employment and income among Ontarians related to visible minority and immigration status. The well-being of Ontario's multiple identities depends on the Ontario government's ability to rise to such challenges. Perhaps equally urgently, as societies around the world experience greater demographic diversity, we need more models of how to make the "politics of difference" work. This is a worthy calling for Canada's most diverse province.

Discussion Questions

1. How does Ontario's history of diversity shape Ontario's political agenda today?
2. What demographic dimensions of Ontario's population today are most significant?
3. What is the nature and significance of Ontario's "diversity gap" in electoral representation?
4. Are recent claims on the Ontario government made by specific identity groups for what they regard as "fair and equitable policies" reasonable? Why or why not?
5. Relative to other issues facing the Government of Ontario, how important is "the politics of difference"?

Notes

1 David K. Foot, "The Policy Implications of Provincial Demographics," in *Provinces: Canadian Provincial Politics*, 2nd ed., ed. Christopher Dunn (Toronto: University of Toronto Press, 2006), 436.

2 Iris Marion Young, *Justice and the Politics of Difference* (Princeton, NJ: Princeton University Press, 1990), 240.

3 Charles Norris Cochrane and William Stewart Wallace, *This Canada of Ours* (Toronto: National Council of Education, 1926), 26.

4 Peter A. Baskerville, *Sites of Power: A Concise History of Ontario* (Don Mills: Oxford University Press, 2005), 1–23.

5 Ibid., 38.

6 Ibid., 43–50.

7 Bryan D. Palmer, *Working-Class Experience: The Rise and Reconstitution of Canadian Labour, 1800–1980* (Toronto: Butterworth & Co., 1983), 304–15.

8 All statistics in this section are from Statistics Canada Census of 2011, as follows: Statistics Canada, *Aboriginal Peoples in Canada: First Nations People, Metis and Inuit*, Catalogue no. 99–011-X2011001 (2013), http://www12.statcan.gc.ca/nhs-enm/2011/as-sa/99-011-x/99-011-x2011001-eng.cfm; Statistics Canada, *Immigration and Ethnocultural Diversity in Canada*, Catalogue no. 99–010-X2011001 (2011), http://www12.statcan.gc.ca/nhs-enm/2011/as-sa/99-010-x/99-010-x2011001-eng.pdf; Statistics Canada, *NHS Focus on Geography Series— Ontario* (2013), http://www12.statcan.gc.ca/nhs-enm/2011/as-sa/fogs-spg/

Pages/FOG.cfm?lang=E&level=2&GeoCode=35); Statistics Canada, *NHS Profile, Ontario, 2011* (2013), https://www12.statcan.gc.ca/nhs-enm/2011/dp-pd/prof/details/Page.cfm?Lang=E&Geo1=PR&Code1=35&Data=Count&SearchText=Ontario&SearchType=Begins&SearchPR=01&A1=All&B1=All&GeoLevel=PR&GeoCode=10

9   Jerome Black and Aleem Lakhani, "Ethnoracial Diversity in the House of Commons: An Analysis of Numerical Representation in the 55th Parliament," *Canadian Ethnic Studies* 29, no. 1 (1997): 2.

10 Myer Siemiatycki, *The Diversity Gap: The Electoral Under-Representation of Visible Minorities* (Toronto: DiverseCity, 2011). All statistics in this section are from this study and subsequent calculations by the author, supported by the excellent research assistance of Ms. Rosalind Gunn.

11 Indigenous Chief Elijah Harper, was elected to the Manitoba Legislature, and in 1990 opposed adoption of a Canadian constitutional reform agreement known as the Meech Lake Accord, because it had not involved consultation with Indigenous people. Since the agreement required unanimous support of the federal Parliament and all 10 provincial legislatures, Mr. Harper's dissent effectively defeated the Accord.

12 Jonathan Malloy, "Double Identities: Aboriginal Policy Agencies in Ontario and British Columbia," *Canadian Journal of Political Science* 34, no. 1 (2001): 153.

13 Lorenzo Cherubini, John Hodson, Michael Manley-Casimir, and Christiane Muir, "'Closing the Gap' at the Peril of Widening the Void: Implications of the Ontario Ministry of Education's Policy for Aboriginal Education," *Canadian Journal of Education* 33, no. 2 (2010): 330.

14 Rand Dyck, *Provincial Politics in Canada*, 3rd ed. (Scarborough, ON: Prentice Hall Canada, 1996), 307.

15 Urban Aboriginal Task Force, *Final Report* (Toronto: The Ontario Federation of Indian Friendship Centres, 2007).

16 Baskerville, *Sites of Power*, 237.

17 For differing accounts of the Caledonia dispute, see Christie Blatchford, *Helpless: Caledonia's Nightmare of Fear and Anarchy, and How the Law Failed All of Us* (Toronto: Doubleday Canada, 2010), and Laura DeVries, *Conflict in Caledonia: Aboriginal Land Rights and the Rule of Law* (Vancouver: UBC Press, 2011).

18 Dawn Zinga, "Ontario's Challenge: Denominational Rights in Public Education," *Canadian Journal of Educational Administration and Policy* 80 (2008): 13.

19 Natasha Bakht, "Were Muslim Barbarians Really Knocking On the Gates of Ontario? The Religious Arbitration Controversy—Another Perspective," *Ottawa Law Review* (2006): 67.

20 Cited in Sherene Razack, "The 'Sharia Law Debate' in Ontario: The Modernity/Premodernity Distinction in Legal Efforts to Protect Women from Culture," *Feminist Legal Studies* 15, no. 1 (2007): 15.

21 Anna C. Korteweg, "The Sharia Debate in Ontario," *ISIM Review* 18 (2006): 50.

22 Cited in ibid., 51.

23 Cited in ibid., 50.

16

The Politics of Labour and Labour Relations in Ontario

LARRY SAVAGE

O NTARIO HAS WITNESSED SIGNIFICANT POLICY shifts in the realm of labour relations in the last few decades, with governments of every political stripe modifying aspects of the province's labour relations regime in the name of "fairness" and "balance." To be sure, these legislative changes have all been highly contested and both labour unions and employer groups have challenged the competing normative assumptions associated with each round of labour law reform. A series of competing labour relations policy changes throughout the 1990s prompted some researchers to argue that the province's labour relations regime had succumbed to an ideological "pendulum effect" wherein the New Democratic Party (NDP) government swung the policy pendulum far to the left, while the Progressive Conservative (PC) government that followed swung it back forcefully to the right. Implicit in this line of argumentation was the idea that ideology and partisanship had replaced fairness and balance as the driving force behind changes to the province's labour laws.[1] While particular governments undoubtedly play a facilitative role in either encouraging or discouraging unionization and collective bargaining, we must be careful to resist the urge to draw a direct correlation between the party that forms government and the relative strength of unions or employers in any given period. This chapter advances the argument that the pendulum analogy is flawed insofar as it assumes an artificial, "balanced," middle ground and, further, that such a middle ground represents sound public policy. This chapter takes a decidedly different approach, arguing that the last few decades are best understood as a roller-coaster ride for labour unions in Ontario, with the drops far more pronounced and enduring than the ascents. The roller-coaster analogy allows us to break from the analytical straightjacket of the pendulum by making it clear that the relationship between business and labour is always in flux, with both sides experiencing ups and downs, often unevenly, and sometimes while the same government is in power. For example, in the early 1990s, Ontario witnessed the passage of unprecedented pro-union labour law reforms under the province's first NDP government, including the adoption of an anti-scab law, which banned the use of replacement workers in the event of a legal strike. However, a year later, the same government temporarily removed the collective bargaining rights of unionized public sector workers by unilaterally reopening their negotiated contracts and forcing them to take unpaid vacation days. In other words, unions both gained ground and lost ground during the NDP's term of office.

Almost immediately upon taking office in 1995, the Harris Conservatives erased all of the NDP's pro-union reforms, and then some, shifting the entire terrain of labour relations in Ontario decisively in favour of corporate interests. In response, an unprecedented number of unions embraced strategic voting as a tactic to oust the governing Conservatives in the 1999 provincial election. While initially unsuccessful, such a strategy helped to forge stronger ties between the Ontario Liberal Party and specific segments of the labour movement, causing a lasting division in the electoral approach of organized labour. When the McGuinty Liberals were elected to a majority government in 2003, they set out to undo some of the previous government's labour relations changes, but stopped short of repealing a number of key measures adopted by the Conservatives, preferring instead to broker ad hoc deals with the specific unions which had come to share close ties with the Liberals. The uneven ascent of the union movement during the McGuinty years was shaken in the aftermath of the Great Recession of 2008, in a climate of government austerity that destabilized many Liberal-labour links. When McGuinty's successor, Kathleen Wynne, took over as premier in 2013, some unions flocked back to the Liberals, if only because her party was best positioned to block the election of the Ontario PCs in the 2014 provincial election.

This chapter documents the labour relations roller-coaster ride described above, which has steadily, albeit unevenly, weakened the political power of Ontario's labour movement over the course of the last few decades. The chapter begins with a contextual overview of labour relations in Ontario before investigating the shifting terrain of labour law reform and labour politics during the life of respective NDP, PC, and Liberal governments. The chapter concludes with some thoughts on the future of labour politics and labour relations in Ontario.

Contextualizing Labour Relations in Ontario

Due to the constitutional division of powers in Canada, responsibility for labour law is divided between 14 different jurisdictions (one federal, 10 provincial, and three territorial). While the federal government is responsible for labour relations in federally regulated industries such as banking, airlines, telecommunications, and radio and television broadcasting, most Canadians (roughly 90 per cent of them) work in provincially regulated workplaces like retail outlets, schools, and hospitals. Therefore, provincial governments play an incredibly central role in managing everyday labour relations, employment standards, and workplace conflict.

Ontario, like other jurisdictions in North America, uses a "Wagner model" of labour relations, modelled after the 1935 Wagner Act adopted as part of President F.D. Roosevelt's New Deal package in the United States. The Canadian version, Privy Council Order 1003, formally recognized the right of workers to organize unions and engage in collective bargaining and (limited) strike activity. This highly regulated system of labour relations created a system of rules governing strike votes, the certification and decertification of unions, unfair labour practices, and other aspects of the labour-management relationship.[2] The province's labour relations regime is governed by the Ontario Labour Relations Act (OLRA) and other sector-specific collective bargaining legislation. The Ontario Labour Relations Board (OLRB), created in 1948, is a government-appointed, quasi-judicial tribunal responsible for adjudicating labour relations disputes that arise from the interpretation of the OLRA and other labour-relations statutes.

Unions are not monolithic entities. There are dozens of unions operating in Ontario, representing a wide variety of workers in practically every sector of the economy. They each have different cultures, different approaches to labour relations, and different political perspectives. Roughly 28 per cent of the non-agricultural workforce in Ontario is unionized. That compares to a national average of approximately 30 per cent, with a high of 39.3 per cent in Quebec and a low of 23.2 per cent in Alberta.[3] As Table 16.1 demonstrates, however, Ontario's level of union density was marginally lower throughout the 2000s than it was in the early 1990s, partly because of the different labour law regimes that existed in each period and partly due to the spread of precarious work arrangements and the onslaught of deindustrialization since the 1990s, which has crippled union membership levels in the private sector. Union membership losses in the private sector have been somewhat offset by union growth in the public sector, thereby masking important demographic changes in the composition of the province's labour movement. In the immediate postwar period, union membership was heavily concentrated in the private sector and the overwhelming majority of members were men. Today, the reverse is true. The majority of union members work in the public sector and women in unions now outnumber men.[4]

While union density cannot be used as a proxy for union power, it does point to the potential for union power both at the bargaining table and in society more generally. At the level of the workplace, unionized workers tend to earn higher wages and greater benefits than their non-union counterparts in similar sectors of the economy. Unions, for example, were instrumental

Table 16.1 Union Density in Ontario (%), 1985–2012

Year	Members	Density	Year	Members	Density
1985	1,282,900	31.8	1999	1,334,300	28.1
1986	1,323,400	31.6	2000	1,394,800	28.3
1987	1,362,300	31.0	2001	1,412,900	27.9
1988	1,402,100	31.3	2002	1,446,600	28.0
1989	1,427,200	31.2	2003	1,498,700	28.2
1990	1,419,600	32.2	2004	1,494,000	27.7
1991	1,399,900	32.5	2005	1,572,900	28.7
1992	1,369,100	32.3	2006	1,546,700	28.7
1993	1,357,000	32.1	2007	1,573,100	28.1
1994	1,370,200	31.4	2008	1,582,300	27.8
1995	1,408,700	32.1	2009	1,516,900	27.6
1996	1,407,900	32.0	2010	1,559,000	27.8
1997	1,326,600	29.8	2011	1,583,200	27.7
1998	1,344,700	29.3	2012	1,620,100	28.2

Source: Statistics Canada Table 2820078—Labour force survey estimates (LFS), employees by union coverage, North American Industry Classification System (NAICS), sex and age group, annually (Persons).

in securing maternity leave benefits, pay equity, occupational health and safety laws, and protections against sexual harassment and workplace discrimination. Historically, this "union advantage" helped to grow the ranks of the labour movement. In recent years, however, union members' negotiated workplace entitlements have become the target of conservative forces which have seemingly mastered the art of "reverse class resentment." In the words of Tom Walkom, "The new resentment is based on the presumption that if I don't have something, neither should you. Its aim is not to improve anyone's lot but to cut down to a common level of misery those uppity enough to think they deserve better."[5] In short, by stoking divisions between union and non-union workers, the union advantage, seen as a badge of honour for labour in a previous era, is increasingly cast as a symbol of greed and excess by those who seek to weaken and undermine unions.

There was a time when unions commanded more public support and wielded greater political, economic, and social power. In the aftermath of World War II, unions established a real capacity to demand and win better wages and working conditions for their members and broader redistributive social programs for working-class people in general.[6] While employers actively opposed the demands of organized labour during this period,[7] unions worked as an effective counterweight to the free market dogma of Ontario's capitalist class, as evidenced by the key role played by unions in securing public health care, unemployment insurance, and minimum employment standards during the PC dynasty of 1943–85.

These reforms, passed in an effort to ease growing unrest among workers, were the product of what some have termed the golden age of capitalism, a period of impressive economic growth between World War II and the mid-1970s. During this period, labour unions made impressive wage gains for workers, thanks in part to a combination of comparatively low levels of unemployment and comparatively higher levels of industrial militancy. This was true both in the private sector and in the public sector. Unionized teachers, for example, launched a mass resignation campaign in 1973 in order to secure the right to strike.[8]

However, by the end of the PC dynasty, the postwar model of labour relations had taken a coercive turn as governments began to experiment with right-wing and anti-union neoliberal reforms precipitated by a global inflationary crisis. Strongly promoted by US President Ronald Reagan and British Prime Minister Margaret Thatcher, neoliberal political and economic reforms were designed to reorient government policy to meet the needs of corporations through privatization, deregulation, globalization, and the weakening and gradual elimination of the social safety net.[9] This shift in government policy resulted in a fundamental reversal of roles. In the postwar era, the demands of labour unions were appeased to maintain capitalism as a viable economic system. The government's new approach shifted the focus by forcing unions to take responsibility for maintaining capitalism.[10] In the case of Ontario, soaring inflation rates and double-digit unemployment posed serious challenges to Bill Davis's PC government. Taking his cue from the federal government, Davis clamped down on public sector wage increases in 1982 through a series of temporary measures that nullified collective bargaining in the public service in all but name.[11]

However, the shift to neoliberalism was not entirely linear and was riddled with contradictions. Organized labour, while clearly on the defensive, was still able to secure some legislative victories, even though the overall terrain of labour relations was becoming more inhospitable to unions. For example, in 1980, the PC government conceded to a long-standing demand from the labour movement to include mandatory union security provisions in the Ontario Labour Relations Act.[12]

The Peterson Liberal government, which toppled the PC dynasty in 1985 through an accord with the New Democrats, arguably tried to reverse the growing neoliberal tide with an expansion of the social safety net and social housing and, importantly for the labour movement, the adoption of pay equity legislation and other socially progressive measures. However, the labour movement continued to experience both ups and downs in the mid to late 1980s, as evidenced by the introduction of legislative measures to end strikes by Toronto Wheel Trans workers, construction workers, and Toronto Transit Commission workers.[13] At the federal level, the labour movement's unsuccessful campaign to defeat Prime Minister Brian Mulroney's proposed Canada–US Free Trade Agreement was a particularly bitter pill to swallow for union members in the industrial heartland of Southern Ontario who rightfully feared for their jobs as a result of the introduction of free trade.[14]

By the end of the 1980s, the tide was clearly turning against organized labour. However, when the Ontario NDP unexpectedly formed a majority government in September 1990, many within the labour movement expressed confidence that unions might regain their footing and significantly bolster their economic and political power.

Labour Relations under the Rae NDP Government

The province's labour movement had very high hopes for Ontario's first NDP government. Some unionists hoped the NDP, under newly elected Premier Bob Rae, would pursue a social democratic approach to government, with an emphasis on strengthening workers' rights, expansion of the social safety net, and the improvement of equality through tax reforms and other measures.[15] There was reason to believe that the labour movement would have unprecedented influence in the Rae government. After all, the NDP was created in 1961 with the assistance of the labour movement and a number of important industrial unions were officially affiliated to the party.[16]

The party's parliamentary caucus of 74 MPPs included at least two dozen union officials or activists who were committed to pursuing a number of pro-union legislative initiatives designed to create a more "level" playing field in the realm of labour relations. The NDP government's first minister of labour, Bob Mackenzie, famously set the tone for the government's labour relations agenda when he insisted that he was Ontario's first minister *for* labour.[17]

After a long consultation process with various stakeholders, the New Democrats passed Bill 40 in 1992. The new pro-union law amended the Ontario Labour Relations Act in several important ways by expanding and facilitating the right to organize, strengthening provisions for first contract arbitration, expanding successor rights, and altering the powers of the OLRB to the benefit of labour.[18] Most controversially, the bill banned the use of replacement workers during the course of strikes or lockouts, prompting the business community to complain that the NDP government had been captured by the labour movement.[19] In reality, the NDP had severely watered down its reform package in face of business opposition by weakening proposed anti-replacement worker provisions and by eliminating requirements for employers to disclose financial information to unions and to grant greater access to their properties for organizing purposes. The government also backed down from proposals to extend collective bargaining frameworks on a sectoral level.

Despite these perceived shortcomings, unions were generally very happy with the government's labour law reforms. The business community, on the other hand, argued that the NDP reforms would deepen the province's growing economic recession by driving away business and private investment. The global economic recession had hit Ontario particularly hard due to the export-led nature of the province's economy and the introduction of the Canada–US Free Trade Agreement in 1989. Between 1989 and 1992, the unemployment rate had more than doubled from 5 to 10.2 per cent.[20] The NDP government's Keynesian-inspired decision to fight the recession through increased budgetary spending in 1991 won praise from the labour movement but was politically unpopular with the general public and business community that expressed concerns about the province's growing budgetary deficit. The NDP's resistance to neoliberal policy prescriptions was hampered by a federal PC government that was deeply committed to neoliberalism and by a business community that refused to play ball with the NDP's economic agenda. With the provincial debt and deficit at record high levels in 1993, the Rae government succumbed to the pressure and announced the introduction of its now infamous Social Contract Act—a fiscal austerity program which rolled back wages through unpaid days off (dubbed Rae Days by critics) and suspended collective bargaining rights in the broader public sector. The Social Contract was met with fierce opposition by public sector unions and had repercussions for the NDP's relationship to organized labour across the country.[21] Ontario Secondary School Teachers' Federation (OSSTF) President Liz Barkley called on the government "not to abandon its social democratic principles in favour of a destructive neo-conservative agenda," and Canadian Auto Workers (CAW) President Buzz Hargrove pledged to "stand side by side with the Public Sector Unions against any attacks on their rights by the Government of Ontario."[22]

The Social Contract represented a significant political and economic shift to the right for the NDP and caused legions of union activists to quit the party in disgust. The Ontario Federation of Labour voted to officially condemn the NDP government at its 1993 convention.[23] However, some private sector unions remained loyal to the party, pointing out that the Social Contract was only one (albeit significant) blight on an otherwise pro–union legislative record and that public sector unions would have faced a much worse situation under a Liberal or PC government.

After the Social Contract debacle, the Rae government tried to mend fences by extending collective bargaining rights in the senior Ontario public service and granting public service workers the right to strike.[24] The NDP also implemented employment equity legislation in order to remove employment barriers to women, racialized minorities, Indigenous people, and people with disabilities. Finally, in 1994, the NDP extended rights to unionize and bargain collectively to agricultural workers.[25] However, for some of the party's traditional allies in the labour movement, these pro-union initiatives were not enough to reverse the damage caused by the Social Contract. The Ontario NDP government's defeat in the 1995 provincial election was decisive. The party finished a distant third in both seat count and popular vote. While unions had arguably experienced both ups and downs under the NDP, the election of a rabidly anti-union right-wing alternative, in the form of the Mike Harris PCs, meant that labour was about to experience a dramatic and sustained decline.

Labour Relations under the Harris PC Government

Upon taking office, the Harris Tories wasted no time undoing the NDP's pro-union reforms, including a repeal of the Rae government's ban on replacement workers. However, the Harris government's amendments to the OLRA in Bill 7 went far beyond restoring the pre-NDP status quo in the realm of labour relations. Instead, the bill, which was passed with little to no consultation with the province's unions, undid many of the postwar reforms implemented by previous PC governments, limiting unions' ability to call strike votes, eliminating card-based union certification, and instituting mandatory secret ballot votes for all union organizing drives.[26] This latter amendment had long been championed by anti-union employers in the name of "democracy," but also served the purpose of weakening unions' organizing efforts.[27] Bill 7 also made it easier to decertify unions and imposed a year-long organizing ban on unions that lost a certification vote.

Beyond its amendments to the OLRA, the Harris government dumped a number of key NDP appointments to the OLRB, leading some to challenge the independence of the board.[28] The Tories followed up on Bill 7 with Bill 31, the Economic Development and Workplace Democracy Act, dubbed the Wal-Mart bill by its opponents. Passed in 1998, Bill 31 repealed the OLRB's power of automatic certification after the OLRB certified a union at a Wal-Mart store in Windsor in which workers voted against unionization after the company threatened to close down the store if the workers opted for union certification. The board reasoned that Wal-Mart had poisoned the well with its unfair labour practice and because a clear majority of employees had originally supported unionization through card-signing, the most appropriate remedy would be to automatically certify the union despite the secret ballot vote results.[29] Outraged by the decision, Wal-Mart called on the provincial government to change the law and the Tories obliged.[30] The Harris government's package of reforms accompanied a number of other work-related public policy initiatives, including the capping of pay equity agreements, the freezing of the minimum wage, and the ill-fated introduction of a system of work for welfare.

The Harris years also featured significant labour unrest as unions attempted to reverse their precipitous descent through strike action. The Ontario Public Service Employees Union (OPSEU) launched its first-ever province-wide strike in February 1996 in response to the Harris government's downsizing of the Ontario public service and to demonstrate in support of protecting job security.[31] Province-wide illegal teacher strikes were launched in 1997 in response to the Harris government's proposed education reforms.[32] However, the greatest mass labour mobilization against the Harris government came in the form of a series of rotating general strikes across the province known as the Days of Action.[33] After the Ontario NDP government's defeat in June 1995, the province's labour movement, momentarily disillusioned with electoral politics, sought to build alliances with progressive community organizations and social movements as part of a broad-based coalition in opposition to the neoliberal policies of the new PC government. Between 1995 and 1998, organized labour and its allies launched one- to two-day protests in an effort to strengthen links between social movements, cause economic disruption, and highlight the damage being done by the Harris government.[34] The CAW and many of the public sector unions which had opposed the NDP government's Social Contract took a leadership role in organizing the Days of Action and decried the Ontario Federation of Labour's (OFL) controversial and divisive decision to jettison the rotating protests in favour of reconciliation with the NDP in the run-up to the 1999 provincial election.

The OFL's decision to pull the plug on the Days of Action had the effect of pushing unions back into the electoral arena, but in an unexpected way. While most industrial unions and CUPE Ontario decided to give the NDP (now led by Howard Hampton) a second chance, another group of unions, cognizant of the fact that the party was performing poorly in public opinion polls, came together under the umbrella of the Ontario Election Network (OEN) in an effort to promote strategic voting.[35] The Network, made up of teachers' unions, CAW, OPSEU, the Ontario Nurses' Association, and the building trades unions, took the position that defeating the Harris Conservatives was labour's first electoral priority. The OEN targeted 26 key swing ridings, endorsing 14 Liberals and 12 NDP candidates. In the words of OPSEU President Leah Casselman, "Strategic voting means voting NDP in strong NDP ridings, voting Liberal in strong Liberal ridings, and defeating Tories in both."[36]

However, participation in the OEN was highly divisive within the labour movement, especially among unions traditionally loyal to the NDP. While there was virtual unanimity within the labour movement on the need to defeat the Tories, union activists were sharply divided over strategy. While many long-time NDP activists in the labour movement were prepared to forgive the party for its past sins, others complained that the NDP would simply split the "non-right" vote and allow the Harris Tories to be re-elected.[37] There were also divisions within the OEN, with unions such as OPSEU deciding to endorse candidates above and beyond the list agreed upon by the organization.[38] In the end, as a purely instrumental intervention, the Network's electoral strategy ultimately failed when the Conservatives were returned to power with an even larger share of the popular vote than in 1995 and the NDP lost official party status.

Relations between the NDP and some of the OEN unions went from bad to worse in the aftermath of the 1999 election campaign. Ontario NDP leader Howard Hampton accused the CAW of having handed Harris a second term through its promotion of strategic voting. The party even flirted with the idea of revoking Hargrove's membership, but in the end decided against it.[39] Unrepentant, Hargrove suggested that if just a few thousand more voters had bought into the strategic voting campaign, the Liberals would have defeated the Tories, and "we would have had a minority government with our party [the NDP] in control of the agenda."[40]

Disillusioned with the NDP, the CAW launched an internal taskforce in late 1999 to reconsider its engagement with electoral politics. Despite the best intentions of some of its framers, who saw the project as a way of laying the foundation for a more radical working-class politics, in May 2002, the Task Force on Working Class Politics in the Twenty-first Century unveiled a number of recommendations[41] that in effect legitimized the CAW leadership's call for strategic voting and set the stage for a closer relationship to the Liberal Party in subsequent election campaigns.

The Tories did not let up in their second term, gutting the Employment Standards Act, making pro-employer changes to the Workers Compensation Board, and introducing new legislation requiring employers to post information in unionized workplaces on how to decertify a union. While the minister of labour justified the legislation by arguing that the provincial government was simply informing workers of their rights, union leaders argued that the government's position was hypocritical. "He is going to be posting in workplaces for employees who are unionized how to decertify, yet he will not be posting in a non-unionized location, how to certify," complained Leah Casselman, president of OPSEU.[42]

The Harris government's anti-union restructuring of the province's system of labour relations was driven entirely by the corporate sector. By the end of the PC government's second term, union density had dropped from 32.1 per cent in 1995 to 28.3 per cent in 2003 (see Table 16.1) and real average weekly wages dropped by 0.4 per cent, despite an economic growth rate of 3.7 per cent during the same period.[43]

In the run-up to the 2003 provincial election, under the banner of the newly formed Working Families Coalition,[44] the CAW joined forces with building and construction trades, nurses' and teachers' unions to launch a major third-party anti-Conservative advertising blitz.[45] Riding a wave of anti-PC sentiment, Dalton McGuinty's Liberals handily defeated the Tories, then led by Ernie Eves. The defeat of the PC government was one of the few bright spots for a labour movement that had experienced steep and significant descents between 1995 and 2003.

Labour Relations under the McGuinty Liberal Government

Determined to avoid the labour unrest that characterized the previous government's time in office, the newly elected McGuinty Liberals promised to restore "fairness and balance" to the province's system of labour relations. In practice, that meant reversing some (but by no means most) of the previous government's anti-union labour law reforms.

Passed in 2005, Bill 144, the Labour Relations Statute Law Amendment Act, returned remedial certification authority and other powers to the OLRB and repealed the Harris government's law requiring employers to post notices explaining how to decertify their unions. However, much of the previous government's anti-union labour law reforms went untouched. For example, the Liberals maintained the Harris government's imposed year-long ban on organizing in the event a union lost a certification vote. The Liberals also refused to restore the right of farm workers to unionize and flat out rejected calls to bring back the NDP's anti-scab law, which had been repealed by the Harris government.

Despite the McGuinty government's uneven record, the Liberals managed to satisfy the expectations of the unions which had backed the ostensibly pro-Liberal Working Families Coalition. Strategically, the McGuinty government fostered quid pro quo relationships with the unions associated

with the Coalition. As a result, teacher union support for the Liberals trans-
lated into unprecedented investments into the province's education system.
In return, the provincial government won education sector labour peace.
Autoworker support for McGuinty through strategic voting irked the New
Democrats, but helped to secure the premier's support for the province's ail-
ing automobile industry. Building and construction trades unions, the key
actors in the Working Families Coalition, were rewarded with the restoration of card-based union certification on construction sites. In many ways,
the Liberals were let off the hook for their general lack of pro-union initiatives on the labour relations front because they managed to retain support
from a number of influential unions whose sectionalist priorities had been
addressed by the government. While even these unions may have been critical of the McGuinty Liberals from time to time, they also recognized that
the return of a PC government would surely undo many, if not all, of the
gains organized labour had managed to make during this period.

No doubt satisfied with the McGuinty government's first term in office,
the Working Families Coalition redoubled its efforts in the 2007 provincial
election, making explicit its desire to see the Liberals re-elected, much to
the dismay of unions such as the United Steelworkers (USW), the Canadian
Union of Public Employees (CUPE), and the Communications, Energy
and Paperworkers (CEP), all of which continued to share strong ties to the
NDP.[46] The coalition spent $1.1 million on a third-party advertising cam-
paign trumpeting the Liberal government's achievements and warning voters not to turn back to the Tories.[47] In the end, the Liberals were easily
re-elected after the Ontario Tories fumbled badly during the campaign with
an ill-fated promise to extend public funding to private religious schools.

The relative "labour peace" that characterized the McGuinty government's first term in office was shaken somewhat after the Liberals were
returned to power in 2007 and the Great Recession of 2008 hit. In 2009, the
Liberals legislatively ended an 85-day-long strike by part-time instructors
and teaching assistants at York University in Toronto and, in 2008, McGuinty
legislated striking Toronto Transit Commission (TTC) employees back to
work before removing their right to strike entirely in 2011. In March 2011,
the McGuinty government established the Commission on the Reform of
Ontario's Public Services, headed by former TD Bank chief economist Donald Drummond, in order to recommend ways of eliminating the mounting
provincial deficit. The establishment of the Commission sent a clear signal
that the Liberals would target public sector workers to pay for an economic
crisis that originated in the banking sector.

While the commission did its work, the Liberals sought re-election with
the continued support of the Working Families Coalition. Ontario PC Party

leader Tim Hudak's 2011 campaign pledge to allow union members to opt out of having their dues spent for political action purposes was aimed squarely at undermining the Coalition, which launched a $2.1-million advertising blitz against Hudak, portraying the PC leader as the puppet of Bay Street capitalists.[48] The Coalition's third-party advertising budget was so impressive that the unions involved actually outspent the Ontario NDP's entire advertising campaign budget during the 2011 election campaign.[49] While the unions involved credit the Coalition for denying the Ontario PC Party power in 2003, 2007, and 2011, it is at best unclear what impact their third-party advertising campaigns have had on Ontario provincial elections or whether most union members actually follow the electoral advice of the union leadership. What is clear, however, is that the existence of the Working Families Coalition has created a lasting fissure in the politics of the province's labour movement, which has helped to forestall a resurgence of union support for the traditionally pro-labour NDP.

Reduced to a minority after the 2011 provincial election, the McGuinty Liberals, still reeling from the economic impact of the recession, turned their attention to the findings of the Drummond Commission. The final report of the Commission called for massive cuts in public spending and public services. Unsurprisingly, the recommendations were universally panned by the labour movement. According to an analysis by the Ontario Confederation of University Faculty Associations, "Drummond's model of labour relations consists primarily of hard bargaining on the part of broader public sector (BPS) employers, with government ... supporting the employer when the going gets tough."[50] The analysis continued by observing that Drummond "is counting on the devastating size of his cuts to the funding of public services to force the parties to bargain concessionary agreements, eliminate jobs, and find 'efficiencies,' which obviously can only translate into dramatically higher workloads for the remaining public sector workers."[51]

With the Commission's finding in hand, the Liberals shifted gears on the education front, teaming up with Tim Hudak's PCs to pass Bill 115, the Putting Students First Act, in August 2012. The new law implemented a wage freeze, clawed back sick days, and extinguished meaningful collective bargaining rights for the education workers who refused to follow the lead of the Catholic and French-language teachers' unions in negotiating concessionary agreements with the provincial government.[52] Teachers' unions had been a reliable ally of the McGuinty Liberals since the late 1990s, but his government's attack on collective bargaining rights in the education sector changed the party–union dynamic overnight. After convincing long-serving PC MPP Elizabeth Witmer to resign her seat with the offer of a patronage appointment, the Liberals hoped to win her vacated Kitchener–Waterloo riding in order to regain its majority. However, in an unexpected twist, the NDP managed to effectively tap into the anger of teachers and other unionized public sector workers and scored a decisive victory in the September 2012 by-election.[53] The NDP's stunning by-election victory, combined with mounting teacher protest and a number of constitutional challenges to Bill 115,[54] convinced the Liberals to re-evaluate their strategy. In the wake of all this turmoil, McGuinty announced his resignation, providing the Liberals with an opportunity to recalibrate and potentially repair their tarnished relationship with teachers and other groups of unionized workers.

Labour Politics under the Wynne Liberal Government

In the days leading up to the January 2013 Liberal leadership convention, where delegates chose Toronto MPP and former education minister Kathleen Wynne to replace McGuinty, the government hastily announced it would repeal Bill 115 in an effort to dampen growing teacher opposition to the party. The tactic, which was more symbolic than substantive given that the Bill had served its purpose, represented an olive branch of sorts. In the weeks and months that followed, the Wynne government was able to convince teachers' unions to drop their work-to-rule campaigns. A short time later, OSSTF President Ken Coran stunned political observers and members of his own union by announcing he would vacate his position to run for the Wynne Liberals in an August 2013 by-election in the Liberal-held riding of London West. On election day, however, the NDP candidate unexpectedly scored a decisive victory. Coran, who finished a distant third, could not overcome accusations that his candidacy was both opportunistic and unprincipled. The former union leader's disastrous campaign demonstrated that, while segments of the union leadership were prepared to give the Liberals a second chance, the rank-and-file was not quite ready to forgive and forget. Another by-election victory for the NDP, in February 2014 in the Liberal-held riding of Niagara Falls, struck a blow to both the government and the opposition Tories.

The PC Party's controversial commitment to implement right-to-work legislation in Ontario, in order to weaken labour organizations by making the payment of union dues voluntary, became a flashpoint in that campaign and the party's loss convinced PC leader Tim Hudak to jettison the policy plank in advance of the 2014 general election.

While the NDP was riding high on a string of impressive by-election victories, the party's decision to precipitate the general election by toppling the minority Wynne government in May 2014 proved wildly unpopular in labour movement circles. In Kathleen Wynne, union leaders saw progressive potential and, more importantly, feared that defeating her government would open the door to a PC Party majority. While Hudak had backed off on right-to-work legislation, labour leaders argued that he had a hidden anti-union agenda which he would no doubt implement if elected. Livid with NDP leader Andrea Horwath for pulling the plug on the minority Liberal government, important sections of the labour movement mounted a well-financed #StopHudak campaign, which explicitly asked union members to vote for whichever candidate was best positioned to defeat the Tories at the riding level. The campaign was backed by resources to key ridings where unions thought they could influence the outcome. In most cases, that meant supporting Liberals. The NDP's electoral ambitions had, in effect, driven many unions back into the arms of the Liberal Party. On June 12, 2014, the Wynne Liberals were re-elected with a majority, winning seats from both the NDP and the PC Party. Union leaders were quick to take credit for the bruising defeat of the Hudak Conservatives. The party's ill-advised commitment to cut 100,000 public sector jobs fed directly into the labour movement's portrayal of Hudak as anti-labour and the job cut issue became a focal point of the campaign.

In the wake of the 2014 provincial election, Ontario has become home to the most divided labour movement in Canada. While some unions continue to give their unwavering support to the NDP, other segments of the labour movement have managed to craft meaningful, yet sectionalist, ad hoc relationships with the Liberals. Given this context, the penchant for some unions to call for strategic voting in an effort to block the election of the Ontario PCs will likely continue for the foreseeable future, despite its limitations as an electoral tactic—not the least of which is the tendency of strategic voting advocates to exaggerate ideological differences between existing parties.[55]

Although there have been important policy differences between respective Liberal, PC, and NDP provincial governments in the realm of labour relations, each of those governments operated, more or less, within a neoliberal public policy sphere. While the Harris government, and to a lesser extent the McGuinty government, openly embraced such a policy direction, the social democratic Rae government seemed to reluctantly and unevenly surrender to neoliberal economic imperatives. In short, to revisit the roller-coaster analogy presented in the beginning of this chapter, unions have experienced far greater and far more pronounced descents than ascents since the mid-1990s, never entirely recovering from the steep declines of the Harris years. Understanding this broader political economic context is critical because it suggests that the competing electoral tactics and party–union alliances promoted by various labour movement constituencies may be overlooking a much bigger strategic problem—namely, that neoliberalism has successfully shifted the entire political terrain upon which Ontario's system of labour relations was built. In short, unions arguably face strategic dead ends in every electoral direction with all major political parties in Ontario having internalized, to varying degrees, neoliberal imperatives that are reproduced in policy positions, campaign platforms, and legislation. Andrea Horwath's pro-union NDP is no exception in this regard. In the words of Bryan Evans, "the politics of the centre-left now express little more than a more moderate and pragmatic management of neoliberalism."[56] Given this context, whether unions can re-establish even a modicum of the political and economic influence they displayed in the postwar era remains an open question. However, in the short term, the prospects for significant pro-union labour law reforms look bleak and unions are likely to continue fighting defensive rather than offensive legislative battles as governments and employers continue to rewrite the book on "balance" and "fairness" in the workplace.

Discussion Questions

1. What are the political difficulties in determining what constitutes "fairness" and "balance" in labour relations?
2. What impact did the Rae government's Social Contract Act have on the relationship between the Ontario NDP and the union movement, in both the short and long term? Why did unions take such offence at the legislation?
3. Is strategic voting an effective political strategy for unions or would organized labour be better served uniting behind a single party at election time?
4. What is "reverse-class resentment" and what are its political implications for the labour movement?

Notes

1   See Kevin Burkett, "The Politicization of the Ontario Labour Relations Framework in the 1990s," *Canadian Labour and Employment Law Journal* 6 (1998): 161–84; Timothy Bartkiw, "Manufacturing Descent? Labour Law and Union Organizing in the Province of Ontario," *Canadian Public Policy* 34 (2008): 111–31; and Michael Lynk "Labour Law and the New Inequality," *Just Labour: A Canadian Journal of Work and Society* 15 (2009): 125–39.
2   Charles W. Smith, "The Politics of the Ontario Labour Relations Act: Business, Labour, and Government in the Consolidation of Post-War Industrial Relations, 1949–1961," *Labour/Le Travail* 62 (2008): 112.

3   CBC News, "How Canadian Unions Are Changing," 1 March 2012, http://www.cbc.ca/news/interactives/labour-demographics

4   Stephanie Ross and Larry Savage, "Introduction: Public Sector Unions in the Age of Austerity," in *Public Sector Unions in the Age of Austerity*, ed. Stephanie Ross and Larry Savage (Halifax: Fernwood, 2013), 11.

5   Thomas Walkom, "The Art of Reverse Class Resentment," *Toronto Star*, 27 February 2010, http://www.thestar.com/news/insight/2010/02/27/walkom_the_art_of_reverse_class_resentment.html

6   Stephanie Ross and Larry Savage, "Rethinking the Politics of Labour in Canada: An Introduction," in *Rethinking the Politics of Labour in Canada*, ed. Stephanie Ross and Larry Savage (Halifax: Fernwood, 2012), 7.

7   Charles W. Smith, "The Politics of the Ontario Labour Relations Act," *Labour/Le Travail* 62 (2008): 124–28.

8   Robert Laxer, *Canada's Unions* (Toronto: James Lorimer, 1977), 217–24.

9   David Harvey, *A Brief History of Neoliberalism*, 2nd ed. (New York: Oxford University Press, 2009), 64–81, 160–65.

10 Leo Panitch and Donald Swartz, *From Consent to Coercion: The Assault on Trade Union Freedoms* (Toronto: University of Toronto Press, 2003), 30.

11 Ibid., 35–36, 131.

12 Pat McNenly, "Union Dues Check-Off Called Long Overdue," *Toronto Star*, 5 June 1980.

13 Panitch and Swartz, *From Consent to Coercion*, 133.

14 Andrew Jackson, "Tarnished Anniversary: Why the Free-Trade Deal Didn't Deliver," Broadbent Institute Blog, 5 October 2012, http://www.broadbentinstitute.ca/andrew_ajackson/tarnished_anniversary_why_the_free_trade_deal_didn_t_deliver

15 Ontario New Democratic Party, *Agenda for the People*, 1990, https://www.poltext.org/sites/poltext.org/files/plateformes/on1990ndp_tax._26122008_90238.pdf

16 Thomas Walkom, *Rae Days: Rise and Follies of the NDP* (Toronto: Key Porter, 1994), 6–8.

17 Wayne Roberts and George Ehring, *Giving Away a Miracle: Lost Dreams, Broken Promises and the Ontario NDP* (Oakville, ON: Mosaic Press, 1993), 327.

18 See Christopher Schenk, "Fifty Years after PC 1003: The Need for New Directions," in *Labour Gains, Labour Pains: 50 Years of PC 1003*, ed. Cy Gonick, Paul Phillips, and Jesse Vors (Halifax: Fernwood, 1995), 197–98; Leo Panitch and Donald Swartz, *From Consent to Coercion*, 168–71; and Harish Jain and S.P. Muthuchidambaram, *Ontario Labour Law Reform: A History and Evaluation of Bill 40* (Kingston: IRC Press, 1995), 31–95.

19 Walkom, *Rae Days*, 130.

20 Statistics Canada, Table 2820086; Unemployment; Both Sexes; 15 years and over; Ministry of Treasury and Economics, Sectoral and Regional Policy Branch, Statistics Section, *Ontario Statistics 1986* (Toronto: Queen's Printer, 1986).

21 Panitch and Swartz, *From Consent to Coercion*, 172–81; Buzz Hargrove, *Laying It on the Line: Driving a Hard Bargain in Challenging Times* (Toronto: HarperCollins, 2009), 120.

22 Quoted in George Martell, *A New Education Politics: Bob Rae's Legacy and the Response of the Ontario Secondary School Teachers' Federation* (Toronto: James Lorimer, 1995), 79, 83.

310   SAVAGE

23 Walkom, *Rae Days*, 121–22.
24 David Rapaport, *No Justice, No Peace: The 1996 OPSEU Strike against the Harris Government in Ontario* (Montreal: McGill-Queen's University Press, 1999), 28.
25 Bradley Walchuk, "Ontario's Agricultural Workers and Collective Bargaining: A History of Struggle," *Just Labour: A Canadian Journal of Work and Society* 14 (2009): 152.
26 Government of Ontario, "Government Acts to Repeal Bill 40 to Spur Economic Growth and Create Jobs," *Canada Newswire*, 4 October 1995.
27 Charles W. Smith, "Fairness and Balance? The Politics of Ontario's Labour Relations Regime, 1949–1963" (PhD diss., York University, 2009), 395; and Sara Slinn, "The Union Certification Experience in Ontario: 1993 to 1998" (PhD diss., University of Toronto, 2003), 156.
28 Kevin Burkett, "Ontario Labour Relations Framework," 78–81, and Judith McCormack, "Comment on 'The Politicization of the Ontario Labour Relations Framework in the 1990s,'" *Canadian Labour & Employment Law Journal* 7 (1999): 350.
29 Judith McCormack, "Shopping for a Remedy: The Wal-Mart Case," *Canadian Labour & Employment Law Journal* 5 (1997): 341–58.
30 Bill Schiller, "Tough Labour Bill Approved Law Will Restrict Rights of Unions," *Toronto Star*, 24 June 1998.
31 Rapaport, *No Justice, No Peace*, 107–10.
32 Alan Sears, *Retooling the Mind Factory: Education in a Lean State* (Toronto: University of Toronto Press, 2003), 6, 233–34.
33 Marcella Munro, "Ontario's 'Days of Action' and Strategic Choices for the Left in Canada," *Studies in Political Economy* 53 (1997): 125–40.
34 Yonatan Reshef and Sandra Rastin, *Unions in the Time of Revolution: Government Restructuring in Alberta and Ontario* (Toronto: University of Toronto Press, 2003), 133.
35 Ibid., 166–82; and Brian Tanguay, "Parties, Organized Interests, and Electoral Democracy: The 1999 Ontario Provincial Election," in *Political Parties, Representation, and Electoral Democracy in Canada*, ed. William Cross (Don Mills: Oxford University Press, 2002), 145–60.
36 Carmela Patrias and Larry Savage, *Union Power: Solidarity and Struggle in Niagara* (Edmonton: Athabasca University Press, 2012), 128.
37 Canadian Auto Workers, *Contact* 28 (38), 15 November 1998, and Reshef and Rastin, *Unions in the Time of Revolution*, 168.
38 Patrias and Savage, *Union Power*.
39 Reshef and Rastin, *Unions in the Time of Revolution*, 178.
40 Ibid.
41 CAW National Executive Board, *CAW Task Force on Working Class Politics in the 21st Century*, May 2002, 16–17.
42 Larry Savage, "Organized Labour and the Politics of Strategic Voting," in *Rethinking the Politics of Labour in Canada*, ed. Stephanie Ross and Larry Savage (Halifax: Fernwood, 2012), 78.
43 Ontario Ministry of Finance, *Ontario Outlook and Fiscal Review* (2004), 96, Table 2; 121, Table 27.
44 The Working Families Coalition, widely considered a union-sponsored Liberal Party front group, was backed by the Ontario English Catholic Teachers Association, the Canadian Auto Workers, the Ontario Secondary School

Teachers' Federation, the International Brotherhood of Boilermakers Local 128, the International Brotherhood of Electrical Workers, Millwrights, the International Union of Operating Engineers Local 793, the Ontario Provincial Council of Painters and Allied Trades, the Ontario Pipe Trades Council, and Ironworkers Local 721.

45 Larry Savage, "Organized Labour and the Politics of Strategic Voting," 80; Bradley Walchuk, "Changing Union-Party Relations in Canada," *Labour Studies Journal* 35 (2010): 38.

46 Larry Savage, "Contemporary Party-Union Relations in Canada," *Labour Studies Journal* 35 (2010): 15–16; Walchuk, "Changing Union-Party Relations in Canada," 38–41.

47 Rob Ferguson, "Campaign Finance Rules 'Too Loose' Study Says," *Toronto Star*, 3 October 2011, http://www.thestar.com/news/canada/2011/10/03/campaign_finance_rules_too_loose_study_says.html

48 Ferguson, "Campaign Finance Rules"; and Rob Ferguson and Richard Brennan, "Elections Ontario Head Calls for Limits to Advertising by Interest Groups," *Toronto Star*, 8 April 2013, http://www.thestar.com/news/queenspark/2013/04/08/elections_ontario_head_calls_for_limits_to_advertising_by_interest_groups.html

49 Ferguson and Brennan, "Elections Ontario Head Calls for Limits to Advertising by Interest Group."

50 Ontario Confederation of University Faculty Associations, "OCUFA Analysis of the Drummond Report: Long on Cuts, Short on Insight," 22 February 2012, 3, http://ocufa.on.ca/assets/OCUFA-Drummond-Report-Analysis-Feb.-22-2012Final.pdf

51 Ibid.

52 Louise Brown and Richard Brennan, "Ontario High School Teachers, Government Agree to Meet," *Toronto Star*, 7 November 2012, http://www.thestar.com/news/canada/2012/11/07/ontario_high_school_teachers_government_agree_to_meet.html

53 Martin Regg Cohn, "Dalton Mcguinty's Decision and Timing Were All Wrong," *Toronto Star*, 23 October 2012, http://www.thestar.com/news/canada/2012/10/23/dalton_mcguintys_decisions_and_timing_were_all_wrong.html

54 Louise Brown, "Ontario Teachers Have Strong Case in Court Challenge, Legal Expert Says," *Toronto Star*, 11 October 2012, http://www.thestar.com/news/canada/2012/10/11/ontario_teachers_have_strong_case_in_court_challenge_legal_expert_says.html

55 Savage, "Organized Labour and the Politics of Strategic Voting," 85–86.

56 Bryan Evans, "The New Democratic Party in the Era of Neoliberalism," in *Rethinking the Politics of Labour in Canada*, ed. Stephanie Ross and Larry Savage (Halifax: Fernwood, 2012), 63.

17
Toronto and the GTA: Changing Contours of Governance in Ontario's Global City

MARTIN HORAK

T HE GREATER TORONTO AREA (GTA) is a rapidly growing urban region of more than 6 million people. It includes the City of Toronto, with a population of 2.7 million, as well as 28 surrounding suburban municipalities.[1] This chapter looks at the changing nature of governance and policy in Toronto and the GTA, with brief forays into a variety of matters, including the political career of Toronto's most (in)famous political figure, Rob Ford. The main focus, however, is on provincial–local relations in Toronto and the GTA. The GTA is home to almost half of Ontario's population, so it looms large in Ontario politics. Since the late 1990s, long-standing patterns of provincial–local interaction in the region have been swept aside. In 1997, the provincial government of Mike Harris amalgamated the municipalities of Metropolitan Toronto into a single City of Toronto. The new city has since emerged as a significant intergovernmental actor. Meanwhile, GTA population growth has shifted from Toronto itself to the surrounding suburbs, whose residents now outnumber those in the central city. And globalization, immigration, and the rise of a postindustrial economy have transformed the region, giving rise to new policy issues. In this context, Toronto and the GTA have become sites of a variety of policy and governance experiments. These range from a new City of Toronto Act to provincial growth management policies for the GTA. The contours of governance in Toronto and the GTA are in flux, with little stability on the horizon.

The Demographic and Electoral Significance of the Greater Toronto Area

Any Ontario provincial government that ignores the issues and concerns of GTA residents does so at its peril. The Toronto area's significance in the provincial context has increased steadily over time. In 1951, the Toronto metropolitan region had about 1 million residents—20 per cent of Ontario's population.[2] By 2011, the GTA had more than 6 million residents, and accounted for 47 per cent of Ontario's population (Table 17.1). In recent years, the annual population growth rate in the GTA has been triple that in the rest of the province; between 2006 and 2011, the region accounted for

Table 17.1 Population of Toronto Area in Millions (% of Ontario population), 1986–2011

	1986	1991	1996	2001	2006	2011
Toronto	2.19 (24)	2.28 (23)	2.39 (22)	2.48 (22)	2.50 (21)	2.62 (20)
GTA	3.73 (41)	4.24 (42)	4.63 (43)	5.08 (45)	5.56 (46)	6.05 (47)
Ontario	9.10	10.09	10.75	11.41	12.16	12.85

Note: The area that is now Toronto was, until 1998, the Municipality of Metropolitan Toronto.

Source: Calculated from Statistics Canada data tables.

71 per cent of Ontario's population growth (as calculated using Table 17.1). These trends are expected to continue. By 2036, the GTA is expected to have 9.2 million residents, well over half of Ontario's population.[3] Until the 1970s, most population growth in the GTA occurred in what is now the City of Toronto, especially the "inner suburbs" that surround the old city core. Since then, however, the bulk of the population growth has shifted to the outer suburbs of the GTA.

The GTA looms large in Ontario electoral politics. As Table 17.2 shows, both the central City of Toronto and the outer GTA suburbs have shifted partisan allegiances more than once since 1990. With some 40 per cent of Ontario ridings located in the GTA, such swings can make or break the electoral fortunes of a provincial political party. Indeed, since 1990 no

Table 17.2 Distribution of Toronto/GTA Seats in Legislature by Party, 1990–2011

Election Year	City of Toronto			Outer GTA Suburbs			Total GTA			Ontario		
	PC	Lib.	NDP	PC	Lib.	NDP	PC	Lib.	NDP	PC	Lib.	NDP
1990	3	9	18	4	8	6	7	17	24	20	36	74
1995	16	9	5	18	0	0	34	9	5	82	30	17
1999	8	11	3	16	0	0	24	11	3	59	35	9
2003	0	19	3	4	12	0	4	31	3	24	72	7
2007	0	18	4	4	15	0	4	33	4	26	71	10
2011	0	17	5	4	14	1	4	31	6	37	53	17
2014	0	20	2	2	15	2	2	35	4	27	59	21

Note: Prior to 1998, the area noted as "City of Toronto" was the Municipality of Metropolitan Toronto. Some provincial electoral districts cross the boundaries of the GTA; only results from ridings fully within GTA boundaries are included in this table.

Source: Author's calculations based on Elections Ontario data.

political party has formed a government without securing a majority of seats in the GTA. While the City of Toronto remains an important political battleground, the rapid growth of the outer suburbs has made them especially critical to provincial electoral success in recent years. The resounding victories of the Progressive Conservatives in 1995 and the Liberals in 2003 were both built on a near-sweep of outer suburban seats in the GTA. The GTA's role as a linchpin of Ontario electoral politics ensures that Toronto-area issues receive significant provincial attention.

The Economic and Social Transformation of the GTA

The past two decades have fundamentally changed the economic and social fabric of the GTA. After the recession of the early 1990s, Toronto reinvented itself as a hub of Canada's new postindustrial, globally integrated economy. The outer suburbs retain major industrial capacity in sectors such as automotive, energy, and food processing, but the central City of Toronto is largely de-industrialized, and the relative size of the manufacturing sector has declined in the GTA as a whole. Postindustrial economic sectors such as finance, cultural production, research, and development and postsecondary education have emerged as major drivers of the region's economy. The Toronto region is home to 40 per cent of Canada's corporate headquarters and has the country's largest stock exchange; it has 12 colleges and universities; and it is the largest film and television production centre in the country.

Along with economic change, international immigration has transformed the social structure of the GTA. International immigrants make up the vast majority of the 100,000 or so new residents who settle in the GTA each year. Since the 1980s the Toronto area has become one of the most ethnoculturally diverse city-regions in the world. By 2011, 49 per cent of the City of Toronto's residents were members of visible minorities. Some outer suburban municipalities, such as Brampton (66 per cent) and Markham (72 per cent), have even higher percentages of visible minority residents.[4] The GTA today houses large populations of many ethnocultural groups, including Chinese, South Asian, Filipino, and Jamaican.

Rapid economic and social change has brought with it new policy challenges. The continued outward growth of the GTA's suburbs has politicized the issue of suburban sprawl. Growth also places major demands in the region's aging infrastructure, especially in the transportation sector, where congestion has become a big problem. Meanwhile, the rise of the postindustrial economy and the decline of the provincial welfare state have increased the gap between the rich and the poor, which is now among the largest of any city in Canada. Increasingly, this gap is reflected in the spatial segregation of rich from poor neighbourhoods. This trend is especially strong in the City of Toronto, where the area around the downtown core is now largely wealthy, but parts of the inner suburbs have become impoverished.[5] Many new immigrants are well educated and relatively well off, and most of these settle in the GTA's outer suburbs. However, poor immigrants and those who are unable to find good employment increasingly concentrate in 1960s-vintage high-rise apartments in the inner suburbs. A strong correlation between concentrated poverty and visible-minority status has emerged in the City of Toronto, raising serious concerns about ethnoracial segregation.[6]

The GTA's transformation and the policy challenges that it raises have compelled the provincial government, as well as the City of Toronto, to try new governance arrangements and to experiment with new policy instruments. David Siegel argues that the provincial government has increasingly treated Toronto as a "special case" that demands custom-made governance and policy solutions.[7] There is no doubt that the role of Toronto and the GTA in Ontario politics has shifted in recent years. Yet the province has long treated the region differently than others in Ontario. So to understand recent developments in GTA governance, we need to look back at what came before.

The Province and GTA Governance, 1954–1998[8]

During the second half of the twentieth century, the Ontario government repeatedly used local government restructuring as a means of dealing with Toronto-area governance issues. In 1954, the province established a two-tier local government system called Metropolitan Toronto. It consisted of the upper-tier regional government (Metro), which encompassed 13 (later consolidated into six) lower-tier local governments. Metro was responsible for developing major public infrastructure such as freeways, subways, and sewers. It also delivered policing, transit, social housing, and provincially mandated social services. The lower-tier municipalities—which included the old core City of Toronto and postwar suburbs such as Scarborough and North York—had control over local planning and development, and community services such as parks, libraries, and waste collection. In 1974, as suburbs outside the boundaries of Metro began to grow quickly, the province replicated the two-tier system there, setting up four upper-tier regional governments—Peel, Halton, Durham, and York—that still exist today.

The emergence of two-tier local government had a big impact on provincial–municipal relations in the Toronto area. Upper-tier regional governments were at the front lines of interaction with the province, whereas lower-tier governments were insulated. As a result, the province could influence the development of the Toronto region without appearing to trample on local autonomy. In the 1960s and early 1970s, Metropolitan Toronto delivered several large provincially funded public infrastructure projects, including more than 15,000 units of public housing and extensions to the subway system. As Frances Frisken argues, Metro spread the costs and benefits of such development across various parts of the city, which helped to prevent the inner-city decline that many American cities experienced in the 1960s and 1970s.[9]

The suburban regional governments of Halton, Durham, Peel, and York did not deliver large provincial infrastructure projects, since they were established at a time when provincial investment was declining.[10] However, like Metro, they delivered (and still deliver) a variety of provincially mandated social services. Despite the province's extensive involvement in GTA governance, no fully fledged GTA regional policy emerged during the twentieth century. GTA issues were managed by general-purpose provincial ministries—especially the Ministry of Municipal Affairs and Housing—and sporadic efforts to develop provincial-level regional policies and institutions for the GTA did not get far.[11] The one exception was GO Transit, a provincial commuter rail system established in 1968 that still exists today.

Unlike upper-tier municipalities, lower-tier local governments—both those in Metro and those in the outer suburbs—were quite insulated from interaction with the province. In most cases, lower-tier governments focused heavily on property development and services to property. Development was often pursued through tight coalitions between elected officials and private developers. Two classic examples are North York during Mel Lastman's tenure as mayor (1973–97), and Mississauga, whose rapid growth was steered for 36 years (1978–2014) by Mayor Hazel McCallion.[12] The former lower-tier City of Toronto took a different direction. In 1972, a "reform" movement led by young middle-class professionals swept Toronto's local elections, ushering in several decades during which the city used its rich commercial property tax base in order to pursue historical preservation, affordable housing development, neighbourhood planning, generous arts funding, and various other innovative local policies.[13]

Amalgamation and the New City of Toronto

By the 1990s, GTA governance seemed ripe for a new round of structural reform. There was frequent conflict between upper- and lower-tier governments in Metro, and Metro as a whole was showing signs of social and economic decline, with business and residents moving to the booming outer suburbs. In 1993 the provincial NDP government appointed a GTA task force, which recommended that Metro and the outer suburban regional governments be replaced with an upper-tier government covering the whole GTA. But by the time the task force report came out, the NDP had been swept aside by the Conservatives under Mike Harris. The task force's proposal was a political non-starter for the Conservatives, since their key support base in the outer suburbs strongly opposed the idea of a GTA-wide upper-tier government. So the Harris government left the two-tier systems in the outer suburbs untouched. Instead, in 1997, it amalgamated all of the municipalities within Metro into one new City of Toronto. This move was vociferously but unsuccessfully opposed by many local politicians and residents within Metro, especially those in the old lower-tier City of Toronto.[14]

The reasons behind Toronto's amalgamation remain unclear. The Harris government's main rationale—that amalgamation would save money—was not well justified at the time, nor has it been borne out in practice. Some scholars argue that the real reason had more to do with the Harris government's desire to abolish the old central City of Toronto, whose politicians were bitterly opposed to the Conservatives' cost-cutting agenda.[15] Regardless of why it happened, amalgamation has transformed the landscape of GTA governance in ways that the Harris Conservatives did not anticipate or intend. It has created a new asymmetry in local governance structures in the GTA. Whereas the outer suburbs retain two-tier governing systems, the central city is now a huge, unified municipality. The new City of Toronto is home to over 20 per cent of Ontario's population, and has a larger budget than most Canadian provinces. It has a vast and professionalized bureaucracy. Its mayor is elected by more people than any other politician in Canada. All these things give Toronto the potential for exercising much greater influence on the intergovernmental stage than its predecessors.

Yet the City of Toronto has also faced significant fiscal challenges. Far from inducing savings, amalgamation produced upward pressure on the municipal budget due to wage and service harmonization across the new city. In addition, the Harris government's Local Services Realignment (see Chapter 7) increased municipal fiscal responsibility for a number of services, including social assistance and social housing, which are in above-average demand in Toronto.[16] Fear of losing businesses and residents to the outer suburbs limits the extent to which Toronto politicians are willing to raise local taxes to cover rising costs. As a result, for much of its existence post-amalgamation, Toronto has operated in an atmosphere of fiscal shortage.

The city also has a divided, volatile local politics. It is run by a 44-member, non-partisan council, in which councillors focus heavily on ward concerns.[17] In this context, political coalitions are built on an issue-by-issue basis, and bigger-picture policy initiatives are typically led by the mayor and supported by the bureaucracy. But Toronto's mayor does not have significant executive powers, so he or she must rely on his or her city-wide electoral mandate as the foundation for his or her activity. And the city's electorate is geographically divided in a way that reflects the city's Metro-era history. Downtown voters tend to favour an expansive local government that pays attention to social policy concerns; voters in the postwar suburbs (the former municipalities of Scarborough, Etobicoke, and North York) tend to favour low-tax local government that focuses on property services.[18] Toronto's first three post-amalgamation mayors each represented one or the other of these "two solitudes" of Toronto politics. The brash and entrepreneurial Mel Lastman (1998–2003) was elected mainly with support from the inner suburbs; support for David Miller (2003–2010), a left-leaning, big ideas mayor with a long-term policy orientation, was strongest in the city core; the election of Rob Ford in 2010 marked a dramatic swing back to a populist-conservative mayor with a suburban support base.

Rob Ford's 2010 mayoral campaign took advantage of a wave of deep discontent among middle-class inner-suburban residents with the allegedly elitist and spendthrift politics of David Miller. As Taylor notes, "Ford's platform constituted an almost systematic repudiation of Miller's legacy,"[19] and included a focus on cutting public spending, privatizing public services, ending "the war on the car," and building subways instead of light rail. This platform helped Ford, a political outsider prone to public gaffes and controversy, to secure the largest direct electoral mandate of any politician in Canadian history.[20] Ford's policy initiatives while in office largely held true to the populist-conservative vision. Growth in spending slowed during his time as mayor (although not dramatically so),[21] garbage collection was partly contracted out, the much-loathed vehicle registration tax was axed, and Miller's signature transit focus on building light rail was weakened, although not derailed entirely (see below).

Yet, by late 2011, the council consensus in support of Ford's policies was crumbling, and the mayor's controversial persona and personal activities began to overshadow his policy priorities. Ford became globally famous for his alleged alcohol and drug abuse, as well as his outrageous statements about his political rivals, women, and minority groups. Nonetheless, throughout his term Ford retained substantial support from "Ford Nation"—the angry, politically disaffected residents who saw him as a man of the people. In 2014 Ford ran a serious campaign for re-election. He eventually dropped out due to serious health troubles, and his equally controversial brother, Councillor Doug Ford, took his place as mayoral candidate.

Ultimately, a critical mass of Torontonians had had enough of the Ford years and, in an election that saw a record voter turnout of more than 60 per cent, Doug Ford was defeated by John Tory. Tory, a moderate conservative whose past career included several years leading the provincial Progressive Conservatives, ran on a platform that promised to address the city's transportation needs (see below). While his electoral base was strongest in the city's core, he also secured solid support in some suburban areas, eroding the previously stark downtown–suburban electoral divide. During the early part of his time in office, Tory retained broad popular appeal, solid council support, and an image as a competent and uncontroversial (if somewhat uninspiring) mayor that stood in stark contrast to the profile of his predecessor.

The Promise and the Limits of Increased Local Autonomy

For a brief time after amalgamation in 1998, the idea of establishing some kind of "city-state" of Toronto received significant public attention. Early proposals—like the idea of a GTA-wide "Province of Toronto"—proved little more than wishful thinking, since the outer suburbs of the GTA were opposed to any institutional connection with the urban core. As a result, the focus of the autonomy debate soon shifted to the City of Toronto itself. In 2002, city administrators proposed that the province pass a new City of Toronto Act that would grant the city additional powers and sources of revenue. The provincial Conservatives were not interested, but the election of the McGuinty Liberals in the fall of 2003 opened a new window of opportunity.

In a successful bid to recapture key Toronto seats, the Liberals promised to work with Toronto to implement a new City of Toronto Act. Until 2004, the City of Toronto was represented in its dealings with the province by the Association of Municipalities of Ontario (AMO). But shortly after the election of McGuinty, the city left the AMO, which paved the way for direct negotiations with the new Liberal government. In October 2004, the province and the city constituted a joint task force to develop a new act. The act came into force at the beginning of 2007. It modestly expanded the city's authority in a number of domains, including planning and development. More importantly, it granted Toronto new revenue tools, including the right to levy sales taxes, a property transfer tax, a vehicle registration tax, and road tolls.[22]

Despite its significance on paper, the real impact of the City of Toronto Act has been limited. One reason for this is that the city has not actually used all of the new revenue tools granted in the act. In 2007, after intense campaigning by David Miller, city council did approve new land transfer and vehicle registration taxes. However, the measures were unpopular. In his 2010 mayoral campaign, Rob Ford promised to scrap the vehicle registration tax, and council did so shortly after he was elected. The land transfer tax has remained in place and has become an important source of revenue in a city with a booming real estate market.[23] But many of the other new revenue tools have remained entirely unused since they are politically unattractive, all the more so since the city competes with the outer GTA suburbs for businesses and residents. In a context where the outer suburbs are politically independent from the central city, the city's push for more local autonomy appears for now to have run its course.

Multilevel Policy Initiatives in the City of Toronto

Since 1998, the City of Toronto has been the site of a number of multi-level policy initiatives. These are initiatives in which the local, provincial, and federal governments coordinate their jurisdiction and resources to pursue a common policy goal. The Canadian federal government has historically been reluctant to interact directly with municipalities, which are in the provincial sphere of jurisdiction. But many complex urban governance problems might benefit from tri-level policy coordination, and since amalgamation, the City of Toronto has used its new intergovernmental clout to actively pursue such coordination on a number of fronts. The extent and emphasis of multilevel initiatives in Toronto since 1998 has varied along with shifts in local, provincial, and federal political leadership.

One of the earliest and most enduring multilevel initiatives post-amalgamation Toronto focused on waterfront redevelopment. For decades, Toronto's central waterfront area languished in a largely derelict state. Most of this land is publicly owned, but ownership is divided among the municipal, provincial, and federal governments and their associated special-purpose authorities. Many plans for revitalization came and went between 1960 and 2000, and all foundered on the competing land interests of various public agencies.[24] In 1999, city and provincial officials anxious to boost the global profile of Toronto launched a bid for the 2008 summer Olympics. Toronto lost the bid, but in the process, a tri-level Toronto Waterfront Revitalization Corporation (TWRC) was created and given $1.5 billion in government funding—$500 million from each of the three levels of government.[25]

Over the past decade the TWRC (now called Waterfront Toronto) has had significant success in realizing waterfront redevelopment. It has developed new parkland and public infrastructure, new office buildings, a waterfront campus for George Brown College, and a new residential neighbourhood, the West Don Lands (which began its life as the athletes' village for the 2015 Pan Am Games). Yet much of the waterfront remains derelict, and Waterfront Toronto's future prospects are uncertain. The initial $1.5 billion in funding is now fully committed, and in order to advance redevelopment Water-front Toronto would require the authority to expropriate land and borrow money—powers that its political masters at all three levels of government have thus far been unwilling to grant.

The fall of 2003 brought tri-level political change to Toronto. David Miller was elected mayor; Dalton McGuinty's Liberals came to power provincially; and Paul Martin replaced Jean Chrétien as prime minister. Unlike his predecessor Mel Lastman, David Miller embraced a local governing agenda that included significant attention to social policy concerns. McGuinty promised new provincial attention to Toronto's needs; and Martin spoke of a federal "New Deal for Cities." These changes opened a new window of opportunity for multilevel policy initiatives in Toronto. Between 2004 and 2006, a number of significant initiatives were developed in policy fields such as immigrant settlement,[26] transit funding,[27] and neighbourhood revitalization. We cannot examine them all here, but we will briefly look at the Strong Neighbourhoods Strategy as an example.

As discussed earlier on, since the 1980s, deep pockets of concentrated poverty have emerged in Toronto's inner suburbs. These areas, heavily populated by recent immigrants, feature poor-quality high-rise apartment housing, as well as poor access to public services and public transit. Since recent immigrants are politically marginalized in Toronto,[28] this development was for a long time ignored by local politicians. However, in 2003 and 2004, a series of events—a rash of gun violence by young black men in poor neighbourhoods, the election of David Miller, and the publication of a landmark United Way report on neighbourhood poverty in Toronto—put the issue on the political agenda.[29] In 2005, Toronto City Council approved the Strong Neighbourhoods Strategy (SNS), which called for investment in public infrastructure, social services, and community capacity building in 13 inner-suburban "priority neighbourhoods" (PNs). The main delivery mechanism was a proposed five-year, $500-million investment agreement between the municipal, provincial, and federal governments.[30]

In January 2006 the federal Liberals were replaced by the Conservatives, who had no interest in tri-level agreements, so the proposed agreement did not materialize. The provincial government went ahead and rolled out policy initiatives in the PNs in the fields of policing and youth services, but it retained full control over these initiatives rather than coordinating control with municipal officials. The city introduced some initiatives of its own, but the politics of fiscal restraint on council meant that municipal investment was limited, leaving the non-profit United Way of Toronto as the dominant local funder in the PNs. The net result was a significant ($200 million) but poorly coordinated series of policy interventions that pursued sometimes incompatible policy goals.[31] Like many other Miller-era policy initiatives, the SNS faced a political backlash with the election in 2010 of Rob Ford. City administrators responded to criticism by producing an updated "SNS 2020" initiative, but this initiative got little political attention or funding, and neighbourhood revitalization has remained on the back burner.

Multilevel policy initiatives in Toronto have achieved some results, but these initiatives have been vulnerable to political change. The key problem is that—with a few exceptions, such as Waterfront Toronto—they have not been institutionalized. In other words, they have not included any durable governing structures that could sustain them in the face of political change. With the demise in 2006 of federal involvement in local and urban policy, Toronto and GTA governance has once again become mainly a matter for provincial-local interaction.

The Rise of Provincial Regionalism

The City of Toronto is the most active municipality on the intergovernmental stage in the GTA, but most GTA residents do not live in the city. Instead, an ever-increasing majority of them live in the outer suburbs. The GTA's rising social inequities may be most intense and visible in the City of Toronto, but its growing pains are most glaring in the outer suburbs, where the car commutes are long and farmland is being paved over at breakneck pace. Public dissatisfaction with the problems of growth in the outer suburbs has mounted in recent years. Around 2000, serious conflicts between environmentalists and developers emerged concerning plans to build housing on the Oak Ridges Moraine, a wooded area north of Toronto (discussed more extensively in Chapters 7 and 13 of this book). By 2003, residents of the outer suburbs identified land development, traffic, and transit infrastructure (in that order) as the three most important local problems.[32] In this context, the Liberals under Dalton McGuinty captured many suburban constituencies in the 2003 provincial election, promising to deal with the problems of urban growth.

Since 2003, the provincial Liberals have introduced a series of regional growth management policies in the Toronto area. These policies reach well beyond the GTA in geographical scope, spanning the entire Greater Golden Horseshoe (GGH), an area that stretches around the western end of Lake Ontario from Niagara Falls to Oshawa, and is home to about two-thirds of Ontario's population. In 2004 the provincial government passed the Greenbelt Act, which froze most development in a wide arc of rural and forested land surrounding the urbanized core of the GGH. In 2005, it passed the Places to Grow Act, which authorized the province to establish growth plans

for designated areas in Ontario. The growth plan for the GGH was promulgated in 2006. Focusing on intensification as the main tool of regional
growth management, this plan stipulated that by the year 2015, at least
40 per cent of all new residential development in each GGH municipality
would take place in existing built-up areas.

Ontario's new GGH policies have been called "the boldest attempt to
address urban sprawl in Canada, and arguably North America."[33] They are
certainly the strongest provincial effort at regional growth planning that we
have ever seen in the GTA. Yet it is too early to judge the extent to which
these policies will achieve their aims. For the most part, municipal governments in the GGH have not resisted them, and many now have new land
use plans that focus on intensification. But as the new policies begin to affect
actual decisions about what can be built where, resistance may grow. An early
warning sign came in January 2013, when developers successfully appealed
the Region of Waterloo's new intensification-focused growth plan to the
Ontario Municipal Board on the grounds that it overly limited the scope of
single-family housing development.[34] If enough local actors resist the new
density requirements, growth management may turn into a political liability
that future provincial governments are reluctant to enforce.

The provincial government has also pursued ambitious efforts to build new
public transit infrastructure in the GTA. In 2006 it established Metrolinx, a
provincial agency designed to coordinate, plan, finance, and develop an integrated transportation network for the Toronto region. Metrolinx's primary
emphasis has been on planning and developing public transit infrastructure.
In 2007, the City of Toronto unveiled Transit City, a multibillion-dollar proposal for building light rail lines in the inner suburbs, and asked the federal
and provincial governments to help fund it. The new Conservative federal
government of Stephen Harper was not interested; but the provincial Liberals were. They promised a remarkable $17.5 billion in transit funding for
the Toronto region, which included funding for four of the eight proposed
Transit City light rail lines, as well as for new bus rapid transit systems in the
outer GTA suburbs.[35] The implementing agency for these new projects was
Metrolinx.

Since 2008, Metrolinx has grown into an important regional transportation agency. It has constructed busways in York Region and a new rail link
from Pearson Airport to downtown Toronto; it has taken over management
of the GO Transit commuter rail system; and it is implementing Presto, a
regionally integrated electronic fare card system. But Metrolinx has also
faced resistance. Between 2008 and 2012, Metrolinx found itself in a stalemate with the city's public transit agency, the Toronto Transit Commission
(TTC). The TTC resisted what it saw as a looming provincial takeover, and

wanted to retain control over the construction and operation of the Transit City light rail lines. Meanwhile, the election of Rob Ford in 2010 raised the question of whether these lines would be built at all. Ford promised to scrap the Transit City lines and replace them with subways, mainly on the grounds that subways would not take away road space from other vehicles. City council at first deferred to Ford, then changed its mind in early 2012, when it became clear that Ford's subway vision was financially unsound.

In November of 2012, the TTC and Metrolinx agreed that Metrolinx would build and own the four new Transit City lines, but the TTC would operate them.[36] The lines then moved to the detailed design stage, with completion planned for around 2020. However, in fall 2013 Mayor Ford secured a promise of federal money to help fund construction of a subway instead of the planned Scarborough light rail line, and Toronto Council voted to endorse this change. During the 2014 local election campaign, John Tory in turn unveiled yet another priority urban rail project—a "SmartTrack" line that would link downtown Toronto to the outer suburbs along upgraded GO Transit lines. Since Tory's election as mayor, discussion of SmartTrack has overshadowed previously approved projects and, by the end of 2015, only one of the four lines approved in 2012—the Eglinton-Crosstown—was actually under construction. In short, while Metrolinx is gradually consolidating its position as the regional transit authority for the GTA, the inability of City of Toronto politicians to settle on a clear transit vision continues to present obstacles to the realization of a new regional transit system.

The Future of Toronto and the GTA

The governance landscape of Toronto and the GTA has changed dramatically since the 1990s. The region's rapid growth and its emergence as a globalized, multiethnic metropolis have produced new policy challenges for local and provincial governments. Since amalgamation, the City of Toronto has emerged as a major player in its own right in reshaping the contours of governance. And since the election of the McGuinty Liberals in 2003, the provincial government has taken Toronto and GTA governance in new directions. It has collaborated with the City of Toronto on legislative reform and on multilevel policy initiatives, and it has developed an ambitious regional governance agenda.

The governance of Toronto and the GTA stands at a crossroads. One thing is fairly sure, though: full-scale regional government for the GTA on the Metro model is no longer a viable option. The region is simply too large, too diverse, and too rapidly changing. As a result, GTA-wide metropolitan government is politically and practically infeasible. Beyond this, however, much remains uncertain. Toronto's intergovernmental activism was in low ebb during the Ford years, but there are signs that it may yet re-emerge as a significant force under John Tory. At the provincial level, Premier Kathleen Wynne has indicated that she aims to stay the course on the province's regional growth and transit infrastructure agenda. But this agenda is vulnerable to reversal. There is no strong dedicated Toronto-area unit within the provincial bureaucracy. Regional growth management faces the prospect of local resistance. Meanwhile, while the Wynne government has promised increased funding for transportation infrastructure, the crucial challenge of identifying sustainable revenue sources for infrastructure development has not been resolved. The concerns of Ontario's dominant global city-region will continue to occupy much of the province's political and policy attention in the years and decades to come.

Discussion Questions

1. How has the economic and social structure of Toronto and the GTA changed in recent years, and what new policy challenges have these changes produced?
2. How have electoral considerations influenced the province's approach to Toronto and GTA issues since the early 1990s?
3. Should the City of Toronto allow political parties on council? How might governance and leadership in Toronto change if this happened?
4. Is the provincial government too involved in GTA governance? Justify your position.
5. Are we likely to see the emergence of a GTA-wide local government unit in the near future? Why or why not?

Notes

1   The outer suburbs of the GTA comprise four upper-tier regional municipalities—Halton, York, Peel, and Durham—and 24 lower-tier municipalities, including major population growth centres such as Mississauga, Brampton, Markham, and Richmond Hill.
2   Albert Rose, *Governing Metropolitan Toronto: A Social and Political Analysis, 1953–1971* (Berkeley, CA: Institute of Governmental Studies), 164.
3   Ontario Ministry of Finance, *Ontario Population Projections Update* (Toronto: Queen's Printer for Ontario, 2012).
4   Statistics Canada, "National Household Survey 2011: NHS Focus on Geography Series" (2013), https://www12.statcan.gc.ca/nhs-enm/2011/as-sa/fogs-spg/?Lang=E
5   David Hulchanski, "The Three Cities within Toronto: Income Polarization in Toronto's Neighborhoods, 1970–2005" (Toronto: Cities Centre, 2010), 6.

Overall, the percentage of middle-income neighbourhoods in Toronto declined from 66 per cent in 1970 to 29 per cent in 2005.

6   Hulchanski, "The Three Cities within Toronto," 20; United Way of Greater Toronto, *Poverty by Postal Code: The Geography of Neighbourhood Poverty 1981–2001* (Toronto: United Way of Greater Toronto, 2004), http://www.unitedwaytyr.com/document.doc?id=59

7   David Siegel, "Ontario," in *Foundations of Governance: Municipal Government in Canada's Provinces*, ed. Andrew Sancton and Robert Young (Toronto: University of Toronto Press, 2009), 21.

8   The definitive account of the provincial government's role in governing the Toronto region in the twentieth century can be found in Frances Frisken, *The Public Metropolis: The Political Dynamics of Urban Expansion in the Toronto Region, 1924–2003* (Toronto: Canadian Scholars' Press, 2007).

9   Ibid., Chapter 7.

10   Ibid., 122–23.

11   Ibid., 143–47, 191–94.

12   For a detailed account of McCallion's remarkable career, see Tom Urbaniak, *Her Worship: Hazel McCallion and the Development of Mississauga* (Toronto: University of Toronto Press, 2009).

13   For a summary, see Martin Horak, "The Power of Local Identity: C4LD and the Anti-Amalgamation Mobilization in Toronto," *Research Paper 195* (Toronto: Centre for Urban and Community Studies, 1998).

14   Ibid.

15   Julie-Anne Boudreau, *The MegaCity Saga: Democracy and Citizenship in the Global Age* (Montreal: Black Rose Books, 2000).

16   The added cost was partly, but not entirely, offset by GTA-wide tax pooling for social services and social housing, instituted in 1998 and phased out between 2007 and 2013.

17   Aaron A. Moore, "Trading Density for Benefits: Toronto and Vancouver Compared," IMFG Papers Series (Toronto: Institute on Finance and Governance, 2013).

18   Zack Taylor, "Who Elected Rob Ford, and Why? An Ecological Analysis of the 2010 Toronto Election" (paper presented at the Canadian Political Science Association Annual Conference, Wilfrid Laurier University, Waterloo, ON, 2011), https://www.cpsa-acsp.ca/papers-2011/Taylor.pdf

19   Ibid., 2.

20   Christie Blatchford, "383,501 People Voted for Rob Ford—Not One Voted for the Men Behind His Ouster," *National Post*, 26 November 2012.

21   Matt Elliott, "Debunking Ford Nation's Favourite Budget Chart," *Metro*, 23 January 2013.

22   For a detailed discussion, see Martin Horak, *Governance Reform from Below: Multilevel Politics and Toronto's "New Deal" Campaign*, Global Dialogue Series, No. 4 (Nairobi: UN-Habitat, 2008), 28–31.

23   The land transfer tax will generate close to $500 million in revenue in 2015. James, Royson, "Land-transfer Tax Keeps City from Return to Cash Crises," *Toronto Star*, 28 August 2015.

24   Gabriel Eidelman, "Landlocked: Politics, Property, and the Toronto Waterfront, 1960–2000" (PhD diss., University of Toronto, 2013).

25 Martin Horak, "Multilevel Governance in Toronto: Success and Failure in Canada's Largest City," in *Sites of Governance: Multilevel Governance and Policy Making in Canada's Big Cities*, ed. Martin Horak and Robert Young (Montreal: McGill-Queen's University Press, 2012), 248–50.

26 See Kristin Good, *Municipalities and Multiculturalism: The Politics of Immigration in Toronto and Vancouver* (Toronto: University of Toronto Press, 2009).

27 Horak, "Multilevel Governance in Toronto," 234–38.

28 Myer Siemiatycki, "Governing Immigrant City: Immigrant Political Representation in Toronto," *American Behavioral Scientist* 55 (2011): 1214–34.

29 Martin Horak and Marilyn Dantico, "The Limits of Local Redistribution: Neighborhood Regeneration Initiatives in Toronto and Phoenix," *International Journal of Canadian Studies* 49 (2014): 135–58.

30 Strong Neighbourhoods Task Force, *Strong Neighbourhoods: A Call to Action* (Toronto, 2005), http://www.unitedwaytyr.com/research-and-reports

31 Horak and Dantico, "The Limits of Local Redistribution."

32 Gabriel Eidelman, "Managing Urban Sprawl in Ontario: Good Policy or Good Politics?" *Politics & Policy* 38, no. 6 (2010): 1211–36.

33 Ibid., 1212.

34 Terry Pender, "OMB Decision Undermines Region's Authority, Prof Says," *The Record*, 29 January 2013.

35 Tess Kalinowski, "A $17.5B Transit Promise," *Toronto Star*, 16 June 2007.

36 Tess Kalinowski, "TTC, Metrolinx Finally Sign Off on LRTs," *Toronto Star*, 28 November 2012.

Index

Blake, Edward, 193
Bliss, Paul, 168
Blizzard, Christina, 158, 164, 168–69
Bloc Québécois, 199
Boyd, Marion, 217, 290
Bradley, Jim, 262
Brampton, 6–7, 44, 314
British Columbia, 141–42
    party system, 195, 198
    voter turnout, 72
    women as premiers, 209
British Columbia Liberal Party, 200
British Columbia Social Credit, 199
Broadbent, Ed, 68
Brookfield Asset Management, 46
Brown, Patrick, 200
Bruce nuclear station, 43
Buddhism, 52, 278
building trades unions, 302
bullying, 55, 72
Burak, Rita, 112, 220

cabinet
    institutionalized cabinet system, 100,
        104, 106, 109
cabinet committee system, 100, 103,
        106–8, 185
Cabinet Office, 100–103, 105–7
cabinet secretary, 107
Caledonia, 51, 236, 286
Calgary Herald, 149
Campbell, Margaret, 215
Canada/US different value orientations,
        59–60
Canada Assistance Plan, 143–44. See also
        federal transfers
Canada Health Act, 140
Canada Job Grant, 135
Canada Pension Plan (1966), 140
Canada-US Free Trade Agreement (FTA),
        143–44, 299
Canada West Foundation, 146
Canadian Alliance, 215
Canadian Auto Workers (CAW), 299,
        301–3
Canadian Business, 45
Canadian dollar, 31, 33–34, 44, 142
Canadian National, 41, 286

Canadian Pacific, 41
Canadian Parliamentary Press Gallery.
        See press gallery
The Canadian Press, 166
Canadian Shield, 38, 43
Canadian Tire, 46
Caplan, David, 236–37
Caribbean Carnival, 4, 7
Carter, Alan, 166
Casselman, Leah, 302–3
Catholic school system, 52, 55, 61, 65, 69
Catholic secondary schools
    funding to, 65, 203
Catholics, 8, 52
    constitutional guarantee of separate
        system, 287
    largest religious group in Ontario, 278
CBC, 158
CCF, 64, 194, 205
Celestica, 46
census (1951), 6
census (2006), 7, 49–50
census (2011), 7–8, 50, 52–53, 55, 165,
        175, 178, 277–78
central agencies, 100–101, 103, 106–7
Central region, 40
CFPL (London), 164
Charlottetown Accord, 67
Charter of Rights and Freedoms, 10, 52,
        142–43, 157, 222, 290
Chatham, 120
CHCH (Hamilton), 164
Chiarelli, Bob, 264
chief administrative officer (CAO), 122
Chief Electoral Officer, 84
child care, 53–54, 210–11, 220–21
    Liberals reinstated funding, 222
    municipalities, 123
child welfare policy (1950s), 12
Chinese cabinet ministers, 283
Chinese immigrants, 7, 50
Chinese languages, 49, 278
Chinese representation in the Legislature,
        280
Chrétien, Jean, 68, 251
Christopherson, David, 200
Chrysler, 33, 44, 67
citizenry as "customers," 14

publicly funded school systems, 52, 61,
    287–88, 304. *See also* Catholic
    school system
pulp and paper, 43, 251
Punjabi, 49, 278
Pupatello, Sandra, 216, 263
Putting Students First Act, 305

Quebec, 59, 142
    acid rain control, 251
    attempt to bring Quebec back into
        constitution, 145
    banned corporate and union donations
        to parties, 197
    cap and trade system, 265
    on federal-provincial issues, 67
    party system, 195, 199
    women as premiers, 209
Quebec Liberal Party, 200
Quebec nationalism, 199
Quebec referendum (1980), 142
Québec Solidaire, 199
Queen's Park Briefing (QP Briefing),
    165–66, 168
Queen's Park This Week, 167
Question Period, 87, 159
Quiet Revolution, 49

racial discrimination, 70
radio, 41, 45
Radwanski, Adam, 169
Rae, Bob, 8, 67, 137, 143–44, 199–200,
    205–6. *See also* NDP government
    attempts to balance business and
        labour, 70
    centralized in response to fiscal stress,
        108
    leadership role in Charlottetown
        negotiations, 145
    PO under, 104
    support for federal constitution
        attempts, 145
Rae Days, 299
"rape culture," 224
Reagan, Ronald, 297
real estate sector, 21
recession (2008), 20, 31, 33, 44, 47, 56, 67,
    110, 125, 137, 149, 241, 261, 304

government austerity, 294
impact on Ontario's manufacturing
    sector, 239, 257
Red Lake, 43
Red Tories, 65
Reeves, Andrew, 158, 161
Region of Waterloo, 120, 323
regional disparities, 56
regionalism, 38–40
regionalization, 63
Regulations and Private Bills committee,
    93
religion, 52–53
religion and school funding, 287–88,
    304
religious affiliations, 7–8
ReNew Ontario, 126
renewable energy resources (wind and
    solar), 255, 258, 261
rent control, 205
research and development, 314
Research and Innovation MO, 113
resource boom. *See* commodities boom
    (early 2000s)
resource sectors, 9, 177, 253. *See also*
    natural resources
responsible government, 83, 86, 94, 193
results tables, 106
retail sales tax, 14. *See also* harmonized
    sales tax
retirement homes, 55
"reverse class resentment," 296
Richmond Hill, 6
Ring of Fire, 43, 136, 184–85, 187, 259,
    267
Ring of Fire Secretariat in Ministry of
    Northern Development and Mines,
    185–87
riots in Canadian cities (1820–1850), 277
Rittenberg, Jason, 167
Robarts, John, 16, 64–65, 69, 202
robotics, 30
Rogers Communications, 46
role of state, 15, 73, 254
    "Common Sense Revolution"
        rolled back, 103
    social investment state, 211
    state intervention, 61–62

visible minority cabinet ministers, 282–83
visible minority women, 218

Wagner Act (1935), 295
Wal-Mart, 300–303
Walkerton disaster, 252, 257, 260
Walkom, Tom, 296
Wallace, Peter, 220
War of 1812, 60
Waterfront Toronto, 320–21
Waterloo referendum (2010) ending
    fluoridation, 127
webcasting in Legislative Assembly, 167
welfare state, 15–16, 139–41, 143. *See also*
    social assistance
welfare support (1950s), 12
Welland Canal, 41
Weller, Geoffrey, 177, 181–83
West
    economic engine of the country, 147
    neocolonial status, 139
West Don Lands, 320
Westminster parliamentary systems, 81,
    83, 111, 157, 217
Weston, Galen, 46
Whitby, 6
White, Graham, 159, 166
white collar, 6
Whitney, James, 69
wholesale trade, 22
Williams, Danny, 200
Wilson, John, 64, 66, 69
wind turbines, 64, 238
    local opposition to, 130, 261–62
    rules on siting of, 261
    rural unhappiness with, 260
    subsidization, 44
Windsor, 40, 44
Windsor-to-Cornwall corridor, 40
Witmer, Elizabeth, 305
women
    average earnings, 54
    disproportionately affected by
        neoliberal trends, 211
    in nonstandard employment, 24
    participation in the workforce, 9, 53
    poverty, 48
    representation in cabinet, 217–18

representation in Canadian House of
    Commons, 210
representation in elected and appointed
    political office, 209–10, 212–21,
    279
second wave of women's movement,
    53
violence against (*See* violence against
    women)
visible minority, 218
women and politics research in
    neoliberal/post-neoliberal era, 211
women as premiers, 209
women deputy ministers and assistant
    deputy ministers, 219–20
women in legislature, 11, 54, 88
    critical mass, 211, 213, 217
women in senior officer and top earning
    positions, 53
women in the public service, 11
women in unions, 295
women party leaders, 54
Women's College Hospital, 54
women's issues, 210–11
Woodstock, 44
Workers Compensation Board, 303
workfare (Ontario Works), 48, 301
working class, 47–48, 64, 66
Working Families Coalition, 303–5
Workman's Compensation Act, 62
workmen's compensation (1950s), 12
World Trade Organization (WTO), 24
Wynne, Kathleen, 4, 54, 216, 219
    agriculture portfolio, 42
    apology to voters during leaders'
        debate, 239, 241
    attempt to work with other parties to
        pass legislation, 83, 96
    breakthrough for women in politics,
        209, 225
    concessions to NDP (2013), 83
    differences with Stephen Harper,
        135–36, 146, 241
    established Cabinet Committee on
        Northern Ontario (CCNO), 185
    first female premier, 209, 282
    first openly gay premier, 55, 83, 209,
        217, 282

gains with teachers, 240
majority victory (2014), 205–6, 216,
   229, 241
policies differentiating from McGuinty,
   241
prefers government intervention over
   austerity, 241
premiership, 112–13
on province's regional growth and
   transit infrastructure agenda, 325
ran for leadership as a progressive, 112
reached out to opposition leaders, 240
on sexual education, 241
success at getting bills passed, 92
success in GTA suburbs, 196
Sudbury 2015 by-election, 183
support for Justin Trudeau, 136, 151
won leadership, 83, 240, 262–63, 306
Wynne government
accessibility to press, 161
activist inclinations, 267
budget (2014), 113
collaboration with Premier Couillard,
   265
demands to eliminate the deficit, 113
emphasis on need for additional
   revenues, 263
environmental agenda, 262–67
gas plant controversy, 238
labour politics under, 306–8

lack of gender attention in Throne
   Speeches, 224
majority (2014), 83, 95, 264–67, 307
party financing legislation, 197
policy areas (environment, education,
   health care), 241
positioned away from PCs, NDP, Ford
   and federal Conservatives, 263
poverty reduction strategy, 48
provincial-municipal relations under,
   129
public transit in GTA and Hamilton, 263
relationship with teachers, 113
retreat from McGuinty's green energy
   initiatives, 264–65, 267
Sexual Violence Action Plan, 224
support for Transit City, 323
time allocation, 90
transportation infrastructure, 241, 263
union support, 294, 306–7
visible minority cabinet ministers, 283

York, 316
Young, Iris Marion, 274
younger citizens voting, 72
youth outmigration, 179
youth suicide crisis, 180
Yukon, 150

zoning by-laws, 126